ENGLAND AND NORMANDY IN
THE MIDDLE AGES

ENGLAND AND NORMANDY IN THE MIDDLE AGES

EDITED BY

DAVID BATES AND ANNE CURRY

THE HAMBLEDON PRESS

LONDON AND RIO GRANDE

Published by The Hambledon Press 1994

102 Gloucester Avenue, London NW1 8HX (U.K.)

P.O. Box 162, Rio Grande, Ohio 45674 (U.S.A.)

ISBN 1 85285 083 3

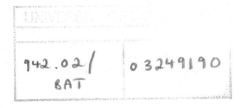

Typeset by York House Typographic Ltd

Printed on acid-free paper and bound in
Great Britain by Cambridge University Press

Contents

Illustrations

Text Illustrations

Tables

Acknowledgements

Illustrations are reproduced by kind permission of the following: London,
British Library, Fig. 19; London, Conway Library, Courtauld Institute of
Art, University of London, Figs 7-16, 24, 25; Oxford, Bodleian Library, Fig.
26; Paris, Bibliothèque Nationale, Figs 20-23; Reading, Reading University
Library, Fig. 18; Rouen, Bibliothèque Municipale, Figs 1–6.

Preface

The Norman victory at the battle of Hastings created a relationship between England and Normandy which, as Donald Matthew's account in this book illustrates, has ever since been a source of consistent reflection and searching enquiry. The essays in this volume, taken together, demonstrate beyond any doubt just how alive and significant the subject remains. It is not just that the Norman victory established a dominant northern French aristocracy in Britain and that the consequences of this event had an undeniably profound impact on Britain's history. The Norman Conquest created a framework of relationships and ideas which greatly influenced the history of Britain, Normandy and France throughout the medieval period and, arguably, beyond. It created a symbiosis which must on any reckoning be seen as one of the more important themes in British and French medieval history. If the two traditional supposed turning-points of 1066 and 1485 are selected, England and Normandy were under the control of the same rulers for a longer time than were England and Wales, and for almost as long as Normandy was an integrated part of the French kingdom.

It is with these general considerations in mind that the two editors decided that it would be both a valid and an exciting idea to bring together many of the foremost specialists on the relationship of medieval England and Normandy to a unique conference, held at Reading in September 1992. The result was an undoubted success, not only because of the quality of the papers given, but also because (inevitably) it showed through cross-fertilisation, how many aspects of the subject could be profitably developed. The essays by Philippe Contamine, Anne Curry and Mark Ormrod all open up new perspectives on the links between what might be called 'the first phase', that is the period from 1066 to 1204, and the fourteenth and fifteenth centuries. The essays by David Bates, Lindy Grant, Vincent Moss and Kathleen Thompson all, in their different ways, show how far twelfth-century Normandy remains an unexplored area of enquiry and how necessary is further fundamental research on the Angevin period. Equally deserving of historical investigation is the question of economic links between duchy and kingdom both before and after 1204.

The influence of the late John Le Patourel's University of Reading Stenton

Lecture, 'Normandy and England 1066-1144' (1971) and his book *The Norman Empire* (Oxford, 1976) is readily apparent in the essays on the period from 1066 to 1204. Even where disagreements with his general thesis are proposed, the central and profound importance of his ideas on cross-Channel relationships must be acknowledged. In addition to the four essays mentioned at the end of the preceding paragraph, Majorie Chibnall's wide-ranging discussion of monasticism in Normandy and England brings new dimensions to knowledge of Normandy and England's relationship between 1066 and 1189. The potential for deepening understanding of this relationship through the study of monasticism and monastic patronage is also highlighted in the papers by Emma Cownie, Véronique Gazeau and Béatrice Poulle. David Crouch contributes a provocative discussion of the cross-Channel aristocracy. Eric Fernie looks at architectural change in the context of the effects of the Conquest. Peter Noble provides a wide-ranging study of Anglo-Norman literature and Anne Lawrence of Anglo-Norman book production, while Henry Loyn takes a thoughtful look at the new Norman abbots of post-conquest England.

The fifteenth-century links between England and Normandy consequent upon Henry V's conquest of the duchy have already been the subject of considerable interest by historians on both sides of the Channel. It is not surprising, therefore, that this volume should contain four essays on this period. Christopher Allmand complements his magisterial study of *Lancastrian Normandy* (Oxford, 1983) with a review of the Norman church under English rule. Robert Massey focuses on English settlement in Rouen, the result of Henry V's policy of granting lands in the duchy to his supporters and thereby encouraging long-term interest and commitment to its tenure. This has even been seen as a 'Norman Conquest in reverse'. The evidence for a conscious harking back to a supposed or real Anglo-Norman past by Henry V and his contemporaries is reviewed by Anne Curry. Finally, Catherine Reynolds examines the implications for artistic patronage of the English occupation of Normandy.

It would be dangerously misleading to dismiss the period between John's loss of the duchy and Henry V's conquest of it as lacking in Anglo-Norman connections. Mark Ormrod reminds us of issues which persisted after 1204 before examining Edward III's policies in the duchy in the 1350's where, alongside his continuing claim to the French throne, Edward adopted the title 'duke of Normandy', a title last held by an English king in 1259. Andrew Ayton traces the organisation of Edward's first incursion into Normandy in 1346, a significant yet controversial campaign. Philippe Contamine alerts us to the French side of things. The English could advance claims and even invade the duchy in the fourteenth and fifteenth centuries but, as Contamine shows, there can be no doubt that after 1204 French kings did their utmost to integrate Normandy into royal France. He demonstrates that the duchy in the later medieval period cannot be viewed as a separatist oddity, but must be studied within the context of French history as a whole. Studies by the English contributors all show how late medieval ambitions in Normandy relate to the path of English royal history. In these later centuries, Normandy stood as an interface between the increasingly divergent and conflicting nations of England and France.

This volume originated at a conference held in Reading in September 1992. It might seem ironic that the idea of a conference on England and Normandy in the middle ages was first mooted in an Italian restaurant in the capital of Wales but it emphasises the fact that a collaborative element between Reading and Cardiff was present right from the start. When an initial core of potential speakers was established, it drew heavily on these two universities, both of which had strong and lengthy traditions of Anglo-Norman interest. The venue, Reading Town Hall, was the result of a further collaborative venture, and was a more appropriate location for the conference than might at first appear. Reading Museum, which forms part of the Town Hall complex owned by Reading Borough Council, houses the only woven facsimile of the Bayeux Tapestry, produced in Victorian Staffordshire but given to the town of Reading nearly a century ago. It was against this backdrop that delegates were welcomed by representatives of the town, of both universities and of the French Embassy, as they steered their way around the splendours of real Anglo-Norman workmanship, the capitals of Reading Abbey. That the conference proved such a success was due not only to the ambience of the location but also to the hard work of its staff. We would like to thank in particular John Rhodes, of Reading Museum, who had to cope with our intrusion into a museum which was still in the process of refurbishment, and Laura Milner and her staff at the Town Hall for their ceaseless concern for our comfort. We are also grateful to Sir David Wilson for helping to cement town-gown relations further by means of his splendidly illustrated public lecture on the Bayeux Tapestry, presented under the auspices of both the conference and the Town Hall. Thanks are also due to the University of Reading (which included the event in its centenary celebrations) and to the University of Wales College of Cardiff, as well as to the French Embassy, the British Academy, the Royal Historical Society and the Society for the Study of French History for their generous financial assistance, particularly in facilitating the attendance of postgraduate students and our speakers from France. Publication has been facilitated by a grant from the Scouloudi Foundation in association with the Institute of Historical Research. We are also indebted to Adrian Bell for his indexing and proofreading services. Finally, we must thank Martin Sheppard of Hambledon Press for his unfailing enthusiasm and encouragement.

Abbreviations

AD	Archives Départementales
ADSM	Archives Départementales de la Seine-Maritime
AN	Archives Nationales
A-NS	*Anglo-Norman Studies: Proceedings of the Battle Conference*, ed. R.A. Brown and M. Chibnall
BAACT	*British Archaeological Association Conference Transactions*
BL	British Library
BM	Bibliothèque Municipale
BN	Bibliothèque Nationale
Bod Lib	Bodleian Library
CCR	*Calendar of Close Rolls*
CFR	*Calendar of Fine Rolls*
CIPM	*Calendar of Inquisitions Post Mortem*
CP	G.E. Cockayne, *The Complete Peerage of England, Scotland, Ireland, Great Britain and the United Kingdom, new edn. revised V. Gibbs et al.*, 13 vols (London, 1910-59)
CPR	*Calendar of Patent Rolls*
DB	*Domesday Book: seu liber censualis Willelmi primi regis Angliae inter archivos regni in domo capitulari Westmonasterii asservatus*, ed. A. Farley, 2 vols (London, 1783).
DKR	*Annual Report of the Deputy Keeper of the Public Records*

EETS	Early English Text Society
EHR	*English Historical Review*
Froissart	Froissart, *Oeuvres*, ed. Kervyn de Lettenhove, 25 vols (Brussels 1867-77)
l.t.	livres tournois
Orderic	*The Ecclesiastical History of Orderic Vitalis*, ed. and trans. Marjorie Chibnall, 6 vols (Oxford, 1969-80)
PRO	Public Record Office
Rot. Parl.	*Rotuli parliamentorum, ut et petitiones et placita in parliamento, 1278-1503*, 6 vols

1

The English Cultivation of Norman History

D.J.A Matthew

Among the many surviving medieval books of Reading Abbey is a copy of the Norman abbot Robert of Torigny's version of William of Jumièges' *Gesta Normannorum ducum* made late in Henry II's reign. This is the only known copy of the text to make full use of Torigny's own final revisions to this work.[1] Even by that time, however, Anglo-Norman relations were three centuries old. The earliest notice we have of any relationship between England and Normandy is for March 991 when Pope John XV ratified the agreements reached in Rouen by his envoy between representatives of King Æthelred II and the duke. This agreement was followed by alliance in 1002 when Æthelred married Emma, sister of Duke Richard II.

Since the English and the Normans have been living on opposite sides of the Channel for over 1,000 years, it is natural for them to have shown some interest in one another, but the English relationship with Normandy owes its special *frisson* to the fact of the Norman Conquest. For a 150 years thereafter the English kingdom and Norman duchy remained closely bound together. After an interval of 200 years the relationship was renewed when Henry V conquered Normandy. David Hume observed soothingly in 1762 that 'the present rights and privileges of the people who are a mixture of English and Norman can never be affected by a transaction which passed seven hundred years ago',[2] but 200 years on from Hume the matter of Normandy still seems to arouse more excitement and controversy than any other episode of English history.

Over the past hundred years, writing about the Conquest has become a mainly academic interest but, before that, it had been a long-standing issue of public concern. Apart from the intrinsic interest of the topic, the main reason why so much historical effort has had to be put into the study of the Norman Conquest is that the sources of information have always proved to be inadequate for answering the kind of questions different generations have asked,

---

[1] *The Gesta Normannorum Ducum of William of Jumièges, Orderic Vitalis and Robert of Torigni*, ed.and trans. Elisabeth M.C. van Houts, i, (Oxford 1992), pp. cxii-cxiii, for BL, MS Cotton Vitellius A viii.

[2] David Hume, *The History of England from the Invasion of Julius Caesar to the Accession of Henry III* (London, 1762), i, p. 201.

even though by eleventh-century standards the historical source material is surprisingly abundant. If it cannot yield satisfactory answers, it is mainly because questions like 'How can such a great kingdom as England have passed enduringly into foreign hands as a result of one great battle?' are never likely to be given uncontroversial explanations. Opinions about it also change over periods of time, in response to new situations.

The best evidence we have of English perceptions of Normandy during the eleventh century is the *Anglo-Saxon Chronicle*. When this was copied at Peterborough after 1121, it was clearly puzzling to find that the existing text made no reference at all to the early history of Normandy. Appropriate insertions, in Latin, were therefore made, giving first the arrival of Rollo and his men in Normandy in 876, and after Rollo's reign of fifty-three years, the succession of later dukes William Longsword, the Richards, I, II and III, Robert and William. While the chronicle was being written in England, it had not become aware of Normandy until recording Æthelred's marriage in 1002. Oddly, the annalists did not mention Normandy as such, which is referred to only as Richard's realm. Even later, when the Chronicle notices the return of Emma's son Edward, he is said to have come from France, not Normandy, so the word Normandy does not appear in the text until 1066 itself. After the Conquest, the English annals still write of the French rather than of the Normans, emphasising their difference of speech and this also explains why they notice separately both Bretons and Flemings.[3] The English did not adopt the Normans' own preferred way of speaking of themselves as Normans. Royal charters were addressed to the king's faithful men, French and English.

However resolutely foreign the Normans seemed in England, the chroniclers still had no difficulty about accepting the legitimacy of William's kingship. God had granted him victory as a punishment for the nation's sins. For his part, William also showed no hesitation in counting on the loyalty of his English subjects. As early as 1072 he called on naval and land levies to deal with English rebels in Ely and in Scotland; and in 1073 he took English forces to France where they laid waste the county of Maine and subjected it to William's authority. At his death, William was acknowledged as a man of great wisdom and power who surpassed in honour and strength all those who had gone before him. Though both he and his leading men were criticised for their love of gold and for their unlawful and unjust acts, the chronicler did not imply that foreigners as such were wicked to conquer and oppress English people. The English chroniclers certainly recognised that the Norman Conquest had been a real calamity. As Matthew Hale wrote six centuries later, 'it must be evident to any Man that considers Things of this Nature that there were great Outrages and Oppressions committed by the Victor's soldiers and their

---

[3] *The Anglo-Saxon Chronicle*, trans. by G.N. Garmonsway (London, 1953). What mattered was not 'nationality' but the language spoken.

Officers, many false Accusations made against innocent Persons, great Disturbances and Evictions of Possessions'.[4] Hale had lived through the English Civil War: he knew. Domesday Book confirms that there had been a complete sweep of those in possession of landed estates. But the way the chronicle was written does not help us to penetrate to the mood of the nation in that critical generation that survived the Conquest.

In order to review English historical understanding of the Conquest since the eleventh century, I shall concentrate on three separate periods. In the first of these, the medieval, the most important achievement was the preservation of evidence about the event. Without these essential materials, it would be impossible for modern historians to write about the Conquest at all. English monasteries also acquired copies of the major Norman historical writers, Dudo, Jumièges, William of Poitiers and Torigny. Put together, all this amounts to impressive evidence of the interest the English continued to take in the Norman Conquest; without them some texts of importance, like Poitiers and the *Encomium Emmae*, would not be known today.[5] Even so, medieval historians were clearly already dissatisfied with what they had. To judge from Matthew Paris, who wanted to enhance the role of St Albans (his own monastery) at the time of the Conquest, they were even prepared to use legendary material, if not actually invent it.[6]

These early monastic chroniclers tended to see events very much from the point of view of their own community. Though this could mean preserving valuable local stories, it is important not to draw general conclusions from single case histories, as seems to have happened with Eadmer's memories of pre-conquest Canterbury.[7] Another disadvantage of clerical historians was their inclination to interpret historical events as they had been taught to read Old Testament history – in religious and moral terms. Yet by the time historians began to write about the Conquest, the English and Normans had already tried to put confrontation well behind them. Henry I's marriage to Matilda of the old royal house had been calculated to symbolise the reconciliation of the two peoples. Malmesbury's history made the Norman kings direct heirs of the earlier English kings. Malmesbury is himself proof that, despite having one Norman parent, he thought of himself as English. He never speaks

---

[4] Matthew Hale, *The History and Analysis of the Common Law of England* (London, 1713), p.94.

[5] The only known manuscript of William of Poitiers' *Gesta Gulielmi* was transmitted from England by William Camden to André Duchesne for use in his edition of 1619 and was thereafter lost. The only manuscripts of the *Encomium Emmae* known are all of English origin.

[6] *Gesta abbatum monasterii Sancti Albani a Thomas Walsingham . . . compilata*, ed. H.T. Riley, Rolls Series (London, 1867), pp. 41-51. On Abbot Fretheric, see R. Vaughan, *Matthew Paris* (Cambridge, 1958), pp. 203-4.

[7] Eadmer, *Historia novorum in Anglia*, ed. M. Rule, Rolls Series (London, 1884), p. 12. M.D. Knowles *The Monastic Order in England* (Cambridge 1949), p. 80, argued that this was the basis of the more general comments made by William of Malmesbury.

of Normandy as though he had been there and may indeed have known little about it.[8]

The inattention of Englishmen to the continuing history of Normandy can be easily demonstrated. Inspired perhaps by Henry V's victory at Agincourt, Thomas Walsingham, historian of St Albans, decided to compile a history book for the king as a warning against men's faithlessness, by showing how earlier treaties had been violated and Henry's predecessors cheated of their rights by deceitful and hypocritical enemies. Completed by early in 1419, it was given a very learned title *Ypodigma Neustriae*, chosen specially to emphasise how instructive the example of Normandy should be.[9] Most of the historical matter only summarises Walsingham's own earlier histories of England but it begins with a long section on Norman history between 911 and 1066, about one eighth of the whole book, taken for the most part verbatim from Jumièges. Walsingham obviously made every effort to put into the text all he knew about Normandy; the fact that he found almost nothing to put down in the later parts of the text illustrates the depth of English ignorance about what had happened in the thirteenth and fourteenth centuries. Henry V himself may have hoped to change this, for he is said to have brought over a copy of part of Orderic's history from Caen and a copy of Torigny's chronicle was made for Henry's monastic foundation at Syon. After Henry's death copies of both Dudo and Jumièges were made at All Souls College in 1445.[10] The English occupation of Normandy appears to have stimulated fresh interest in Normandy.

Given what the English medieval histories had to tell them, men may have had little chance of obtaining a good understanding of the Norman Conquest and its impact, but it cannot be denied that they had quite a lot of information about it. The popular general chronicles of the late middle ages, like the Brut or Higden's *Polychronicon*, give very full accounts, conflating snippets from a host of sources, good and bad.[11] Although it is difficult to imagine how such books were used, even for purposes of reference, they were certainly popular and the main source of general information about the past. When these came to be printed in the late fifteenth century they must have had considerable

[8] William of Malmesbury, *De gestis regum Anglorum*, ed. W. Stubbs, Rolls Series (London, 1886-89), pp. 304-5. The slightness of even Malmesbury's intellectual links with Normandy is shown in Rodney Thomson, *William of Malmesbury* (Woodbridge, 1987).

[9] Thomas Walsingham, *Ypodigma Neustriae*, ed. H.T. Riley, Rolls Series (London, 1876). The word was coined by the author from the Greek and what he intended to mean is not certain. Perhaps the idea was that Norman history should be understood as a paradigm.

[10] BL, MS Harley 3742: John Norfolk copied Dudo and Jumièges at All Souls College, Oxford, *c*. 1445; the fourteenth-century Caen manuscript of Orderic (BL, MS Cotton, Vespasian A xix) used by Camden, who published extracts from it, is said by him to have been brought to England by Henry V. The Syon copy of Torigny is now Bod Lib, MS Bodley 212.

[11] *The Brut or the Chronicles of England*, ed. F.W.D. Brie, EETS, original series, 131, 136; 1906, ch. cxxxi – ch. xli; Ranulf Higden *Polychronicon*, ed. J.R. Lumby, Rolls Series (London, 1879), vii.

impact on the wider dissemination of historical information. Most English-men's knowledge of Norman England must have been derived from them. It is notable, for example, that Shakespearean references to Normans present them as both fine soldiers and horsemen.[12]

The best known of the sixteenth-century vernacular chronicles, because of its use by Shakespeare, was that of Holinshed, first printed in 1577.[13] This work, still essentially a compilation from previous authors, profited in particu-lar from Polydore Vergil's *Historia anglicana*, published in 1534,[14] which had introduced Italian humanist ideas about history into England. He dealt roughly with the earlier tradition of compilation and offended many by summarily rejecting familiar stories, notably those about Brutus and the Trojans as the original Britons. Unfortunately, his motive was not so much scholarly scepticism but excessive reliance on his own ideas of how things must have been. This is particularly true of his approach to the Norman Conquest, which he naturally saw as another example of foreign conquest familiar to him from the Roman historians. He presents William as an arbitrary tyrant who had imposed the curfew in England, had tried to force the English to speak French and deliberately issued his laws in that language so that the poor English would not be able to understand them. Later historians, impressed by Vergil's confidence in his own opinions and by his new approach to making sense of events, cheerfully adopted him as a new authority.

His was a new kind of history, begun at the behest of King Henry VII, who wanted a dignified Latin history of England. Many later historians also wrote specifically for princes and their works naturally narrowed the historical focus to affairs of state. The new historians, moreover, were expected to compose coherent narratives capable of holding the attention of the well-educated: a mere rag-bag of information was no longer acceptable.

Even more important than this change in the character of the historical work itself was the fact that from the late sixteenth century a vast amount of original historical source material was put into print. The availability of the sources enabled any educated person to judge historians' opinions for themselves. The new surge of interest in historical sources had begun under Elizabeth I with more general problems connected with the English Reformation, particularly in trying to understand the position of the church in England before the assertion of Roman claims, plausibly attributed to Gregory VII.[15] In effect this meant England before the Conquest. The Dissolution of the Monasteries had itself been an important event for historical scholarship. It had in the first place

---

[12] Shakespeare's Normans, in *Love's Labour's Lost*, II (Longavill); *Hamlet* IV, 7.

[13] Raphael Holinshed, *The First Volume of the Chronicles of England*, 3 vols (London,1577); now usually read in the edition of 1807-8, 6 vols (London, 1807-8).

[14] Polydore Vergil, *Historia anglicana* (Basel, 1534).

[15] Parker's interest in the parallels between the pre-Conquest church and the post-Reformation church of England made him aware of how much innovation in the Roman position was caused by Gregory VII.

broken up the old libraries: this eventually made it possible to accumulate the first national collection of medieval texts in Cotton's library.[16] In addition, antiquarian enthusiasm for the medieval past may have owed something to a sense of nostalgia for the world that had vanished with the monasteries. Although the antiquaries were not crypto-papists, they did want to believe in a basic continuity of English history. This applied not only across the Reformation divide but to the Conquest itself, which was, after all, the only other occasion when there had been a wholesale change in the lordship of English property in England. A society of antiquaries was formed under Archbishop Parker and survived into James I's reign, when it was broken up by the new king as a potentially dangerous cabal.[17]

The first tangible evidence of the new scholarship was Parker's publications of major medieval chroniclers, including Matthew Paris and Walsingham's *Ypodigma Neustriae*.[18] In 1596 Henry Savile continued this work with editions of Malmesbury, Huntingdon, Hoveden and, less happily, the fifteenth-century fabrication of the Croyland chronicle attributed to Abbot Ingulph, called the Conqueror's secretary.[19] Only six years later Camden issued extracts from Orderic (which he thought was written by William of Poitiers), Jumièges, Gerald of Wales and Walsingham, again.[20] About the same time, a comparable movement had begun in France when the French scholar Pierre Pithou began to publish French medieval royal chronicles.[21] André Duchesne's publication of Norman chroniclers in 1619 actually owed much to the interest of his English contemporaries. Camden procured manuscripts of both the *Encomium Emmae* and William of Poitiers from Cotton's library for Duchesne and fascicules of the *Scriptores Normannorum* were sent to Camden as they came off the press.[22]

Cotton's library also provided the source materials for English historical scholars, such as Selden and Spelman. The result was works including Selden's valuable edition of Eadmer published in 1623.[23] Works of contemporary scholarship became authoritative opinions, quoted not only by later writers

---

[16] The use made of Cotton's library by all the scholars of the age demonstrates its national importance in the early seventeenth century.

[17] For an account of the society established by Parker in Elizabeth I's reign see *Archaeologia*, 1 (1770).

[18] Matthew Parker published four volumes of chronicles in London 1567-74.

[19] Henry Savile, *Rerum anglicarum scriptores post Bedam praecipui* (London, 1596).

[20] William Camden, *Anglica Normannica Hibernica Cambrica a veteribus scripta* (Frankfurt, 1602).

[21] Pierre Pithou, *Historiae Francorum ab anno Christi 900 ad annum 1285 scriptores veteres XI* (Frankfurt, 1596). Pithou had published the Carolingian material earlier: *Annalium et historiae Francorum scriptores* (Paris, 1588).

[22] André Duchesne, *Normannorum historiae scriptores* (Paris, 1619). For Camden's part in this publication see *Camdeni et illustrium virorum epistolae* (London, 1691), especially letters clxxvi, clxxxv.

[23] *Eadmeri monachi Cantuariensis historiae novorum*, ed. John Selden, (London, 1623).

but cited in law suits.[24] Historians soon began to appreciate the importance for history of using texts from official sources rather than just relying on chronicles. Spelman began by publishing his collection of materials relating to ecclesiastical synods, the *Concilia* (1639); Dugdale's *Monasticon* (1655) documented monastic history.[25] The historical significance of documents was already fully appreciated by Robert Brady, who had been keeper of the records in the Tower of London before writing his history of England, published in 1685.[26] It was the publication of documents in Rymer's *Foedera* from 1704 which made it much easier for historians to make use of documentary material.[27] The French historian Rapin was the first scholar to exploit Rymer's texts in his history of England; this was immediately translated into English and set a new standard of historical scholarship.[28] The development of English views about the Norman Conquest during the seventeenth century therefore owed much to changes in historical practice between Savile and Rymer.

The importance of England's Norman connection was recognised by scholars in a number of ways. Just as Duchesne had made use of Cotton's library, Dugdale, while in France during the Civil War, made use of Duchesne's papers to copy documents relating to Norman monastic property in England. A more common reason, however, for English historical interest in Normandy was the perception of lawyers that there was much more to the relationship of English law to Norman customs than the mere curiosity of its using so many French technical terms. Several editions of the Norman customary with commentaries, published in the sixteenth and seventeenth centuries, were accordingly acquired, read and quoted by English writers.[29] In 1629 Richard Zouche, an Oxford jurist, actually published a little treatise on civil law where the English law of land tenure was elucidated by comparing it with the Italian *Libri feudorum* and the Norman customs.[30] The rules of English and Norman law were obviously so closely related that any discussion of the origins of English law necessarily involved reference to Norman practice. Opinions were naturally divided as to how the connection should be explained. Not all scholars

---

[24] Henry Spelman, *Reliquiae Spelmanniae* (Oxford, 1698), pp. 1-46: The original growth, propagation and condition of feuds and tenure by knight service (1639).

[25] Henry Spelman, *Concilia decreta leges constitutiones in re ecclesiarum orbis britannicae* (London, 1639); William Dugdale, *Monasticon anglicanum*, 3 vols (London, 1655-73).

[26] Robert Brady, *A Complete History of England from the Entrance of the Romans under the Conduct of Julius Caesar unto the End of the Reign of King Henry III* (London, 1685).

[27] T. Rymer, *Foedera, conventiones, literae . . . ab anno 1101* (London, 1704).

[28] P. Rapin de Thoyras, *The History of England*, translated from the French of 1723 in 1726 and provided with notes by N. Tindal for the third edition of 1743 (London).

[29] The seventeenth-century library catalogues of the Bodleian Library (T. James, 1605, 1620 and T. Hyde, 1674) show that the library continued to add to its copies of Norman customary law-books.

[30] Richard Zouche, *Elementa iurisprudentiae definitionibus regulis et sententiis selectoribus iuris civilis illustrata* (Oxford, 1629).

thought Norman law must have been imported ready-made into England. Some thought Edward the Confessor had taken his laws to Normandy.[31] History was seen to be of importance for the training of lawyers, and lawyers accordingly made serious contributions to the study of English history. The lawyers' own attention to the past tended to sharpen historical focus on issues of law, government and the constitution. In the long term it helped to secularise a subject that had, in the medieval period, been mainly of interest to monks and moralists. All this created a new public for history books, which authors and publishers were not slow to satisfy.

Christopher Hill, in his famous essay on the Norman Yoke,[32] drew attention to those English political visionaries who blamed the Normans for introducing class, property and lordship into an original English Eden, but he did not consider where these publicists got their ideas about the Conquest from. Seventeenth-century authors gave considerable prominence to the Norman Conquest in their general histories. They recognised its importance for English law and government, as matters of concern to their readers. From Vergil's example they had learned about the historian's duty to arrange materials into rational discourse and to write persuasively. They did not necessarily endorse Vergil's hostile interpretation of the reign, but they accepted that history books had to be readable and not just works of reference. An early example of this is the popular little history book on England till Stephen's reign which appeared in 1612-13, written by Samuel Daniel, better known as a poet.[33] In his account of the Conqueror, Daniel made use of the printed Norman chronicle recently republished at Rouen in 1610, so he must have made some effort to do some fresh reading for the book.[34] He gives prominence to the matter of the law but in his view the Conqueror found better laws established in England 'by the wary care of our former kings then any he could bring' with him. Daniel did not, however, believe in an old English Eden. The Normans had introduced many beneficial changes with 'innovation in most things but Religion. So that from this mutation which was the greatest it ever had wee are to beginne with a new account of an England more in dominion abroad, more in State and abilitie at home and more of honour and name in the world.' This was possible because of the way the Normans were prepared to become blended with the English, 'the Normans having more of the sun and civility by

---

[31] According to Spelman 'William Roville of Alenzon in his preface to the Grand Customier of Normandy taught that all those customs (among which these tenures are) were first brought into Normandy out of England by Edward the Confessor. This is Guillaume Le Rouillé of Alençon whose *Grand coustumier de pays et duché de Normandie* was issued in 1520, 1534 and 1539. Spelman, *Reliquiae*, pp. 1, 26 and preface – fifth page (unnumbered).

[32] Christopher Hill, 'The Norman Yoke', *Democracy and the Labour Movement: Essays in Honour of Dona Torr*, ed. J. Saville (London, 1984).

[33] Samuel Daniel, *The First Part of the Historie of England* (London, 1612), pp. 128, 73, 74.

[34] *L'Histoire et cronique de Normandie* (Rouen, 1610), a reprint of the Rouen edition of 1578; the text was first printed at Rouen in 1487.

their commixtion with the English begat smoother fashions with quicker motions. And being a nation free from that dull disease of drink induced a more comely temperance with a neere regard of reputation and honour.'

The same year as Daniel's account of the Conquest was published, Sir John Hayward wrote a whole book on the reigns of the three Norman kings – the first book in English entirely devoted to the Normans.[35] It was originally commissioned by Henry, Prince of Wales, who died in 1612. The new dedicatee, Prince Charles, was supposed to read it as a kind of manual to prepare him for the kingship. In this sense the Stuart monarchy was explicitly linked with the idea of Norman authority. Hayward had, however, little real sense of history. He used the events of the three reigns only to demonstrate matters of legal principle or political wisdom, which he also illustrated by reference to events in biblical or classical history, as in his discussion of what rights the Conqueror might have to bequeath the kingdom to his second son. Perhaps surprisingly, Hayward was even prepared to defend Rufus, who, he said, had been criticised by monastic writers 'because he was not so credulous to Rome'. He went so far as to consider Rufus as a model ruler because he never wasted time: 'So effectuall is celeritie for the benefit of a service, that oftentimes it more availeth then either multitude or courage of Souldiers.' More appropriate still for Charles I was Hayward's opinion of extravagance: 'costly apparel and dainty fare' are 'two assured tokens of a diseased state; as in fishes, so in families and likewise in states putrefaction commonly begineth at the head'.

How Norman history was studied and presented during the Civil War is indicated by Nathaniel Bacon's *Historical Discourse of the Uniformity of the Government of England* (1647).[36] The first third of its 323 pages is devoted entirely to an exposition of the Anglo-Saxon polity 'a beautifull composure, mutually dependant in every part', which actually developed an idea of Daniel's as to the merits of the surety or tithing system. Bacon argued, however, not only that the Conqueror could not undermine the old English constitution, but that he never wanted to. He buttressed his case by inserting marginal references to his authorities, the chroniclers Matthew Paris, Malmesbury, Eadmer of course, but also to laws and statutes, and to recent scholarship – Spelman's *Glossary* and Selden's *Eadmer*. For the first time a historian of Norman England set out an elaborately conceived argument supported by meticulous reference to his sources. According to Bacon:

> A private debate concerning the right of an English king to Arbitrary rule over English subjects as Successor to the Norman Conquerour (so-called) first occasioned this Discourse . . . He that knoweth the secrets of all mens hearts doth know that my aime in this Discourse is neither at Scepter or Crosier, nor after popular dotage, but that Justice and Truth may moderate in all. This is a Vessell I

[35] John Hayward, *The Lives of the Three Normans, Kings of England* (London, 1613), pp. 153, 186, 210.

[36] Nathaniel Bacon, *An Historical Discourse of the Uniformity of the Government of England* (London, 1647), pp. 112, 148, 150; and introduction 'To Consideration'.

confesse ill and weakly built, yet doth it adventure into the vast Ocean of your censures, Gentlemen, who are Antiquaries Lawyers and Historians, any one of whom might have steered in their course much better than my selfe.

Bacon saw the importance of aiming for objectivity and of understanding the nature of his readership. His history is a work of learning and integrity. He perceived that the Normans had genuine virtues and was able to defend aspects of their government often criticised in his day. The Norman feudal rules on marriage, dower and wardship were 'customs rationally and with great wisdom upholden' and 'this point of honour must be given to the Normans that their sword had eyes and moved not altogether by rage but by reason'. After the Restoration attempts to suppress later editions, because of Bacon's political support of Cromwell, were ineffectual because his book was much too substantial to be disregarded. It influenced Matthew Hale's history and analysis of the common law of England,[37] and inspired Robert Brady's attempt to interpret the English past in a sense much more favourable to the monarchy. Brady's book was dedicated to James II. He aimed 'to prove by Authentic Testimony' and 'convince men of Impartial and Unbyassed minds' of what 'the ancient government of this Famous Kingdom was'. His book was to be read as an 'impregnable Rock against the pretended Sovereignty and Power of the People in this Nation which the Republicans can never climb over'.[38] Brady was unfortunate in the timing of his publication. His work immediately provoked fury and, for all its merits, it is still easy to see why. The sheer readability of his text is impeded by excessively elaborate annotation; and its physical bulk added to the difficulty of trying to read it for pleasure and enlightenment.

After 1689, when the constitutional issues were abated, interest in the Norman Conquest did not fade. The Whig statesman Sir William Temple wrote an *Introduction to the History of England* (1695) which actually got no further than 1087.[39] Temple took over 200 pages to sing the praises of William I: 'the last and great period of this kingdom leaving the succession and constitution since that time so fixed and established as to have lasted for the space of above six hundred years without any considerable alteration', a surprising conclusion, to say the least. All this was the Conqueror's doing.

He owed his greatness to his birth (as issue of a sudden and strong inclination) and his fortune to his personal merit, from the strength of his temper and vigour of his mind, for he had a body of iron as well as a heart of steel. Yet his intellectuals were at least equal to his other natural advantages and he appears as wise in his politick institutions as he was bold in his enterprises and brave and fortunate in the achievement of his great adventures.

[37] Matthew Hale, *History and Analysis of the Common Law* (London, 1713).
[38] Robert Brady, *Complete History*, 'Dedication' and 'To the Reader'.
[39] William Temple, *An Introduction to the History of England* (London, 1695).

Temple aimed to vindicate 'the memory of this noble prince and famous conqueror from the aspersions and detractions from several malicious or partial authors who have more unfaithfully represented his reign than any other period of our English history'. Author and readers in 1695 may have established some kind of link in their minds between the Norman William and the Dutch William III.

During this second great phase of historical study, the Normans had acquired, for Englishmen, many of those features that they have retained until now. By the early eighteenth century it was already possible to form sensible opinions about the outcome of the Norman Conquest. Yet from the late eighteenth century and over the succeeding hundred years, the third phase of my analysis, the study of the Normans in England was completely transformed. The subject was, as it were, transferred from black and white to colour, and the first blush of Romanticism in the eighteenth century gradually deepened till it became as crimson as maps of the British empire. The earliest scholar to be identified with this movement was Andrew Ducarel, who had been born in Normandy but brought to England at a young age. In 1752 he made a tour of monuments in Normandy of which he published an account two years later.[40] He acknowledges the inspiration provided by Montfaucon's *Monuments de la monarchie française*, a translation of which had appeared in 1750.[41] He explains his reasons for choosing Normandy. 'Having formerly been so nearly allied to the kingdom it particularly deserves the attention of an English antiquary.' Normandy, he wrote, 'so nearly resembles old England that we could scarce believe ourselves to be in France'. He made many observations about the countryside and the state of agriculture. The way of life at the academy of Caen compared with Eton, both founded, as it happened, by Henry VI. His main interest in Normandy, however, was in Norman building. He came to the conclusion that similar architectural features in England assumed by his learned friends 'to have been Saxon' must, on the contrary, have been brought over from Normandy by the Conqueror, 'who introduced as much as in him lay the laws, customs and language of the Normans and most probably their method of building'. Ducarel began the study of medieval architecture in England by the comparative method. While at Bayeux he had, he says, the satisfaction of also seeing the famous historical tapestry known to him from Montfaucon's book. According to Ducarel no one in Bayeux at the time connected the tapestry in any way with William the Conqueror. Ducarel is the first English writer known to have himself seen the tapestry and his book helped to make it better known. Ducarel also helped to give more general currency to the term 'Anglo-Norman'. Whereas until then it had been used of

---

[40] Andrew C. Ducarel, *A Tour through Normandy* (London, 1754). This was reissued with plates in *Anglo-Norman Antiquities Considered* (London, 1767).

[41] Bernard de Montfaucon, *Les monuments de la monarchie française*, 5 vols (Paris, 1729-33).

Normans in England, Ducarel gave it a new sense to cover whatever England and Normandy might have in common.

Ducarel's personal observations in Normandy made him aware rather early of the nature of Norman influence on English architecture. From this time English enthusiasts began to write passionately about medieval building, pouring out both learning and speculation on a subject barely discussed before. It was till then generally believed that Gothic architecture had been imported more or less ready-made from the Muslims at the time of the Crusades but, as early as 1771, Bentham had argued in his study of Ely Cathedral for an English origin for Gothic architecture since, according to him, it could be traced to the effect of intersecting semi-circular arches, of which the earliest examples were found in England.[42] The idea of Gothic architecture being an English innovation may have helped to make the study of the subject that much more attractive; whether Gothic was first invented in England or not, there is no doubt that the English invented the new historical study of monuments.[43]

The study of monuments was accompanied by the lavish publication of architectural plates by the engravers of the day and both aspects of this had general appeal for cultivated gentlemen. Their interest in picturesque buildings and landscapes reflected contemporary taste in Britain. Particularly after the Napoleonic wars, antiquarians and the artists began to pour across the Channel to study Norman buildings and to paint them.[44] All this gave quite a new meaning to the word 'Norman'. One of its principal meanings still in English is post-Conquest Romanesque architecture.

Something of the same enthusiasm felt by artistic amateurs also animated the intellects of the age. The Society of Antiquaries, which had been revived in early eighteenth-century London, received a royal charter in 1750 and began to publish the proceedings of its meetings regularly in *Archaeologia* from 1770. There was a trickle of studies on Norman subjects from the first: ancient castles, Odo of Bayeux, even Reading Abbey.[45] Gentlemen antiquaries brought to their study of the Normans quite different perceptions from those of the great seventeenth-century legal antiquaries. They had no pressing political problems to resolve; they pursued very personal, even idiosyncratic

---

[42] James Bentham, *History and Antiquities of the Conventual and Cathedral Church of Ely* (Cambridge, 1771).

[43] Notable contributions were: J. Milner, *A Treatise on the Ecclesiastical Architecture of England during the Middle Ages* (London, 1811); G.D. Whittington, *An Historical Survey of the Ecclesiastical Antiquities of France,*(2nd edn, London, 1811); J. Britton, *The Architectural Antiquities of Great Britain*, v (London, 1826), ch. 1 discusses the contributions made to the development of the history of medieval architecture by earlier writers.

[44] The most famous of these Norman picture books is that of J. S. Cotman, *Architectural Antiquities of Normandy*, 2 vols (London, 1822).

[45] *Archaeologia*, vol. 1 (1770) S. Pegge on a document of Odo of Bayeux; vol. 4 (1777) E. King on ancient castles; vol. 6 C. Englefield on Reading Abbey (1782).

interests. Within a century they had nevertheless transformed the meaning of Norman for English history.

When Englishmen began to travel in Normandy regularly they began to require detailed guide books, so many new books about Normandy itself were published in these years, including handsome books with plates and various accounts of travel.[46] The possibility of travel did not diminish interest in simply reading about the Normans. On the contrary, words had never been more important to stir the emotions. The new Romanticism throbbed in the literature, most notably the works of Sir Walter Scott. *Ivanhoe* (1820), though set in the reign of Richard I, dealt with the problem posed for English society by the Conquest: how had the English reacted to the French? The historical novelist made a genuine attempt to think through the social implications of known events and realise in fiction how things must have been.[47] The romantic concern for the feel of the past has still a very powerful hold on the way the contemporary imagination deals with the problems of history. The main effects of such works were to transform public expectations of what historians ought to explain about the past, and to put new faith in the powers of the imagination to conjure the past to life.

The rediscovery, at this time, of medieval vernacular literature did much to help liberate the historical imagination. For the Normans this meant, in particular, the revelations provided first by the Icelandic sagas and secondly by the work of the poet Wace. The British public was first made aware of the importance of Icelandic sources by Thomas Percy, whose *Northern Antiquities* came out in 1770.[48] The earliest application of the new materials for historical purposes was, however, made by James Johnstone, one time British embassy chaplain at Copenhagen. He profited from recent publications there of Snorri Sturlason to write of the Norse connection with Orkney in 1784-86.[49] From this time English interest in the Vikings grew apace and though, according to the *Oxford English Dictionary*, the word Viking itself was not used in modern English until 1807, since that time the resonance of the term has profoundly affected historical assessments of the Normans. As to Wace and his vernacular version of Norman history written in the mid twelfth century, the earliest

[46] According to the *Indicateur de Dieppe* of 1824, there was then a twice-weekly sailing between Brighton and Dieppe. The crossing took nine hours. The twice-daily service by *diligence* between Dieppe and Rouen took six hours. By 1847 *A Handbook for Travellers in France* shows that the journey from Dieppe to Rouen could be completed in four hours and that it took another four hours in the train from Rouen to Paris.

[47] Walter Scott's *Ivanhoe* (1820) inspired Julia Pardoe to write *Lord Morcar of Hereward* (1829), a romance set in the Conqueror's own reign.

[48] Thomas Percy, *Northern Antiquities* (London, 1770), was a translation from P.H. Mallet's *Introduction à l'histoire de Dannemarc* (Copenhagen, 1755-56).

[49] James Johnstone, *Antiquitates Celto-Scandicae* (Copenhagen, 1784); idem, *Antiquitates Celto-Normannica* (Copenhagen, 1786).

detailed account of him in English was the essay about four English manuscripts of Wace contributed to *Archaeologia* in 1796 by Gervais De La Rue,
then in exile from the Revolution in London.[50] Earlier discussion of Wace had
been made in France, but his work was still little known. When a text of the
Roman de Rou was published at Rouen in 1828, the editor, Pluquet, used one
of the London manuscripts as being the oldest and most complete.[51] When
Edgar Taylor published an English translation of Wace in 1837, he likewise
acknowledged the help he had received from Le Prévost, 'a resident antiquary
of great and deserved reputation'.[52] The Normans, as the English had long
understood them, were by these various means transformed into intrepid
adventurers, innovative in art and literature. They became the great heroes of
English nineteenth-century romance.

The efforts of antiquaries and archivists in this same period to make public
the extraordinarily fascinating documents of the medieval past must also be
considered in this context. There is undeniably something romantic about the
modern scholar plunging into dusty archives in search of hidden treasures
which have somehow survived the centuries, neglected and unknown but often
monuments as important in their own right as cathedrals and castles. The
greatest of all Norman monuments is surely Domesday Book. It was not at all
easy to understand even what it was until the wish, often expressed earlier, to
have it printed, was realised in 1783.[53] Within twenty years this publication had
opened up a new era in British history. In the first place, it certainly helped to
prompt the British government to order the first census of the population since
1086; secondly, it inspired the House of Commons to set up a Record
Commission to survey the state of British archives and to proceed with the
publication of other medieval documents on the pattern of Domesday Book.[54]
Ponderously, over the succeeding decades, the Record Commission went
about its task. Out of this experience developed the realisation of a need for
the Public Record Office resolved on in 1837. While in London, De La Rue
himself is said to have copied out 4,000 documents amongst the chancery
records in the Tower of London, relating to Norman history. His example was
not lost on English contemporaries. It was Charles Abbott, the lawyer
archivist and later Speaker of the Commons, whose resolutions of 1800

---

[50] Gervais De La Rue, *Archaeologia*, 12 (1796), pp. 50-79.

[51] Wace's *Roman de Rou* was first published in French with a Danish translation by P.C.
Brønsted at Copenhagen, 1817-18. A German edition appeared in 1824 and F. Pluquet published
his text in 1827, using the oldest surviving manuscript from London, BL, Royal MS 4 C xi,
formerly at Battle Abbey.

[52] Edgar Taylor, *Master Wace his Chronicle of the Norman Conquest from the Roman de Rou*
(London, 1837), p. xxiii.

[53] *Domesday Book*, ed. Abraham Farley (London, 1783).

[54] The reports of the Record Commission give a comprehensive view of its activities. Some of
the background can be read about more conveniently in M.D. Knowles, 'Great Historical
Enterprises, iv, The Rolls Series', *Transactions of the Royal Historical Society*, 5th series, 11
(1961), pp. 137-59.

brought about both the census and the Record Commission.[55] Nor were important changes of this kind confined to England. In Normandy itself the Revolution had brought all the surviving monastic archives into the care of the state. Once the Napoleonic wars were over, local antiquaries set about the task of working through them. The Normans were particularly eager to make progress on this front and, in 1824, a new Society of Norman Antiquaries was set up in Caen, almost certainly modelled on that of London.[56] From its early days it had a number of affiliated British members, such as Sir Walter Scott himself and the architect Pugin.[57] The English interest in Normandy was sardonically acknowledged by Auguste Le Prévost in connection with the study of medieval architecture:

> Né en Angleterre, il est natural qu'il soit particulièrement répandu dans notre province, dans cette terre des châteaux et des églises où nos voisins de l'autre côté de la Manche sont obligés de venir chercher le berceau de leurs arts, aussi bien que celui de leur monarchie, de leurs familles et de leurs institutions.[58]

The changing cultural and intellectual conditions of England and France in the nineteenth century had provided new institutional forms for the study of texts and documents. This is turn affected the way historians themselves wrote about the past.

One of the earliest demonstrations of what careful study of ancient charters could do for the transformation of historical understanding of the past was provided by Sharon Turner's account of Anglo-Saxon England which he started to publish in 1799. Turner was encouraged by the favourable reception of this work to extend the history from the Norman Conquest to the reign of Edward I, the first part of which was issued in 1814.[59] Despite his own earlier appreciation of Anglo-Saxon achievements, he could still regard the advent of the Normans as 'a moral earthquake'. It had 'suddenly shook England's polity and population to their centre: broke up and hurled into ruin all its ancient aristocracy'. Nevertheless, according to Turner, 'it raised from the mighty ruins with which it overspread the country that new and great character of government, clergy, nobility and people, which the British history has never ceased to display'. Turner had shown the native English party a way to restore their faith in the sound old-English polity. As the century moved forward, the study of the Normans became once again an acrimonious arena where English traditions were now stoutly defended against those of foreign importation. A

---

[55] See Charles Abbot, Baron Colchester, *Dictionary of National Biography*, i, pp. 3-5.

[56] *Mémoires des antiquaires de Normandie* 1 (1825).

[57] The members are listed in ibid., 5 (1828).

[58] Ibid., 1 (1825), pp. 11, 79.

[59] Sharon Turner, *History of England from the Norman Conquest to the accession of Edward I* (London, 1814), p. 57.

fresh element was actually introduced by the French historian, Auguste Thierry, whose *History of the Conquest of England by the Normans* first appeared in French in 1825.[60] Thierry probably took from Scott the idea that there had been no blending of the two peoples: the Normans had created a governing class, who kept the English in subjection. In Thierry's view, this class system had persisted for centuries. He saw the English past as resembling that of the Greeks under Turkish lordship, a comparison of considerable contemporary importance in both France and England, since in the 1820s the Greeks were trying to obtain their independence. Thierry was not a Norman. His main purpose, as a historian, was to rescue the history of peoples from the neglect into which previous emphasis on governments had thrust it.

The best known of nineteenth-century English historians of the Norman Conquest was E.A. Freeman, whose comprehensive account of it, in five volumes, was published between 1867 and 1879.[61] It must now be one of the most cited but least read historical monuments written on any historical subject. Even at the time of publication its genuine learning was not sufficient to allay suspicions that it was wrong-headed and unreliable.[62] Its passionate defence of the Teutonic cause made it seem excessively partisan. For all its limitations, its sheer weight gave it status as an authoritative account. Since Freeman's time, however, Norman historians have, on the whole, rejected the grand historical manner. Later Norman scholarship owed, in fact, more to the work of scholars like Thomas Stapleton, whose edition of the Norman exchequer rolls is still invaluable.[63] His meticulous attention to detail can be easily illustrated from the map of Normandy he provided there, which Powicke used for his own book on the loss of Normandy seventy years later.[64] The English scholar who did most to work the new Norman history into the fabric of English history at this time was, however, Francis Palgrave, father of the anthologist. His account of the Conquest was published posthumously and unsatisfactorily in 1864, only three years before Freeman's.[65] Palgrave had been, for many years, Deputy Keeper of the Public Records, and his professional background gave him a perception of the past quite different from Freeman's. Even so his historical works were still written for the general public. He too favoured the narrative form. But he began not so much with a

---

[60] J.N. Auguste Thierry, *History of the Conquest of England by the Normans*. C.C. Hamilton's translation appeared in the same year as the French original, 1825.

[61] E.A. Freeman, *The History of the Norman Conquest of England, its causes and its results*, 6 vols (Oxford, 1867-79).

[62] For a twentieth-century assessment of Freeman, see H.A. Cronne, 'Historical Revision: E.A. Freeman, 1823-1892', *History*, 28 (1943), pp. 78-92.

[63] Thomas Stapleton, *Magni rotuli scaccarii Normanniae sub regibus Angliae* (London, 1840).

[64] F.M. Powicke, *The Loss of Normandy, 1189-1204* (Manchester, 1913). Palgrave had much earlier written appreciatively of Stapleton's map.

[65] Francis Palgrave, *The History of Normandy and England* (London, i, 1851; ii, 1857; iii-iv, 1864).

great idea, like Freeman, but with the sources. He realised what great advantages English historians of the middle ages enjoyed on account of English historical records being so much better preserved than those of other nations. He saw that it was a serious shortcoming for early Norman history to be obliged to use Dudo as its main source. Although he sensibly preferred Wace to the Norse sagas, because Wace wrote earlier, he appreciated above all the testimony of the document, saying of the only charter of Duke Richard I known to him, the one for Saint-Denis, 'that it affords more insight into the political position of Richard than can be obtained from any history'. All the same, Palgrave managed to write 900 pages on tenth-century Normandy. The scale of his history of Normandy and England, had it ever been completed, would have far exceeded Freeman's. Palgrave set out to write it because in his view English history was the joint graft of Anglo-Saxon history and Norman history. 'The History of Normandy is as essential a section of English history as the history of Wessex. We must adopt Rollo equally with Cerdic.' Palgrave's thoroughness is what Freeman aimed to emulate, and his Norman enthusiasms to deflate. Both authors, interestingly enough, demonstrate that commercial publishers then had great confidence in the public's willingness to purchase big books on Normandy.

If we ask why the English took such an interest in the Norman Conquest at that time, we have to recognise that no one answer will do. The English were not united in their views about what the Normans had brought with them in 1066 or what they had done with their Conquest. Had the Normans remained an alien aristocratic elite? Or had they been rapidly absorbed into society? Were they representative of allegedly more advanced French culture? Or barely civilised descendants of Viking pirates? There were even Victorian Englishmen prepared to believe that the Normans were still an identifiable element in the population. According to an author writing in 1876,

> The Norman Conquest involved the addition of a numerous and mighty people equalling probably a moiety of the conquered population and the people thus introduced has continued to exist without merger or absorption in any other race and as a race it is distinguishable now as it was a 1,000 years since and at this hour its descendants may be counted by tens of millions in this country and in the United States . . . [66]

The Normans are still almost universally credited with extraordinary mental and physical energies, so that by the late nineteenth century it is hardly surprising if so many Englishmen were eager to regard themselves as the Normans' natural heirs. Just as the Normans had once acquired a great empire

---

[66] *The Norman People and their Existing Descendants in the British Dominions and the USA* (London, 1874). The author has not been identified.

overseas in England and Italy so, in modern times, the English had spread themselves across the globe. This imperialistic phase of Norman study, which took off in the late nineteenth century, has hardly yet exhausted its potential. From the late nineteenth century there have also been American historians eager to stress the Norman capacity to borrow from many cultures and create new masterful authorities.[67] Although the Norman historians of the twentieth century are another topic all together, they prove that after a thousand years the Normans have still not lost their fascination.

[67] The first American scholar to establish a reputation for Norman history was C.H. Haskins, after whom a society dedicated to Norman studies has recently been named. However, S.O. Jewett, who contributed a book on the Normans to the Story of the Nations series issued by Putnam of New York in 1886, had already perceived a link between the Normans and the Americans: 'the people of the young republic of the United States who might be called the Normans of modern times' (1891 edn, London), p. 360.

2

The Rise and Fall of Normandy, *c.* 911-1204

David Bates

The idea that we can think of Normandy's history in terms of 'rise and fall' is not a new one – it was suggested by Professor Lucien Musset more than a decade ago.[1] It is certainly premature to propose general hypotheses on such a large theme, when so many aspects of it need thorough examination. Thus, for example, the politics of the Norman frontier await a systematic analysis which will build on important regional studies.[2] The evolving structure of the cross-Channel estates requires further research.[3] There is also, and above all, the great problem of the mass of unprinted evidence in Normandy (with which I cannot claim even to have begun to come to terms for the period after 1100); a mass which should be astonishing to English historians accustomed to the steady appearance of charters and cartularies from national and local record societies. It seems to me, nonetheless, that an attempt to understand the relationship of England and Normandy in the Anglo-Norman and Angevin periods requires that we start to think about the continuum of Norman history from the earliest Scandinavian settlements to the collapse of 1204.

Scholars have arguably been too ready to follow the Normans to their conquests in England and Italy and to forget about their original home; it is notable how little general surveys of the history of the Normans after 1066 take Normandy into account.[4] The assimilation of the Normans into the societies

---

[1] L. Musset, 'Quelques problèmes posés par l'annexion de la Normandie au domaine royal français', in R.-H. Bautier, ed., *La France de Philippe Auguste: le temps des mutations*. (Paris, 1982), pp. 291-94. Versions of this essay have also been given at the University of Wales College of Cardiff, to the Lancaster Branch of the Historical Association, and to the Early Medieval Seminar at the University of London. I am grateful for all the helpful comments which were made on these occasions as well as at Reading. I must in particular thank Matthew Bennett, John Gillingham, Diana Greenway and Janet Nelson, without in any way associating them with the views expressed. It should also be noted that in an essay which ranges over three centuries, I have generally not given references to well-known events in Anglo-Norman history.

[2] See, J.A. Green, 'Lords of the Norman Vexin' in *War and Government in the Middle Ages*, ed. J. Gillingham and J.C. Holt (Woodbridge, 1984), pp. 47-62, and the articles by K. Thompson cited in note 13.

[3] See, however, David Crouch's contribution to this volume, below pp. 51-67.

[4] D.C. Douglas, *The Norman Achievement* (London, 1969), devotes only pp. 22-29 directly to Normandy; there are only five index references to 'Normandy' in *The Norman Fate, 1100-1154* (London, 1976).

they conquered is a much discussed subject. Concentration on it has even led to the idea, inaugurated apparently by Charles Homer Haskins, whereby we think in terms of the 'ultimate extinction' or 'disappearance' of the Normans.[5] As a corrective to this, we need only refer to Graham Loud's persuasive reaction to the central thesis of R.H.C. Davis' *The Normans and their Myth* and his justified emphasis on the vitality of the medieval *gens Normannorum*.[6] Norman identity was not extinguished; it simply changed over time and it is still very much with us. This continuum of identity and self-identity becomes important once we consider the problem, not of how the Normans came to be assimilated in England, southern Italy and elsewhere, but of how Normandy became, and then ceased to be, the centre of a movement of conquest, colonisation and domination: the problem of 'rise and fall'.

It is important to define terms. By 'rise and fall', I obviously mean to tell a story with a beginning and an end. It is also a story with a middle. The fact that I pronounce it a single story means that I regard 'rise' and 'fall' as connected ideas, part of a single process, with factors which were present during the first influencing the second. It is important also to recognise that 'the rise and fall of Normandy' can be taken to mean both the rise and fall of a conquering power and the rise and fall of a viable, independent northern French territorial principality. This essay's ultimate emphasis is on the rise and fall of a territorial principality. However, it must be accepted that the two types of 'rise and fall' are so closely related that they cannot be neatly disentangled. It is, for instance, unlikely that Normandy would have been so ferociously attacked had its aristocracy not been at the heart of a wide-ranging movement of conquest.

Numerous aspects of the subject are controversial. It is, for example, arguable whether 'rise', as opposed to 'establishment', is the best term to describe the creation of the future duchy of Normandy in the late ninth and early tenth centuries; and arguable whether the rise of the dominant colonising power developed out of the earliest Scandinavian settlements, started in the reign of Duke Richard II (996-1026), was the opportunistic creation of William the Conqueror, or, indeed, was a combination of all three. It seems likely that Normandy's role as a dominant colonising power was over by 1144, when the duchy was acquired by Count Geoffrey of Anjou during the war of succession between Stephen and Matilda. It is possible also to suggest that its role as an independent principality was also over by that date, since its fate was there-after largely determined by outsiders. However, the fact that there are powerful echoes and continuities from the time of domination in the Angevin period justifies continuing the discussion of 'rise and fall' until 1204: it was only then that the wholesale abandonment and confiscation of Norman estates, associated with the duchy's absorption into the French king's demesne, finally

---

[5] C.H. Haskins, *The Normans in European History* (Boston and New York, 1915; repr., 1959), p. 247; R.H.C. Davis, *The Normans and their Myth* (London, 1976), pp. 9, 132.

[6] G.A. Loud, 'The *Gens Normannorum* – Myth or Reality?', *A-NS*, 5 (1982), pp. 104-16.

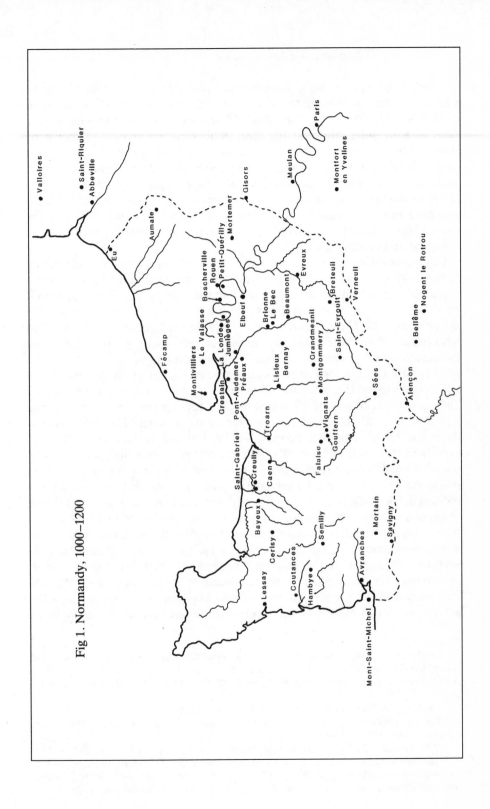

Fig 1. Normandy, 1000–1200

destroyed the principality's independence and that its role within a cross-Channel realm was brought to a definitive end.[7] It is also possible to argue, as does John Gillingham, that 'the loss of Normandy' in 1203-4 was mainly the fault of King John, and that the term 'fall' is inappropriate and should be replaced by 'collapse', since no long-term process was involved.[8] Gillingham may well be right in placing a heavy responsibility on John's shoulders, but it must surely be accepted that – at the least – factors existed which were always likely to disrupt or destroy the Anglo-Norman realm; that some of its rulers grappled more successfully than others to overcome them; and that the principality's capacity for survival may have declined after the great days of conquest and domination.

Contemporaries commented on the process I am discussing. Gerald of Wales devoted a section of his *De principis instructione* to it.[9] He did so in a report of a conversation he supposedly had with Henry II's justiciar, Rannulf de Glanvill, which, if it took place, must have happened before Rannulf's departure on the Third Crusade. Essentially Rannulf argued that France had been weak when Normandy rose to power; her young warriors had been exhausted by other preoccupations. The situation had been reversed by the later twelfth century for two main reasons: the tyranny of the Angevin kings which had sapped the Norman will to resist; and the French love of learning and more civilised way of life which made them superior, just as the Greeks and Romans had once been superior for similar reasons. This evidence was discussed in Sir Maurice Powicke's *The Loss of Normandy*.[10] Powicke remarked that each of Rannulf's (or Gerald's) reasons contains 'a profound truth'. As will become clear, I am not sure I agree, or think that such truths as might be involved are all particularly profound. As Robert Bartlett has indicated, Gerald's remarks fit in neatly with his personal prejudices.[11] The composition of the *De principis instructione* continued throughout the period from 1190 to *c.* 1217. It may be that Gerald's ideas belong with other assessments made after the catastrophes of 1203-4, such as William Marshal's supposed opinion that the Normans became as chaff because of lack of leadership after Richard the Lionheart's death or St Hugh of Lincoln's 'death-bed' speech which 'prophesied' the collapse of power whose origins lay in the achievements of a bastard.[12] The former sentiments were written down in the

---

[7] On this theme, see, above all, J. Le Patourel, 'What Did Not Happen in Stephen's Reign', *History* 58 (1973), pp. 10-17; J.C. Holt, 'The End of the Anglo-Norman Realm', British Academy Raleigh Lecture On History (London, 1975), pp. 23-30, 43-44; Musset, 'Quelques problèmes', pp. 295-301.

[8] J. Gillingham, *The Angevin Empire* (London, 1984), pp. 65-76.

[9] 'De principis instructione liber', in *Giraldi Cambrensis opera*, ed. G.F. Warner, Rolls Series, (London, 1891), viii, pp. 257-59.

[10] F.M. Powicke, *The Loss of Normandy* (2nd ed, Manchester, 1961), pp. 297-303.

[11] See the commentary in R. Bartlett, *Gerald of Wales, 1146-1223* (Oxford, 1982), pp. 84-100.

[12] *Histoire de Guillaume le Maréchal*, ed. P. Meyer, 3 vols (Paris, 1891-1907), iii, p. 58; *Magna vita sancti Hugonis*, ed. D.L. Douie and D.H. Farmer, 2 vols (Oxford, 1985), ii, pp. 184-85.

1220s and the latter in 1213. It is nonetheless interesting that Gerald focused on structural factors of strength and weakness and on an historical process.

A single event can for the moment be taken as typical of the long-term historical process which is, I think, basic to any definition of Normandy's 'rise and fall'. In examining this event, I rely mostly on recent work by Kathleen Thompson, interpreted within a theoretical framework which owes much to Karl Ferdinand Werner and the late Jacques Boussard.[13] The event concerned is the defection of Robert, count of Alençon, to Philip Augustus in January 1203, which, according to Powicke, marked 'the beginning of the end'.[14] Powicke said this because King John was never able to make a serious military effort thereafter: Robert's large estates controlled the road from Normandy to Maine and Anjou and his change of sides opened Normandy up to the Capetians. Yet Count Robert's treachery can be seen as the last event in a sequence which goes back into the early eleventh century and – in all probability – to an even earlier date. In 1173 Count Robert's predecessor, Count John, joined the revolt against King Henry II. In December 1135, even before King Stephen's coronation in England, his father William Talvas joined Matilda; the base she thereby secured in southern Normandy launched the Angevin conquest of the duchy. And so on and so on – or rather back and back – through the history of the Bellême family to, and beyond, the point where the late Jacques Boussard opined – surely rightly – that their ancestors were introduced into the region in the tenth century by the *dux Francorum* Hugh the Great to restrain the Normans.[15] The family's earlier history may well be traceable through the much-discussed 'biological continuity' which has demonstrated the descent of so many of the region's families from the elite of the Carolingian Empire.[16] We have a continuum of instability in and around southern Normandy which stretches from the formation of the territorial principalities within the west Frankish kingdom in the tenth century through to the early thirteenth.

The Bellême family history, as much as Normandy's, has a place at the heart of the volatile politics of the 'age of the principalities' in France. At times the

[13] K. Thompson, 'Family and Influence to the South of Normandy in the Eleventh Century', *Journal of Medieval History*, 11 (1985), pp. 215-26; 'Robert of Bellême Reconsidered', *A-NS*, 13 (1991), pp. 263-86; and her contribution to this volume, below, pp. 169-84; K.F. Werner, 'Untersuchungen zur Frühzeit des französischen Furstentums', *Die Welt als Geschichte*, 18 (1958), pp. 256-89; 19 (1959), pp. 146-93; 20 (1960), pp. 87-119; J. Boussard, 'L'origine des familles seigneuriales dans la région de la Loire moyenne', *Cahiers de civilisation médiévale*, 5 (1962), pp. 303-22.

[14] Powicke, *Loss of Normandy*, p. 158.

[15] J. Boussard, 'Les destinées de la Neustrie du IXe au XIe siècle', *Cahiers de civilisation médiévale*, 11 (1968), pp. 25-26.

[16] Werner, 'Untersuchungen', passim. See also the remarks of C.B. Bouchard, 'The Origins of the French Nobility: A Reassessment', *American Historical Review*, 86 (1981), pp. 501-32.

Bellêmes were drawn profitably into the Normans' orbit – witness the collaboration between Robert de Bellême and King William Rufus[17] – but the needs of
the moment or opportunism might equally orientate them towards Anjou, as
in the 1050s or the late 1130s, or towards the Capetians. These events illustrate
the politics of territorial lordship and the frontier, and they also show both the
relativity and multiplicity of loyalty which could be involved and the magnetic
character of royal and princely military households, all much studied topics in
recent times.[18] The defection of Robert, count of Alençon, is in fact mirrored
by a multitude of other similar actions by many individuals and families
throughout several centuries: the dilemmas are well-illustrated by recent
studies of other powers who operated on the fringes of the great French
principalities and by recent work on twelfth-century Anglo-Norman lordship.[19] From the point of view of Normandy, the nature of the political game in
northern France had barely changed in its fundamentals between 1000 and
1200 – I am tempted to say between 900 and 1200. Although it was modified by
the conquest of 1066, it remained essentially unaffected. Normandy remained
strong as long as its rulers exploited effectively the *'zone interne'* – a term
borrowed from Dominique Barthelémy – of the principality,[20] competed on
equal or superior terms with other princes, attracted neighbours into their
court and retained the strength which was the basis of good lordship. They
were entangled in a web of alliances, relationships and feuds which alternately
advanced or threatened the duchy's power and, sometimes, its very existence.

  Both the creation of the Norman principality and the rise of the conquering
power of the Normans are currently controversial subjects. On the one hand,
we have the late John Le Patourel's thesis of a 'continuous and consistent'

---

[17] F. Barlow, *William Rufus* (London, 1983), pp. 379-85; Thompson, 'Robert of Bellême', pp.
275-76.

[18] The literature is extensive. See especially, J. Boussard, 'L'origine des comtés de Tours, Blois
et Chartres', in *103e congrès national des sociétés savantes. Colloque de Nancy-Metz (1978), section
de philologie et d'histoire* (Paris, 1979), pp. 85-112; J.-F Lemarignier, *Le gouvernement royal aux
premiers temps capétiens* (Paris, 1965), pp. 60-65; J.A. Green, 'Aristocratic Loyalties on the
Northern Frontier of England, c. 1100-1174', *England in the Twelfth Century: Proceedings of the
1988 Harlaxton Symposium*, ed D. Williams (Woodbridge, 1990), pp. 83-100; M. Chibnall,
'Mercenaries and the *Familia Regis* under Henry I', *History*, 62 (1977), pp. 15-23; J.O. Prestwich,
'The Military Household of the Norman Kings', *EHR*, 96 (1981), pp. 1-35. See also, Green, 'Lords
of the Norman Vexin', passim; Holt, 'End of the Anglo-Norman Realm', pp. 36-40.

[19] On Anglo-Norman lordship, see now the stimulating suggestions by D. Crouch, 'Debate.
Bastard Feudalism Revised', *Past and Present*, 131 (1991), pp. 165-77. For the fringes of
Normandy, in addition to the works on Bellème cited in note 13, see D. Bates, 'The Family of the
Counts of Amiens, Valois and the Vexin in France and England during the Eleventh Century', *The
Sudeleys: Lords of Toddington*, the Manorial Society of Great Britain (London, 1987), pp. 34-48;
D. Crouch, *The Beaumont Twins* (Cambridge, 1986), pp. 58-79; Green, 'Lords of the Norman
Vexin'; C. Potts, 'Normandy or Brittany? A Conflict of Interests at Mont Saint-Michel, 996-1035',
A-NS, 12 (1990), pp. 135-56; H. Tanner, 'The Expansion of the Power of the Counts of Boulogne
under Eustace II', *A-NS*, 14 (1992), pp. 251-86.

[20] D. Barthelémy, *L'ordre seigneurial, XIe-XIIe* (Paris, 1990), pp. 15-16.

process of colonisation from the early tenth century onwards. I have taken issue elsewhere with this view, suggesting that in northern Europe, Norman expansion and colonisation were not 'continuous and consistent', but episodic and controlled by the political balance between the various French territorial principalities.[21] Eleanor Searle's recent argument for a more powerfully Scandinavian character to Norman society up until the mid eleventh century has suggested a very definite antipathy between Viking and Frank and a distinctive Germanic social structure. I am both fascinated and, ultimately, not persuaded by either of these ideas. However, the details of her thesis of 'predatory kinship' can mostly be left for another occasion.[22] It is the common ground in the controversies which matters as much as anything here – the violence which surrounded the creation of Normandy and the competitiveness of the principalities in the tenth and eleventh centuries; in particular, the rise of Blois, the great conflict between Anjou and Blois which started in 977 and ended in Angevin victory in 1044, and the period of Angevin supremacy in northern France in the mid eleventh century. These conditioned and limited Normandy's so-called rise and indicate that, in northern French terms, Normandy was little, if anything, more than the political and military equal of its neighbours. Searle's emphasis on the political cohesion created within the duchy by real or imagined kindred networks is also of central importance in explaining the conquest of England. Although the role she assigns to female kindred may be more accidental than deliberate, since paternally descended ducal kindred were in distinctly short supply in the middle of the eleventh century, the resultant unity of purpose and the political domination of a small group were crucial.

What also matters, much more than Searle would allow, in the rise of Normandy, however defined, is the manner in which all territorial princes, the Normans included, picked up parcels of rights once exercised on behalf of Carolingian rulers and exploited them to their own advantage. These supplied the fiscal foundations of Norman ducal power, whose full significance can only be grasped from the late twelfth-century exchequer rolls, and which were exploited within a region whose economic prosperity is beyond doubt. If the species of 'continuity' devised for the tenth century by Werner, Musset and Yver is now justifiably unfashionable among English-speaking scholars, we can still, I suggest, think in terms of a creative use of existing resources.[23] The construction by princes of fortresses and new centres of power, a process now well known for Anjou, Brittany, Flanders and Normandy, was also a crucial factor in the rise of Normandy, as also is the formation of an active, organised

[21] D. Bates, 'Normandy and England after 1066', *EHR*, 104 (1989), pp. 853-61.

[22] E. Searle, *Predatory Kinship and the Creation of Norman Power, 840-1066* (Berkeley and Los Angeles, 1988), passim. See further, the forthcoming 2nd edition of D. Bates, *Normandy before 1066* (London, 1982).

[23] The literature on this topic is vast. For a survey, D. Bates, 'West Francia: The Northern Principalities', *The New Cambridge Medieval History*, iii, ed. T. Reuter, forthcoming.

church.[24] Finally, a recent article by Simon Keynes has shown that the Norman dukes had a much more developed English policy than I believed when I wrote *Normandy before 1066*.[25] His conclusions are reinforced by Elisabeth van Houts' redating of William of Jumièges' first redaction of the *Gesta Normannorum ducum* to the late 1050s.[26] Both show conclusively that the diplomatic prelude to the Conquest of 1066 was a long one, even if the aim of conquest was only formulated by William the Conqueror.

If the Normans possessed the techniques, the material base and the policies which were conducive to conquest, we need nevertheless to retain perspective. There were weaknesses within the Norman principality related to rivalries within and between kindred groups, to the frontier, to competition with neighbouring principalities, and to the retention of a conservative language of power. The tenth-century evolution from Viking settlement to Normandy was turbulent and uncertain. On occasion, as in both the 940s and the 960s, Frankish armies penetrated deep into the new settlement. As I have already noted, in the eleventh century, the families around the Norman frontiers peeled away into other allegiances in times of stress. The language of power remained fundamentally Carolingian throughout northern France – *regnum*, *dux*, *comes*, *fidelitas* can serve as examples. The terms acquired new meanings, but they retained old ones which might be revived to effect; in particular, it is important to recognise that the Norman rulers, like other princes, remained within a framework of fidelity to the French kings.[27] Duke Richard II (996-1026), the Conqueror's grandfather, was a great prince, renowned for keeping the peace, and a great patron of the Christian church. But he was not a great conqueror: aside from some kind of superiority over the Bretons, his achievements in northern French politics were mostly those of a weighty participant in the wars of others.[28] He was followed in quick succession by his sons Richard III and Robert the Magnificent. There looks to have been a succession dispute between them and in Robert's reign considerable pressure was exerted on Normandy's frontiers. When Robert died on pilgrimage, leaving the duchy to his young, illegitimate son William, there was another succession dispute within the ducal kindred and the duchy was plunged into civil war.

When we come to define the processes of 'rise and fall', we can accept that the Norman principality was the creation of its tenth- and early eleventh-century rulers and that they and their aristocracy shaped the base from which the great conquests were made. From the early eleventh century, Normans were also prominent in the social mobility which was characteristic of other northern French peoples at this time. If John France is right to place the

---

[24] On the church, see Bates, *Normandy*, pp. 189-235, and the references supplied there.

[25] S. Keynes, 'The Æthelings in Normandy', *A-NS*, 13 (1991), pp. 173-205.

[26] *The Gesta Normannorum Ducum of William of Jumièges, Orderic Vitalis and Robert of Torigni*, ed. E.M.C. van Houts (Oxford, 1992), i, pp. xxxii-xxxv, xlv-1.

[27] Bates, *Normandy*, pp. 58-62, and 'The Northern Principalities', forthcoming.

[28] Idem, *Normandy*, pp. 65-68.

earliest Norman settlements in southern Europe in Richard II's reign, we are dealing with an initial small migration which gathered pace in the 1040s and 1050s.[29] The numbers involved in the southern Italian conquests are difficult to estimate. They cannot have been very large, since the greatest exodus can probably be related to political crisis in the duchy, and individual departures to personal disagreements and rebellions against the reigning duke. The Normans were at most only a majority among peoples from various regions of northern France.[30] It is surely undeniable that significant expansion came suddenly and dramatically under a great war-leader, William the Conqueror. He undoubtedly harnessed some of the forces which were already fuelling the much smaller migration to southern Italy, but, as with Anjou under counts Fulk Nerra and Geoffrey Martel, or Blois-Chartres under Count Odo II, the relationship between the rule of a warrior prince and large-scale military expansion is transparently obvious. The numbers involved in the so-called 'Norman' Conquest of England are likewise hard to estimate; it seems reasonable to suggest that in demographic terms they were insufficient to sustain long-term domination.

It is also important to remind ourselves that the conquest of England took place during a very special and very fortuitous hiatus in the power-struggle in northern France, when the French royal principality and the county of Anjou were ineffective and Flanders was friendly. The remarkable cohesion which the Normans achieved through kinship networks was by its nature temporary; Eleanor Searle's title, *Predatory Kinship*, aptly indicates the disruptive, as well as the cohesive, aspects of kindred politics. As Jane Martindale has shown, the resultant succession disputes were manifestations of a phenomenon which affected not only Normandy, but all French princely and aristocratic families.[31] With this in mind, we can point out that, as is frequently the case with powers which expand militarily, the expansion does not cure existing structural flaws. The other major principalities of northern France revived during the 1070s and made the last years of the Conqueror's reign notably difficult. William's conquest of Maine, very different in execution from his English

[29] J. France, 'The Occasion of the Coming of the Normans to Southern Italy', *Journal of Medieval History*, 17 (1992), pp. 185-205.

[30] L.-R. Ménager, 'Pesanteur et étiologie de la colonisation normande de l'Italie', *Roberto il Guiscardo e il suo tempore*, Fonti e studi del corpus membranorum Italicarum, 11 (Rome, 1975), pp. 189-214; also reproduced in *Hommes et institutions de l'Italie normande* (London, 1981); G.A. Loud, 'How "Norman" was the Norman Conquest of Southern Italy?', *Nottingham Medieval Studies*, 25 (1981), pp. 19-21; D.J.A. Matthew, *The Norman Kingdom of Sicily* (Cambridge, 1992), p. 140; L. Musset, 'Autour des modalités juridiques de l'expansion normande au XIe siècle: le droit d'exil', in L. Musset et al, *Autour du pouvoir ducal normand, Xe-XIIe siècles* (Caen, 1985), pp. 45-59.

[31] J. Martindale, 'Succession and Politics in the Romance-Speaking World, *c.* 1000-1140', in *England and her Neighbours, 1066-1453*, ed. M. Jones and M. Vale (London and Ronceverte, 1989), pp. 19-41.

achievement, brought additional headaches as well as territorial gains.[32] The break-down of order in Normandy after the Conqueror's death in 1087 and the feud between his sons for the succession were, in all fundamental aspects, a replay of an old tune. As is well known, they were followed by several similar conflicts in the twelfth century. In the same way, Norman expansion into England was an expression of the drive to expand that was typical of all eleventh-century northern French territorial principalities. As far as Normandy was concerned therefore, its results were unlikely to alter the fundamental characteristics of northern French princely politics.

The Norman expansion into Britain added a fresh set of problems to those which already existed. The Conquest brought divergent interests from many parts of northern France together in a common enterprise. Once the initial campaigns were over, divergent interests remained and divergent interests reemerged. In 1075, for example, the Breton, Ralph, earl of East Anglia, rebelled against William the Conqueror. Expelled from England he established himself at Dol near the Norman frontier, brought the French King Philip I to his aid, and inflicted on the Conqueror the first major military defeat he had ever suffered. As a result of the marriage which prefaced Ralph's revolt, he had a son who in the early twelfth century had a claim to the southern Norman honour of Breteuil. This again led to war.[33] The disruptive impact of such cross-principality family connections needs clarification and quantification; it has already been significantly advanced by Katherine Keats-Rohan's study of the Bretons in England.[34] A good case study involving cross-principality ties is supplied by the history of the counts of Boulogne. Ambivalent towards Normandy before 1066, richly rewarded in England after the Conquest and more closely integrated when Henry I arranged the marriage of his nephew Stephen to the heiress Matilda of Boulogne, the family's loss of the honour of Boulogne after 1159 initiated another period of hostility. Richard I bought the alliance of Rainald de Danmartin in 1198,[35] but in 1203-4 he was on the side of Philip Augustus.[36]

There can be no doubt about the devastating significance for the future of one aspect of this phenomenon, namely the Norman rulers' practice of marrying daughters into the families of other northern French princes. It is necessary only to point to the combined long-term results of the marriage of the Conqueror's daughter Adela into the family of the counts of Blois and the courting of Anjou by Henry I and William Clito. The alliance with Blois

[32] See the remarks in D. Bates, *William the Conqueror* (London, 1989), pp. 137-38.

[33] Crouch, *Beaumont Twins*, pp. 102-14.

[34] K.S.B. Keats-Rohan, 'The Bretons and Normans of England, 1066-1154', *Nottingham Medieval Studies*, 36 (1992), pp. 42-78.

[35] *Pipe Roll 10 Richard I*, ed. D.M. Stenton, Pipe Roll Society, 47 (1932), pp. xv-xvi.

[36] For an account of the twists and turns in the relationship between the counts and the Norman and Angevin rulers, J.H. Round, 'The Counts of Boulogne as English Lords', *Studies in Peerage and Family History* (Westminster, 1901), pp. 163-89.

provided Henry I with an important ally in his wars against other northern French rulers, gave Stephen his opportunity to seize England and Normandy, and produced a war which resulted in the Angevin conquest of Normandy in the 1140s. Normandy's rulers, both Norman and Angevin, showed little inclination or instinct to escape from the double-edged political game created by marriages and kinship ties within northern France. One last such marriage, arranged between Henry II's third son Geoffrey and Constance the Breton heiress in 1166, had even more devastating consequences as a result of the rivalry between their son Arthur and John for succession to the 'Angevin Empire'. In 1203-4 Breton forces joined Philip Augustus in the decisive two-pronged assault on Normandy after the 'disappearance' of Arthur of Brittany.

The Norman settlement of Britain created an overarching cross-Channel aristocracy whose dominant role in Anglo-Norman politics has been analysed by John Le Patourel, Warren Hollister and others. Le Patourel's *The Norman Empire* remains the essential survey of Norman colonisation.[37] However, as Judith Green and myself have suggested, it also left behind a substantial Norman/French aristocracy whose interests were concentrated in France and whose policies were conditioned accordingly.[38] The cohesion of the duchy's aristocracy was thereby threatened by another potentially disruptive factor, whose contribution was especially significant during Henry I's reign in support of his nephew William Clito. Modern discussion of the period of Henry I's rule in Normandy has differed somewhat on the effectiveness of Henry's rule within the duchy; the common ground in the debates nonetheless stresses his basic control, despite set-backs; the essential defensiveness of his policies; and the stresses imposed by war finance.[39] Ideas on both the momentum and rhythm of Norman colonisation and on cross-Channel politics have also developed significantly since Le Patourel's book was published. For example, a rough-and-ready demographic survey suggests that the majority of the enfeofments in England recorded in the *Cartae baronum* of 1166 had been made before 1086. Afterwards such migration as took place was to the northern and westerly fringes. Important recent studies of the 'Norman' (a most questionable term in this context) settlements in Wales and Scotland have shown that the majority of settlers came from families already established in England. The evidence for migration from Normandy to England after 1135 is

---

[37] J. Le Patourel, *The Norman Empire* (Oxford, 1976); C.W. Hollister, 'Normandy, France and the Anglo-Norman *Regnum*', *Speculum*, 51 (1976), pp. 202-42.

[38] Bates, 'Normandy and England', pp. 858-9; J.A. Green, 'Unity and Disunity in the Anglo-Norman State', *Historical Research*, 63 (1989), pp. 128-33.

[39] See, from among a considerable literature, C.W. Hollister and T.K. Keefe, 'The Making of the Angevin Empire', *Journal of British Studies*, 12 (1973), pp. 3-19; Chibnall, 'Mercenaries', pp. 20-22; J.A. Green, *The Government of England under Henry I* (Cambridge, 1986), pp. 17-18; eadem, 'King Henry I and the Aristocracy of Normandy', in *Actes du IIIe congrès national des sociétés savantes, section d'histoire et de philologie, i* (Paris, 1988), pp. 161-73.

very weak indeed.[40] The pattern of the southern migrations is similar; a falling-away by the early twelfth century.[41]

These conclusions also raise questions about the changing nature of Norman domination in the lands they settled, and about Normandy's changing role within the Norman conquests. A well-known literature, at whose heart is Orderic Vitalis, emphasises a Norman world with Normandy at its centre until the middle of the twelfth century and beyond. We read also of attitudes which historians of more recent times would identify as colonial. Richard Basset, for example, who had grown rich in England in the service of Henry I, is said by Orderic to have built a stone castle on 'the little fief' which he had inherited from his parents at Montreuil-en-Houlme in the modern Norman *département* of Orne.[42] Yet recent research in England on topics as diverse as aristocratic burials, personal names, saints' cults and monastic patronage by Brian Golding, the late Cecily Clark, Susan Ridyard and Emma Cownie demonstrates conclusively how newcomers became entrenched in English society and established local loyalties from a notably early date.[43] Southern Italy presents a similar picture of a dominant elite becoming quite quickly 'domiciled' in a new land.[44]

A Norman world undoubtedly did exist in the first half of the twelfth century around which individuals moved and made careers.[45] At the very same time, Normandy was gradually, imperceptibly but inexorably, being displaced from centre-stage. We should note that the 'Normans' employed by King Roger II of Sicily, like Thomas Brown or Robert of Selby, were in fact of English origin. Also that the *Gesta Normannorum ducum* had ceased to be written by the 1140s. A loss of dynamic is also suggested by Lindy Grant's work on Gothic architecture: such originality as eleventh-century Norman Romanesque possessed was displaced by dependence on the new styles of the Ile-de-France.[46] The history of the provincial synod of the archdiocese of Rouen points in a similar direction: in the eleventh century, the frequency of its meetings set it apart from the rest of the French kingdom, but after 1118 such gatherings ceased to take place.[47] There can be no doubt that Normandy remained the

---

[40] Bates, 'Normandy and England', pp. 853-57.

[41] Matthew, *Norman Kingdom*, p. 140.

[42] Bates, 'Normandy and England', pp. 865-69.

[43] B. Golding, 'Anglo-Norman Knightly Burials', *The Ideals and Practice of Medieval Knighthood*, ed. C. Harper-Bill and R. Harvey (Woodbridge, 1986), pp. 40-48; C. Clark, 'Women's Names in Post-Conquest England: Observations and Speculations', *Speculum*, 53 (1978), pp. 223-51; S. Ridyard, '*Condigna Veneratio*: Post-Conquest Attitudes to the Saints of the Anglo-Saxons', *A-NS*, 9 (1987), pp. 179-206. See also Emma Cownie's essay, below, pp. 143-57.

[44] The word 'domiciled' is employed in Matthew, *Norman Kingdom*, p. 140.

[45] See most recently, R.V. Turner, 'Les contacts entre l'Angleterre normanno-angevine et la Sicile normande', *Etudes normandes*, 35 (1986), pp. 39-60.

[46] See Lindy Grant's essay, below, pp. 117-29.

[47] R. Foreville, 'The Synod of the Province of Rouen in the Eleventh and Twelfth Centuries', *Church and Government in the Middle Ages*, ed. C.N.L. Brooke et al (Cambridge, 1976), pp. 34-37.

subject of a sentimental affection for an ancestral homeland well on into the second half of the twelfth century; note, for example, Wace's massive vernacular French poem the *Roman de Rou et des ducs de Normandie* written for the court of King Henry II, celebrating the achievements of the ancestors of a large number of Norman families.[48] It is also important to recognise that declining colonial momentum is not synonymous with political weakness. The duchy's continuing strength is shown by its aristocracy's effective resistance to the Angevins during the first years of Stephen's reign.[49] Multiple signs of vitality and of a powerful desire to sustain the connection with England are supplied by the alacrity with which the Normans accepted Stephen's coup in England and by the manner in which Norman bishops were prepared to shore up Stephen's kingship; it was Bishop Arnulf of Lisieux who represented him at the papal court and Archbishop Hugh of Rouen who came to his assistance after the arrest of Bishop Roger of Salisbury and his relatives. Collapse came only after the battle of Lincoln and, even then, Rouen did not capitulate until 1144. It is, however, becoming clear that Normandy's history at the centre of a movement of colonisation and conquest was a comparatively short one. Marjorie Chibnall has observed that the ideas of common descent and of the unity of the *gens Normannorum* were 'fast becoming an illusion in Orderic's active life-time'.[50] It must also be significant that John Gillingham has discerned the emergence of a new sense of Englishness at precisely the same period.[51]

Normandy occupied an important place in the Angevins' rule of their far-flung territories. Members of the urban elite of Rouen put up money which assisted Henry II to secure the English kingdom. Geoffrey, Matilda and Henry II all flattered and patronised the city, granting it its earliest surviving charter of liberties, and financing the construction of the first stone bridge across the Seine. They generally supported the process which elevated it to the status of the second city of France in the late twelfth and thirteenth centuries. Treaties between Henry II and the kings of France in the 1170s and 1180s placed Rouen on the same level as Paris and the explanations of the young king Henry's burial in Rouen Cathedral emphasised his Norman ancestry.[52] Henry II's itinerary brought him to Normandy more often than to any other part of his

---

[48] M. Bennett, 'Poetry as History? The *Roman de Rou* of Wace as a Source for the Norman Conquest', *A-NS*, 5 (1983), pp. 21-39.

[49] Crouch, *Beaumont Twins*, pp. 31-38; M. Chibnall, *The Empress Matilda* (Oxford, 1991), pp. 72-74; J. Bradbury, 'The Early Years of the Reign of Stephen', *England in the Twelfth Century*, pp. 26-7.

[50] M. Chibnall, *The World of Orderic Vitalis* (Oxford, 1984), pp. 213-14.

[51] J. Gillingham, 'The Beginnings of English Imperialism', *Journal of Historical Sociology*, 5 (1992), pp. 392-409.

[52] For a survey of Rouen's history, D. Bates, 'Rouen 900 to 1204: From Scandinavian Settlement to Angevin "Capital" ', *Medieval Art, Architecture and Archaeology at Rouen*, ed. J. Stratford, *BAACT*, 12 (1993), 1-11.

vast lands and the scarcely understood development of the Norman *baillis* shows a capacity for major governmental reform. Aside from the participation in the 1173 revolt of a small number of men with lands which straddled the frontier, the duchy remained solidly on the side of Henry II.[53] Statistical calculations made by Léopold Delisle from the Norman Pipe Roll of 1180 suggest a comfortable superiority of resources over the Capetians. This last proposition will eventually be given a renewed and thorough discussion by Vincent Moss.[54] In the short term, Angevin rule may have brought a security to Normandy which it had enjoyed only when the Conqueror was at the height of his power; this may well have been a result of the restoration of ducal power in the Norman Vexin in 1160 and the associated policy of seizing castles near and beyond the Norman frontier.[55] This security seemingly became greater still when Brittany was absorbed in 1166.

All was not prosperity under the Angevins. Although the *Etablissements*, the urban constitution of Rouen, was exported to other towns in the Angevin Empire and Norman diplomatic forms influenced charters in Anjou, Normans drew little personal benefit from the Angevin Empire. The Rouen financiers who had supported Henry II in 1154 soon ceased to have dealings with the English exchequer; he preferred to borrow from Flemings and Jews.[56] Only one among the Angevin administrative servants in England studied by Ralph Turner turns out to have been of Norman origin.[57] David Crouch has shown that, despite his possession of a cross-Channel estate, only one rather obscure member of the predominantly English military household of William Marshal came from Normandy.[58] Few Normans obtained bishoprics in the non-Norman regions of the Angevin Empire; my impression is that those who did, did so in the first years of Henry II's reign.[59]

During the revolt of 1173-74, despite apparent strong Norman support for Henry II, the defences of Upper Normandy collapsed after the count of Flanders had captured Eu and King Louis VII's army was able to lay siege to Rouen. The estates of the cross-Channel magnates during this period deserve careful study. Two of them, one recreated for Robert II, earl of Leicester, and held by his descendants and one created for William Marshal, were held by men whose origins were not Norman. Lucien Musset has suggested that the

[53] J. Boussard, *Le gouvernement d'Henri II Plantagenêt* (Paris, 1956), p. 477 n. 5.

[54] See M. de Bouard, ed., *Histoire de la Normandie* (Toulouse, 1970), pp. 152-53.

[55] W.L. Warren, *Henry II* (London, 1973), pp. 90-91, 235-36; Robert of Torigny, pp. 206, 208, 209, 211-12, 223, 227.

[56] L. Musset, 'Une aristocratie d'affaires anglo-normande après la conquête', *Etudes normandes*, 35 (1986), pp. 10-11.

[57] R.V. Turner, *Men Raised from the Dust: Administrative Service and Upward Mobility in Angevin England* (Philadelphia, 1988), p. 21, calls William de Sainte-Mère-Eglise 'one of the rare native Normans to join England's royal administration under Henry II and his sons'.

[58] D. Crouch, *William Marshal* (London, 1990), pp. 136, 141.

[59] D. Walker, 'Crown and Episcopacy under the Normans and Angevins', *A-NS*, 5 (1983), pp. 227-31.

centre of gravity of the Tosny's cross-Channel estate had shifted towards England by the later twelfth century.[60] Musset has argued that the process of migration moved into reverse in the later twelfth century and had produced several examples of Englishmen making careers and fortunes in Normandy.[61] The chronology of this whole development deserves closer examination. What may have been a trickle at the beginning had certainly become a stronger flow by 1200, when the archbishop of Rouen and the mayors of Caen and Evreux were Englishmen. There were of course exceptions to this pattern; Bishop Arnulf of Lisieux, for example, acquired lands in England in Henry II's reign and, most unsuccessfully, the Norman William Longchamp enjoyed brief power in England. It is nonetheless my impression that the structure rather than the substance of Normandy's wide-ranging connections was recreated after 1154. At the end of the twelfth century, as disaster loomed, Normandy was submerged in the defence of the entire Angevin Empire. As Powicke long ago suggested, by the end its people had mostly lost control over their own destiny, as its defences were organised by mercenary captains and such key strong-points as the counties of Eu and Aumale passed respectively to an Aquitanian and a Fleming.[62]

The continuities beneath this survey of ducal Normandy are striking. It was William the Conqueror who first shipped English money across the Channel to finance a campaign in France and it was William the Conqueror who first used English troops to fight his wars there. Henry I's use of the same techniques is, as we have seen, well known. Stephen imported Flemish mercenaries; Henry II, Flemish and Welsh. William the Conqueror was not the first Norman ruler to fight a war against members of his own kindred whose ambitions had received support from other northern French principalities; and he was certainly not the last. Gisors, the site of a splendid castle on the frontier of the Norman and the French Vexin, began its shuttle-cock career from Norman to French hands and back again before 1066, when William the Conqueror granted it to Ralph, count of Amiens, Valois and the Vexin.[63] William the Conqueror, Henry I and Henry II all invested heavily in castle-building around the Norman frontier. Yet invading armies penetrated deep into Normandy during the reigns of all three. Problems connected with families on Normandy's frontiers were endemic throughout: it is salutary to remember that our written evidence shows the lords of Bellême causing difficulties for every Norman ruler from the tenth century to the thirteenth. Likewise there were arguments between every Norman ruler and contemporary Capetian king about the *fidelitas* they owed. No Norman ruler developed either the ritual or

---

[60] L. Musset, 'Aux origines d'une classe dirigeante: les Tosny, grands barons normands du Xe au XIIIe siècles', *Francia*, 5 (1977), pp. 62-66.

[61] Musset, 'Quelques problèmes', pp. 292-94.

[62] Powicke, *Loss of Normandy*, pp. 228-31; see also J. Gillingham, *Richard the Lionheart* (London, 1978), pp. 256-57.

[63] ADSM, G 8739.

the ideology with which to compete on equal terms with the French kings; the first stirrings came in the later twelfth century, as disaster loomed.[64] Another continuity is that each separate problem was in one way or another resolved. Each invasion was beaten back. Henry I solved his problems about fealty to Louis VI by permitting his son to perform the ceremony. Waleran, count of Meulan, reached a settlement in 1157 whereby he did liege homage to Henry II and had this arrangement accepted by Louis VII.[65] The lords of Bellême reached accommodations with a succession of Norman dukes, Angevin counts and Capetian kings.

It is well known – and was indeed clearly shown by Powicke – that Normandy in the later twelfth century was utterly unable to meet the costs of defence without a substantial English contribution. Richard I's great castle of Château-Gaillard cost approximately 46,000 *livres angevins*, almost half the receipts at the Norman Exchequer in 1198, a year apparently of high income (98,000 *livres angevins*). In the accounting year 1202-3 at least around £15,000 sterling (60,000 *livres angevins*) was despatched from England into Normandy. The English pipe rolls show thousands of men being transported to Normandy.[66] These financial issues have been well-researched and are currently a matter of controversy.[67] They suggest to me that the occasional injections of earlier times had turned into addiction. This happened because, in the 1190s and 1200s, Normandy faced a transformed Capetian monarchy and a ruthless opponent in Philip Augustus. In 1202-3 the amount of money which Philip could use to finance war exceeded anything that John could apparently deploy.[68] The conflict was also no longer one between principalities, but one with an overlord determined to enforce what he regarded as his rights. In these circumstances the negotiated settlements possible in earlier times were no longer possible: no wonder that men like Hugh de Gournai, Robert, count of Meulan and William Marshal attracted accusations of treachery as they sought to find ways out of what became in 1203-4 an appalling predicament.[69] Yet the key consideration when we contemplate 'the rise and fall of Normandy' is that the catastrophes in which all were involved had been foreshadowed many times before. Richard the Lionheart's return to Normandy in May 1194 stilled, for the last time, the massive defections to Philip Augustus among families

[64] H. Hoffman, 'Französische Fürstenweihen des Hochmittelalters', *Deutsches Archiv*, 18 (1962), pp. 98-102; D. Crouch, *The Image of Aristocracy in Britain, 1000-1300* (London, 1992), pp. 200-02.

[65] Idem, *Beaumont Twins*, p. 77.

[66] Powicke, *Loss of Normandy*, pp. 232-41.

[67] J.C. Holt, 'The Loss of Normandy and Royal Finances', *War and Government in the Middle Ages*, ed. Gillingham and Holt, pp. 92-105; Gillingham, *Angevin Empire*, pp. 71-74.

[68] J.W. Baldwin, *The Government of Philip Augustus*, (Berkeley, Los Angeles and London, 1986), pp. 166-75.

[69] Powicke, *Loss of Normandy*, pp. 160-61, 285-86, 344-45; Crouch, *William Marshal*, pp. 82-88.

around the Norman frontier. In all this, I am reminded of Geoffrey Barrow's comments on the Anglo-Scottish frontier to the effect that the ultimate solvent of plural loyalty and cross-border landholding was long-enduring and devastating war.[70]

Gerald of Wales (and Sir Maurice Powicke) may be said to have had a point when they associated Normandy's rise with French weakness. The hiatus in the power-struggle in northern France in the 1060s provided a superb opportunity for a well-organised and structured territorial principality. Their thesis of cultural decline might even be supported by what we often call the transformation from 'the Age of the Principalities' to 'the Age of the Cathedrals'. Normandy's decline is paralleled by the rise in wealth and prestige of Paris. Yet there is much more to the rise and fall of Normandy than this. Joined in 1066 to a kingdom four or five times its size, Normandy was from then on open to domination by an economically stronger partner; after 1154, it was a less significant part of a still larger territorial combination. Attitudes to the succession to the combined lands of Normandy and England were persistently disruptive. Whatever, for example, William the Conqueror was planning in his last years, it most certainly was not a smooth, healthy transition of his lands. The interests of family predominated over those of 'the state' and continued to do so throughout. Normandy's rulers continued to accept a relationship of *fidelitas* to the French kings. They lacked the framework of ideas required to release their principality from the feudal structure of the French kingdom to create a genuine cross-Channel state. All is summed up in Robert of Torigny's blunt statement that the 'ducatus Normannie est de regno Francorum'.[71] Because of this, I prefer in broad terms to see Normandy's rise and fall in terms of the 'politics of the principalities'. In the 1190s Philip Augustus changed the rules by which a centuries-old game had been played. Richard the Lionheart coped heroically. John failed disastrously and the increasingly fragile structure shattered.

---

[70] G.W.S. Barrow, 'Frontier and Settlement: Which Influenced Which? England and Scotland, 1100-1300', *Medieval Frontier Societies*, ed. R. Bartlett and A. MacKay (Oxford, 1989), p. 21.

[71] Robert of Torign, p. 208.

3

Monastic Foundations in England and Normandy, 1066-1189

Marjorie Chibnall

Writing from a Cluniac monastery in the early eleventh century, Raoul Glaber proclaimed with amazement and joy that the whole world was clothing itself in a white mantle of churches.[1] A century later William of Malmesbury described with equal wonder the changes he was witnessing in England, as new churches sprang up in villages, towns and cities.[2] But if the metaphors were similar, the explanation (in part at least) was different. Glaber was observing the upsurge of reform inspired in particular by Cluny; Malmesbury was most conscious of the consequences of the Norman conquest in redistributing the wealth of England in the wake of the new reform movement. Almost before the ink was dry on his parchment a white mantle of a different kind was spreading over Europe: the (nominally at least) white habits of the new orders of monks and regular canons. Socially too changes were taking place. The Conquest brought new wealth on an unprecedented scale to Norman baronial and knightly families. It changed the balance of wealth between patrimony and acquisitions. The conquerors – Normans and their allies – had lands that might become new centres of family piety for either the main stem or some of the branches of their family; and the churches they founded enabled them to put down roots more firmly in newly-conquered territory. In the early years of the Conquest the greater tenants-in-chief were the conspicuous beneficiaries of surplus wealth; their vassals followed more modestly, directing their charitable gifts mostly to houses founded by their lords. In time, however, the honorial barons too became settled landholders and, during the twelfth century, the ranks of potential new monastic founders were swollen by the new class of administrative officers who throve in the royal service. Changing patterns of monastic life helped even the less wealthy to become founders of new, smaller religious houses. The history of foundations in the period from the Conquest

---

[1] Rodulphus Glaber, *The Five Books of the Histories*, ed. John France, Oxford Medieval Texts (Oxford, 1989), iii, 13, pp. 114-16.
[2] *Willelmi Malmesbiriensis monachi de gestis regum Anglorum*, ed. William Stubbs, Rolls Series (London, 1887), ii, p. 306.

to the death of Henry II provides a mirror of the interplay of religious and social change during those years.

The monastic reforms of the tenth century in England, and the impetus received in Normandy from Lotharingia, the Loire Valley and above all from Cluny by way of Dijon, had established a solid core of great Benedictine houses on both sides of the Channel. In England the revival owed as much to bishops and monks as to the king. On the eve of the Conquest there were some thirty-five houses of men and nine of women, all well-endowed but unevenly distributed. Most were in Wessex, the Fens and the basin of the Severn. They were autonomous houses, with hardly any dependent priories or cells, and most followed the customs of the *Regularis concordia*.[3] In Normandy the dukes, from the time of Richard II, had played a leading part in furthering the foundation or restoration of Benedictine houses. Under Duke William II his leading vassals vied with one another to follow his example. The greatest abbeys were independent but, to a greater extent than elsewhere, they were in the general protection of the duke. Certain characteristics stand out: patrons from the duke down were willing to adopt the customs of the abbey that provided a nucleus of monks, particularly the customs of Cluny which William of Dijon did so much to promote. They were not, however, prepared to accept any kind of permanent subjection.[4] This was appropriate in the period when Cluny was rather a model and an inspiration than an order. By the mid eleventh century, however, and particularly during the abbacy of St Hugh, Cluny began to impose stricter control on its daughter priories. It was a symptom of the change, and of Duke William's view of his relations with the church, that no dependent Cluniac priories were founded in Normandy at this time.[5]

In contrast to England, however, small dependent priories and cells were beginning to proliferate by the middle of the century. Outside Normandy, Marmoutier was a favoured centre of excellence, and the Angevin abbeys of Saint-Nicholas Angers and Saint-Florent-près-Saumur also established cells, some in Normandy. This movement resulted from the wish of feudal lords of

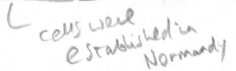

[3] David Knowles and R. Neville Hadcock, *Medieval Religious Houses, England and Wales* (London, 1971), pp. 11-14. David Knowles, *The Monastic Order in England* (2nd edn, Cambridge, 1962), remains fundamental for all aspects of monastic history in this period.

[4] See J. Laporte, 'Les origines du monachisme dans la province de Rouen', *Revue Mabillon*, 31 (1941), pp. 1-13, 25-41, 49-68, esp. pp. 57-64; David Bates, *Normandy before 1066* (London, 1982), pp. 194-98, 207-8, 218-25; Marjorie Chibnall, *The World of Orderic Vitalis* (Oxford, 1984), pp. 48-49. Details of Norman religious houses are given in Dom Beaunier, *Recueil historique des archévêchés, évêchés, abbayes et prieurés de France*, ed. J.M. Besse, Archives de la France monastique, 4 (Ligugé and Paris, 1906).

[5] On Cluniac foundations see Brian Golding, 'The Coming of the Cluniacs', *A-NS*, 3 (1981), pp. 65-77.

relatively modest means to enjoy the prayers and services of religious, and to secure a burial-place for themselves among the monks they regarded as their own. Many small priories were founded at the caput of an honour, often in or near a castle.[6] The smaller cells were not founded as conventual priories; they resulted from the need of abbeys to administer distant properties received from benefactors. The movement of reform also touched the communities of secular canons, some of whom followed an adaptation of the *Regula* of St Chrodegang, but many of whom treated their prebends as hereditary private property. They were being replaced by groups of monks from a Benedictine house, and frequently became subject priories.

The Norman Conquest led to a somewhat different pattern of Benedictine monasticism spreading over England, while at the same time changes continued in Normandy. Although many of the great English abbeys such as Glastonbury, Malmesbury, Worcester and Canterbury were centres of learning and piety, new Norman abbots found much to criticise (not always justly) and to change, from liturgy and libraries to architecture and estate management. Except in parts of the country which had not felt the reform movement, there was little need for major new independent Benedictine houses. Moreover, some great continental houses were not prepared to send their monks overseas to a newly-conquered and still turbulent country, unless they could maintain some kind of control over the new foundations.

The Conqueror's own abbey of Battle was a special case, though it was not easy to persuade Marmoutier, the abbey which supplied the first colony of monks, to relinquish all control over the new house: the monks of Battle finally achieved total independence only with the aid of a masterful royal patron (Henry II) and a handful of forged charters.[7] Two other abbeys in the Welsh marches secured independence without serious difficulty.[8] Durham, the most important Benedictine house in the north, belongs to a category peculiar to England: the cathedral priories. Since England was very unusual in providing Benedictine monasteries instead of colleges of secular canons for the service of some cathedral churches, it may seem surprising that the Conquest actually led to an increase in their number. In fact, the Norman settlers in southern Italy had already shown themselves willing to found a bishopric in an abbey, as the example of the restored Benedictine abbey of Venosa, which served as the

[6] D.J.A. Matthew, *The Norman Monasteries and their English Possessions* (Oxford, 1962), pp. 50-51, 55-57.

[7] Eleanor Searle, *The Chronicle of Battle Abbey*, Oxford Medieval Texts (Oxford 1980), pp. 20-23, 309-13.

[8] St Werburgh, Chester, was founded as an independent Benedictine abbey peopled with monks of Bec-Hellouin with the full support of Anselm. Roger of Montgomery secured monks from Sées for his new abbey at Shrewsbury without seriously compromising its independence, Marjorie Chibnall, 'Forgery in Narrative Charters', *Fälschungen im Mittelalter*, Monumenta Germaniae Historica, *Schriften*, 33, iv, pp. 335-45.

cathedral church of the city with the sanction of Pope Nicholas II, shows.[9] The Normans in England also took the wealth of their new cathedrals where they could find it. Some sees were moved to more important urban centres, and taking over the property of an older religious house was a convenient way of providing for their endowment. If Chester, which was for a time one of the seats of the first Norman bishops in Mercia, had become a permanent episcopal centre, St Werburgh's might have been added to the number of cathedral priories. Instead it was Coventry that, after a struggle, submitted to that fate. In East Anglia the great abbey of Bury St Edmunds successfully fought off the threat of annexation, and the see finally settled under Herbert Losinga in a new priory at Norwich. Rochester was another new foundation. But the earliest of all was Durham, where the see was not moved. There the secular clerks were replaced by twenty-three monks, drawn partly from the newly restored small houses of Jarrow and Wearmouth to take over the patrimony of St Cuthbert; it became a centre of Benedictine culture and influence in the semi-independent north of England.[10]

The other important new Benedictine houses belonged to the family of Cluny and were not fully independent.[11] However strong the Norman influence on the church might be, the Norman kings had not quite the same protective function in the kingdom as in the duchy. William the Conqueror was an admirer of Cluny, and even wrote to ask St Hugh for Cluniac monks to help him to reform the church. His letter, however, tactlessly offered money in terms that produced from the great abbot a somewhat testy reply that his monks were not for sale, and that he would not send them overseas to their perdition. St Hugh had, in fact, just provided communities of monks for three houses in Castile,[12] and he may have felt his human resources depleted; if he was really daunted by the need to go overseas his objections were soon overcome by another would-be benefactor. William of Warenne and his wife Gundreda, who visited Cluny when on pilgrimage and were impressed by the splendour of the liturgy, succeeded in persuading him to send monks for the priory they wished to found at Lewes. The generosity of their endowment, which made Lewes by far the richest of the Cluniac houses in England, and their willingness to allow their new priory to be subject to the mother-house of Cluny, no doubt helped to persuade the abbot. A few years previously Roger of Montgomery had turned not to Cluny but to a daughter house at La-

---

[9] For the cathedral priories see Knowles, *Monastic Order*, pp. 129-34. For Venosa, L.-R. Ménager, 'Les fondations monastiques de Robert Guiscard, duc de Pouille et de Calabre', *Quellen und Forschungen aus italienischen Archiven und Bibliotheken*, 39 (1959), 1-116, at pp. 36-57.

[10] Knowles, *Monastic Order*, pp. 168-69; Marjorie Chibnall, 'Le problème des réseaux monastiques en Angleterre', *Naissance et fonctionnement des réseaux monastiques et canoniaux*, C.E.R.-C.O.R., Travaux et Recherches, 1, (Saint-Etienne, 1991), pp. 345-46.

[11] Golding, 'Coming of the Cluniacs'.

[12] Frank Barlow, *The English Church, 1066-1154* (London and New York, 1979), pp. 184-85; Richard Fletcher, *The Quest for El Cid* (Oxford, 1989), pp. 71-72.

Charité-sur-Loire for monks to enable him to use the endowments of a former double house at Wenlock to found a priory there. Other, mostly smaller, Cluniac houses quickly sprang up in England; they were all content to allow their priors to be appointed by the mother house and to attend the general chapters of the Order. One result was that they were later to be classed as alien priories, with all that this entailed.

Because the new wealth of the Conquest brought an unprecedented flood of small foundations, and because in the later middle ages the loss of Normandy and the wars with France forced the cells of many French abbeys into a category of alien priories, the group has attracted special attention.[13] But it was part of a widespread movement, whereby many of the greater Benedictine houses in north-west Europe acquired a network of dependent priories and cells. Not all the mother houses of the English priories were in Normandy, or indeed in the regions from which individual Bretons, Angevins, Poitevins or Flemings who fought in the Conqueror's army, came; and many had other dependencies in regions outside the Anglo-Norman realm. Much depended on the reputation for piety and sound discipline in the founding houses, or on their fame as centres of pilgrimage. A rough guide to the scale of this type of monastic colonisation is given by Pierre-Roger Gaussin;[14] his figures, however, include the most minute cells and even administrative centres that housed a monk or two for a few years. They need to be pruned. For instance, his count of twenty dependencies of Le Bec in England and twenty-two elsewhere should be reduced to eight conventual and two or three non-conventual priories in England, with a corresponding reduction for Normandy. However the figures give some indication of scale and distribution. Among prominent non-Norman houses, Saint-Nicholas Angers, with four priories in England, had thirty in the Loire region; Saint-Florent-près-Saumur had four priories in England and twelve conventual priories in western France, of which one (Briouze) was in Normandy. Marmoutier's numerous dependencies included thirteen in England and seventeen in Normandy; Jumièges and Saint-Wandrille, with only one or two priories in England, each had over a dozen in Normandy. This is but a small sample of a movement that scattered hundreds of small cells over Europe. It is worth remembering that at least seventeen houses in other parts of France had possessions in Normandy.[15]

Not all the colonising Norman abbeys sent colonies of monks across the Channel. Saint-Evroult, whose monastic history is particularly well known through the work of Orderic Vitalis, provides an interesting example of expansion in which England played only a small part.[16] Some of its Norman

---

[13] For the alien priories see Matthew, *Norman Monasteries*.

[14] Pierre-Roger Gaussin, *L'Europe des ordres et des congrégations* (Saint-Etienne, 1984), passim.

[15] C.H. Haskins, *Norman Institutions* (Cambridge, MA, 1918), p. 245.

[16] Orderic, ii, pp. 150-55; iii, pp. xviii-xx, 170-211.

priories were established before the conquest; Neufchâtel, on the Vexin frontier, replaced a small secular college when Hugh of Grandmesnil, one of Saint-Evroult's leading patrons, was made castellan of Neufchâtel and wished to have monks from his family monastery around him. The attempt to press Norman conquests in the Vexin region led to the establishment of Norman monks from the same abbey at La Chapelle-en-Vexin and Parnes; Moulins and Bon-Moulins were similarly associated with the devotion to Saint-Evroult of aggressive lords on the southern frontier. Other motives played their part in the expansion. Among the *conversi* who took the habit after a career in the world was Goisbert of Chartres, at one time Ralph of Tosny's doctor, who had many grateful and wealthy former patients. One of these, Peter of Maule the son of Arnold le Riche of Paris, founded a conventual priory at Maule in the Ile-de-France. Though the Grandmesnil gave generously from the estates they acquired in England, these were all administered from a small priory at Ware, in the heart of the estates. Perhaps the failure of the family to thrive stunted any possible cross-Channel development. Moreover, the patrons of the monks included some who deliberately turned their backs on England; one of these was Gilbert of Auffay, who fought at Hastings but declined the offer of lands in England, returning home to found a priory on his patrimonial lands at Auffay in Normandy.[17]

The great reputation of Bec-Hellouin, and the appointment of both Lanfranc and Anselm to the see of Canterbury, ensured that the expansion of Le Bec would be almost as important in England as in Normandy and France, in spite of Anselm's initial reluctance to send his monks so far. By contrast, some abbeys had no hesitation in sending out little colonies of monks to distant and isolated houses, as did some of the pilgrimage centres. Robert fitz Walter and his wife Sybil seem to have had no difficulty in securing monks from Conques in Rouergues for their priory of Horsham St Faith in Norfolk, founded out of gratitude to St Faith.[18] George Beech has shown the part played by Aquitanians and Flemings in the foundation of Bardney Abbey as a daughter house of Charroux – a Poitevin house with relics related to the cult of the Holy Saviour, which attracted over 200 dependencies.[19] Some abbeys were favoured for different reasons. Jane Martindale has shown how Saint-Florent-près-Saumur had already considerable experience of administering its castle priories in Anjou before it acquired its English dependencies, two of which were in castles.[20] The alien priories at the time of their origin need to be seen in the context of wider monastic movements.

[17] Ibid., iii, pp. 254-57.

[18] *Cartulaire de l'abbaye de Conque en Rouergues*, ed. G. Desjardins, (Paris, 1879), pp. cxv-cxvi, 359, 368-72.

[19] George Beech, 'Aquitanians and Flemings in the Refoundation of Bardney Abbey', *Haskins Society Journal*, 1 (1989), pp. 73-90.

[20] Jane Martindale, 'Monasteries and Castles: The Priories of Saint-Florent de Saumur in England after 1066', *England in the Eleventh Century*, ed. Carola Hicks, Harlaxton Medieval Studies, 2 (Stamford 1992), pp. 135-56.

After the Conquest some of the English abbeys began to imitate continental practice, though none had more than eight or nine dependencies, not one of which was in Normandy. St Albans, Gloucester and Durham acquired the largest families; each was under the rule of a vigorous Norman, or at least continental, abbot in the early years after the Conquest. It is noteworthy that the great abbey of Bury, whose abbot Baldwin was not Norman, had no dependencies. All St Albans' cells were in England; the influence of Durham and Gloucester extended only into other regions open to the advance of Norman settlement. Durham had one cell north of the border at Coldingham; Gloucester for a time had three in Wales. Monastic expansion tended to move with settlement.[21]

The origin of the various new orders that appeared from the late eleventh century onwards was the need felt by many individuals for a simpler, different and – to them – better way of life than that provided by the older types of monasticism. The speed with which these orders spread was due to the response they offered to the social and economic no less than the religious needs of all classes, from kings and dukes downwards.[22] At the same time, houses of regular canons following the Augustinian rule attracted recruits and endowments. Many remained independent; others were drawn into groups through devotion to the austere ideals of some leader, such as Norbert, founder of Prémontré; and these established their own general chapter, like the Cistercians. They appealed to all patrons more concerned with the austerity of life of the men who prayed for them than with the solemnity and beauty of their liturgy; some appealed specially also to those without the resources to found an independent Benedictine or a Cluniac house. Their communities could be smaller, though the great Cistercian houses attracted and supported dozens of postulants. Their preference for remote settlements meant that they gladly accepted untilled or barren land and often made it fertile: indeed they spear-headed economic conquest of the waste as the Benedictines had contributed to the advance of feudal conquests. Many of the houses of regular canons, and some of Cistercian or other stricter orders of monks, began as small groups of hermits, turning from the world for various reasons: knights, sickened by battle, or secular clerks and laymen, disillusioned with the life of a court. Initially growth might be slow and uncertain; a small group could practise an ascetic life for as much as twenty years before a priory was actually founded or a definite rule adopted. They were also willing to recruit men and women from all walks of life. Bernard of Tiron welcomed

[21] These small groups are discussed in Chibnall, 'Réseaux monastiques en Angleterre', pp. 342-48.

[22] The motives that inspired laymen to found religious houses have been discussed in many places, most recently by Christopher Holdsworth in his Stenton Lecture, *The Piper and the Tune: Medieval Patrons and Monks* (Reading, 1991); see also idem, 'The Cistercians in Devon', *Studies in Medieval History Presented to R. Allen Brown*, ed. C. Harper-Bill et. al. (Woodbridge and Wolfeboro, 1989), pp. 189-90.

craftsmen of all kinds as well as literate *conversi*; so did Norbert, and after him the Arrouasians. The Cistercians were the greatest recruiters of lay brethren within their order.

If one looks at the spread of these newer orders in Normandy and England slightly different priorities become apparent. Normandy continued to resist large, tightly organised orders. The great Cistercian expansion proceeded apace in England, whereas no Cistercian house appeared in Normandy until Henry I's foundation at Mortemer accepted subordination to the Cistercian general chapter in 1137. Only two more Cistercian houses appeared before 1147, when Savigny, which had attracted many benefactions, became affiliated to the Cistercian order.[23] Savigny, in Mortain, was indeed equally popular in both Normandy and England. Tiron, so near to the duchy in the diocese of Chartres, also appealed strongly to Norman patrons. The keen interest in these new movements felt by monks in the older Benedictine houses in Normandy can be seen in the sympathetic and tolerant accounts given by Orderic Vitalis and Robert of Torigny. In England William of Malmesbury's chapter on the newer orders was confined to Cîteaux, and formed a digression in his account of the life of the English abbot, Stephen Harding.[24] His special interest may have arisen from the dramatic impact of the Cistercians in England; there the general pattern of expansion was much more in line with that of western Europe as a whole, whereas Normandy was different.

Sometimes personal influence was important in introducing a new order. Although St Norbert, founder of Prémontré, had previously served in the court of the Emperor Henry V and spent the whole of his life in the Empire, his influence was carried to Normandy by his disciples. Ardennes had as its first prior Gilbert, one of Norbert's followers, who also had some influence in the founding of La Lucerne. Ulric, who first gathered a small, ascetic community in a little chapel and later moved to Marcheraux, was another disciple.[25] So too was Drogo, one of the knights of the Empress Matilda, who returned with her to Normandy and abandoned the world to become in time the first abbot of Silly in Gouffern.[26] Even without these personal contacts, the extreme austerity of the way of life of the white canons was attractive to donors – the order spread rapidly in England also from 1143, after the foundation of Newhouse.[27] The one order to remain exclusively English was the double order of Gilbertines, founded by Gilbert of Sempringham.[28]

---

[23] Lindy Grant, 'The Architecture of the Early Savigniacs and Cistercians in Normandy', *A-NS*, 10, (1988), pp. 113-24.

[24] Orderic, iv, pp. 311-35; Malmesbury, *GR*, ii, pp. 380-85.

[25] Emmanuel Rigaud, 'Les origines de l'ordre de Prémontré en Normandie: recherches sur la filiation des abbayes de La Lucerne et d'Ardennes', *Analecta praemonstratensia*, ii (1926), pp. 159-76.

[26] Marjorie Chibnall, *The Empress Matilda* (Oxford, 1991), p. 180.

[27] For the Premonstratensians see H.M. Colvin, *The White Canons in England* (Oxford, 1951).

[28] *The Book of St Gilbert*, ed. Raymonde Foreville and Gillian Keir, Oxford Medieval Texts (Oxford, 1987), pp. xix-xxxii.

Monastic reform stimulated lay piety; changing social conditions determined the direction it should take. As H.M. Colvin has shown, patrons still took for granted that their spiritual obligations included the foundation of religious houses.[29] The need for prayers was still deeply felt, particularly with the development of the doctrine of purgatory; but there were many other ways of expiating sins, and many of the magnates already had their own family monasteries and mausolea. Later, modest benefactions were more inclined to go to establish chantries or support lights to burn before a particular altar than to found a new, small priory. At all times the royal family helped to point the way, but its alms were distributed to old and new orders alike.[30] Henry I chose his own foundation at Reading, a Benedictine abbey following Cluniac customs while remaining independent, as his place of burial; that his heart and entrails were buried at Bec-Hellouin's priory of Le Pré outside Rouen was probably due to the accident of his death in Normandy. Stephen's foundation at Faversham was in the same mould as Reading. But the royal family had increasingly important spiritual stakes in the newer orders also. Henry's first wife, Queen Matilda, helped to promote the foundation of an Augustinian house at Llanthony with the help of St Anselm; and with her husband's encouragement she founded Holy Trinity Priory, London (also Augustinian) in 1107, 'the only major religious house to find a home within the city walls'.[31] Henry himself showed a preference for Augustinian canons rather than Benedictines or seculars in cathedral chapters. He established them at Carlisle in 1133, two years after he had obtained papal permission for the replacement of seculars by Augustinians in the cathedral of Sées. The canons of Sées received endowments from him in both Normandy and England.[32] It may seem strange to see the foundation of a cathedral priory of regular canons in Normandy; yet again there is a parallel in southern Italy, for in 1130 the church of Cefalù in Sicily was colonised by Roger II with Augustinian canons from Bagnana.[33] Henry's children and grandchildren were similarly eclectic in their patronage, with a growing preference for the more austere orders.

Throughout the whole of this period feudal ties had some influence on the choices of patrons, whether magnates or lesser feudatories, in making new foundations. A further complication was added in Stephen's reign, when the succession was in dispute. So we may ask, how far did feudal ties, or the union or separation of England and Normandy determine the direction of endowments? In the main, at least up to the death of Henry I, the presence of

[29] Colvin, *White Canons*, pp. 32, 38.

[30] Christopher Brooke, 'Princes and Kings as Patrons of Monasteries: Normandy and England', *Il monachesimo e la riforma ecclesiastica 1049-1122*, Miscellanea del Centro di Studi Medievali, 6 (Milan, 1971), pp. 125-44.

[31] Brooke, 'Princes and Kings', p. 142.

[32] Haskins, *Norman Institutions*, pp. 300-3, 307.

[33] L.T. White, *Latin Monasticism in Norman Sicily*, Medieval Academy of America, Monograph, 13 (Cambridge, MA, 1938), pp. 194-201.

numerous daughter houses of Norman abbeys in England helped to bind together kingdoms and duchy. But, at the same time that cross-Channel estates, secular and ecclesiastical, were helping to promote union, the tensions caused by the cross-border estates in Normandy and France were liable to pull the other way. Some of the new monastic foundations in Normandy in the twelfth century were made by lords with one foot in France. When William Talvas of Bellême, count of Ponthieu, secured the restoration of the former family castles in Maine, forfeited by his father, he established an Augustinian priory in the forest of Gouffern, near to Vignats. Political motives may have prompted the placing; after the death of Henry I he was as eager to declare his allegiance to Geoffrey of Anjou as to press his claim to rights in his father's former castle of Vignats and the forest of Gouffern. His charter of gift, if correctly dated to September 1143, calls Geoffrey duke of Normandy several months before Geoffrey had conquered Rouen and begun to use the title himself.[34] The lords of Beaumont, whose wealthy honours lay in England and France as well as in Normandy, were powerful enough to bestow their largesse in all three.[35]

During the course of the twelfth century, however, many Norman families established separate branches in England, and those with roots in England founded houses which were either independent or attached to larger, not specifically Norman, orders. The family of Tosny, studied by Lucien Musset, shows how endowments might change. Benefactions in England began shortly after the Conquest with gifts to the Benedictine abbey of Conches of lands at Wootton Wawen and Monkland, which became small cells of the abbey – typical alien priories. By the middle of the twelfth century a small, independent nunnery for up to thirteen religious had been founded at Flamstead, probably by Roger III of Tosny.[36] The family of Roumare, while carefully husbanding its Norman patrimony, was willing to use its acquisitions in England for pious donations. After William of Roumare, castellan of Neuf-marché, acquired some of his mother Lucy's lands in England and became earl of Lincoln, his one foundation (in 1142) was the Cistercian abbey of Revesby, a daughter house of Rievaulx.[37] It was an appropriate action for an earl of Lincoln (with a somewhat precarious title); he did not forget his origins in Normandy but preferred to retain the patrimony there intact.

The history of the Paynel family shows the gradual separation of two branches, in spite of a determined effort to retain an interest on both sides of

---

[34] *Gallia christiana*, xi, pp. 743-44; instrumenta, pp. 162-63.

[35] For their foundations see David Crouch, *The Beaumont Twins* (Cambridge, 1986), pp. 55, 83, 198-99, 201-2 and passim; A.A. Porée, *Histoire de l'abbaye du Bec*, 2 vols (Evreux, 1901), i, pp. 401-02.

[36] Lucien Musset, 'Aux origines d'une classe dirigeante: les Tosny', *Francia*, 5 (1978), pp. 45-80.

[37] The foundation of Revesby is discussed by Holdsworth, *The Piper and the Tune*, pp. 6-7.

the Channel.[38] Their original home was at Les Moutiers-Hubert in Calvados, to which Hambye was added later, probably by marriage. Fulk, the follower of the Conqueror, was rewarded with substantial estates in England, principally in Yorkshire and Lincolnshire. At a time when endowments were directed to found cells of great Benedictine abbeys, he and his son Ralph replaced the secular canons of Holy Trinity, York, with monks from Marmoutier, and Ralph later founded a small cell at Tickford as a dependency of Holy Trinity. By the 1130s William Paynel, who had succeeded to some of the family lands in Drax and Normandy, wishing to found a priory in Yorkshire, took counsel with Archbishop Thurstan and established a house of Augustinian canons at Drax. War soon divided the family. William gave his allegiance to Geoffrey of Anjou and retired to his Norman lands. By 1143 he may have felt that his end was near but that his body could not be taken for burial to the turbulent north of England, then in the hands of Stephen and his nominal adherents. Again he took counsel with his diocesan bishop, Algar of Coutances. Algar had been a clerk at Laon, and had himself established regular canons in the churches of Saint-Laud in Rouen and Coutances.[39] Drax too was a house of regular canons; nevertheless William, with Algar's encouragement, brought Benedictine monks from the reformed abbey of Tiron to begin monastic life in the abbey he founded at Hambye. Probably, like many of his contemporaries, his chief wish was to secure men admired for the austerity of their life (as were the monks of Tiron), without having a clear idea of the kind of religious house they might establish. William was dead within a year or two and was buried as he wished at Hambye. By 1154 free communication between England and Normandy had been restored. But the foundation of Hambye had deepened the Norman roots of at least part of the family. Fifty years later, when Hugh Paynel of Les Moutiers-Hubert and West Rasen (Lincs.) adhered to John and lost his Norman lands, his cousin Fulk Paynel of Hambye and Drax supported the king of France, so forfeiting Drax. No single family can typify all the influences that swayed the choice of religious benefactions made by all middle-ranking Anglo-Norman barons, but the Paynels illustrate the diversities of religious motive and feudal pressure.

The religious needs of women were met in very similar ways. At the time of the Conquest a number of great Benedictine nunneries, many of royal or ducal foundation, already existed; they included Romsey, Wilton and Shaftesbury in England and La Sainte-Trinité, Caen, in Normandy.[40] Magnates often preferred to make donations to these houses, as unacknowledged 'dowries' for

---

[38] For the Paynels and their monastic foundations and the division of their lands, see C.T. Clay, *Early Yorkshire Charters*, Yorkshire Archaeological, Society, record series, 6 (Wakefield, 1939), pp. 3-7, 25-26; for Hambye, *Gallia christiana*, xi, p. 931; instrumenta, p. 241.

[39] *Gallia christiana*, xi, p. 874.

[40] There is an excellent recent account of the founding of houses for women religious in England by Sally Thompson, *Women Religious: The Founding of English Nunneries after the Norman Conquest* (Oxford, 1991).

daughters who took the veil, rather than attempting to found new houses, especially in the more unsettled parts of the newly conquered country. The list of gifts to Shaftesbury, many of which accompanied the entry into religion of a kinswoman, shows an interesting cross-section of both English and Norman families who supported the abbey partly to provide for one of their number.[41] A similar list for Caen is naturally purely continental.[42] Within a generation or two communities of women were emerging inside most of the great new orders in spite of the resistance of some, the Cistercians in particular. Some houses were founded by wealthy women in part at least to provide a refuge for their own widowhood or retirement from the world. One such founder was Amicia, countess of Leicester, who withdrew to the family's Fontebraudian priory of Nuneaton; another was the Countess Lucy of Lincoln, who probably ended her days in the house she founded at Stixwold.[43] Fontevraud attracted the daughters of the highest in the land; Henry I contributed payments from the royal revenues, possibly inspired by the withdrawal of his widowed daughter-in-law to the abbey, as well as by the marriage of his daughter Matilda to the count of Anjou. The Angevin connection certainly strengthened royal interest thereafter: Henry II was to restore Amesbury as the greatest of Fontevraud's English priories, and it was Amesbury that, after the loss of Normandy, attracted the first royal princess not to gravitate towards the mother houses in Anjou.[44]

For the less wealthy or influential families the newer orders such as the canons offered the possibility of endowing a family nunnery with modest means. Sometimes the diocesan bishop contributed financial no less than spiritual support and service. The double order of the Gilbertines proved particularly attractive to the many smaller Lincolnshire families, who might combine to make a house financially viable. Most of the Gilbertine priories owed their existence to lesser landowners, though Watton, one of the two Yorkshire houses, was founded by a prominent magnate, Eustace fitz John, as reparation for having fought with the Scots at the battle of the Standard.[45] Reparation, a continuing motive, was particularly prominent during the Anarchy.

There is room for much further research on the interplay of piety and politics in the century when the Anglo-Norman realm was being established, and in the period of the Anarchy when the future of the duchy must have seemed to

---

[41] Kathleen Cooke, 'Donors and Daughters: Shaftesbury Abbey's Benefactions, Endowments and Nuns, *c.* 1086-1130', *A-NS*, 12 (1990), pp. 29-45.

[42] *Les actes de Guillaume le Conquérant et de la reine Mathilde pour les abbayes caennaises*, ed. Lucien Musset, Mémoires de la Société des Antiquaires de Normandie, 37 (Caen, 1967), pp. 129-31.

[43] Thompson, *Women Religious*, pp. 173, 169.

[44] Ibid., pp. 113-32; Victoria a History of England *Wiltshire*, iii, pp. 242-48.

[45] Knowles and Hadcock, *Medieval Religious House*, pp. 194-96; Foreville and Keir, ed., *The Book of St Gilbert*, pp. xxxi-xxxii.

many to hang in the balance. With the accession of Henry II the widening interests of the Angevins placed new strains on the structure, though up to the end of his reign serious cracks did not appear. Among many topics of interest for further investigation would be a comprehensive study of the motives behind monastic foundations in Normandy during these years. The much more integrated organisation of the new Orders, with their system of chapters general and regular visitation, provided support for their subject priories that far outweighed any strains due to changing feudal allegiance. The smaller, independent houses of canons enabled the rising administrative families, such as the Glanvilles and the lesser feudatories to become an integral part of their regional society. As Howard Colvin remarked, 'the patronage of a religious house was as much a part of feudal privileges as the possession of a mill or a fishery'.[46] Much has been written on the history of the religious Orders during this period; a general survey of the trends under the Normans and early Angevins clearly demonstrates that much still remains to write.

[46] Colvin, *White Canons*, p. 32.

4

Normans and Anglo-Normans: A Divided Aristocracy?

David Crouch

In the 1970 Stenton Lecture, Professor John Le Patourel first explored the phenomenon of the 'cross-Channel' estate. The fact that there were complexes of great estates straddling the Channel in the hands of great Norman or French barons was of particular significance to Professor Le Patourel. He fashioned this truism into one of the staples that knit together his vision of England and Normandy as a unified realm in the Norman period. Le Patourel left us in no doubt of his interpretation, 'there could not be an "English baronage" and a "Norman baronage" at this time; only one ambitious, acquisitive and often ruthless Norman-French baronial society established in both countries'.[1] Six years later, when Le Patourel published his *Norman Empire*, it was this unified, common aristocracy which was one of the most compelling and drawn out of his arguments in favour of the unity of the Norman condominium on either side of the Channel.

Now, over two decades after his Stenton Lecture, we find that Le Patourel's construct has not convinced the next generation of Anglo-Norman historians. But in that one component of his model – the cross-Channel aristocracy – his vision still survives, like the chimney-stack of an otherwise flattened cottage. Hence David Bates' reservation in his comprehensive reassessment of Le Patourel's work, 'there is . . . no doubt that Le Patourel was substantially correct in emphasising that the Anglo-Norman aristocracy would exert itself at times of political crisis to try to reunite Normandy and England.'[2]

The Le Patourel construct of a cross-Channel aristocratic community has survived because it is built of sound materials. The sources are happily explicit. The key source is Orderic Vitalis, in particular Orderic when he describes the aftermath of the death of Henry I in December 1135. While the king's corpse lay awaiting transport to England and burial, a group described by Orderic as 'the Normans' met at the castle of Le Neubourg, south of Rouen. There they resolved to offer the duchy of Normandy to Count Theobald of Blois. But then

---

[1] J. Le Patourel, *Normandy and England, 1066-1144* (Reading, 1971), p. 8.
[2] D. Bates, 'Normandy and England after 1066', *EHR*, 104 (1989), p. 871.

a messenger from the hastily crowned Stephen, Theobald's younger brother, announced that their decision had been forestalled by events, and that a group described as 'the English' had accepted Stephen as king. At this news, and with Theobald's pained acquiescence, the Norman barons withdrew their offer wishing 'to serve one lord on account of the honors which they held in both lands'.[3] The barons gathered at this Norman meeting followed the imperative which their self-interest dictated. Le Patourel, and Warren Hollister along with him, have amply demonstrated that the same imperative can be deduced from the behaviour of many of the dominant cross-Channel magnates during earlier crises in the reigns of William Rufus and Henry I.[4] It has also been suggested as a motive for baronial behaviour in England in 1153, when the supporters of Henry fitz Empress and King Stephen compelled their principals to negotiate a single succession.[5]

I am not now going to dispute what Le Patourel called the 'vested interest' of the highest level of Anglo-Norman society in keeping the two realms under one ruler. What I am going to analyse is Le Patourel's next step. In 1976 he apostrophised the aristocracy of Henry I thus: 'one homogeneous, aristocratic community'. A little later he stated that 'the upper levels of society in England and Normandy were completely assimilated, indeed merged into one community'.[6] Was he justified in developing his cross-Channel polity into a cross-Channel aristocratic culture, united in attendance on a single sovereign? Judith Green thinks not. She is willing to accept that 'kinship and shared culture bound the families settled in England to Normandy', but she has reservations whether cross-Channel holdings were quite as widespread in society as Le Patourel believed. Le Patourel was happy to believe that cross-Channel holdings could be found at every level of landholding society. Dr Green, however, points out how little we can know about the lesser cadre of the aristocracy, those characterised variously as 'undertenants' or 'honorial barons'; the Norman followers of the Norman magnates to whom they granted fees in England.[7] Le Patourel was fashioning generalities out of a few examples.

Le Patourel has confronted us with a vision of the self-image of a past aristocratic society. We may have doubts about it, but if so it is up to us to find a better one. Dr Green has pointed out the obstacles in the way of an answer. The principal ones are to do with numbers and the nature of the evidence. At any one time, there were over a hundred magnates of substance in England and Normandy in the late eleventh and twelfth century. They all controlled

---

[3] Orderic, vi, p. 455.

[4] C. Warren Hollister, 'The Anglo-Norman Civil War, 1101', *EHR*, 88 (1973), pp. 315-43; J. Le Patourel, *The Norman Empire* (London, 1976), pp. 197-201.

[5] Ibid., pp. 108-9.

[6] Ibid., p. 195.

[7] J.A. Green, 'Unity and Disunity in the Anglo-Norman State', *Historical Research*, 62 (1989), pp. 129-32, quotation from p. 131.

networks of power and influence which often included several dozen of lesser landowners. The mathematics of isolating and tracing these networks through several generations are prohibitive. Most scholars interested in the job produce only one such study in their academic lifetime. But added to this is the patchiness of the documentation. In England, there is a troublesome hiatus in evidence between Domesday Book and the sudden surge in written evidence later in the reign of Henry I: a gap of some forty years which makes the study of an entire generation of landholders in England rather difficult. In Normandy, there is a teasing patchwork of evidence. There are few surveys and accounts. Private deeds and cartularies are our only constant resource. Some areas, such as central Normandy, are well covered, but others, such as western Normandy are difficult to penetrate. It is a salutary reflection that the succession of one of the greatest and noblest of Norman families, the Grandmesnil, is irrecoverable after Orderic Vitalis lost interest in its fortunes in 1103.[8]

The final answer to the nature of Anglo-Norman society will therefore only be an approximation but, such as it is, it lies in reconstructing the fortunes of a great number of families and their relationship to their acknowledged lords. In the meantime what we have are hints, and it is a parade of hints which I am going to review. The first consists of a brief look at two English shires – Warwick and Leicester – between the Conquest and the loss of Normandy. These shires were outside the first wave of Norman conquest in England, but otherwise they were by no means exceptional in the mode of Norman settlement. Indeed the counties show examples of both main types of aristocratic settlement: the concentrated castellanry and the diffuse centreless lordship.[9] Of the former type (the castellanry) the region contained examples at and around Belvoir and Leicester. Two more, at Dudley and Tamworth, stood on the borders of Warwickshire, and their tributary manors took in ample corners of the shire. Of the dispersed lordships, we have the Domesday honor of the count of Meulan, which rambled about the Avon valley and the Cotswolds, and spilled across Watling Street. Honors of such a type sprawled into the two shires from outside: dispersed estates dependent on Chester,

[8] The Grandmesnil, one of the founding families of Orderic's abbey of Saint-Evroult, divided their estates on the death of Hugh de Grandmesnil; the Norman lands went to one Robert (III) de Grandmesnil, whom we lose sight of in 1106, Orderic, vi, p. 84. The next news of the family comes early in the reign of Henry II, when Robert de Breteuil, son of Earl Robert II of Leicester, married Petronilla, heiress of Grandmesnil; a bald commemoration notice tells us that her father was called William de Grandmesnil, but to link this William to the earlier Robert de Grandmesnil has not yet proved possible, D. Crouch, *The Beaumont Twins* (Cambridge, 1986), pp. 90-91.

[9] For a debate about the creation and perpetuation of lordships in England, see P. Sawyer, '1066-1086: A Tenurial Revolution?', *Domesday Book: A Reassessment*, ed. P. Sawyer (London, 1985), pp. 71-85; R. Fleming, 'Domesday Book and the Tenurial Revolution', *A-NS*, 9 (1986), pp. 87-102. R. Fleming, *Kings and Lords in Conquest England* (Cambridge, 1991), pp. 210-14, suggests a mechanism for the creation of compact honors as that of magnate enterprise outside royal supervision.

Stafford, Northampton, Tutbury and Richard's Castle occupied pockets of land across the counties.

These shires are characteristic examples of the pattern of Norman settlement in England. Those aristocrats and their followers who settled them are also a good representative sample. The fact that both Leicestershire and Warwickshire are exceedingly well-documented add to the value they have in disentangling precisely how Anglo-Norman they were. Both shires demonstrate how long after the initial conquest Normandy continued to send out surges of colonists to England. The Norman magnates who took power in the region in the late 1060s and early 1070s were all men with cross-Channel possessions, men great in Normandy, men therefore with communities of followers already dependent on them before they came to England. Chief of them were Hugh de Grandmesnil (lord of Grandmesnil and Leicester), Count Robert of Meulan (lord of Warwick), Robert Marmion (lord of Fontenay and Tamworth) and Robert de Tosny, lord of Belvoir. The only significant character amongst the landholders of Leicestershire and Warwickshire who did not belong to the cross-Channel aristocracy was Thurkil son of Æthelwine, needless to say, an English survivor of the Conquest.

With these men came their followers. This can be demonstrated from the way that the principal tenants of these magnates in England carried surnames derived from places in the neighbourhood of their Norman centres. Hugh de Grandmesnil had settled several of this sort of dependent around Leicester by 1086. Amongst them were the Burdet brothers, Hugh and Robert, who hailed from Rabodanges, a Grandmesnil fee in western Normandy. A family called Neufmarché must have derived from the castle of the Grandmesnil of that name in the Norman Vexin. The Grandmesnil settled the famous family of Beaumeis at Ashby de la Zouche in Leicestershire; the Beaumeis derived from a large fee of that name near Grandmesnil itself.[10] What happened around Leicester was also happening around the Tosny lordship of Belvoir and the Marmion lordship of Tamworth. The Tosnys brought to Leicestershire men

---

[10] For the Burdets, Crouch, *Beaumont Twins*, pp. 127-28. For Neufmarché (Seine-Maritime, cant. Gournay-en-Bray) as a Grandmesnil fee, A.A. Porée, *Histoire de l'abbaye du Bec*, 2 vols (Evreux, 1901), ii, p. 648. The Neufmarché family fee was held by a certain Osbern in 1086 and included lands held of Leicester in Leicestershire, Warwickshire and Northamptonshire. It was divided between the daughters of William de Neufmarché (II) in the mid twelfth century, see *Domesday Book*, i, fos 224v, 242r; Register of Leicester Abbey, Bod Lib, MS Laud misc. 625, fos 81v, 128r; *The Cartulary of Daventry Priory*, ed. M.J. Franklin, Northamptonshire Record Society, 35 (1988), p. 159; *Curia Regis Rolls*, xvi, p. 453. For the identification of Beaumeis (Calvados, cant. Morteaux-Couliboeuf), see L.C. Loyd, *The Origins of Some Anglo-Norman Families*, Harleian Society, 103 (1951), pp. 13-14; Loyd identifies the Beaumeis as Montgomery tenants, and it may be that a branch of the family did follow the Montgomeries, but a Walter de Beaumeis was a principal tenant of Ivo de Grandmesnil, lord of Leicester, and continued to hold Ashby into the time of Robert of Meulan as earl of Leicester, BL, MSS Harley 4757, fo. 11r, Cotton Julius, C vii, fo 221r; *Registrum Antiquissimum of the Cathedral Church of Lincoln*, ed. C.W. Foster and K. Major, Lincoln Record Society (1931-73) ii, pp. 10-11.

from their Norman fees of Bosc-le-Hard, Noyers and Thierceville.[11] The Marmions brought to Warwickshire men from their fees of Meisi and Quilly.[12] Domesday Book also demonstrates how widely the tenantry of Leicestershire and Warwickshire had been colonised by men of French extraction (apart from those whose village of origin can be identified). The incidence of Franco-Germanic Christian names amongst the tenants of the two shires in 1086 is over 75 per cent of the total, even allowing for names such as Alfred and Osbern which might have belonged as much to men of English as Norman extraction.

We have, twenty years after the Conquest, a region densely settled with Norman magnates and their tenants. Both magnates and the top echelon of their tenants enjoyed cross-Channel estates. There is no doubt that in many cases the Norman magnates who were dominant in the two shires were continuing in England relationships of dependence formed in Normandy. This situation of Le Patourel-style unity did not erode gently away in the years after the Domesday survey. New colonists continued to arrive from Normandy; and Leicestershire and Warwickshire continued to accommodate them. Two years after the survey, Warwickshire's pattern of lordship was fundamentally reordered when King William Rufus created the earldom of Warwick for his crony, Henry de Beaumont. Amongst other consequences, this brought a fresh wave of cross-Channel personalities into Warwickshire. The new Earl Henry was himself a cross-Channel magnate. He held that same castle of Le Neubourg in which the Norman magnates were to meet in 1135 to decide on the successor to Henry I.[13] As a result, it was natural for the earl to select his principal tenants from families long connected with his own in Normandy. He generously endowed his kinsmen, Robert de Harcourt and Thurstin de Montfort, with substantial lands in his earldom.[14] But he also drew other tenants from his family's lordships in central Normandy: members of the families of Beaumont, Saint-Samson and Luvet.[15]

---

[11] Loyd, *Origins*, pp. 18-19, 74, 103.

[12] Ibid., pp. 64, 84.

[13] For the creation of the earldom of Warwick, see D. Crouch, *The Earliest Earls of Warwick*, forthcoming.

[14] For the Harcourts and Montforts of Beaudesert, and their kinship with the earls of Warwick, see Crouch, *Beaumont Twins*, pp. 20-23; *CP*, viii, p. 120 and n.

[15] For the family of Beaumont as tenants of Warwick, *Red Book of the Exchequer*, ed. H. Hall, Rolls Series, 3 vols (London, 1896), i, p. 326; M.O. Harris, 'Feet of Fines of Warwickshire and Leicestershire for the Reign of John, 1199-1214' (unpublished M.A. thesis, University of Reading, 1956), nos 60, 117. For the family of Saint-Samson (Saint-Samson-de-la-Roque, Eure, cant. Quillebeuf), domiciled in Warwickshire, cartulary of Préaux, AD Eure, H 711, fo. 48v. The Luvet family were to be found at Condé-sur-Risle (Eure, cant. Pont-Audemer) until the loss of Normandy, *Recueil des historiens des Gaules et de la France*, ed. M. Bouquet and others, 24 vols (Paris, 1869-1904), xxiv, p. 11 and held at Oxhill, Warwicks, in the time of Earl Roger of Warwick, cartulary of Kenilworth, BL, MS Add. 47677, fos 271r-272r, and were frequent attestors to acts of Earl Roger.

Twenty years on again, King Henry I did for Leicestershire what his brother had done for Warwickshire. He created an earldom of Leicester for Henry of Warwick's elder brother, Count Robert of Meulan (who was a landholder in the area back in 1086). The core of the new earldom was made up of the estates of the Grandmesnil family in England, centred on Leicester itself.[16] Count Robert added to the Grandmesnil tenantry which came along with the estate (tenants he does not seem to have deprived) a new cadre of Anglo-Normans. The name of Harcourt appears as prominent in the earldom of Leicester as it had been in the earldom of Warwick. Other new tenants included the families of Tourville, Vatteville and Thibouville, principal tenants of Count Robert's Norman lordships.[17] The famous midlands family of Mallory arrived in Leicestershire at this time, drawn from the French county of Meulan.[18] All these immigrants were nobly rewarded for consenting to take on English estates; all belonged to the pre-existing community of barons dependent on the count in Normandy and France. We can only regard them as reinforcements to the Le Patourel thesis, forty years after Hastings.

The arrival of such immigrants, on the face of it, did not disrupt local communities, even when they arrived (as they did in Leicestershire and Warwickshire) in communities which had French settlers already established in them for a clear generation. I am inclined to think that there may have been more tension involved in the process than the sources reveal (and I will return

---

[16] Orderic, vi, pp. 18-20, says unequivocally that Robert was 'consul in Anglia factus'. *CP*, vi, p. 525 and n., genuflects to John Horace Round's doubts as to whether there was ever an earldom of Leicester created for Count Robert. The doubts hover round the fact that Count Robert is never credited with the title *comes Legrecestrie*, except in one late charter, noted in an inspeximus of Edward I, which is an obvious fabrication, cartulary of the duchy of Lancaster, PRO, DL42/2 fos 225v-226r. However, there does survive (or at least until recently there survived) an impression of a double-sided seal of Count Robert, which on one face apparently bore the partial legend [+ SIGILLVM ROB]ERT[I COMITIS DE] LEIC[ESTRIE], till 1986 in the Keele University Library, Raymond Richards Collection (now lost). An engraving of the seal is in J. Nichols, *History and Antiquities of the County of Leicester*, 4 vols in 8 (London, 1795-1815), i, pt 1, appendix, p. 48. There is also a description in the catalogue of the Hatton Wood MSS. Although it has been put forward as an objection that double titles were unknown at this date, there is a well-attested instance of Odo of Bayeux being styled *Baiocensis episcopus et Cantie comes*, Canterbury D. & C., Carta antiqua S 246. The king of England was also duke of Normandy at this time, of course. For the creation of the earldom generally, L. Fox, 'The Honor and Earldom of Leicester: Origin and Descent, 1066-1399', *EHR*, 64 (1939), pp. 385-88.

[17] For the Harcourt in the earldom of Leicester, Crouch, *Beaumont Twins*, pp. 123-25; for the Tourville (who may have been kinsfolk of the Beaumonts), ibid., pp. 116-19; for the Vatteville, ibid., p. 110 and n. The Thibouville family was, like the Harcourt, one of the principal tenant families of the counts of Meulan and in 1210 the head of the family, Robert, was described as a banneret, *Recueil des historiens de la France*, xxiii, p. 684. William de Thibouville held Weedon Bec, Northants., of Earl Robert II in 1126, and clearly had held it before 1118 too, *Select Documents of the English Lands of the Abbey of Bec*, ed. M. Chibnall (Camden Society, 3rd series, 73, 1951), pp. 22-23. Robert de Thibouville, the banneret, lost a manor at Syston and Croxton Kerrial (Leics.) in 1204, *The Book of Fees, Commonly Called Testa de Nevill*, 3 vols (London, 1920-31), ii, p. 1392.

[18] For the Mallory family, Loyd, *Origins*, p. 56.

to this in due course). If there were such tensions, the great power in the localities possessed by the sponsoring magnate might well account for the muting of complaints. The process of settlement continued well into the twelfth century, whatever the case. As late as the 1120s organised movements of Norman knightly families were affecting Warwickshire and Leicestershire. The second earl of Leicester (who succeeded his father in 1118) came by the great Norman honor of Breteuil in 1120 by marriage. To recruit the friendship of its chief barons, the earl lavishly endowed certain of the barons of Breteuil with estates in Warwickshire and Leicestershire. The most notable of these newcomers was Arnold du Bois, on whom the earl conferred a dozen manors before 1130. Arnold's son received a dozen more by means of a marriage granted him by the earl not long after 1130. The result was a complex of estates in the Midlands big enough to maintain the state of the peers of the realm which Arnold's descendants became at the end of the thirteenth century. It is interesting, although a little beside the point, to observe how it was still possible, sixty years or so after Hastings, for a Norman not previously connected with England to find space to settle there in style. Other families from Breteuil shared the earl's generosity with Arnold: those of Fresnel, Charneles, Cierrey and Bordigny. Again, under the earl's protection they seemed to have settled easily into Leicestershire life, so much so that, when their master lost his Norman lands in 1141, many apparently abandoned Breteuil for Leicestershire.[19]

So far we have what looks like rather impressive evidence supporting Le Patourel's 'Grand Unified Theory' of the Norman aristocracy. A periodic renewal of landholding ties did take place between England and Normandy in the sixty years after Hastings, at least as far as Leicestershire and Warwickshire were concerned. It happened at the level of the magnate, and also at the level of the magnate's followers, the people who we may rightly begin to call the county knights in the mid twelfth century. The surges of immigrants were small in numbers but large in proportion to the aristocratic communities they penetrated. But if there were evidence that such surges *disrupted* communities and caused animosities, even possibly xenophobia, then the self-satisfied Anglo-Normanness of the English end of the Anglo-Norman aristocracy would look less convincing. Le Patourel's model of society did not allow for particularism. In the 1120s and 1130s we find such evidence in Warwickshire. In 1124 Geoffrey de Clinton, a rising courtier of Henry I, was established by the king in Warwickshire as a counterweight in local affairs to the out-of-favour earl, Roger. Earl Roger would not have welcomed this intruder, despite Geoffrey's Anglo-Norman credentials, as he had to provide most of the manors with which to endow Geoffrey in the county. The earl and his followers would have been even less welcoming to the influx of Norman settlers Geoffrey imported

---

[19] For the family of Bois-Arnault, Crouch, *Beaumont Twins*, pp. 106-7, 109-11; for the other families, p. 111.

to settle his new estates. These were Normans who (from the evidence of their names) derived from the forested hills between the rivers Vire and Elle in western Normandy, around Geoffrey's Norman castle of Semilly. The local resentment can be deduced from what happened after the deaths of Geoffrey and his patron, Henry I. In the political instability of the new reign, Earl Roger of Warwick chose to strike back at the Clintons and their imported tenantry. There was a small war in Warwickshire in which not many may have been killed, but the Clinton base at Kenilworth was attacked and the family's lands confiscated.[20]

Although this local upset was resolved in 1138, it does indicate that by the 1120s large-scale Norman penetration of an established English society might be unwelcome. It was certainly unwelcome to one resident magnate who saw his network of power and influence built up patiently over the years disrupted. It was easy for magnates to stir up their followers to more decisive action than mere sulking at the county court, as the Clinton problem demonstrates.

Norman colonisation indubitably slackened after 1135, although local communities found much to resent in the new reign in the companies of foreign mercenaries which roamed England in Stephen's reign. One of Henry II's first and most popular actions when he attained power was to oust them from England.[21] Newcomers in Leicestershire and Warwickshire were a rarity after Stephen's time. At the very end of the century we can observe one new Norman family, the Sainevilles, establishing themselves at Lockington on the River Trent in Leicestershire.[22] It is of course unlikely that Normans stopped coming because they were unwelcome. Magnates simply had less reserved demesne land to give away in the second half of the twelfth century. Although the magnates remained cross-Channel in their interests, they began – long before the fall of Normandy – to work with existing pieces in the local game of power, rather than add new and unpredictable pieces to the board. Surprisingly, the growth of xenophobia matched the slackening of the colonisation of England from Normandy.

I have been describing English society in terms of local communities, assuming these communities had a capacity for common action when led to it by magnates. Such a community was the body of knights of the earldom of

---

[20] For a reconstruction of the Clinton-Warwick confrontation, D. Crouch, 'Geoffrey de Clinton and Roger, Earl of Warwick: New Men and Magnates in the Reign of Henry I', *Bulletin of the Institute of Historical Research*, 55 (1982), pp. 113-24.

[21] Gervase of Canterbury, *Opera Historica*, Rolls Series, 2 vols (1879-80) i, p. 161.

[22] Sainneville (Seine-Maritime, cant. Saint-Romain de Colbosc) was held by one William in 1195, *Magni Rotuli Scaccarii Normanniae sub Regibus Angliae*, ed. T. Stapleton, 2 vols (London, 1840-44), i, p. 58. It is probable that this William was the William de Sainneville who became a household knight of Earl Robert III of Leicester and who was granted the earl's manor of Lockington (Leics.) by Earl Robert IV between 1199 and 1204, PRO, E13/76, m. 72d. William de Sainneville abandoned his ancestral Norman fee in 1204; see also J. Le Maho, 'L'apparition des seigneuries châtelaines dans le Grand-Caux à l'époque ducale', *Archéologie Mediévale*, 6 (1976), p. 41.

Warwick roused against the Clintons by Earl Roger. Judith Green has pointed out how the existence of such communities rather imperil Le Patourel's vision of an homogeneous, unified Anglo-Norman aristocracy. In her study of the region known as the Norman Vexin, she found just such a community of barons and their tenants sufficient unto themselves. They formed a border aristocracy; their lands and dynastic interests sprawling over the frontier into France, rather than forming links with the Norman hinterland. The fact that two of the baronial families of the Norman Vexin, the Gisors and the Baudemont, actually had land holdings in Sussex, Hampshire and Suffolk was an irrelevance to their pattern of marriage, politics and religious patronage. Dr Green found that the border aristocracy of English Northumbria behaved in the same way – looking to the king of Scotland to counterbalance the local pretensions of the king of England.[23] I have recently finished a study of the aristocratic society of the southern march of Wales, which behaved in a way which encourages the belief that it was more concerned with its own regional peace than national affairs.[24]

That such communities existed at all within the Anglo-Norman realm is disruptive to any idea of homogeneity. Dr Green sees them as exceptional border phenomena, but they had ominous and worrying consequences for the king who sat in Westminster and aspired to control Normandy and Wales. It was the Marcher community of Wales which, by embracing the cause of Matilda and allying with the Welsh kings, toppled King Stephen at the battle of Lincoln in 1141. The Norman border community could be quite as disruptive. The magnates of the Norman Vexin described by Dr Green could be termed *Franco-Normans* as much as *Anglo-Normans*, and as we track along the borders of Normandy to the west of the Vexin we find other such Franco-Normans. Principal amongst them were the counts of Meulan, who ruled a small county on the River Seine, to the east of the Norman border. The counts combined great estates in central Normandy with the county of Meulan from 1080 to the fall of Normandy in 1204. In 1142 the counts augmented this cross-border agglomeration of lands with the honor of Gournay-sur-Marne to the east of Paris. Whenever in the twelfth century the kings of Paris and Rouen were in conflict, the count of Meulan was more often to be found on the French than the Norman side.[25] What was true of the counts of Meulan was equally true of the counts of Evreux and Alençon. Until 1118 an Anglo-Norman dynasty possessed Evreux, although its English estates were not particularly large. On the death of Count William, his nephew, Amaury de Montfort,

[23] J.A. Green, 'Lords of the Norman Vexin', *War and Government in the Middle Ages: Essays in Honour of J.O. Prestwich*, ed. J. Gillingham and J.C. Holt (Woodbridge, 1984), pp. 47-61; eadem, 'Anglo-Scottish Relations, 1066-1174', *England and her Neighbours, 1066-1453*, ed. M. Jones and M. Vale (London, 1990), pp. 53-72. Dr Green summed up her ideas on this point in 'Unity and Disunity', pp. 131-32.

[24] D. Crouch, 'Stephen, the March and the Welsh Kings', *The Anarchy of King Stephen's Reign*, ed. E. King (Oxford, 1994), forthcoming.

[25] Crouch, *Beaumont Twins*, pp. 64-79.

changed the orientation of the county. Amaury was lord of Montfort-en-Yvelines in the Méresais, the frontier area south of the Seine. King Henry I was alive to the potential problem of the Montforts' divided allegiance, and for some time tried to prevent the succession. He was defeated by the barons of the county who wanted Amaury as lord, as the nephew of their late lord. In their struggle against the king on their chosen lord's behalf we find yet more evidence of fragmentation amongst the Norman aristocracy – a local community was willing to defy royal ambitions for its locality, for it had its own interests and views.[26]

An example of how the Franco-Norman group amongst the aristocracy of Normandy could disrupt the equilibrium of the Anglo-Norman realm can be found in the troubles of Normandy in Henry I's time. For the king, his nephew, William Clito, was a constant rival and source of trouble in the second half of his reign. William hovered around the Norman frontiers with the support of Louis VI, ever probing for a means to unseat his uncle. He was a constant focus for dissenters from Henry I's rule. The great crisis of Henry's struggle with William occurred between 1118 and 1124. Unlike earlier crises in the succession, there seems to have been no desire amongst the rebel magnates to act to remove one claimant or other and keep England and Normandy under one ruler. The rebels of 1118 to 1124 were quite intent on the opposite aim, the separation of England and Normandy and the installation of Clito as duke of their choice. When we look at who they were, we find this an unsurprising aim: they were few of them men with much to lose in England – mostly they were our Franco-Normans or, if not, Norman magnates, pure and simple.

Prominent in the troubles of 1118-19 were the lords of the Vexin, with Amaury de Montfort and other Norman border magnates: the counts of Eu and Aumale; Richer de L'Aigle; Eustace de Breteuil; and some lesser barons including Robert, the lord of Le Neubourg, whose interests were substantially Norman. In the troubles of 1123-24, the rebels were the Franco-Norman counts of Evreux and Meulan, the barons of the Vexin (once again) and the Norman, Hugh de Montfort. Orderic Vitalis characterises the dissidents as 'castellani proceres Neustrie', 'noble castellans of Normandy'.[27] There was no awareness here of a feeling of Anglo-Normanness. Their rebellions were purely Norman affairs, although it is fair to point out that the reported behaviour of Richer de L'Aigle demonstrates how the king might display cross-Channel enticements to make at least one rebel safe. Richer's father had combined the English lordship of Pevensey with the Norman border lordship of L'Aigle, but Richer was not allowed to succeed to Pevensey because Henry I chose to take up the claims of Richer's younger brother to it. Richer then felt justified in allying with Clito and Louis VI. But as soon as the possibility of

[26] Orderic, vi, pp. 188, 260-64, 276-78.
[27] Ibid., p. 194.

acquiring Pevensey was dangled before him, Richer abruptly ditched the cause of Clito and embraced Henry I.[28]

Le Patourel failed to comment on these troubles except in reference to his own framework of society. Not surprising that he did not, for they demonstrate that a powerful body of magnates was to be found in Normandy which could afford to be mercurial in its allegiance, lacking any cross-Channel incentive to keep England and Normandy together. It was a group disengaged from royal aspirations. We may see in the Franco-Norman magnate a shadow of the nemesis of the later Angevin empire. If the Franco-Normans were not quite a third column in Norman aristocratic society, they always formed a powerful group of floating voters, with ears ever open to Capetian blandishments. It is no surprise that we find amongst those magnates who defected to Philip Augustus *even before* the fall of Normandy, the counts of Meulan and Alençon, the lords of Baudemont, Gisors and Le Neubourg; all descendants of those who had favoured William Clito and Louis VI half a century and more before.

Magnates are not the whole question here. What made them magnates was that their activities embraced a realm, or even realms. Their potential for disruption was realised when their cross-border activities led to action against the ruler of one realm or another. There is no doubt that there was a cross-Channel component of the aristocracy the activities of which tended to keep England and Normandy together. The recognition of the existence of another group with a tendency to spin the two realms apart does not alter that. What it does do, in my opinion, is to discredit Le Patourel's wider views on the homogeneity of magnate society in England and Normandy. I want now to try to penetrate lower social orders to assess the Anglo-Normanness and homogeneity of the so-called 'knightly class'.

I suspect that local aristocracies in England and Normandy rapidly became particularist after 1066. Le Patourel did not believe this. He believed that Anglo-Norman solidarity stretched down to all levels of free landed families. Even the knightly level underpinned it: 'examples of cross-Channel estates and interests at almost all levels can be quoted; that as they are sought for, more are found; and . . . one can trust the impression that they were in sufficient number to be entirely characteristic of the Norman lands and lordships'.[29] What lies behind this remark seems to be an optimistic reading of Lewis Loyd's study, *Anglo-Norman Families* (1951). Loyd set out to look for families in England which could be linked to places in Normandy. He found a good many, but not quite enough to justify Le Patourel's enthusiasm. The generation after the Conquest might have looked on Normandy as the motherland, but it is doubtful whether the second generation – the one born in England – would have, unless it retained estates in Normandy to confuse its sense of identity.

---

[28] Ibid., pp. 196-98.
[29] Le Patourel, *The Norman Empire*, p. 194.

How many such cross-Channel estates were to be found at the level of county society? Back to the central midlands. In the twelfth century only the greatest of the county knights of Leicestershire and Warwickshire had cross-Channel interests. Of the families domesticated in the counties, seven can be proved to have enjoyed Norman estates at some time in that century: Clinton, Burdet, du Bois, Montfort of Beaudesert, Tourville, Butler of Oversley and Curli of Budbrooke. Of the seven, the Norman connections of the Butlers and Clintons are lost sight of long before 1204. Of the five left, the Montforts, Burdets, Tourvilles and Curlis unloaded their Norman interests on cadet branches by the end of the twelfth century, at the latest.[30] When Normandy was lost to King John, only the du Bois family took losses (admittedly heavy losses) in Normandy.

The reason why these midlands families parted with their Norman estates can only be a matter of speculation, but there are at least some grounds on which to speculate. We know that the Montforts, Tourvilles and Curlis divided their estates at the end of the twelfth century. It could be suggested that they did so foreseeing the end of the Anglo-Norman *regnum*. It might then be suggested that these families partitioned their estates against their own wishes, as being constrained by severe political pressure. But this suggestion would not fit the case of the Tourvilles. They partitioned their estates at the Channel as a result of a routine family division between male heirs. Arnold, the younger Tourville, took the ancient family fee near Pont-Audemer; his elder brother, Simon, took the family's English interests. No expectation that Normandy and England were about to separate entered into the Tourville family's calculations. The partition was just another example of the natural impulse within landed families to rationalise the problems caused by holdings separated by the Channel, an impulse which served to increase particularism.[31] The Du Bois family made no division of its inheritance in its various generations, because there was (apparently) never any more than one son able to succeed; only Arnold IV du Bois had a brother, and that brother was a clerk.

[30] For the Clinton castle of Semilly (Manche, cant. Saint-Clair-sur-Elle), see Bod Lib, MS Dugdale 13, p. 149, and Crouch, 'Geoffrey de Clinton', p. 119n. For the Burdets, see above, n. 10. For the du Bois, above, n. 19. For the lands of Montfort of Beaudesert at Pithienville (Eure, cant. Evreux Nord et Sud, comm. Bernienville), Gauville and Claville (Eure, cant. Evreux Nord et Sud), *Report on the Manuscripts of Lord Middleton*, Historical Manuscripts Commission (1911) pp. 35-36; they were granted by Henry de Montfort, lord of Beaudesert to his younger brother Hugh in the later twelfth century. For the Tourville lands in Normandy, Crouch, *Beaumont Twins*, pp. 116-17, 119n. The Butler family had rents at Beaumont-le-Roger (Eure, cant. Beaumont) in the early twelfth century, cartulary of Beaumont priory, Bibliothèque Mazarine, MS 3417, fo. 2r. The Curli family of Budbrooke, Warwicks, held unknown lands in Normandy until the late twelfth century, *Book of Fees*, ii, p. 1280.

[31] Crouch, *Beaumont Twins*, pp. 218-19. For a resumé of the practice of divided magnate and knightly successions in the twelfth century, and some consideration of their significance. E.Z. Tabuteau, 'Law in the Succession to Normandy and England, 1087', *Haskins Society Journal*, 3 (1991), pp. 155-69.

On the other side of the coin are those families domesticated in Normandy with interests in the central Midlands. The *Terrae Normannorum* inquests are patchy, but they reveal nine Normans holding manors in Leicestershire and Warwickshire who decided for Philip Augustus when the time came to choose which king to follow. It is known in some cases, and likely in the others, that the eight held more land in Normandy than they had in England.[32] Were they then much of a loss to the county communities of Leicestershire and Warwickshire? Seventy or so knights were active in the two shires in the first decade of the thirteenth century, by my estimation. Although eight out of such a number may seem quite a loss, the fact was that none of the Normans played any active part in Midlands society. They appeared neither as jurors nor justices in either county; they attested no known local charters. We know that three of the eight (Robert de Harcourt, William de Thibouville and John d'Ajou) can be identified as men of weight in Norman society; the activities of John d'Ajou were centred on the household of the Norman magnate, Count Robert II of Meulan.[33]

Cross-Channel holdings were therefore likely to be the concern of only a small elite of county knights, and even amongst them, a clear orientation to one realm or other had developed long before 1204. The great majority of the knightly families of the shires, even if of French extraction, would have become exclusively 'English' in attachment. Those of English extraction (and Christopher Lewis has now produced evidence that they could have been at least half the landed families of a shire) may never have considered themselves Anglo-Norman at all.[34] I do not want to start off on the red herring trail of the

[32] For the names of most of these we are indebted to an inquest of 1247 carried out in the county court of Leicester and entered on the eyre roll, PRO, JUST 1/455, mm. 6d-13, printed in, *Book of Fees*, ii, pp. 1392-93. This source gives the *Normanni* as Robert de Thibouville (Syston and Croxton Kerrial, Leics.), Richard de Harcourt (Sileby and Burstall, Leics.), William de Ouville (unknown), Hugh le Porter (Croxton Kerrial, Leics.), William Paynel (Garthorpe, Leics.), William Mene Duraunt (Normanton, Leics.), John d'Ajou (Thurnby and Ilston-on-the-Hill, Leics.) and William de Rollos (Saddington, Leics.). From other sources we know that Richard de Harcourt *Normannus* held land in Warwickshire at Ilmington (and succeeded in securing its restoration), *Book of Fees*, ii, pp. 1356, 1394; Bod Lib, MS Dugdale 13, p. 256. A small estate at Wilmcote, Warwicks., belonged to Brito the chamberlain *Normannus*, P.R. Coss, *Lordship, Knighthood and Locality: A Study in English Society, c. 1180-c. 1280* (Cambridge, 1991), p. 229. Of these nine, Richard de Harcourt and Robert de Thibouville are noted as bannerets of Normandy, although most of their estates were held of the Beaumont family in Normandy.

[33] Richard de Harcourt and Robert de Thibouville, originally from Beaumont tenant families, had raised themselves to magnate status in the Normandy of King John and Philip Augustus, when they are noted as *banneretti*, *Recueil des historiens de la France*, xxiii, p. 684. Richard de Harcourt secured by 1207 the former Beaumont honor of Elbeuf on the Seine from Philip Augustus; for him see F.M. Powicke, *The Loss of Normandy, 1189-1204* (Manchester, 1913), pp. 342-3; *Recueil des historiens de la France*, xxiv, p. 38; cartulary of Le Valasse abbey, ADSM, 18 H, fos 160v-161v. John d'Ajou attests at least fourteen Norman acts of Count Robert II of Meulan before 1204.

[34] C.P. Lewis, 'Domesday Jurors', *Haskins Society Journal*, 5, (for 1993), forthcoming.

early county community, but it seems to me undeniable that local loyalties were already a feature of English landed society in the mid twelfth century. It might have focused on the regular meetings of the county and hundred courts, or on the honor courts of particularly powerful local magnates, but the feeling is there and is stated. John de Saint-Omer, a monk of Peterborough in the late twelfth century, defends his home county in strong terms: 'Whoever once enters Norfolk will not wish to leave as long as he lives, for once he sees so good a land, he will declare it a little Paradise!'. It is undoubtedly significant that he goes on to say: 'Where in the world are knights valued so highly as in Normandy? If the English are lukewarm about knightliness, Norfolk surpasses all others in it!'[35]

This monk, seemingly from a knightly background, loved his home county and was antagonistic to Normans. The sentiment was returned on the other side of the Channel. England puzzled those living in Normandy, even infuriated them. Such a feeling lay behind the frustrated letter of a monk of Fécamp marooned in Oxfordshire on his abbey's business. Describing local society he complains, 'The land has as many lords as it has neighbours, and what is more burdensome than anything, you can get nothing by which to pay the host of dues.'[36] Another story survives which puts the feeling of alienation more graphically. A Norman knight rode to the hunt with a king of England in one of the ducal forests of Normandy. A wolf was started by the dogs, but when it was cornered the Norman waded in and freed the wolf. When the king demanded to know why the knight had done this, he said bluntly that he loved Norman wolves better than English dogs.[37] There is other casual abuse. The French (as is well known) characterised the English as *caudati*, having tails hidden about their clothing; and as being abstracted and dreamy because of the damp and foggy land they inhabited.[38] But a more particularly Norman insult thrown at the English was their lack of martial prowess. The English knew the Normans thought this of them and detested it. Take for instance the mocking words placed by Jordan Fantosme in the 1170s in the mouth of the great Norman noblewoman, Petronilla de Grandmesnil, countess of Leicester, when she and

---

[35] *Norfolchiae descriptionis impugnatio*, in *Early Mysteries and other Latin Poems of the Twelfth and Thirteenth Centuries*, ed. T. Wright (London, 1838), p. 106. One can compare this with the feeling comments on Norfolk by Jordan Fantosme, *Jordan Fantosme's Chronicle*, ed. R.C. Johnston (Oxford, 1981), p. 30. For a suggestion that the political mechanism of a county community (as suggested by early modern historians) went back beyond the thirteenth century, see J.R. Maddicott, 'Magna Carta and the Local Community, 1215-59', *Past and Present*, 102 (1984), p. 25.

[36] J. Laporte, '*Epistulae Fiscannenses*: lettres d'amitié, de gouvernement et d'affaires (XIe et XIIe siècles)', *Revue Mabillon*, 43 (1953), pp. 29-30.

[37] *A Selection of Latin Stories*, ed. T. Wright, Percy Society, 8 (1842), p. 126. The story is to be found in BL, MS Royal 7 E iv, a manuscript of the fourteenth century, but it seems to derive from political conditions much earlier than the manuscript.

[38] For this, see particularly R.W. Southern, 'England's First Entry into Europe', *Medieval Humanism and Other Studies* (Oxford, 1970), pp. 141-47.

her husband led a Flemish invasion force into East Anglia. 'The English are great boasters, but poor fighters; they are better at quaffing great tankards and guzzling.'[39] The joke was that the countess and her husband were routed soon afterwards by a force of English townsmen in arms.

The verse biography of William Marshal is one of the best measures of the antagonism between English and Norman knights. It was composed, almost certainly in the southern march of Wales, in the mid 1220s. The composer was an aged *trouvère* whose own memory stretched well back into the reign of Henry II. He drew much of his material from the recollections of the old Marshal's squires and household knights. It was they who told him that the reason for their master's fall at the court of Henry, the Young King, in 1182 was the hatred and envy felt by the Norman majority of the royal household that William, an Englishman from Wiltshire, was placed above them in the king's affections. The biography cannot resist its own glee that it was William Marshal, an Englishman, who laid low the finest knights in France during his career on the tournament field in the 1170s.[40] The biographer also records the sentiment attributed to William de Tancarville, the young Marshal's cousin and mentor, that he should avoid England as it was a poor place for a warrior, and that military exercises were unimportant there.[41] He does so to blacken Tancarville, with whom the young Marshal apparently fell out, but he hugs the insult to his bosom with the enthusiasm of the xenophobe; it excused his hatred.

English knightly society was certainly localised and particularist, and was (to a degree which is difficult to assess) xenophobic also. Even English counties were in competition with each other in the twelfth century. There are numerous indications that Norman knightly society returned the feeling. At the level of the magnates, this feeling was probably absent. William Marshal, although from Wiltshire, himself demonstrated his love and affection for Normandy on several occasions in a way his biographer could not disguise. The jibe about England being a poor place for a warrior might even be the Marshal's own. His household, younger than himself, had grown up in England in Henry II's reign and thought differently about the duchy. Although rejoicing in their master's French triumphs, they loved not France.

We hear a lot about the international culture of the twelfth century aristocrat, and I am not going to deny that English and French aristocrats shared many aspirations and ideas. French was the language of the English aristocrat,

---

[39] *Jordan Fantosme's Chronicle*, p. 72. This calumny (Fantosme wrote *c.* 1175) is prefigured by a punning canon of Reims who wrote that the English were fonder of their *gula* (gullet) than their *galea* (arms) some fifteen years before Fantosme's report, see Southern, *Medieval Humanism*, pp. 145-46.

[40] D. Crouch, *William Marshal: Court, Career and Chivalry in the Angevin Empire* (London, 1990), pp. 34, 44, 115, 141.

[41] *Histoire de Guillaume le Maréchal, comte de Pembroke et Striguil*, ed. P. Meyer, Société de l'histoire de la France, 3 vols (1891-1901) i, lines 1530-48.

whether his ancestry was English or immigrant. That does not alter the fact that some aspects of this international culture served to divide rather than unite Englishman and Norman. One of the great manifestations of international knightly society was the tournament. We hear of English knights travelling over to Normandy to participate in tournaments as early as the 1130s. Yet when we find the first decent descriptions of the way tournaments were carried out, in the 1170s (just at the point when magnates were taking up the pursuit), we find that large tournaments divided up on national lines. Despite the union between England and Normandy, English and Norman knights fought in separate teams. Since the tournament was in origin a pursuit developed by household knights and not their masters, we must be seeing a facet of the perception of the world of the knights of the earlier twelfth century.[42]

Another striking cultural phenomenon of the twelfth century was the propagation of what we now call 'heraldry'. It arose, as far as anyone can tell, in north-west France in the later eleventh century amongst the competing counts of Picardy. It was a means of boosting family pride by adopting symbols relating to lordship and lineage. It spread outwards to northern France and England early in the twelfth century.[43] At this stage, until the 1160s, heraldry was confined to the greatest noblemen, and the use of symbols was indifferent to national boundaries. One of the best examples of this was the device borne by a group of families which claimed descent from the Emperor Charlemagne. Following the lead of the counts of Vermandois, all these families took a device of a blue and gold check. The counts of Vermandois were based on Picardy, their cousins, the counts of Meulan and the earls of Warwick, Leicester and Surrey also took this same device. Heraldry was not merely cross-Channel, it was quite international. By the mid twelfth century other cross-Channel clans sported such devices: the chevrons carried by the related families of Clare, Montfichet, fitz Robert and Monmouth are a case in point; their territories ran from the Welsh march to the southern border of Normandy. Another group

---

[42] For the tournament in the twelfth century generally, J.R.V. Barker, *The Tournament in England, 1100-1400*, (Woodbridge, 1986), pp. 4-16; G. Duby, *Le dimanche de Bouvines* (Paris, 1973), pp. 100-44. That English knights were crossing to the Continent to tourney is known from the remarkable charter of Osbert of Arden, discussed by Barker. *Tournament in England*, p. 7. A tournament of *c.* 1168 recorded in *Histoire de Guillaume le Maréchal*, i, lines 1208-12, divided up into two sides of several companies: Angevins, Manceaux, Poitevins and Bretons against French, Norman and English. This sensitivity to nationality in warfare is perhaps prefigured by a passage in the *Song of Roland* (*c.* 1100) where Charlemagne's army rode in companies by nation (French, Bavarians, Allemans, Normans, Bretons, Auvergnais, Poitevins, Flemings, Frisians, Lotharingians and Burgundians). Significantly, Charlemagne himself headed the French company, as the most distinguished, *La chanson de Roland*, ed. F. Whitehead (Oxford, 1946), lines 3014-95.

[43] For the origins of heraldry generally, M. Pastoureau, 'L'origine des armoiries: un problème en voie de solution?', *Genealogica & Heraldica*, ed. S.T. Achen (Copenhagen, 1982), pp. 241-54; A. Ailes, 'The Knight, Heraldry and Armour: The Role of Recognition and the Origins of Heraldry', *Medieval Knighthood*, 4 (1992), ed. C. Harper-Bill and R. Harvey, pp. 1-21.

was made up of those families related to the Mandeville earls of Essex, which included the families of Vere and Saye and lands from Flanders to the Welsh March.[44]

In its earliest stages heraldry was a good support for Le Patourel's view of an homogeneous aristocracy bridging the Channel. Since it affected the higher aristocracy at that point, this should be no surprise. When the processes of diffusion brought heraldry to the level of the county knight, the symbols taken by knightly families give us a view of these families' place in the political world which is by no means that of the upper aristocracy. What many knights did was to take devices which alluded to the particular magnate they followed; taking symbols which advertised local lordship not international kinship. Thus many of the followers of the earls of Hertford took chevrons; those of the earls of Leicester, five-petalled flowers; those of the earls of Chester, wheat sheaves; and those of the earls of Pembroke, linked wings (allures). For the knight, his local concerns produced a regional heraldry, in the way the heraldry of his master, the magnate, had produced a heraldry which spanned kingdoms. The knight did not see the big world, and had no concern with it.[45]

I take that as my final demonstration of what I find faulty with Le Patourel's vision of the aristocracy of the twelfth century. It was not an homogeneous cross-Channel elite with common political aspirations, embracing several levels of wealth. The section of it that did have transcendent political characteristics was represented by the magnates, but if this group was socially homogeneous it was also politically divergent, with a Franco-Norman lobby within it as liable to pull away Normandy from England as the Anglo-Normans were trying to keep the two countries together. The twelfth-century local elites of England (and I would believe this of Normandy too) were local in aspirations and concerns. When each considered the other at all, their image of English knight and Norman knight was coloured by xenophobia. From this we could go on to conclude that it was only the fraction of the magnates with Anglo-Norman interests which supported the king of England's desire to keep Normandy. This fraction's commitment to a wider Angevin Empire must be suspect. Hence the fatal nature of the separation of England and Normandy in 1204. Once the magnates were forced to abandon one realm or the other, once compensation had been sought or offered for the loss, or the loss simply absorbed, the magnates would no longer exert themselves amongst the knights who were their dependants to support the uncongenial task of reconquering alien Normandy. By 1236 Henry III might well have been alone in England in sincerely wanting to regain Normandy. What little Anglo-Norman feeling there ever had been around the king was quite gone.

[44] D. Crouch, *The Image of Aristocracy in Britain, 1000-1300* (London, 1992), pp. 222-23.
[45] Ibid., pp. 229-35.

5

Romance in England and Normandy in the Twelfth Century

Peter S. Noble

How to divide the literature of the twelfth and thirteenth centuries between England and Normandy is a question which poses a variety of problems.[1] Scholars such as the late Dominica Legge and Constance West distinguished between insular and continental texts on linguistic grounds, dividing the texts between those written in Anglo-Norman and those written in the dialects of France, such as Picard, Champenois, Francien etc.[2] This is a perfectly valid distinction, although even Professor Legge found herself in her books about Anglo-Norman writing about texts which were not strictly in that dialect, but which had such obvious links with England that she could not omit them.[3] There is also the problem that some texts which must have started life as Anglo-Norman are not preserved in that dialect, as they had been copied by Picard (or other) scribes who had erased all traces of the original dialect to render the text more acceptable to their audience.[4] Are these texts to be counted as part of the Anglo-Norman inheritance or not? Yet another problem is that, as England and Normandy were usually under the same ruler, more or less, from 1066 and throughout the period under consideration, the distinction is in some ways artificial. Texts must have been known on both sides of the Channel and appreciated to some extent by individuals who had lands or contacts in England and Normandy. Indeed for the first half-century after the Conquest there was very little difference between the dialects.[5] It is well into the twelfth century when the dialects can be seen to separate. Even then we have examples of texts by authors from France who wrote for the Anglo-Norman

---

[1] I would like to thank my colleague Wolfgang van Emden and my wife, who both read drafts of this paper and whose advice certainly improved it.

[2] M. Dominica Legge, *Anglo-Norman in the Cloisters* (Edinburgh, 1950) [henceforth *ANC*]; C.B. West, *Courtoisie in Anglo-Norman Literature* (Oxford, 1938); M. Dominica Legge, *Anglo-Norman Literature and its Background* (Oxford, 1963) [henceforth *ANL*].

[3] See *ANL*, p. 59.

[4] Ibid., p. 109.

[5] Ibid., p. 7, points out that the first surviving Anglo-Norman text is the *Voyage of St Brendan* by Benedeit probably written for Matilda, queen of Henry I.

court. One of the earliest examples is the *Brut* by Wace, the Channel Islander, who wrote for the court of Henry II and Eleanor of Aquitaine. His subject was the 'matter of Britain', his patrons were the king and queen of England but his dialect was not Anglo-Norman. In fact because of the title of this essay, he does not need to be included as he was a chronicler rather than a romance writer, but he does indicate the sort of problem which can arise in defining the area to be discussed.

In spite of all these reservations it is possible to establish a rather rough distinction between romances written for English consumption as opposed to those with a continental origin. Anything written in Anglo-Norman must belong to the English category and should be joined by anything obviously written for an English patron or the English court, using English in the very broad sense of all the French or Anglo-Norman speaking families based in England. Such a definition immediately brings in the *Romance of Horn* (I follow the editor's opinion in including it in the romances and not in the *chansons de geste*); both the longer surviving fragments of the Tristan legend; the two romances by Hue de Rotelande, perhaps one of the romances by Chrétien de Troyes, *Cligès*, which Constance Bullock-Davies, for example, thought was probably written for the court of Henry II after a visit to England; and *Guillaume d'Angleterre*, which may have been written by Chrétien and seems to have been designed to appeal to an island audience.[6] By way of contrast the romances in the twelfth century which seem to have little or no connection with England are the *Conte de Floire et de Blancheflor*, the other romances of Chrétien de Troyes, the two romances of Gautier d'Arras, the massive romance *Partonopeu de Blois*, *Li Bel Inconnu* by Renaut de Beaujeu, *L'Escoufle* by Jean Renart and *Galeran de Bretagne*, which may be twelfth century and which used to be attributed to Jean Renart but is now thought to be by an imitator called Renaus.[7]

Professor Legge and Miss West were able to point out some differences between Anglo-Norman literature and that produced by continental writers of the same generation. Anglo-Norman is more didactic and tends to moralise more than continental writers according to Professor Legge,[8] while Miss West, despite devoting a whole book to the subject, had little success in finding much evidence of *courtoisie* or *amour courtois* in island writers.[9] Love is of course very much present in the romances. Horn is the beloved of two princesses, Rigmel, the daughter of King Hunlauf of Brittany, whose love he eventually returns, and Lenburc, the daughter of the King of Ireland, whose love he rejects because he remains faithful to Rigmel. In each case the girl takes the

---

[6] C. Bullock-Davies, 'Chrétien de Troyes and England', *Arthurian Literature*, 1 (1981).

[7] See Introduction to Sweetser's edition of *L'Escoufle*. Full details of all the texts used are given in the list of editions which follows.

[8] *ANC*, p. 2.

[9] West, *Courtoisie*, p. 167.

initiative, offering herself to Horn whose good looks and valour are irresist-ible. Horn keeps them at arm's length only gradually allowing himself to be won over by Rigmel, accepting first a pennon and then a ring as a pledge of her troth. Lenburc accepts that she has no chance of winning him, once she realises that the man she has known as Gudmod is actually Horn, the beloved of Rigmel, whose beauty is famous everywhere. Meekly Lenburc accepts as her husband Modin of Fenenie, whom Horn bestows on her father after rescuing Rigmel from a forced marriage to him. Despite their readiness to declare their love and to seek the man that they want, the princesses are wholly at the mercy of the men who surround them and are expected to marry the man chosen for them. This is a feature shared with the Tristan romances. Iseut is married to Mark as a pawn in the political struggle between Ireland and Cornwall. We do not have the parts of Beroul and Thomas in which the marriage is negotiated, but there is nothing in Beroul to suggest that she was particularly opposed to the match until after she had drunk the potion. In Thomas, however, Tristan quite clearly suggests that their love had started before they drank the potion, at the point when Iseut was nursing him during his stay at the court of Ireland as he convalesced from his poisoned wound. Iseut would in this version presumably be a reluctant bride even before she embarked on the voyage to Cornwall. Unlike Rigmel and Lenburc she does not end by marrying either the man she wants or a man who is acceptable to her, with the tragic results that are so well known. Her namesake, Iseut aux blanches mains, is also married to please the political needs of her family, who are eager to attach Tristan firmly to them. In fact Iseut aux blanches mains is in love with Tristan and not at all averse to the marriage, but it brings her little happiness in the end as Tristan is not in love with her and is using her for his own purposes. In neither Beroul nor Thomas is there any evidence that the love of Tristan and Iseut is conceived as a courtly love. In *Horn* male dominance, the submission of the ladies and their readiness to confess their love to an unresponsive suitor are all alien to the ideas of courtly love. In *Tristan* the role of the potion, the lack of secrecy, the relationship between the lovers are all at variance with courtly love, Beroul and Thomas were both familiar with courtly love and it can be argued that Thomas in particular was writing a poem that was deeply hostile to courtly love, despite the signs of courtly influence in the vocabulary and in the interest in the analysis of the nature of love.[10] The author of *Horn* shows little interest in courtly love and only rarely uses the vocabulary associated with it.

Chrétien, on the other hand, is generally associated with courtly love and certainly knew a great deal about it. Opinions differ as to whether he was actually in favour of it or against it, but he was familiar with the work of the troubadours such as Bernart de Ventadour and courtly elements do appear in his work, such as the need for the man to woo the lady by his service and

---

[10] T. Hunt, 'The Significance of Thomas's *Tristan*', *Reading Medieval Studies*, 7 (1981), pp. 41-61.

devotion. *Cligès*, however, is a work in which Chrétien demonstrates that it is impossible to resolve the dilemma of Iseut without the use of magic. Fénice, his heroine, is married against her will to the uncle of the man she loves. When she discovers that Cligès returns her love, she refuses to consummate their love unless she can keep her reputation. She refuses to elope with him to the court of his great-uncle, King Arthur. The dilemma is solved only through the near supernatural skill of Cligès's slave, Jean, who constructs a secret garden for the lovers, and the wholly supernatural powers of Fénice's nurse, Thessala, who arranges their escape. Eventually the convenient death from rage of Fénice's husband leaves the lovers free to marry, but the trickery of Fénice is never forgotten and all future empresses of Constantinople are kept secluded so that they can never again be unfaithful in the same way. Throughout the poem there are overt and covert references to the Tristan legend in a way which shows that Chrétien intended to criticise the morality of Tristan and Iseut. There is a clear moral to be drawn and to that extent the poem meets one of Professor Legge's criteria.

Guillaume d'Angleterre, which is not an Anglo-Norman text in either of the surviving manuscripts, must have been written for an English patron and is an edifying – if rather boring – tale of love and devotion surviving through years of separation and hardship.[11] It is difficult to believe that such a boringly pious tale is written by the witty and ironic author of the five famous Arthurian romances and it seems more likely that it was some other Chrétien, as he names himself in the prologue (line 1), who wrote it. It seems reasonable to include it amongst the romances of England since it was probably written for the Lovel family.[12]

Hue de Rotelande is quite clearly an Anglo-Norman writer, probably from Rhuddlan, and writing between 1174 and 1191. *Ipomedon* is set in the Norman areas of southern Italy and was probably inspired by the marriage of Joan, daughter of Henry II to William of Sicily. Ipomedon is the heir to the kingdom of Apulia and falls in love with the duchess of Calabria, whom he eventually wins, but his success is delayed for years by his refusal to woo her openly. Although she is attracted to him physically, the Duchess is unimpressed by his apparent lack of valour and it is only when his identity is betrayed that his true worth is recognised and the couple are able to marry. Hue's second romance *Prothesilaus* anticipates the trend in thirteenth-century Anglo-Norman romance towards family or ancestral romance by relating the adventures of the sons of Ipomedon. Prothesilaus is the heir to his mother's duchy but is cheated of his inheritance by his brother. He is helped in his campaign to recover his lands by the queen of Sicily, Medea. In the end he defeats his brother, marries Medea and produces many children whose adventures Hue hoped to relate. In

---

[11] *ANL*, p. 41.
[12] Ibid., p. 41.

these poems, too, courtly love is not an important element. Although Ipomedon seems to try to win the duchess by serving her, his service is in fact a parody
of courtly service, as he refuses to join in the jousting, preferring always to go
hunting. Of course he then secretly returns to take part in the tournaments.
Some of the ladies are as bold and frank as Rigmel and Lenburc in *Horn* in
declaring their love. Hue is not particularly idealistic about love, which he
views with Ovidian cynicism, and is perhaps more interested in fighting, which
has a particularly large role in *Prothesilaus*.[13] This too is a feature of Horn,
although there is a difference in that in *Horn* the fighting is reminiscent of epic
whereas in *Hue* the fighting is much more typical of romance, with the
individual hero dominating.

When the continental romances are examined, two points immediately
stand out which differentiate them from the romances which have been
discussed so far. Many of the continental romances are set at the court of
Arthur and the concept of love in the romances is different. So too is the
attitude to fighting in many of them. There are, of course, links between the
two groups, but it is worth looking at the differences just mentioned. In the
romances which I have described as belonging to England, Arthur is absent
from almost all of them. He appears in *Cligès* by Chrétien de Troyes, although
the romance is mainly about the adventures of two Byzantine princes, Alexander and his son Cligès, both of whom spend time at the court of Arthur,
whose niece Alexander marries, so that Cligès, their son, is the great nephew
of Arthur. Arthur's court, though not free from treachery and intrigue,
contrasts with the corrupt atmosphere of the Byzantine court and is also
openly stated to be the court where young men must go to measure themselves
and show themselves to be worthy of knighthood. Arthur also appears briefly
in both the versions of the Tristan legend. In Thomas he is mentioned as
belonging to a previous generation. He has no part to play in the romance.
Mark is king of England and the legends of Arthur and Tristan are separate, as
they were in the sixth to ninth centuries. In Beroul the power of the Arthurian
legend can be seen, however, as the legend of Tristan is joined to that of
Arthur. Although the two courts are separate, and Cornwall seems to be an
independent kingdom under Mark, the prestige of Arthur and his knights is
such that he is the obvious arbiter for Iseut's oath and feels able to lecture
Mark on how he should behave towards his wife and his men. Interestingly
Arthur and his knights never doubt for one moment that Iseut is in the right.
They spring to the defence of the most beautiful woman in western Europe
without any hesitation, although the audience knows that her defence against
the charge of adultery is weak.

Contrast this with Arthur's importance in Chrétien de Troyes's other
romances, where Arthur and his court form the background to the adventures
of his knights. Except in the unfinished *Conte du Graal*, his adventures start

---

[13] Ibid., p. 88, describes Hue as 'quizzical'.

from his court, finish there and are punctuated by return visits to the court to seek approval or to mark a stage in the hero's quest for self-knowledge. The characters are all closely connected with the court of Arthur, either through ties of friendship or occasionally through feuds. Similarly Renaut de Beaujeu, who drew heavily on the work of Chrétien and to a lesser extent on that of Wace, structures his romance to a plan not dissimilar to those of Chrétien, as his hero starts from Arthur's court and finishes there. In the meantime he has found a bride and adventured in the world of the supernatural, rather more explicitly than Chrétien's heroes, whose adventures are tinged with a supernatural which is never overt.

The other continental romances are not Arthurian in setting, but most of them are influenced by another of the then popular exotic settings, Byzantium and the formerly Byzantine, currently Norman, territories of Sicily and southern Italy, a setting which they share with the two romances of Hue de Rotelande. *Partonopeu de Blois*, although undoubtedly influenced by two of the romances of Chrétien, is about the empress of Byzantium who is loved by Partonopeu, betrayed by him and eventually reconciled with him. Partonopeu has to regain the love of his lady by proving himself worthy of her, although she had taken the initiative in their original affair, like the princesses in *Horn*. *Floire et Blancheflor* is partly set in Egypt, *Eracle* is the story of the loves of an empress of Rome, *Ille et Galeron* and *L'Escoufle* see much of the action take place in Italy. *Galeran de Bretagne* (based on the lai, *Le Fresne*, by Marie de France) is set in northern France and differs from the other romances in that Galeran is a less active character than some of the other heroes. The happy ending to the romance is brought about by the energy and musical talent of the heroine, who goes in search of her lover and is eventually recognised as the lost twin of the girl who is about to marry him.

In all of these romances the atmosphere is different from that of the first group. All the heroes recognise the merit of their ladies and can be said to serve and honour them in a way that Horn and Beroul's Tristan, at least, do not. The ideas of courtly love and courtly behaviour are apparent in all the poets, even if, like Chrétien, they are not wholly in favour of such ideas which nonetheless did refine the attitudes and the behaviour of the members of the court. Take, the example, the way in which Paridès in *Eracle* strives to impress Athenais once he has realised that she is interested in his good looks and musical talent. Similarly Partonopeu has to prove his suitability to marry Melior by his prowess in the tournament arranged to find her a suitable husband.

The greatest difference perhaps is the focus on the individual, particularly in the fighting, in the continental romances. Each of the romances mentioned is primarily concerned with the development or career of the hero and the heroine and with their attempts to establish themselves in the society to which they belong or to which they aspire. In *Horn* on the other hand, there is a strong sense of societies in conflict. Horn's main enemies are the pagans from the south who killed his father. Horn does not regard himself as a suitable husband for Rigmel until he has avenged his father and proved himself against the pagans. The actual battles are strongly reminiscent of the battles in epic between Christians and Saracens. In Beroul, Tristan and Iseut are at war with the group of barons who are their rivals for power and influence at the court of Mark. Again the conflict is between groups, although on a smaller scale than in many of the other romances, let alone the epics, reflecting perhaps the accuracy of detail which Beroul so often shows. Even in the surviving fragments of Thomas's *Tristan*, the hero joins with Tristan le Nain to fight the ravishers of the latter's beloved, the just lovers versus the unjust lovers, so that again there is the idea of group conflict. In *Cligès* there is the war between Arthur and the treacherous Count Angrès, in which Alexander and his Greek followers distinguish themselves, followed by the war between the Greeks and the Saxons, when the emperor of Germany decides to give his daughter to the emperor of Byzantium rather than to the duke of Saxony to whom she had been promised. In Hue de Rotelande's two romances the focus is almost as much on fighting as on love, particularly in *Prothesilaus*, where the emphasis is more on the individual than the group but not exclusively so.

In the continental romances, however, the emphasis is exclusively on the hero and his advancement through his military prowess. Chrétien's heroes – Erec, Yvain, Lancelot, Perceval and Gauvain – participate in numerous single combats and occasionally even in larger skirmishes and tournaments. Always, however, the attention of the author, and therefore the reader or listener, is fixed on the deeds of the hero. For example Yvain, almost single-handedly, defeats Count Allier and his men who have been attacking La Dame de Noiroison. His example inspires her men to fight better but the victory is entirely due to his inspiration and his efforts. Perceval lifts the siege of Belrepaire by a series of single combats in which he is always the victor, so that Blanchefleur is restored to her lands and freed from the threat of the besieger. There is much fighting in *Partonopeu*, not all of it single combat, but again it is the hero who is normally the focus of attention until the end, when his friend starts to share the limelight so that he is then a suitable candidate for the hand of Melior's sister, Urraque. In *Galeran de Bretagne* there is no fighting, although it is clear that Galeran could fight if necessary. As there is no male rival and no dispute over land, there is no cause for fighting.

This survey of the twelfth-century romances written in French and Anglo-Norman suggests that, while they have certain elements in common, there are clear differences. The most striking difference is the lack of interest in Arthur and the Arthurian legend in the romances which are clearly insular. There are only Chrétien's *Cligès*, the status of which is slightly ambiguous anyway, and the brief references in the two Tristan fragments, in one of which Thomas is clearly concerned to distance his story from Arthur. The Tristan legend is, in fact, the only clear evidence of Celtic influence in the island romances. Otherwise the Anglo-Normans show little taste for the faery, although it must have been readily available. We know from stories, such as the story of Ailred, that there were monks who preferred listening to tales of Arthur when they should have been listening to Scripture, that Arthurian material was circulating in Britain and presumably very popular. It has not survived in written form. Secondly, it is clear that Constance West was right to see an absence of courtly influence in the romances written for an island audience, although island writers were aware of courtly love and courtliness.[14] Thirdly, island romances were slower to respond to the increasing interest in the individual which was such a marked feature of the twelfth century. It was becoming clearer by the time of Hue de Rotelande, but Hue's approach is not quite the same as that of his continental contemporaries.[15]

On the other hand, there are points in common. It is clear that both audiences shared an interest in the Mediterranean lands conquered by or under attack from the Normans. The Norman conquest of southern Italy and Sicily, their attacks on the Byzantine Empire, the marriage between the daughter of Henry II and William of Sicily and the interest in the crusading ideal had all made the names of these lands familiar, although they were, of course, seen as faraway and exotic, which clearly appealed to the audiences of the second half of the twelfth century. In general the audiences were interested in fighting and love, although, as already indicated, there were different interpretations of the roles of the two sexes in love. Magic figures occasionally in both groups, especially in *Partonopeu*, but is not a major feature, something which was to change in the following century.

The following century also saw the rise of the important group of Anglo-Norman romances known as family romances, such as *Gui de Warewic*, *Fouke Fitwaryn* and *Boeve de Hantome*, but none of these survive in twelfth-century versions, although Professor Legge argues forcefully that *Boeve* certainly stems from the twelfth century in its original lost version.[16] These romances have not been discussed here because it seems difficult to fit them into a study of twelfth-century romances, when there is no certain evidence as to what the twelfth-century versions were like. From the surviving romances which are clearly twelfth-century it seems probable that the tastes of the island and continental audiences were not identical. The latter were more interested in courtly love, the rise of the individual and the exotic, whether Celtic or Mediterranean. The former were more matter of fact, less interested in Celtic material and less inclined to idealise their female characters.

---

[14] West, *Courtoisie*, pp. 167-68.
[15] *ANL*, p. 88.
[16] Ibid., p. 160.

Editions Used

Texts in Anglo-Norman or Texts Associated with Britain

The Romance of Tristan by Beroul, ed. A. Ewert (Oxford, 1963), i (dated between 1160 and 1191).

Thomas, *Les fragments du roman de Tristan*, ed., Bartina Wind (Geneva and Paris, 1960) (probable dating around 1170).

La Folie Tristan de Berne, ed. Ernest Hoepffner, Publications de la Faculté des Lettres de l'Université de Strasbourg, 3 (Paris, 1949) (dated towards the end of the twelfth century).

La Folie Tristan d'Oxford, ed. Ernest Hoepffner, Publications de la Faculté des Lettres de l'Université de Strasbourg, 8 (Rodez, 1943) (dated towards the end of the twelfth century).

Marie de France, *Lais*, ed. A. Ewert (Oxford, 1969) (dated most probably to the 1170s but the dating is controversial because of the uncertainty over the identity of Marie).

The Romance of Horn, ed. Mildred K. Pope, Anglo-Norman Text Society, 9-10 (Oxford, 1955) and 12-13, revised and completed by T.B.W. Reid (Oxford, 1964) (dated before 1170 and could be as early as the late 1130s or early 1140s).

Wace, *La partie arthurienne du roman de Brut*, ed. I.D.O. Arnold and M.M. Pelan (Paris, 1962) (dated to around 1154).

Chrétien de Troyes, *Guillaume d'Angleterre*, ed. Maurice Wilmotte, Classiques français du moyen âge, 55 (Paris, 1927). (The dating of Chrétien is controversial with some critics placing him between 1170 and the late 1180s, while the others see his period of activity as starting after 1180 and extending into the 1190s).

Chrétien de Troyes, *Cligès*, ed. Alexandre Micha, Classiques français du moyen âge, 84 (Paris 1957).

Hue de Rotelande, *Ipomedon*, ed. A.J. Holden (Paris, 1979) (Hue is dated between 1174 and 1190).

Hue de Rotelande, *Prothesilaus*, ed. A.J. Holden 2 vols, Anglo-Norman Text Society (London 1991).

Texts with No Obvious Link with Britain

Le conte de Floire et de Blancheflor, ed. Jean-Luc Leclanche, Classiques français du moyen âge, 105 (Paris, 1980) (dated to around 1150).

Chrétien de Troyes, *Le Chevalier de la Charrete*, ed. Mario Roques, Classiques français du moyen âge, 86 (Paris, 1956).

Chrétien de Troyes, *Le roman de Perceval*, ed., William Roach, Textes littéraires français (Geneva and Paris, 1959).

Chrétien de Troyes, *Erec et Enide*, ed. Mario Roques, Classiques français du moyen âge, 80 (Paris, 1955).

Gautier d'Arras, *Eracle*, ed. Guy Raynaud de Lage, Classiques français du moyen âge, 102 (Paris, 1976).

Gautier d'Arras, *Ille et Galeron*, ed. Yves Lefèvre, Classiques français du moyen âge, 109 (Paris, 1988). (dated between 1167 and 1184 but critics do not agree on his exact dates within that period).

Partonopeu de Blois, ed. Joseph Gildea 3 vols, (Villanova, 1965-67) (dated around 1180).

Jean Renart, *L'Escoufle*, ed. Franklin Sweetser, Textes littéraires français (Paris and Geneva, 1974) (dated 1200-1202).

Renaut de Beaujeu, *Le Bel Inconnu*, ed. G. Perrie Williams, Classiques français du moyen âge, 38 (Paris, 1929) (dated before 1228 but after Chrétien).

Jean Renart, *Galeran de Bretagne*, ed. Lucian Foulet, Classiques français du moyen âge, 37 (Paris, 1925) (date uncertain but after Marie de France, probably around the turn of the century).

6

Anglo-Norman Book Production

Anne Lawrence

The production of decorated and illuminated manuscripts in Anglo-Saxon England has been studied in some detail by art historians who have demonstrated the level of production, the degree of technical excellence and the expense lavished on them by the later tenth century. English manuscripts were rivalled at this period only by those of Ottonian Germany. This being the case it is perhaps not surprising that the Norman Conquest, in its art historical impact, has been examined mainly in terms of the effect of Norman style and Norman concepts of book production and layout as they affected English manuscripts. Relatively little attention has been paid to the impact of the Conquest on Norman monasteries, their scriptoria and their output of books, and it is therefore this which will be a central concern of this essay.

It is already well known that Norman abbots and priors coming into English houses showed great concern for building up libraries, for introducing up-to-date corrected versions of important texts, and for filling out collections of patristic works which they regarded as in various ways defective.[1] They went further, however, and it can be clearly demonstrated that they introduced Norman styles of script, book layout and decoration into the manuscripts being produced for the libraries of their new houses. All this makes it possible to use the term Anglo-Norman to describe books produced in England, under the clear influence of Norman styles. What is less clear is whether the term Anglo-Norman can also be applied to the manuscripts still being produced in the Norman houses themselves; that is, whether any reciprocal influence is discernible.

To go back to the beginning, it is necessary to establish the existence of a characteristically Norman style of book production and decoration, against which to compare later developments. This necessitates a brief look at the surviving evidence concerning the building up of libraries and the production of books in the Norman monasteries in the pre-Conquest period.

---

[1] For a discussion of this, see N.R. Ker, *English Manuscripts in the Century after the Norman Conquest* (Oxford, 1960), pp. 7-8.

By the end of the ninth century organised monastic life in Normandy had been effectively destroyed. Most of the existing houses were abandoned and, when regular Benedictine monasticism was revived, the rulers of Normandy found it necessary to look for reformers and leaders from outside the duchy. The first of these was Mainard, a monk from Saint-Pierre's in Ghent who became abbot of Saint-Wandrille in 960 on the invitation of Duke Richard I. He appears to have introduced the monasticism of Ghent and Saint-Omer and is recorded as having brought books together with ornaments and relics from Saint-Pierre to Saint-Wandrille.[2] His reform was extended also to the house of Mont-Saint-Michel in 966. Clearly, there would have been links between the two reformed houses of Mont-Saint-Michel and Saint-Wandrille and these were continued when Mainard's successor, his nephew Mainard II, became abbot of Mont-Saint-Michel, having previously been prior at Saint-Wandrille. A little later, Theodoricus, a monk from Saint-Bénigne, was successively prior of Fécamp, then abbot of Mont-Saint-Michel (1023), as well as having responsibility for Jumièges and Bernay.

It appears to have been Mont-Saint-Michel which demonstrated concern for building up a library at the earliest date. Jonathan Alexander has argued that by the end of the tenth century monks (or at least one monk, who was presumably a scribe and perhaps an illuminator of manuscripts) was sent both to Fleury and possibly to Corbie in order to copy texts and perhaps to obtain books for the library at Mont-Saint-Michel.[3] It appears that a network of intellectual, monastic and artistic connections was being built up and this was further extended when, again by ducal invitation, an Italian, William of Volpiano, who had already been abbot of Saint-Bénigne in Dijon, became abbot of the ducal monastery of Fécamp.

He arrived, with a small group of monks, in 1001 and was very soon given responsibility for the reform of Jumièges, Saint-Ouen and Bernay (founded *c.* 1017), as well as supervision of Mont-Saint-Michel. This pattern of interconnections between the existing ducal monastic houses of the early eleventh century continued as further appointments were made from within the network, and it therefore seems likely that the building up of collections of books involved some cooperation between them. When in the second quarter of the eleventh century the aristocracy began to found a generation of new houses, they drew upon the existing ducal houses for abbots and even the founding communities of their new houses. It seems likely that a similar process of transferral of books or exemplars would have taken place.[4]

---

[2] See J.J.G. Alexander, *Norman Illumination at Mont-Saint-Michel, 966-1100* (Oxford, 1970), pp. 6-7.

[3] Ibid., pp. 35, 39; idem, 'A Romanesque copy from Mont-Saint-Michel of an Initial in the Corbie Psalter', *Millénaire monastique du Mont-Saint-Michel*, ii, (Paris, 1967), pp. 239-45.

[4] For discussions of the development of Norman monasticism, see D. Knowles, *The Monastic Order in England, 943-1216* (Cambridge, 1969); D. Bates, *Normandy before 1066* (London, 1982), pp. 20-22.

Monastic life in Normandy, as it developed in the eleventh century, was distinguished by two features. The first of these was a continuing tendency for the newer houses to be founded from the older Norman monasteries, in particular the ducal houses, and to continue to draw abbots from them. The second was the frequency with which the leading houses adopted men from outside Normandy as their abbots; most frequently Germans and Italians. Perhaps most influential among the latter in the first half of the eleventh century were John of Ravenna, William of Volpiano's nephew, abbot of Fécamp and author of an influential *Confessio fidei*; and Suppo, abbot of William of Volpiano's foundation of Fruttuaria in north Italy and abbot of Mont-Saint-Michel in 1033-48. The latter also is recorded as bringing books, amongst other things, to his new house. His intellectual interests, and perhaps the reputation of Mont-Saint-Michel and its book collection, are further demonstrated by the arrival of two learned monks, Robert of Tombelaine, the author of a commentary on the Song of Songs, and Anastasius, a master in both Latin and Greek. It seems likely that it was the reputation of Mont-Saint-Michel which drew Lanfranc to Avranches for some years during Suppo's abbacy, before he became a monk at Le Bec, in 1042.[5]

By the middle of the eleventh century both the international contacts of the Norman church and its intellectual activities were greatly enhanced by the establishment of first Lanfranc and then Anselm in positions of reputation and influence. From 1059 there are references to both Italians and Germans coming to hear Lanfranc's lectures; and in 1059-63 Pope Nicholas II sent young clerks to study with him.[6] By this time it seems that besides the schools at Fécamp, the possible school at Avranches, and Lanfranc's own schools at Le Bec and Caen there was a school of some standing at Rouen.

There had, then, been a very considerable growth of monastic and intellectual life in Normandy, most clearly marked by the growth in the number of monastic houses, from five at the beginning of the eleventh century to some thirty-three by 1070. This alone would have necessitated a high level of production and acquisition of books. As monastic life developed, the provision of schools for the training of children and novices would have required the acquisition of works on Latin grammar as well as books for the teaching of the monastic office. The importance of such schools is demonstrated by Lanfranc's acting as school-master for the children at Le Bec, soon after he entered that house. Large schools such as those of Fécamp, where it seems that priests also were trained, would have correspondingly greater needs for books.[7] Some three hours a day are specified in the Rule for the *lectio divina*, and Benedict required that each monk should receive a book from the library at the

---

[5] See M. Gibson, *Lanfranc of Bec* (Oxford, 1978), pp. 20-22.
[6] Ibid., pp. 34-37.
[7] For Fécamp, see Bates, *Normandy*, pp. 193-94.

beginning of Lent.[8] This suggests a need for at least as many library books as there are monks; the customary introduced by Lanfranc to Christ Church Canterbury suggests that each novice is to have a book also.[9] Margaret Gibson's analysis of the studies, teaching and writing undertaken by Lanfranc at Le Bec suggests that he had access not only to a good range of biblical and patristic works, from which to prepare his own corrected texts and commentaries, but also to collections of early glosses, and especially to Carolingian compilations.[10]

The surviving evidence supports this picture of rapid growth of book collections in the eleventh century. A library list from Fécamp suggests that it had eighty-seven volumes; and Nortier demonstrates that by the end of the eleventh century Le Bec had some 166 manuscripts, Saint-Evroult 153 and Lyre 137.[11] It is often possible to demonstrate that Norman houses borrowed and copied texts from one another.[12] This combination of rapid production of books, with reliance upon one another for exemplars, forms the context for the otherwise surprising degree of stylistic coherence in the scripts and decorative elements found in Norman manuscripts by the second quarter of the eleventh century.

This begs the question of how the process started, and of where and when distinctive styles of script and decoration first emerged amongst the Norman monasteries. An attempted answer to these questions is made easier by the relatively high level of survival of Norman manuscripts of the eleventh century. Jonathan Alexander identifies sixty-seven books as coming from Mont-Saint-Michel in the period 966-1100,[13] whilst fifty-one have evidence for a Jumièges provenance in the eleventh century, and at least twenty for Fécamp. From other houses the losses have been greater, but at least twelve each can be identified for Saint-Ouen at Rouen and Saint-Evroult; and there are at least a few surviving manuscripts from most of the main Norman houses.

It seems that the houses to show the earliest signs of activity in building up their libraries were Fécamp, Jumièges and Mont-Saint-Michel. How much, if anything, survived from the pre-Viking libraries of these houses (and of Saint-

---

[8] The amounts of time allocated vary slightly between winter and summer, but some three to four hours would generally be available. The distribution of books is specified in Chapter 48 of the Rule.

[9] See D. Knowles, *The Monastic Constitutions of Lanfranc* (London, 1951), p. 146.

[10] Gibson, *Lanfranc*, pp. 39-61.

[11] G. Nortier, *Les bibliothèques médiévales des abbayes bénédictines de Normandie* (2nd edn, Paris, 1971) passim.

[12] For the spread of Lanfranc's corrected versions of patristic texts, see Gibson, *Lanfranc*, p. 40. Several of Anselm's letters deal with the lending of books from Bec to other abbeys: see for instance M. Gibson, 'Lanfranc's *Commentary on the Pauline Epistles*', *Journal of Theological Studies*, new series, 22 (1971), pp. 86-112. Numerous specific textual connections are noted by F. Avril in his *Manuscrits normands, XI-XIIème siècles* (Rouen, 1975), under entries for individual manuscripts.

[13] Alexander, *Norman Illumination*, pp. 212-32.

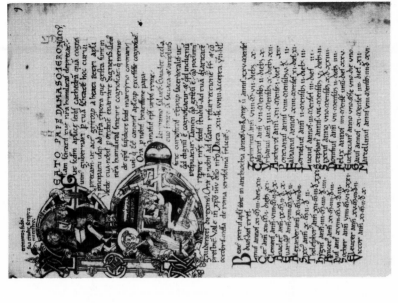

2 Rouen, BM, MS A 24 (31), fo. 9v. A Gospel book made at Saint-Evroult and partly written by Orderic Vitalis (*Rouen, Bibliothèque Municipale*).

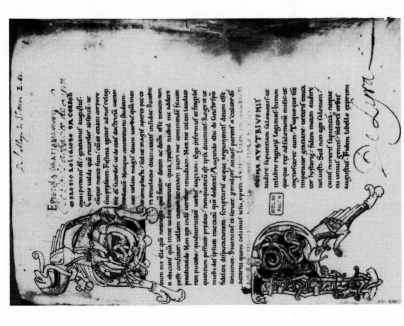

1 Rouen, BM, MS A 342 (430), fo. 1v. A copy of St Ambrose, *De fide*, from the end of the eleventh century (*Rouen, Bibliothèque Municipale*).

3 Rouen, BM, MS A 278 (513), fo. 53. A copy of St Gregory's *Commentary on the Gospels* from Jumièges, late eleventh century. The colours are reminiscent of Hugo Pictor's (*Rouen, Bibliothèque Municipale*).

4 Rouen, BM, MS A 21 (32), fo. 3. A copy of the Gospels, apparently made at Abingdon after the Conquest, for presentation to Jumièges (*Rouen, Bibliothèque Municipale*).

6 Rouen, BM, MS U 66 (1124), fo. 1v. A Josephus, from Lyre, early twelfth century (Rouen, Bibliothèque Municipale).

5 Rouen, BM, MS A 102a (458), fo. 11v. A copy of St Augustine's *Commentary on Psalms One to Fifty*, Jumièges, late eleventh century (Rouen, Bibliothèque Municipale).

7 Fécamp, choir, respond 14, from north radiating chapel.

8 Fécamp, choir, respond 14, from outer north choir aisle.

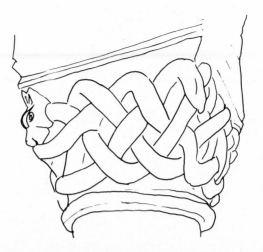

9 Caen, Saint-Etienne, nave clerestory, capital.

10 Falaise, castle, window capital.

12 Evreux Cathedral, nave, west bay, triforium, north side.

11 Reading Abbey, capital from cloister.

13 Canterbury Cathedral, fragment from choir screen.

14 Saint-Martin de Boscherville, abbey of
Saint-Georges de Boscherville, west front, portal,
archivolts.

15 Bayeux Cathedral, nave, arcade spandrels.

16 Salisbury Museum, fragment from Old Sarum.

17 Lincoln Cathedral, west front, central portal, south side, embrasures.

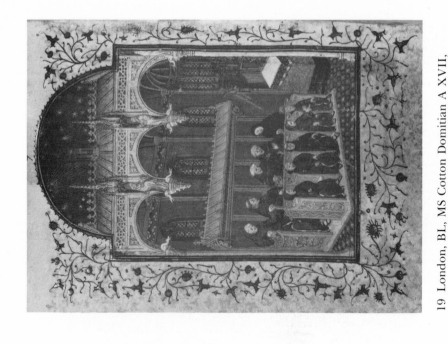

19 London, BL, MS Cotton Domitian A XVII, Psalter of Henry VI (195 × 130 mm.), fo. 122v. Friars in Choir (*British Library*).

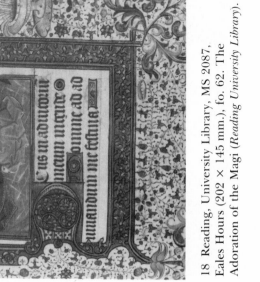

18 Reading, University Library, MS 2087, Eales Hours (202 × 145 mm.), fo. 62. The Adoration of the Magi (*Reading University Library*).

20 Paris, BN, MS lat. 1158, Neville Hours (185 × 129 mm.), fo. 27v. Ralph, earl of Westmorland, and family (*Bibliothèque Nationale*).

21 Paris, BN, MS lat. 1158, Neville Hours (185 × 129 mm.), fo. 34v. Joan Beaufort, countess of Westmorland, and family (*Bibliothèque Nationale*).

22 Paris, BN, MS fr. 126, Treatises (430 × 310 mm.), fo. 121. Laurent de Premierfait presents his translation of Cicero's *De senectute* (*Bibliothèque Nationale*).

23 Paris, BN, MS fr. 126, Treatises (430 × 310 mm.), fo. 7. *Regime des princes* (*Bibliothèque Nationale*).

24 London, Christie's, 2 December 1987, lot 160, Conyers Hours (102 × 70 mm.), fos 43v–44. Annunciation (*Conway Library, Courtauld Institute of Art, University of London*).

25 Malibu, Getty Museum, MS 5, 84 ML.723, Sotheby or
Oxford Hours (120 × 92 mm.), fo. 33v. St Christopher (*Conway
Library, Courtauld Institute of Art, University of London*).

26 A fifteenth-century representation of Alan, count of Brittany, receiving the honour of Richmond from William the Conqueror. Neither the text nor the scene have any eleventh-century foundation (Oxford, Bodleian Library, Ms Lyell 22, fo. 6v: Register of the honour of Richmond, second half of the fifteenth century, probably a copy of the earlier fifteenth-century Register, BL, MS Cotton Faustina BVII) (*Bodleian Library*).

Evroult, Saint-Ouen and Saint-Wandrille) it is now impossible to say; but the revival of old houses, with much of their former possessions, suggests that records of some sort survived. At least one ninth-century book seems to have been in the possession of Jumièges, a copy of the commentary of Paschasius Radbertus, written and decorated most probably in the third quarter of the ninth century, perhaps at Corbie, Paschasius Radbertus' own house. This manuscript is now Rouen, Bibliothèque Municipale, MS 141 (A 244). Amongst other definite contacts with Carolingian illumination, Jonathan Alexander has demonstrated that a Mont-Saint-Michel copy of the Satires of Persius, datable to the early eleventh century (Paris, BN, MS lat 8055) contains an initial which is a copy of one in the famous Corbie Psalter of *c*. 800.[14] That Fécamp also was influenced by such sources has been shown by François Avril, who has demonstrated that initials in a Bible apparently made at or for Fécamp in the second quarter of the eleventh century (now Rouen, BM, MS 1 [A4]) are closely based upon some in the second Bible of Charles the Bald (Paris, BN, MS lat 2)[15] which was made between 871 and 877 probably at Saint-Amand, the centre of the Franco-Saxon school.

There is also evidence that these houses acquired, though rather later, Anglo-Saxon manuscripts of the late tenth or eleventh centuries. Perhaps the best known of these is the sacramentary of Robert of Jumièges, (Rouen, BM, MS 274 [Y6]) given by Robert to his old house, whilst he was bishop of London (1044-50). This luxurious work is decorated with thirteen fully-painted framed miniatures, of a style representative of the best Anglo-Saxon work of the early eleventh century. Moreover, it is possible that Jumièges also possessed an Anglo-Saxon psalter, since such a manuscript was seen there, although it is now lost; as well as an early eleventh-century Anglo-Saxon copy of the *Dialogues* of Gregory the Great (now Rouen, BM, MS A 337 [506]) decorated with one historiated and one minor initial. There is less evidence for Fécamp, but it possibly owned a Gospel Book (now BN, MS lat 272); whilst Saint-Evroult seems to have received the Anglo-Saxon Psalter decorated with pictures, given by Emma to her brother, Archbishop Robert. Saint-Evroult also at some time owned an Anglo-Saxon liturgical manuscript, part of which is now Alençon, BM, MS 14 (fos 91r-114v), but there is no evidence as to when. Finally, another luxuriously decorated Anglo-Saxon manuscript, the Benedictional of Archbishop Robert (Rouen BM, MS 369 [Y7]) was given to the cathedral of Rouen by Archbishop Robert, according to a seventeenth-century inscription (which does not, however, make it clear whether this was Robert, archbishop of Rouen, or Robert of Jumièges, who was archbishop of Canterbury 1051-52). While the manuscripts stated to have been brought from Italy and Flanders do not survive, there does appear to be some stylistic similarity between Norman illumination and decorative features in books from

[14] See above, note 3.
[15] Avril, *Manuscrits normands*, pp. 15-16.

Saint-Bertin and Saint-Vaast, although there is no direct evidence of the borrowing of books.[16]

The monasteries which showed the earliest signs of actual production of manuscripts were again Jumièges and Mont-Saint-Michel. Of the two, Jumièges has the earliest signs of a scriptorium, in the form of a collection of saints' lives, tailored to the interests of Jumièges. This manuscript, now Rouen, BM, MS 1377 (U 108) appears to have been written by a scribe trained in the late ninth century, although its initials, whilst still based on Carolingian types, are more remote from their exemplars and would suggest a date in the early tenth century, by which time communal life had been restored at Jumièges.

The concern to build up a collection of saints' lives is demonstrated by another early manuscript (Rouen, BM, MS 1378[U40]). This has an inscription stating that it was copied on the instructions of Abbot Anno (942-73), and has a large initial A (fo. 152r) which has the distinction of being the earliest known Norman historiated initial, and which opens a treatise by St Augustine. The letter contains not an author portrait but a picture of St Peter, patron of Jumièges. This concept, of combining an initial with a figurative representation, could have been found by the artist of Jumièges in both Carolingian and Anglo-Saxon books. It is interesting in manifesting so early what becomes the very strong Norman preference for confining both decoration and illustration within the bounds of initials.

Equally interesting is another early Jumièges manuscript, containing Smaragdus' *Diadema monachorum* (now Rouen, BM, MS 356 [A 389]). This is dated by F. Avril to the early eleventh century,[17] but is perhaps slightly earlier, as its initial appears to be by the same artist as the previous manuscript and the script is still early in form. Here the text opens with a page (fo. 3r) containing both a competent display script and a large, decorated initial H. Like those of the previous book, this initial is set against areas of coloured ground, though here the Carolingian purple has been replaced by the orange found in Norman initials from all houses. Its structure and decorative motifs are also very important. The H is made up of five panels, two filled with interlace and three with simple, stylised foliage. It has also interlace terminals, embellished with biting heads, of the kind found in Carolingian manuscripts of the Franco-Saxon school. The spaces above and below the bar of the H are filled with foliage scrolls emerging from human heads; up the left side of the letter runs a large dog, chasing a smaller animal.[18]

---

[16] For illustrations of Saint-Bertin illuminations, see H. Swarzenski, *Monuments of Romanesque Art* (London, 1954), plates 69, 70. For links between Mont-Saint-Michel and Saint-Vaast see ibid., plates 74 and 75; and Alexander, *Norman Illumination*, pp. 61-65.

[17] Avril, *Manuscrits normands*, p. 8.

[18] For a reproduction of this initial, ibid., p. 9.

By the end of the tenth century a distinctive type of decoration, confined to initials and a few lines of display capitals, and a distinctive repertoire of motifs, drawing on Carolingian and Anglo-Saxon types, and showing an interest in the use of animal forms, is evident at Jumièges. At Mont-Saint-Michel also the earliest surviving books show a similar concentration on initials, again usually pen drawn and set on coloured grounds, or given touches of colour, and showing a frequent use of orange. Here also these initials are frequently of panelled construction, with interlace terminals and scrolls of stylised foliage.[19] Whilst links with Carolingian initial styles are again strong, it is interesting that there are certain similarities with books from centres in north Italy, though these are generally dated on stylistic grounds to the early eleventh century. One such is a copy of a work by Rabanus Maurus (Bod Lib, MS Bodley 796) from an unknown centre in north Italy, which has an initial with a double-outlined panelled construction, interlace terminals and undulating foliage in relief on a coloured ground, all comparable with the Norman initials.[20]

There are no historiated initials in the early Mont-Saint-Michel books. What does emerge very strongly is a distinctive type of decorated initial, based on the structure and motifs already outlined but using them with more sophistication, and making greater use of animal motifs. A copy of Gregory the Great's *Moralia in Job*, dated by Jonathan Alexander to *c.* 1000 (Avranches, BM, MS 97)[21] demonstrates the latter tendency in a pen-drawn initial Q on fo. 240v, where the letter itself is made up of two birds and a spreadeagled lion. The second volume of this work (now Avranches BM, MS 98) contains an initial P on fo. 132v of a type which combines a clear, simple structure, interlace terminals and coils of foliage with a dragon-mask and clambering lions.[22] This is an early version of a formula which became standard in Norman manuscripts of the first half of the eleventh century.

The basic type of Norman initial, taking its panelled structure and interlace from the Carolingian Franco-Saxon school, was already taking shape by the beginning of the eleventh century. Both at Mont-Saint-Michel and Jumièges there were early signs of artists drawing various types of foliage motifs, beasts and human figures from a range of other sources, both Anglo-Saxon and continental. Rapidly gaining in popularity among these motifs was the dragon, which was increasingly used, not simply to decorate a letter, but to form part, or even all, of it. This is perhaps most clearly marked at Mont-Saint-Michel, where a manuscript containing works by Ambrose and John Chrysostom, dated by Alexander to 1030-1045 (now Avranches, BM, MS 61, fos 112r-343r) has both an initial of the Franco-Saxon type and a B whose stem is formed by

---

[19] For reproductions see Alexander, *Norman Illumination*, plates 7-10.

[20] See O. Pächt and J. Alexander, *Illuminated Manuscripts in the Bodleian Library Oxford*, ii (Oxford 1970), cat. 6 and plate 1 (6).

[21] Alexander, *Norman Illumination*, pp. 220-21, and plate 8c.

[22] Ibid., p. 221 and plate 9c.

two dragons.[23] From Fécamp, closely linked to Mont-Saint-Michel, come more such initials. A volume of works by Ambrose (now Rouen, BM, MS 427 [A 143]), datable to the same period, has an initial R on fo. 1v which is largely Franco-Saxon, but has a dragon forming its diagonal bar. This manuscript is especially interesting since it contains a colophon stating it to have been made at the orders and expense of Suppo, abbot of Mont-Saint-Michel, 1033-48; but the scribe, Antonius, seems to have worked primarily for Fécamp, since his hand appears not only in several other Fécamp books, but also in a contemporary charter of that house.[24] Wherever the initials were painted, the volume was clearly at Fécamp soon after its production.[25]

The emphasis appears to have been on building up collections of good texts of works regarded as important for both the *lectio divina* and other aspects of the life of the monasteries. A number of the surviving books have inscriptions testifying that they were produced, or at least written, by monks; and the production of several is attributed directly to the instructions of the abbot himself. This suggestion of some personal supervision by the Norman abbots corresponds with Orderic Vitalis' statement that Thierry, the first abbot of Saint-Evroult, personally took care that his house was equipped with the most important liturgical and library books within its first ten years.[26] That Saint-Evroult also used the types of initial outlined above is illustrated by Plate 2.

In these circumstances, the rapid formulation and spread of a remarkably coherent style, both of initial construction and of layout of text, across the Norman monasteries is less surprising. It was doubtless further aided by a shared opinion among the Norman abbots on what were the key books to be produced and acquired. Jonathan Alexander's analysis of the surviving books from Mont-Saint-Michel suggests an early interest in such fundamental works as Cassian's *Collations*, St Gregory's *Moralia in Job*, St Augustine's *Commentary on The Psalms*, and the *Revelatio*, the history of the abbey's foundation.[27] There are also works by Alcuin, Boethius and Martianus Capella with, more surprisingly, some classical texts. Dominant in the manuscripts which appear to have been copied in the succeeding period are further commentaries by various patristic authors on books of the Bible; and a set of illuminated disputes against heretics. More specialised interests are represented by further classical texts and by a group of historical works. Similarly at Jumièges, from which some fifty manuscripts survive from the period up to the early twelfth century, the earliest books include fundamental works by Augustine, Cassian and Gregory, as well as more 'old-fashioned' works such as a copy of Paschasius Radbertus' *Commentary on St Matthew's Gospel* and Smaragdus'

[23] Ibid., pp. 216-17, and plate 11d.

[24] For discussions of Antonius, see Alexander, *Norman Illumination*, appendix iv; and Avril, *Manuscrits normands*, pp. 28-29.

[25] The manuscript has a poem to the Trinity copied immediately after the colophon.

[26] Bates, *Normandy*, p. 223 and n. 131.

[27] Alexander, *Norman Illumination*, pp. 34-37.

Diadema monachorum, and a collection of saints' lives. From the second half of the eleventh century comes a collection of twenty volumes of patristic works. An impressive historiated initial, together with a dragon-initial, painted in unusually bold colours, occurs in a copy of St Gregory's *Commentary on the Gospel*, see Plate 3. Biblical and liturgical manuscripts have survived better from Jumièges and number five, although two of the liturgical manuscripts are only fragments.

Few other Norman abbeys have left so many surviving books from this period, but just over twenty are attributable to Fécamp and of these twelve are patristic (of which seven contain works by Augustine). There are also a collection of saints' lives and seven biblical and liturgical books. What survives from the newer houses indicates a similar pattern.

There is, as I have shown, considerable evidence in the surviving books of the care taken by the Norman monasteries to build up their book collections. This is further supported by the overall competence with which the books were produced. There is little uniformity of size, but the overwhelming majority, from all the monasteries, are written in clear, competent (if not always elegant) hands on good quality vellum. Almost all are made up of gatherings of eight folios, regularly arranged. The ruling is in hard point and regularly spaced. Here again the lack of insistence on complete uniformity appears: while a book will always have the same number of columns of script per page throughout, the number of lines per page frequently varies within a volume. Whilst scriptoria from which numerous volumes survive do show recognisable scripts (perhaps especially Mont-Saint-Michel and Jumièges), individual hands can vary quite widely. It is common to find several hands collaborating in one volume.

This general pattern, of variation within coherence, appears again, by the third quarter of the century, in two other areas: the distribution of decoration in relation to text; and the use of colour within the decoration itself. As regards the former, manuscripts of this period very rarely have elaborate title pages or prefatory miniatures. The earlier manuscripts often have no more than a simple title written in one-line capitals at the top of the first text folio, most frequently in orange or red. By the time of the Conquest the display script was becoming more elaborate, and frequently included several lines of capitals, often with small touches of foliate decoration, in red, green or, less often, blue. In every case there is a clear hierarchy of initials, involving variations of size, degree of elaboration and number of colours, so that, as Jonathan Alexander has pointed out, all textual divisions are clearly signalled to the reader.[28] In the case of the range of colours used, the Norman preference for orange and green has already been commented on. That these were prepared by similar methods is also suggested by the fact that a distinctive dark green, with a tendency to eat through the vellum, occurs in manuscripts from several centres. For its effect

---

[28] Ibid., pp. 75-77.

in a manuscript from Saint-Evroult, see Plate 2. Whilst the range of colours used grew, with red, especially, gaining in popularity, yellow remained less used, and brown is rare. A proportion of initials continue to be drawn in simple outline, though black ink does increasingly give way to red. How elaborate these could be is demonstrated by the Gospels given to Jumièges after the Conquest, now Rouen, BM, MS A21, see Plate 4. As would be expected from the emphasis on practicality in these books, there is very little use of gold.

If the account of Norman manuscript illumination so far offered has focused upon areas of relative uniformity, it is necessary also to take account of diversity. This is especially important in the present context, since the most frequent causes of variation from the forms outlined are borrowings of style, motifs or colour-usage from Anglo-Saxon books. There is no sign of the presence of an Anglo-Saxon artist in Normandy, although they were demonstrably present at Fleury and Saint-Bertin.[29] As was stated above, Norman abbeys were in contact with these houses, and several were themselves the recipients of luxuriously decorated Anglo-Saxon manuscripts in the decades before the Conquest.

At Fécamp, Anglo-Saxon influence is already clearly visible in the Bible (Rouen, BM, MS 1 [A4]) which appears to have been made in the 1030s or 1040s. This originally had a large, decorated initial for each book and, though many are now damaged or missing, several show use of foliage motifs, dragon-head masks and inhabited scrolls of types found in Anglo-Saxon manuscripts from the late tenth century (and in those of Saint-Bertin from the turn of the century). Indeed, fo. 186v of this manuscript has an initial S which abandons the usual panelled construction, being formed entirely from Anglo-Saxon acanthus scrolls, while the only human figure in the book, an outline drawing on fo. 199v, although inserted into the script column, in a manner reminiscent of Carolingian illumination, shows Anglo-Saxon influence especially in the handling of the drapery.[30]

By the middle of the century initials constructed of foliage or beast motifs of Anglo-Saxon origin are frequent in manuscripts from all the ducal monasteries, though perhaps especially so at Jumièges. For an example of a type popular at Jumièges, see Plate 5. While many of these are still drawn in simple outline, or given only touches of colours, several, especially at Mont-Saint-Michel and Fécamp, are painted in colour schemes reminiscent of those found in, for instance, the Sacramentary of Robert of Jumièges. These make use of pink, orange, grey, pale blue, yellow, green and mauve, with a heavy use of white.

---

[29] For discussions of the work of these artists see F. Wormald, 'The "Winchester School" before Saint Ethelwold', in *Collected Writings*, i (London, 1984), pp. 77, 82-83; and 'Anglo-Saxon Painting', ibid., p. 118.

[30] For a reproduction, see Avril, *Manuscrits normands*, p. 23.

Perhaps the clearest Anglo-Saxon influence is found in the small number of miniatures, most common in manuscripts from Mont-Saint-Michel, but occurring also in two books from Fécamp and one from Jumièges. Of these the Jumièges miniature, which is drawn in rather dry ink outline, and is a presentation miniature prefacing the text of a *Life of St Aycadre* (now Rouen, BM, MS 1409, fo. 189r), is probably to be dated after the Conquest. Interestingly, it is the manuscripts of the 1050s, several of them having to do with the disputes of St Augustine and others against heretics, which show the strongest Anglo-Saxon influence, in their colours, their frames and their drapery styles. Jonathan Alexander has suggested that the most lavishly illustrated of all, the Sacramentary from Mont-Saint-Michel (New York, Morgan 641), was produced in this house in emulation of the luxurious Anglo-Saxon book recently given to Jumièges. In other words this manuscript, perhaps the most luxurious of all Norman eleventh-century works, like most of the manuscripts with painted miniatures, dates from before the Conquest.

It is a striking fact that, despite the clear admiration of Norman illuminators for Anglo-Saxon book decoration in the decades leading up to the Conquest, the last quarter of the eleventh century is not marked by any great increase in the use of Anglo-Saxon styles, or the imitation of Anglo-Saxon initials or miniatures. Nor is there any evidence that the Norman abbeys made use of their greatly increased income, and their contacts in England, to acquire manuscripts from England. Instead, the new 'Norman' (and Norman-Italian) abbots and bishops in England were at pains to import both Norman manuscripts and Norman scribes and artists. Given the eclecticism and emphasis on practicality of the Norman work already surveyed, it is surprising how rapidly work in purely Anglo-Saxon styles, whether of script or illumination, ceased in England.

N.R. Ker demonstrated that the Norman abbots and bishops devoted considerable resources to the provision of copies of patristic works for the libraries of their new monasteries, looking to Normandy for good editions of the texts.[31] Changes in customs, calendars and liturgical practice would also have made new customaries, calendars, collections of saints' lives and service books necessary. In other words, a rapid production and acquisition of books was required in most of the existing English abbeys, and was integral to the imposition of new norms in monastic life. In these circumstances, the evidence for the importation of Norman books, scribes and artists into England, and into abbeys where organised production of manuscripts was apparently still going on before the Conquest, is less surprising. It is impossible here to give a full account of the Norman importations into all the English abbeys and cathedrals, but some examples will suggest the level and range of activity.

Perhaps the best known of the bibliophiles is William of Saint-Calais, or Carilef, bishop of Durham, under whose guidance Durham became the

---

[31] See above, note 1.

leading monastic house in the north of England. He is recorded as having left some forty-six books to the community, and to have acquired at least some of these during his exile in Normandy from 1088-91. Their texts, as would be expected, show an emphasis on patristic works, together with a Bible, service-books, texts for use in chapter and a copy of Lanfranc's *Monastic Constitution* for Christ Church, Canterbury. Some of these are wholly Norman, including those with initials by an artist who signs himself Robert Benjamin (Durham Dean & Chapter Library, MS B II 13, and perhaps MS B II 21), while the Bible (Durham Dean & Chapter Library, MS A II 4) has initials by an artist who decorated books also for Bayeux Cathedral and Saint-Ouen, Rouen. Not all these 'Carilef' books were imports. The evidence suggests that an active scriptorium had been formed before 1096, producing books in a coherent format, and using styles of script and decorative initial which were fundamentally Norman. In other words, although most of the monks for Durham were drawn from the refounded Wearmouth and Jarrow, some Norman scribes must also have been available.

At Exeter Cathedral, Leofric left the community of clerks fifty-nine books when he died in 1072. These are interesting in including, as well as twenty service-books and ten Books of the Bible, works by Bede, Prudentius, Isidore and Boethius, as well as an impressive classical collection, but nothing by Augustine, Gregory, Ambrose or Jerome. This deficiency seems to have been remedied by Osbern, a royal clerk and the brother of William fitz Osbern, the founder of Lyre. From his time comes a set of the basic patristic works, now in the Bodleian Library, and all Norman in appearance: including one (MS Bodley 301) which has initials by the artist of the Carilef Bible; and MS Bodley 717, which has miniatures and historiated initials by an artist who calls himself 'Hugo, scribe and illuminator' and who decorated several books for Jumièges and a Gospels for Sées.[32] Some of Osbern's books suggest they were produced by an organised group, which may have been located at Exeter itself.[33]

More definite evidence of the arrival of Norman scribes and illuminators survives from Worcester, where a copy of the *Registrum Gregorii* (MS Bodley 223), probably from the abbacy of Samson, a chaplain of the king and protégé of Odo, is written in both English and Norman hands. Here again organised production of books, in a notably plain style, seems to have been established by the beginning of the twelfth century. At Abingdon Abbot Rainald (1084-97), once a monk of Jumièges, seems to have been accompanied by a Jumièges-trained scribe and artist, who produced a copy of the Gospels (see Plate 4), which was encased in a precious cover and presented to Jumièges,

---

[32] For a discussion of his work, see O. Pächt, 'Hugo Pictor', *Bodleian Library Record*, 3 (1950), pp. 96-103.

[33] For a brief discussion of the evidence for an Exeter scriptorium in this period, see T.S.R. Boase, *English Art, 1100-1216* (Oxford, 1953), pp. 28-30.

according to an inscription in the manuscript (Rouen, BM, MS 32 [A 21]).[34] At Lincoln Cathedral, a two-volume Bible and a copy of Saint-Augustine's *Sermons* (Lincoln, Cathedral Library, MSS A 12 and A 317) have historiated initials in a Norman style found at Préaux and Lyre (for a Lyre manuscript in this style, see Plate 6).[35] Books written at Rochester (for instance BL, MSS Royal 6 C vi and 5 D i) also have Norman historiated initials, suggesting the presence of Norman-trained artists.

This brief list will conclude with the two Canterbury houses, whose post-Conquest books have perhaps been the most studied.[36] The new Norman abbot of St Augustine's, Scolland or Scotland, had previously acted as a scribe in his old abbey of Mont-Saint-Michel. Jonathan Alexander has argued that he brought at least two books with him to Canterbury.[37] He seems also to have been accompanied by at least one monk able to act as a scribe, since Corpus Christi College, Cambridge MS 276 contains work in one Anglo-Saxon and two Norman hands. At St Augustine's a group of four or five Anglo-Saxon scribes continued to work in their old style well after the Conquest, and apparently even after the dispersal of the community following the disturbance of 1089. At Christ Church, Lanfranc seems to have been accompanied by two Norman scribes, one of whom may be the Maurice to whom Anselm wrote about books for Le Bec.[38] One of these wrote a very clear, distinctive script which appears in a group of seven manuscripts, and seems to have been made a model for scribes trained at Christ Church, since it was copied by several hands in the impressively uniform books being produced in the last decades of the eleventh century.[39]

There was a considerable movement of books, scribes and artists from Normandy into England, which was not balanced by any flow from England to Normandy, except of wealth. It is tempting to wonder whether this was enough to cause the temporary shortage of scribes able to write both well and fast which Anselm reported to Lanfranc. If this was the case, it seems that the increased wealth of most Norman abbeys, the result of acquisitions of land in England, enabled them to remedy the situation.

By 1100 Norman illumination was at its height, in terms of the number of abbeys producing manuscripts with impressive initials and display scripts and continuing the styles already outlined. Most active, to judge from the surviving books, was Jumièges, where nearly twenty books seem to date from the

---

[34] This is discussed by Avril, *Manuscrits normands*, pp. 40-41.

[35] For reproductions of the Lincoln manuscripts see C.M. Kauffmann, *Romanesque Manuscripts, 1066-1190, Survey of Manuscripts Illuminated in the British Isles*, iii (London, 1975), plates 30-36.

[36] See C.R. Dodwell, *The Canterbury School of Illumination, 1066-1200* (Oxford, 1956); A. Lawrence 'Manuscripts of Early Anglo-Norman Canterbury', *Medieval Art and Architecture at Canterbury*, British Archaeological Association (Oxford, 1982), pp. 101-11.

[37] Alexander, *Norman Illumination*, p. 18.

[38] See Gibson, *Lanfranc*, p. 176; Lawrence, 'Canterbury', p. 107.

[39] See Ker, *English Manuscripts*, ch. 3.

decades either side of 1100. Saint-Evroult is also impressive, with perhaps eleven surviving books from this period; while Fécamp became more active in the first quarter of the twelfth century, with some six volumes. Against this, however, the production of manuscripts at Mont-Saint-Michel seems already to have been slowing by 1100; and by the middle of the twelfth century this slackening is apparent in all the Norman abbeys from which significant numbers of books survive. Jumièges has perhaps nine from the second half of the century, and by the beginning of the thirteenth century was already purchasing manuscripts from a professional workshop in Paris. Unfortunately, while it is clear that Le Bec was active in lending manuscripts throughout the twelfth century, the almost complete loss of its books makes it impossible to draw any conclusions about its scriptorium.

The picture is more complicated than one of simple decline. For instance, at Mont-Saint-Michel, despite the apparent low production of books in the first half of the century, the abbacy of Robert de Torigny saw a very impressive expansion of the library; even the construction of a special tower to hold it. Robert de Torigny built up a collection of forty volumes, which he gave to his abbey, greatly expanding not only its number of books but also the subject areas covered. Evidence of interest in building up a collection of books on the part of at least one individual comes from Fécamp in this period also. Rouen, BM, MS A351 is a copy of the Gospel of Matthew, with two glosses showing an up-to-date, scholarly *mise-en-page*, and having the *ex libris* of Fécamp. The book is very plain, and perhaps of the mid twelfth century, but at the end is a late twelfth-century note of books copied by a clerk called Guilhelmus and of the prices he charged.

The second half of the twelfth century seems to show distinctive changes in the production of books in Normandy. The era of rapid production within monastic scriptoria was fading; books were, it seems, still being made within the monasteries (the evidence for this is primarily stylistic and will be discussed below), but in smaller numbers, and were increasingly supplemented by books purchased from other sources. There was a shift in the type of books being produced. Patristic works continued, but were no longer so dominant. The growing influence of more 'scholastic' ways of reading is suggested by the popularity of glossed books of the Bible, of collections of excerpts from patristic writings, and of recent theological works. The other popular area, not only at Mont-Saint-Michel under Robert de Torigny but also at Jumièges and perhaps, Saint-Ouen and Saint-Evroult, was that of chronicles and histories.

The illumination of Norman manuscripts in the twelfth century continued to be dominated by inhabited and historiated initials, of the traditional types, although with their hierarchies slightly elaborated to take account of the more complex page layouts of the glossed texts. In the first decades of the century, however, the rather one-way direction of movement of books and artists changed. Stylistic developments appear simultaneously on both sides of the Channel. At Durham, for instance, Dean & Chapter Library, MS B II 8, a copy of Jerome's *Commentary on Isaiah*, has historiated initials of a type extremely close to those found in Rouen, BM, MS 444 (A321), a copy of Jerome's *Commentary on Jeremiah*. Neither is dated, but both were perhaps made in the 1120s. Again, the cautery scenes in a medical and astrological manuscript from Durham, usually dated to the early part of the century (Durham Dean & Chapter Library, MS Hunter 100), and stylistically related to other contemporary Durham manuscripts, such as the illustrated *Life of St Cuthbert* (Oxford, University College, MS 165) are also very close to the figure drawings illustrating an astronomical treatise from Mont-Saint-Michel (now Avranches, BM, MS 235). At Rochester also such links appear, this time between the distinctive 'gymnastic' initials and a group of manuscripts from Préaux, such as Rouen, BM, MS 457 (A67).

Stylistically, Norman manuscripts of the second half of the twelfth century are striking in that, whilst their script develops towards Gothic, their initials, both in their structure and in their handling of the human figure, remain clearly linked to eleventh-century types. It is this conservatism which gives the strongest suggestion of continued activity on the part of established scriptoria and which suggests a certain artistic insularity. There is relatively little sign of interest in the more Byzantine-influenced styles being adopted in England; something which is surprising, given the existing links, not only with England, but also with southern Italy. It presumably represents a deliberate choice.

This conservatism was not restricted to manuscripts with only minor decoration. Rouen, BM, MS 22 (A117) is one volume of a mid twelfth-century Bible from Jumièges, and is furnished with a set of decorated initials which continue to make use of the repertoire already described, and to be drawn in plain ink outline. Similarly, at Mont-Saint-Michel, a volume of chronicles, dated to the second half of the century by its association with Robert de Torigny (Avranches, BM, MS 159) has a set of historiated initials still making use of panelled and interlaced letter-types, and with figures drawn in ink outline (touched with red and green) still showing the exaggerated heads and hands and softly-handled drapery hems of the early part of the century. That this conservatism was not due to absence of contact with other styles is demonstrated by the contemporary Cartulary (Avranches, BM, MS 210) which has pen-drawn miniatures decorated with leaf gold, and stylishly elongated figures with up-to-date 'damp-fold' drapery arranged in elegant oval and tear-drop patterns.

It appears that in the century following the Norman Conquest artistic links between England and Normandy went through several phases. The first, that of widespread importation of fundamentally Norman styles into English centres, with little sign of increased interest in Anglo-Saxon styles on the part of Norman artists, lasted roughly until the end of the eleventh century. It was succeeded by a more truly 'Anglo-Norman' phase, in the early twelfth century, showing movement of ideas and artists between the two regions. By the middle of the twelfth century, Norman illuminators were showing a deliberate preference for their 'traditional' styles, whilst 'English' patrons and artists were drawing much more widely on international contacts.

7

Abbots of English Monasteries in the Period Following the Norman Conquest

Henry Loyn

At a conference held at Caen in 1987 I took the opportunity of coming to know English eleventh-century bishops better.[1] Now, some five years later I want to attempt similar things with English abbots. In some respects this is an easier task. There are more of them but the surviving evidence is not so complex. Yet there are also special difficulties, greater than those facing us when we study the episcopate. For one thing it is not so easy to sense a corporate sentiment. The nature of the Benedictine Order with its emphasis on the autonomy of the individual house weakens such sentiment. But some general propositions have been held and I see no reason to refute them. Monasteries were by and large reckoned to be tenacious of Anglo-Saxon sympathy. Norman policy, as rigorous to the regular as to the secular, was directed towards correcting this imbalance by the appointment of new men to the highest office, men committed to the New Order. One might add new women, too, if we take into account the admittedly fragmentary evidence relating to the appointment of abbesses and prioresses in the immediate post-Conquest period.

There is certainly indication enough of the resulting tensions in the records that survive from our leading houses. Most notorious is the situation at Glastonbury where Abbot Thurstan turned his men-at-arms loose in the abbey, slaying some of the monks so that blood ran from the altar to the floor.[2] Passions were aroused elsewhere even if short of bloodshed, though at St Augustine's, Canterbury, it might well be said *non sine sanguinis effusione*.[3] In a powerful letter Archbishop Anselm himself commiserated with Paul, abbot of St Albans, because 'you in your sanctity are lord over barbarians whom you cannot instruct in words because of the diversity of language', and Paul in turn was accused by later historians at St Albans of destroying the tombs of his venerable antecessors whom he was accustomed to describe as rude and

---

[1] H.R. Loyn, 'William's Bishops: Some Further Thoughts', *A-NS*, 10 (1988) pp. 223-35.

[2] *Anglo-Saxon Chronicle*, *s.a.* 1083, ed. and trans. D. Whitelock (London, 1961), p. 160.

[3] *Acta Lanfranci*, ed. C. Plummer, *Two of the Saxon Chronicles Parallel*, 2 vols (Oxford, 1892), i, pp. 290-91.

unlettered (*rudes et idiotas*).[4] Athelelm of Abingdon, in spite of his good Saxon name refused to honour the feasts of Æthelwold and Edmund, dismissing them as English rustics (*Anglicos rusticos*).[5] Tensions between the new and the old cannot be ignored in any full discussion of monastic life in England after 1066.

My brief, however, is more limited, to look at the top layer, mostly themselves in a relatively short time new men, that is to say men loyal to the Norman settlement. We can start with one comforting fact. There is only one order to worry about, the Benedictine, though with Cluniac overtones. And there is further little Benedictine complication in terminology thanks to the nature of the Order: an abbot is an abbot, a prior a prior, an abbess an abbess. But then serious complications set in. Some houses kept better records than others. Some monkish chroniclers had a better sense of chronology than others. The crisis of the Norman Conquest was so acute that it shaped accurate reporting significantly, but it also brought confusion in fact and in record to many distinguished houses. Even so some firm facts can be drawn out which yield a degree of orderly pattern. Consider the facts in October 1066. Of the thirty or so known abbots or priors of cathedral chapters only one was an obvious foreign intrusion, the important and familiar figure of Baldwin, royal physician, former monk at Saint-Denis, abbot of Bury St Edmunds from 1065 till his death in late 1097. By 1087 the picture was vastly different. All the heads of important houses were foreign trained and of foreign birth and blood with only fringe exceptions: Pershore where Thurstan, a former monk of Glouces-ter, died in 1087, and Ælfsige at Ramsey, replaced by Herbert Losinga in the same year.[6] The process was slower than in the case of the episcopate and for the most part, as far as one can judge, the legalities were observed. But the fact of selection and appointment as opposed to the formalities of election rested clearly in the hands of the king and his ecclesiastical advisers. The monks themselves had just as much say in the appointment of a new abbot as the body of non-professorial staff has in the appointment of a vice-chancellor or principal in a provincial university. Surprisingly perhaps this is the state of affairs that Lanfranc's *consuetudines* implies with some approval, if we read it right: 'abbas cum eligitur omnes fratres, vel maior et melior pars in eius electionem consentire debent.'[7]

This is important in explaining the tensions and also in any attempt to assess the strength of the church in the late eleventh century. Martin Brett percepti-vely summed up the general feeling of most who have studied the period when he described it as 'an essentially Anglo-Saxon institution moving slowly

---

[4] *Gesta abbatum Sancti Albani*, ed. H.T. Riley, Rolls Series, 3 vols (London, 1867), i, p. 62.

[5] Discussed by Paul Meyvaert in a valuable and entertaining article on 'Voicing National Antipathy', *Speculum*, 66 (1991), p. 759.

[6] *The Heads of Religious Houses: England and Wales*, 940-1216, ed. David Knowles, C.N.L. Brooke and Vera London (Cambridge, 1972), provides the essential facts.

[7] David Knowles, *The Monastic Constitutions of Lanfranc* (Edinburgh, 1951), p. 72.

towards a later Latin norm'.[8] He recognised the motive power provided to bring this about by the Norman kings and an exclusively alien episcopate, one which he found on the whole (partly for social reasons) to display far less political independence than the Norman bishops at home in Normandy. Can the same or similar comment be applied to the monasteries, to the regular arm of the church, or have we underestimated the revolution caused by the Conquest on the English monks, changes most manifest in harsher secular obligations, the imposition of knight service, and in the literary and social field by the down-grading of the English language?

For the most part Brett's comment remains applicable and basically valid along the main line of Benedictine observance, revitalised and reformed in the tenth century and still far from lifeless in 1066. Acceptance of its validity demands, however, discussion of the intensity of change brought about by the imposition of military service and the difference in language emphasis. English monasticism itself had been far from withdrawn politically from the worldly scene. Many English abbots and monks were prominent in business in the last century of Anglo-Saxon England, advising witans, governing hundreds and wapentakes, looking to finance, geld, coinage and mintage. But the imposition of systematic military service on horseback was new and led, at least in the early stages, to something very like the institution of systems akin to the advocacies which became such a prominent feature of monasticism on the German scene. On language the effect was more subtle. We are rightly conscious of the tenacity with which some houses, Worcester, Exeter and Bury St Edmunds, for example, held on to their Anglo-Saxon studies, copying manuscripts, preserving records, even indulging in some (but not much) creative work. Monasteries provide the basic link if we examine the case for the continuity of English prose. But we should not forget also the continuity of Latin prose. The Anglo-Saxons were not illiterate in the narrow sense: they knew their Latin. We neglect at peril the stimulus given to Latinity in the generations immediately following 1066. In the second quarter in the twelfth century a formidable school of historians appeared in England side by side with the persisting Anglo-Saxon Chronicle. Their training was refined and made more efficient in a world dominated by Gallic abbots and priors. All this speaks well for the inner life of the abbeys. In an age prolific in new institutions – Cistercian, Carthusian, the monks of Saint-Victor, Savigny, the old Benedictine houses, buttressed by Cluny, fared well. The work went on, and the thick strand of spiritual and cultural achievement survived political upheaval and social change.

Our task, however, is to look more coldly at the top-layer changes, and to see if some helpful threads can be drawn together to make more intelligible the consequences of the Conquest. First and foremost we turn to the facts of wealth and power. Domesday Book provides the basic guide, probably more

---

[8] Martin Brett, *The English Church under Henry I* (Oxford, 1975), p. 7.

reliable for the monasteries than for the episcopate.[9] There were seven wealthy houses with an income of over £500 a year; seven solid houses between £200 and £500; seven more between £100 and £200; seventeen between £50 and £100; and eight with an income below £50. Of the seven houses founded between 1066 and 1086 only Battle was of substantial size with a rent-roll over £200, though Shrewsbury topped the £50 and gained much more from the Montgomery interest before the end of the century. Some foreign houses had also benefited, mostly Norman, with Fécamp enjoying revenue of just over £200 and La Sainte-Trinité, Caen at £107. In raw terms the total monastic control of wealth as recorded in Domesday Book was well over £10,000, more than a seventh of the Domesday Book estimate of total landed wealth.

Such figures provide some insight but are not in themselves a satisfactory index to true prosperity. One has to take into account also the question of responsibilities often attendant on wealth and at times associated with the creation of more wealth. Active discussion has ranged from time to time around two special elements in the equation, both leading into perilous country: the question of control of the hundred and the hundred court; and the vexed matter of imposition of knight service. The hundred is rightly recognised as the institutional maid-of-all-work in late Anglo-Saxon England, the chief agency through which local peace was preserved, where routine matters of justice and finance were settled, cattle-theft, the arrangement of tithings, boundary disputes, the apportionment of geld. Shire courts were great formal semi-political occasions, controlled and dominated by the crown. For most of the inhabitants of England the hundred was the outer limit of legal experience, and yet no fewer than some 150 of them, roughly a quarter of the whole, were openly in private hands in 1086.[10] In some areas, notably in the eastern Counties, our monastic houses, Ely, Bury St Edmunds, Peterborough, held a high percentage of the hundreds. Of equal interest, though less recognised, are the intense, localised areas of control, St Albans in the hundred of Cashio or Battle with its massive manor of Wye and sake and soke from no fewer than twenty-two hundreds with all the forfeitures from them that justly belonged to the king.[11] Abbots and discreet men of business attached to the abbeys were useful men from the royal point of view to have exercising vitally important hundredal roles in the judicial and financial work of the local communities.

Deep involvement in the hundredal organisation (or that of wapentakes in the Danelaw) was one aspect of abbatial activity continuous from late Anglo-Saxon days deep into the Norman period. Knight service provides something

---

[9] The figures given here and elsewhere in this paper are based on those given by David Knowles, *The Monastic Order in England* (Cambridge, 1950), appendixes vi, xv, pp. 702-3, 712.

[10] H.R. Loyn, 'The Hundred in England in the Tenth and Early Eleventh Centuries', *British Government and Administration*, ed. H. Hearder and H.R. Loyn (Cardiff, 1974), pp. 1-15. Helen Cam, *Liberties and Communities in Medieval England* (Cambridge, 1944), pp. 59-60.

[11] Domesday Book, i, 135c: *Herts.*, land of St Albans in Cashio hundred; i, 11d: *Kent*, land of Battle church.

of a contrast. It is likely that in 1072 or very shortly afterwards knight service was imposed on the established Benedictine houses, corresponding to similar impositions on the new Norman fiefs awarded the great tenants-in-chief among the conquerors. This was no simple matter. Sir James Holt has clarified the situation by drawing attention by relating the new endowments to the tempo of imposition, but of course the abbeys represented for the most part old endowment, already encumbered estates.[12] Initially it seems certain that knight service was not levied in proportion to gross income (not known before 1086 with any great exactness), but probably in accord with historical precedent of fyrd service and current needs and aptitude. By historical precedent contemporaries probably meant not the current hidage and obligations to geld, but more the nature of the endowment, proportion of royal land involved in patronage, coupled with an offsetting agreed at the time of levy concerning other services rendered, hospitality, secretarial services, and established customs and services associated with storing goods and treasures in the royal interest. Local conditions in the 1070s – could make a substantial difference – the presence of warlike abbots as at Peterborough; the need for constant defence on strategic grounds as at Tavistock or Ely. I suggest, too, from our general knowledge of how bureaucracies work, that the initial bargaining was somewhat prolonged, that it probably reached a moment of crisis with the earls' revolt of 1076, and that it was still in a partially indeterminate state in 1080, though not by the time of the Domesday survey. Some of the variables may never be known but a series of informed guesses may help to make sense of what seems on the surface an irrational and confusing state of affairs where Peterborough was charged with the service of sixty knights and Ramsey, marginally more prosperous, only four; where St Albans owed six and Coventry, with a little more than half its income, owed ten.[13]

All manner of factors, local and national, commonsense as well as inherent military probability, played their part in determining the fixing of manageable units of five or ten knights with supporting apparatus. The Feudal Book of Bury St Edmunds gives the clearest glimpse of the reality behind the abstractions. Frodo, the abbot's brother, took charge, the key man in setting up four constabularies, ten knights apiece: and Frodo has the signal honour of a special section in the Domesday Book, attributed specifically to the abbot's brother.[14] Just as remarkable is the evidence from Peterborough itself, the only non-cathedral monastery to sustain a sixty-knight burden (Glastonbury, the wealthiest monastery of all started with sixty but had its quota reduced to forty). By 1086, as Edmund King has shown us, some 46 per cent of the abbey's property

---

[12] J.C. Holt, 'The Introduction of Knight Service in England', *A-NS*, 6 (1984) pp. 89-106.

[13] David Knowles, *The Monastic Order in England*, p. 712.

[14] *Feudal Documents from the Abbey of Bury St Edmunds*, ed. D.C. Douglas (London, 1932); DB, ii, 354b-355b.

was under the control of knights, selectively, intelligently, but nevertheless a startlingly high proportion. Similar investigation of other monasteries suggests a figure of 15 per cent at Christ Church, Canterbury, of 20 per cent at Winchester, and 30 per cent at Glastonbury. Of all landlords the abbots were best placed to assess the costs of knight service, and the variable nature of the charge is again well brought out by Edmund King who notes that the average fee at Peterborough (£2 10s.0d) was considerably less than the norm of £5-6 elsewhere.[15]

Other near-contemporary documents sometimes sharpen the analysis made possible by Domesday Book. The survival of a *descriptio terrarum* from Peterborough, for example, highlights the impact on the monastic houses of the constant pressure to subinfeudate. Concern with title and the payment of geld was at the heart of the *descriptio* though documents dating from before the Conquest lay behind it. David Roffe in a recent very acute discussion of it notes that at Bury St Edmunds, at Evesham and at Burton we have clear cognates of the *descriptio* (with resemblances to documents from Abingdon, Bath and the Kentish houses), reordering what he sees as a Yorkshire-type summary into feudal *breves*.[16] The same order appears as in the Domesday Book folios but containing geld figures from the time of King Edward. Continuity of written record from Anglo-Saxon days, adapted to the needs of the New Order, enabled the abbeys to cope with the new heavy demands of knight service.

Abbots were therefore, whether they wished it or not, men of influence and power in the secular world. Their appointment had to be carefully vetted, and the Norman kings saw that this was so. Between 1066 and 1135 over sixty foreign appointments were made, mostly from Normandy: seven direct from Caen, seven from Fécamp, with Winchester, Old Minster, and Christ Church, Canterbury, acting as intermediate staging posts for thirteen more (eight from Caen, five from Fécamp).[17] All monastic houses of any size enjoyed or suffered the rule of a Norman or French superior during this period.

Knowledge of the men themselves varies enormously. Some are well known on the national as well as the local stage, others are only names. A glance at the seven wealthiest houses is enough to make the point.[18] Glastonbury with its enormous wealth in the south west had an Anglo-Saxon abbot, Æthelnoth (1053-77/78) for more than a decade after the Conquest, when the over-zealous Thurstan, a monk of Caen, took over. He was sent back, presumably in disgrace, after the 1083 riot, but not fully deposed – indeed he was reinstated by Rufus, though not sent back to Glastonbury. Eventually he was succeeded

---

[15] Edmund King, *Peterborough Abbey, 1086-1310* (Cambridge, 1973), pp. 13-15.

[16] David Roffe, 'The *Descriptio Terrarum* of Peterborough Abbey', *Historical Research*, 65 (1992), pp. 1-16.

[17] Knowles, *The Monastic Order in England*, appendix vii, p. 704.

[18] The basic evidence is clearly set out in Knowles, *Heads of Religious Houses*.

by another monk of Caen (1106-18). At Ely, again with massive resources (no fewer than 105 entries in Domesday Book for Suffolk, sixty-three for Cambridgeshire, twenty-nine for Norfolk), there appears to have been a tortuous struggle to find the right man with Theodwine from Jumièges (to 1075-76), followed by the administrative monk Godfrey (later abbot of Malmesbury to 1082). Full stability was not achieved until Simeon, brother of bishop Walkelin, was appointed (1082-93). Lanfranc was the brooding presence at Christ Church, Canterbury, where one notes solid estates in Suffolk and Sussex were set aside for provision of food and clothing for his monks, but much of the day to day administration was in the hands of the prior, the competent Henry from Le Bec. Bury St. Edmunds remained in the hands of Baldwin with full Gallic apparatus, a survivor but, as has been well emphasised, one who ensured survival (his skill as a doctor helping) without serious loss and without absorption into the secular duties of a bishopric.[19] As for the other three, Westminster was ruled by a succession of able abbots from the Continent in the persons of Geoffrey (*c.* 1068-76), Vitalis (1076-85), and then the scholar Gilbert Crispin (1088-1118); St Augustine's, Canterbury, had the tough monk from Mont-Saint-Michel at its head in the person of Abbot Scotland; and most important of all Winchester Old Minster, was under the direct control of Bishop Walkelin. All saw to the establishment of what they saw as proper monkish stability. Likely men were brought over, especially from Caen and Le Bec, and Winchester rivalled Canterbury as the principal staging-post where promising monks could be installed ready to take high office as opportunity served.

The same pattern is repeated further down the scale of prosperity. At Abingdon, Ealdred (1066-71) was deprived and a monk from Jumièges took over. It may be significant that Ealdred died in the custody of Bishop Walkelin of Winchester. In other houses, sometimes after false starts, tough and capable continentals were moved, many from Le Bec, Caen, Fécamp, or Mont-Saint-Michel, and many exercising their office for long periods at what was clearly a critical time for the development of their monastery: Ingulf from Saint-Wandrille at Crowland (1085/86-1104); Walter of Caen at Evesham (1077-1104); Serlo from Mont-Saint-Michel at Gloucester (1072-1104); Turold from Fécamp at Peterborough, more of a knight than a monk (1070-98); Paul of Caen, nephew of Lanfranc, at St Albans (1077-93); Fulcard at Thorney (1068-75). The lesson is plain. As soon as possible capable men from the French-speaking world were placed in abbatial office. There were exceptions that themselves may well have been significant. One reflects on the loyalty of the active abbot Æthelwig at Evesham (1058-77), Anglo-Saxon by training and a

---

[19] Antonia Gransden, 'Baldwin, Abbot of Bury St. Edmunds, 1065-97', *A-NS*, 4 (1982), pp. 75-76. She quotes (p. 68) with proper approbation the comment of Baldwin's contemporary hagiographer, Hermann, that 'King William implanted the customs of the French throughout England, and began to change those of the English'.

key man in preserving order in the west Midlands in the crisis of 1076.[20] At Bath, Burton, Coventry, Pershore, St Benet Holm and Sherborne long-lived Anglo-Saxon abbots survived (at Sherborne until 1099): and they were substantially left in peace. It is reasonable to assume that such men showed at the very least a willingness to conform to the new Norman-dominated world.

It is desirable sometimes to ask what was precisely involved in such conformity. The answer, as so often, may be found in the work of Archbishop Lanfranc himself. Among his many quiet, unobtrusive contributions Dom David Knowles in 1951 gave us a splendid edition of Lanfranc's *Monastic Constitutions*. He showed how the archbishop proved himself a reformer rather than an innovator, drawing his material from other customaries, principally Le Bec, but not only Le Bec, some older Cluniac customs, some Flemish, though nothing from the native English *Regularis concordia*.[21] The immediate intent, suggested by the covering letter to Prior Henry alone, was to regulate the affairs with all its peculiarity of a cathedral monastery (Christ Church, Canterbury, Winchester, Old Minster, Worcester and Sherborne). The survival of existing manuscripts, however, indicates that the customs came to apply to at least a dozen of existing abbeys and cathedrals in England. At Rochester and at St Albans the influence of Lanfranc was direct and personal. Elsewhere Dom David was inclined to attribute reception to the intrinsic excellence of the customs rather than to external authority. Perhaps weight should also be given to the element of internal authority from each and every abbot. These abbots of the new dispensation belonged to a small intimate group, trained in the same few Norman houses, gifted rulers of men and materials, builders and administrators, for the most part as far as we can judge celibate and tolerably virtuous. They needed a written programme that would set out the Rule in intelligible form, a liturgical calendar from 1 October through Lent and Easter, a statement of a regimen which was strict without savagery. Again we move back to the figure of Lanfranc. If there is one characteristic of the English church that we remember above all other from the late eleventh century it is the truly prodigious building programme. In the 1070s six great ecclesiastical buildings were begun: Canterbury (Christ Church), Lincoln, St Albans, Rochester, Hereford, and Winchester (Old Minster). In the 1080s four more were started: Ely, Worcester, Chichester and Gloucester. In the 1090s another four were added: London, Chester, Durham and Norwich. Such a fabulous programme suggests a degree of central directive, and Lanfranc may well have been the spearhead, so to speak, of the enterprise. His biographer, Eadmer, may possibly have had this in mind when

---

[20] R.R. Darlington, 'Æthelwig, abbot of Evesham', *EHR*, 48 (1933), pp. 177-98. Marylou Ruud makes the shrewd comment that many monk-bishops 'seem to be saintly because they dealt so well with worldly things', and the same comment could well apply to many of our abbots, 'Monks in the World: The Case of Gundulf of Rochester', *A-NS*, 11 (1989), pp. 245-260.

[21] Knowles, *Monastic Constitutions of Lanfranc*, introduction, p. xiii.

he wrote 'postponing all thought of providing for his own convenience, he set out urgently to work and completed (in the seven years (1071-78) the buildings and dwellings needed for the use of the monks'.[22] Others took their time. The great Serlo at Gloucester was in office for some seventeen years before he started work on his abbey church, that spectacular monument to Norman achievement. But Serlo started work from scratch with only two monks and may have had to come to it slowly. The overall picture is impressive. To judge from the ecclesiastical buildings alone, England by 1100 enjoyed the presence under Norman direction of a flourishing and self-confident monasticism, its spiritual and material strength as firm an index as we need to the efficiency and permanent impact of the Norman conquerors.

---

[22] Deborah Kahn, *Canterbury Cathedral and its Romanesque Sculpture* (London, 1991), p. 13, quoting Eadmer, *Historia novorum in Anglia*, ed. M. Rule, Rolls Series, (London, 1884), p. 13.

8

Architecture and the Effects of the Norman Conquest

E.C. Fernie

This essay is synoptic in that it presents a précis of results of the author's research over the last ten years or so. Its aim is to provide an overview of the architectural evidence for the effects of the Conquest on life in England. It is divided into two parts. The first deals with a piece of evidence which supports the view that the Conquest resulted in a widespread imposition of Norman culture on Anglo-Saxon England; the second with the ways in which the Conquest brought to bear a great variety of influences, including aspects of the culture of the Anglo-Saxons themselves.

Evidence for the Imposition of Norman Power and Culture

'There followed the vengeance of God and the Norman disaster and the overthrow of England.'[1] Adam of Bremen's words of *c.* 1070 place him firmly in the camp of those who see the Conquest as a break in the history of eleventh-century England, whereas most historians, while acknowledging breaks in some respects, would now more readily accept a picture of continuity. The archaeological record can contribute one hiatus to this debate as telling in its way as the widely agreed, almost complete destruction of the English landowning classes.[2]

English medieval churches are well known for the mixture of parts of different dates and styles which they frequently contain – the Norman, Early English, Geometric, Decorated and Perpendicular – all often present in the same building. This can be contrasted with the following claim: at the time of writing no English cathedral or large monastic church is known to retain within its fabric any standing masonry of Anglo-Saxon date.

---

[1] Adam of Bremen, *History of the Archbishops of Hamburg-Bremen*, ed. and trans. F.J. Tschan (New York, 1959), iii, p. 14, gloss e.

[2] Frank Barlow, R. Allen Brown, John Le Patourel and Henry Loyn all comment on this removal of a social class. See for example Le Patourel, 'The Norman Conquest, 1066, 1106, 1154?', *A-NS*, 1 (1979), p. 107.

That is, while there are remains of Anglo-Saxon plans extant beneath such Norman churches, and Anglo-Saxon masonry may have been reused in a new building, nothing of a pre-Conquest date is known to survive standing in the churches themselves. It is always possible that a fragment of such masonry will be found, but the significance of the observation would still stand.

Setting aside structures which have no standing Norman masonry, such as Old St Paul's, and those built on new sites, such as Lincoln and Norwich, the large churches in question are presented in Table 1.

The list of cathedrals in this table is complete, but the abbey churches form a much less clearly defined group. The examples listed are those which in the author's opinion can be called large or important, but, even without this proviso, there must be very few monastic churches, of whatever size or importance, which run counter to the rule. In fact it is only in parish churches that incorporated Saxon remains are commonplace. (The cathedrals listed in Table 1 relate to the full list of Anglo-Saxon cathedral sites as indicated in Table 2.)

From the dates of the buildings on the list, it will be clear that the observation does not entail a spasm of destruction on the part of the Normans within a year or two of the Conquest, since the process of rebuilding continued into the early twelfth century. Yet a clean sweep even over the length of two generations is nonetheless strong evidence for the imposition of one culture upon another. Indeed the consistency of purpose which the longer period involves might argue for a clearer wish to dominate than actions carried out in the immediate aftermath of conquest and subjugation.

Evidence for Non-Norman Elements in Post-Conquest England

A standard history of eleventh-century architecture in Normandy and England, such as that of Sir Alfred Clapham written in the 1930s, supports the picture of the Conquest as an imposition of Norman culture on England.[3] The plan types of churches with ambulatorie s and echelon east ends at St Augustine's at Canterbury and at St Albans can be derived from, for example, Rouen Cathedral and Bernay Abbey respectively, and the Norman mason's craft, in particular in its methods of cutting and coursing, almost completely replaces Saxon methods of working stone.

[3] A. Clapham, *English Romanesque Architecture after the Conquest* (Oxford, 1934), chs 1 and 2.

Table 1

Cathedrals and large abbey churches of Anglo-Saxon foundation with standing Norman masonry, in chronological order of Norman rebuilding.[4]

Cathedrals		*Abbey Churches*	
Canterbury	1070	Canterbury, St Augustine's	1071
Rochester	1077	St Albans	1077
Winchester	1079	Bury St Edmunds	1081
York	1080	Ely	1081
Worcester	1084	Tewkesbury	1087
Durham	1093	Gloucester	1089?
Hereford	1107?	Pershore	1090?
Exeter	1112	Crowland	1091
		Romsey	*c.* 1100
		Peterborough	1114

Table 2

Anglo-Saxon cathedral sites in the post-Conquest period[3]

Anglo-Saxon Sees in 1066	*Sites to which Sees were Moved by the Normans*	*Anglo-Saxon Cathedral Sites with Standing Norman Masonry*
Canterbury		Canterbury 1070
Dorchester	Lincoln 1072	
Durham		Durham 1093
Elmham	Norwich 1072	
Exeter		Exeter 1112
Hereford		Hereford 1107?
Lichfield		
London		
Rochester		Rochester 1077
Selsey	Chichester 1075	
Sherborne	Old Sarum 1078	
Wells	Bath 1090	
Winchester		Winchester 1079
Worcester		Worcester 1084
York		York 1080

[4] Some of the sites to which the Normans moved sees, such as Lincoln and Norwich, may have had Anglo-Saxon churches on them; again there is no known case of incorporation of any such earlier masonry.

Examples of Anglo-Saxon masonry surviving the Conquest by at least several centuries, such as that of the pre-Conquest cathedral at Wells and the undercroft of the dormitory of Edward's foundation at Westminster, do not conflict with the claim as they did not form part of the Norman church itself. For Wells see W. Rodwell, 'The Lady Chapel by the Cloister at Wells and the Site of the Anglo-Saxon Cathedral', *Medieval Art and Architecture at Wells and Glastonbury* (*BAACT*, 1978) (1981), pp. 1-9; for Westminster note 6 below. Stow church in Lincolnshire survives as an Anglo-Saxon structure precisely because it was not the subject of a successful refoundation and rebuilding. The Anglo-Saxon cathedral at Sherborne was abandoned by the Normans, but partially rebuilt after its refounding in 1122 incorporating parts of the mid eleventh-century building. If it is deemed to fit the category, despite its loss of cathedral status and its middling size, then it is the exception which proves the rule.

This, however, is a very generalised description of a complex situation, as in addition there are elements of fundamental importance from the Empire, parts of France other than Normandy, and, eventually, from Anglo-Saxon England, as well as social and psychological factors operating only in post-Conquest England and not in Normandy.

An examination of the following six points is intended to illustrate these claims: 1. Scale; 2. Patronage of the Exotic; 3. Cushion Capitals; 4. Spiral Columns; 5. Proportions; 6. Mouldings. Most of the examples cited in what follows are dated between 1030 and 1100, and with one exception all are ecclesiastical.[5]

1. Scale

Great churches built in England after the Conquest are in almost every case of a much larger scale than their counterparts in Normandy, of any date in the eleventh and twelfth centuries.[6] Indeed many Anglo-Norman buildings are as

[5] For the author's publications on these subjects see, on scale, 'Observations on the Norman Plan of Ely Cathedral', *Medieval Art and Architecture at Ely Cathedral* (*BAACT*, 1976) (1979), pp. 4-5; on patronage, 'The Effect of the Conquest on Norman Architectural Patronage', *A-NS*, 9 (1986), pp. 72-85; and 'St Anselm's Crypt', *Medieval Art and Architecture at Canterbury Cathedral* (*BAACT*, 1979) (1982), pp. 27-31; on spiral columns, 'The Spiral Piers of Durham Cathedral', *Medieval Art and Architecture at Durham Cathedral* (*BAACT*, 1977) (1980), pp. 49-58, 'St Anselm's Crypt', *Medieval Art and Architecture at Canterbury Cathedral* (*BAACT*, 1979) (1982), pp. 31-33, and 'The Use of Varied Nave Supports in Romanesque and Early Gothic Churches', *Gesta*, 23 (1984), pp. 111-13; and on proportions, 'Observations on the Norman Plan of Ely Cathedral', *Medieval Art and Architecture at Ely Cathedral* (*BAACT*, 1976), pp. 1-4, 'St. Anselm's Crypt', *Medieval Art and Architecture at Canterbury Cathedral* (*BAACT*, 1979) (1982), pp. 34-36, and 'The Grid System and the Design of the Norman Cathedral', *Medieval Art and Architecture at Winchester Cathedral* (*BAACT*, 1980) (1983), pp. 16-18. Idem, *An Architectural History of Norwich Cathedral* (Oxford, 1993), ch. 4, 'The Context', is also relevant to most parts of this essay. See also the articles by Richard Gem in the BAACT volumes noted above, and the same author's 'L'architecture pre-romane et romane en Angleterre', *Bulletin monumental*, 142 (1984), pp. 233-72, and 'The Bishop's Chapel at Hereford: The Roles of Patron and Craftsman', *Art and Patronage in the English Romanesque*, ed. S. Macready and F.H. Thompson (London, 1986), pp. 87-96.

[6] The nave of the church of Westminster Abbey begun by Edward the Confessor and consecrated unfinished in 1066 was, at 61.76 metres, much longer than contemporary naves in Normandy, such as the 42.86 metres of Notre Dame at Jumièges, and may therefore have been a precursor of the large scale of post-Conquest buildings. Any such claim has now to take account of Tim Tatton-Brown's discovery of twelfth-century masonry in the towers at the west end of the nave, raising the possibility that its length was determined long after Edward's time ('Westminster Abbey: Archaeological Recording at the West End of the Church', forthcoming in *Antiquaries Journal*. I am grateful to Tim Tatton-Brown for allowing me to see his paper in advance of publication). This is not the place to discuss this question in detail, but four points can be made.

continued

large as the two or three largest examples of the eleventh century in the whole of western Europe, all of which seem to be measuring themselves against Constantine's, St Peter's or other Roman basilicas of similar size. The following are the overall lengths and the lengths between the west end of the nave and the chord of the apse of the four biggest buildings: St Peter's (320s), 133 metres and 124 metres; Speyer Cathedral (1030-60), 128 metres and 123 metres; Cluny Abbey (from 1088), 172 metres and 118 metres; and Walkelin's cathedral at Winchester (from 1079), 157 metres and 114 metres.

Each of the large English buildings of the 1070s is larger than its predecessors from, for example, Lanfranc's Canterbury in 1070, to St Augustine's Abbey, Lincoln, St Albans, and Winchester. There was thus no initial intention to make the English buildings rival St Peter's and the increases must rather be seen as the result of competition, up to the point at which the Roman churches were accepted as a benchmark.

2. Patronage of the Exotic

Competition also lies at the root of the next point. There are numerous indications that those who commissioned the great ecclesiastical structures of the decades following the Conquest in England sought out features which would have appeared foreign and even exotic to contemporaries; and the fact that they did this in England and not in Normandy despite their equal involvement there indicates a particular effect of the ambience on this side of the Channel.

Lanfranc's cathedral at Canterbury of the 1070s is often and correctly described as being closely based on Saint-Etienne in Caen, but its design is also characterised by non-Norman elements, such as its raised choir, which has its closest parallels in Lanfranc's native north Italy.

Canterbury, however, appears almost slavishly dependent on precedents in Normandy by comparison with the Minster at York begun by Thomas of Bayeux in 1080, where the plan of the aisleless nave finds its closest parallel in the Loire Valley, at, for instance the mid eleventh-century cathedral of

continued
First, the length of 61.76 metres is that of the nave excluding the western towers; secondly, it appears to correspond to the overall proportional layout of the building; see E.C. Fernie, 'Reconstructing Edward's Abbey at Westminster', *Romanesque and Gothic: Essays for George Zarnecki*, 2 vols (Woodbridge, 1987), i, pp. 63-67; on Westminster see also R.D.H. Gem, 'The Romanesque Rebuilding of Westminster Abbey', *A-NS*, 3 (1981), pp. 33-60; thirdly, the surviving plinths of the western bays are similar to those in the nave at Jumièges, which has an apse and eastern arm almost identical in detail to that at Westminster; and fourthly, the naves of many churches were completed decades after the start of building without there being any sign of a change of plan. Indeed instances of naves being lengthened during the course of construction are very few and far between, with Peterborough Abbey as a certain and Reims Cathedral as a possible example.

Angers, while its east end with a rectangular crypt ambulatory bears a clear resemblance to the same part of the church in the plan of St Gall, of the early ninth century and probably deriving from the Carolingian court; Anselm's extension to the cathedral at Canterbury, begun in 1096, appears to be based on Santa Maria in Kapitol in Cologne, consecrated in 1059 and 1065.

There is therefore a strong likelihood that Anselm was as intent on outdoing Thomas as Thomas had been concerning Lanfranc. It is certain that neither Thomas nor Anselm would have attempted to achieve this result by turning to the unadventurous and traditional architecture of contemporary Normandy.

3. Cushion Capitals

The volute capital was the standard form in use in Normandy throughout the eleventh century. By contrast, buildings erected in England after the Conquest made extensive and in some cases exclusive use of the cushion capital, such as those in the gatehouse of the castle at Exeter and the crypt and north-west tower of Lanfranc's cathedral at Canterbury, begun respectively in 1068 and 1070. The ultimate source of the type is, like so much else, late Roman, as on the sarcophagus at the church of Santo Stefano in Bologna probably of the fifth century. It was revived in the Carolingian Empire (as in the capital from Viernheim, now in the museum at Lorsch) and transmitted via Ottonian examples (such as those in St Michael's, Hildesheim, of the early eleventh century) to the Low Countries (as in St Peter's, Utrecht, consecrated in 1048), whence they were brought to England as it were in the baggage of William the Conqueror's Flemish allies.[7]

4. Spiral Columns

Spiral columns are one of the most prominent elements in the design of the crypt which formed part of Anselm's extension to Canterbury Cathedral. Here again there are no precedents in Normandy. Durham has them on the full scale of the church, but the most obvious parallels are those in analogous positions in the Low Countries, in Utrecht and Deventer. If there is an alternative to this source it is to be found in the crypt of the Anglo-Saxon church at Repton, where the spirals appear to have marked a site of religious importance, but this is more distant in both time and form than the examples from the Empire.[8]

---

[7] To quote Peter Kidson's words. See also R.D.H. Gem, 'Canterbury and the Cushion Capital: A Commentary on Passages from Goscelin's *De miraculi Sancti Augustini*', *Romanesque and Gothic*, pp. 83-102.

[8] Spiral columns were sometimes used purely decoratively, especially on a small scale and before the middle of the twelfth century. The spiral column in the undercroft to Lanfranc's dormitory at Canterbury is an instance of the form being used without liturgical significance.

5. Proportions

The use of the proportion one to the square root of two, or the side of a square to its diagonal, is very common not to say the rule in the large buildings of post-Conquest England. Its presence is most neatly indicated by the odd placing of the west wall of the cloister in a number of examples: whereas one would expect the cloister wall to line up with a convenient buttress marking a bay division in the church, in these cases it lies just a little way off such a buttress. This applies for example at Lanfranc's cathedral at Canterbury, at Worcester Cathedral after 1084, and at Tewkesbury Abbey after 1087, and can be reconstructed at Westminster and Winchester (Fig. 2, a to e). In no case is there an obvious explanation from poor laying out, whereas the position of the wall is correct if the side of the cloister relates to the length of the nave as one to root-two. While this proportion is also common in the Empire and in Anglo-Saxon buildings it has proved difficult to identify many examples of its use in Normandy.

6. Mouldings

This final section differs from the others in being based on unpublished research.[9] It is therefore presented in considerably greater detail. There are only two periods in the history of western architecture in which important and expensive buildings regularly lack mouldings. The first of these is the early middle ages, from the fifth century to the late eleventh, which can be exemplified by buildings such as Charlemagne's Palace Chapel at Aachen of the late eighth century and the church of Saint-Pierre at Jumièges of the late tenth or early eleventh (Fig. 3 a). There must of course have been a great deal of stucco work, of which the late eighth-century remains at Cividale are a reminder, but a clear distinction must be drawn between the technologies of stucco and masonry, and the poverty of the latter in consequence acknowledged. This poverty is usually explained, probably correctly, with reference to economic decline and lack of technical competence, though one has to note that the second period to lack mouldings is the International Style of the twentieth century, where a cause is not normally sought in a backwardness of material culture.

The revival of mouldings began in the early Romanesque buildings of northern France, with simple half-round soffit rolls such as those in the crypt of

---

[9] The substance of this section was presented to the Harlaxton symposium on eleventh-century England in 1990. On mouldings see also E.C. Fernie, *The Architecture of the Anglo-Saxons* (London, 1983), pp. 151-52 and 164-67 and figs 89 and 96-98, and Gem, 'Romane en Angleterre', *Bulletin monumental*, 142 (1984), pp. 255-58 and fig. 13.

around 1030 in the cathedral of Auxerre in north-western Burgundy. This type first occurs in Normandy at Bernay Abbey in the additions of *c*. 1030-40 (Fig. 3b). Saint-Etienne at Caen, begun in the mid 1060s and consecrated in 1077, has angle rolls in the nave arcade arches and a rich combination of a soffit roll and two face rolls forming a trilobe, plus angle rolls, on the arches of the crossing (Fig. 3 c).[10] Next, in England after the Conquest, Durham, after 1093, has rich mouldings similar to those of Saint-Etienne though on a grander scale (Fig. 3 e). Thereafter they stayed rich, except in the churches of the Cistercians, whose preference had an obvious explanation in the puritanical standards of St Bernard.

The examples running from Bernay to Durham form a classic typological sequence, but they conceal a significant oddity: none of the great churches built in England in the quarter-century following the Conquest has any mouldings at all, and Durham is in fact the first. The two churches of the 1070s at Canterbury, and the parts of those at Lincoln, St. Albans, Winchester, Bury St. Edmunds and Ely built before the 1090s all have orders to their arches which are no more complicated than those of Aachen Palace Chapel. Ely makes the point in graphic terms as the parts erected between 1081 and the interregnum in the 1090s lack mouldings, while those immediately adjacent but dating from after 1100 and the resumption of building have angle rolls and hollow rolls on most orders. The sequence (a) to (e) in Fig. 3, with Winchester Cathedral as the odd man out at (d), illustrates the point.

In seeking an explanation for this strange phenomenon it will not suffice to point to the similar lack of mouldings in the abbey church at Jumièges, built between 1040 and 1066 and so at least finished after the additions at Bernay, because this is a single example and the sort of exception one expects in developments of this sort, whereas the English buildings constitute a whole generation of churches of the first rank covering a quarter of a century. It is equally difficult to accept that the lack of mouldings is due to a desire to build as quickly as possible, or to save money, when so much else about the buildings speaks of great expenditure and a wish to rival the best on the Continent.

A possible answer may lie in the fact that mouldings formed an important part of the repertoire of Anglo-Saxon builders, apparently unconnected with the north French developments and indeed starting considerably earlier than them. Thus the church at Earls Barton (Northants.), undated but probably of the late tenth century, has mouldings of some form on most of the arches decorating the exterior; St Lawrence at Bradford-on-Avon (Wilts.), with a

---

[10] For the date of the mouldings at Bernay see J. Decaens, 'La datation de l'abbatiale de Bernay', *A-NS*, 5 (1983), pp. 97-120. The upper parts of the crossing tower of Saint-Etienne were partially rebuilt when a vault was inserted in the first half of the twelfth century, but there is no evidence in the masonry to suggest that the crossing arches belong to this period of work. In any case the Caen mouldings are no more complex than those at Durham in the 1090s.

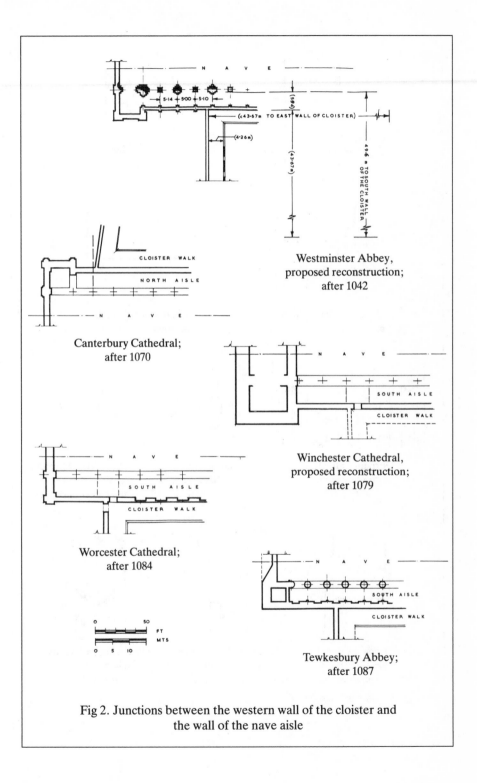

Westminster Abbey,
proposed reconstruction;
after 1042

Canterbury Cathedral;
after 1070

Winchester Cathedral,
proposed reconstruction;
after 1079

Worcester Cathedral;
after 1084

Tewkesbury Abbey;
after 1087

Fig 2. Junctions between the western wall of the cloister and
the wall of the nave aisle

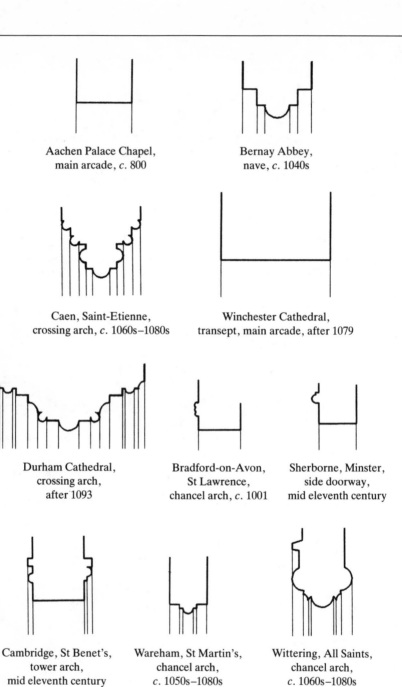

Aachen Palace Chapel,
main arcade, *c.* 800

Bernay Abbey,
nave, *c.* 1040s

Caen, Saint-Etienne,
crossing arch, *c.* 1060s–1080s

Winchester Cathedral,
transept, main arcade, after 1079

Durham Cathedral,
crossing arch,
after 1093

Bradford-on-Avon,
St Lawrence,
chancel arch, *c.* 1001

Sherborne, Minster,
side doorway,
mid eleventh century

Cambridge, St Benet's,
tower arch,
mid eleventh century

Wareham, St Martin's,
chancel arch,
c. 1050s–1080s

Wittering, All Saints,
chancel arch,
c. 1060s–1080s

Fig 3. Arch mouldings

plausible documentary date of *c*. 1001, has mouldings placed strategically on arches in order to make an iconographic point about the greater importance of, for example, the chancel over the nave; while the minster at Sherborne (Dorset) and St Benet's in Cambridge, both probably of the reign of Edward the Confessor, have similarly complex but completely non-Norman mouldings on arches into an aisle and a western tower respectively (Fig. 3 f, g and h).

If the Norman patrons of the great post-Conquest churches were, as we have seen, so intent on excluding masonry of Anglo-Saxon date from their new buildings, it is also possible that they eschewed mouldings as an architectural feature redolent of the old indigenous style.

It only remains to mention a class of small buildings which are Anglo-Saxon in plan, in aspects of the working of the masonry, and in most architectural details, but which have mouldings of Norman rather than Anglo-Saxon type. The chancel arch in St Martin's at Wareham (Dorset), for instance, has a soffit roll like those at Bernay, while that at Wittering (Northants.), despite its unarchitectural appearance, is in section very like the crossing arches at Saint-Etienne in Caen (Fig. 3 j and c). As the mouldings of Bernay and Saint-Etienne are satisfactorily explained by north French precedents, there is no value in postulating an early date for buildings like Wareham and Wittering and suggesting that they are a source for the Norman examples. On the contrary they should be seen as the result of influence from the Norman buildings and dated accordingly between the 1050s and the 1080s, or even later. If this is accepted then we have the interesting situation in the first generation after the Conquest of influence from Normandy making itself felt in *minor* churches while being rejected or avoided in major ones such as Winchester.

The points made in this essay can be summed up as follows. The thoroughness with which Norman culture replaced Anglo-Saxon in at least one sphere is evident in the lack of standing Anglo-Saxon material in the major churches of the first two generations after 1066. Contrariwise, the extent to which the Normans were influenced by their being in England is indicated by the greater scale of their buildings compared with anything they built in Normandy, and their love of the exotic in planning and details which again have no parallels in Normandy. For these exotic elements the patrons or their master masons turned to western France, Burgundy, the pilgrimage route to Santiago and, for a number of plan types, the cushion capital and spiral columns, to the Empire. The proportion one to the square root of two is another aspect of design which the Normans appear to have adopted after the Conquest rather than importing it from Normandy, while, finally, the lack of mouldings in large English churches in the 1070s and 1080s suggests an influence from things Anglo-Saxon, but of an entirely negative character.

The great ecclesiastical buildings of post-Conquest England were built under the aegis of Norman power, being in many respects based on architectural precedent in Normandy. Yet they also indicate massive, detailed and sustained influences from elsewhere, to the extent that one can only talk about designs being 'Norman' in a rather attenuated sense, with aspects of equal importance from the Empire, France and elsewhere and, eventually, from Anglo-Saxon England.

9

Architectural Relationships between England and Normandy, 1100-1204

Lindy Grant

The shame that an older, more xenophobic generation of historians felt about losing anything to the French – only the very worst of English kings or queens ever do it – has established the Loss of Normandy in 1204 as a capital-letter event. This in turn has obscured the fact that, since the Conquest of England in 1066, the king of England lost Normandy on a regular basis, though usually to another member of his own family. Rufus fought for, and then bought, the duchy from Robert Curthose. Henry I fought for it again after Rufus' death, finally reuniting kingdom and duchy in 1106. In 1135 Henry died without a legitimate male heir and kingdom and duchy again parted ways. When Henry's nephew, Stephen of Blois, seized the English throne in 1135, the Norman barons apparently hoped initially that Stephen's brother Theobald, count of Blois, would be duke, though they subsequently accepted Stephen himself. But Stephen's hold on Normandy was always fragile, and by 1144 he had lost it to the Angevins. Normandy and England were not reunited until Henry Plantagenet became king of England in 1154. Thus England and Normandy were not always under the same political management, and their political relationship was not constant, long before the final schism of 1204. Keeping England and Normandy together was possible but, like making mayonnaise, it required skill, judgement, determination and perpetual vigilance.

With the political fluctuations in mind, I am going to explore one aspect of the cultural relationship between the kingdom and the duchy during the century between Tinchebray and 1204. My index is ecclesiastical architecture, that most public and costly of artistic manifestations. The twelfth-century cultural environment in which English and Norman architecture developed was no more constant than the political. Around 1140, at Saint-Denis in the Ile de France, Gothic architecture finally emerged from its Romanesque chrysalis. This was itself but a single element in a major shift which, by the end of the century, established Paris, apparently *ex nihilo*, as the cultural cynosure of western Europe. To this powerful tide the Anglo-Norman world was not immune; it muddies the waters as we try to observe and define the architectural relationship between the kingdom and the duchy.

There is another major problem. Very few of the building projects in

Normandy in the first half of the twelfth century are securely dated. With the eleventh century, with twelfth-century England, and with later twelfth-century Normandy, we reach firmer ground, with relatively substantial documentation which usually coincides with archaeological evidence. But many early twelfth-century Norman works are refashionings of existing buildings, often involving the nave. This sort of work cannot be related to the consecrations, dedications and burials which provide the documentary record. Lessay is one of the few relevant buildings with apparently clear documentary evidence, but there is dispute about how the buildings should be interpreted in relation to it. In 1089 Eudo Capellanus, son of the founder, was buried in the choir. Excavation revealed no evidence of a previous church on the site, and many French archaeologists accept that the present choir of Lessay was complete at that date. Most Anglophone archaeologists, however, prefer a date around 1120. The problem is that the rib vaults belong to an early stage of the design, being integral with the upper walls of the choir.[1] If Lessay really is late eleventh century, it stands right out on its own as the earliest high rib vault.

Extant and reasonably dated buildings in twelfth-century Normandy come down to Saint-Georges de Boscherville, with a *terminus a quo* of 1114, when William I Tancarville refounded it as a Benedictine monastery;[2] and the first campaign of Evreux Cathedral, rebuilt by Henry I after he had burnt it down in 1120.[3] Otherwise it is all rather a moveable feast. The nave at Bayeux has been dated *c.* 1120, and 1163-65.[4] The upper levels of the nave at La Trinité at Caen are dated *c.* 1125-30 by Baylé, and *c.* 1150 by Kahn.[5] The date of the Trinité nave vault affects the dating of a number of associated buildings in the Caen region, including the vault in the nave of Saint-Etienne. Most of these dates have been proposed in the context of monographic studies of single buildings. No one has so far attempted to establish even the most skeletal chronology for early twelfth-century Norman architecture, or considered the implications of the various dates so far proposed in relation to many other buildings in Normandy, let alone outside it. A great deal of early twelfth-century Norman building activity seems to have been concentrated in the Caen area; but are we looking at a single short burst of activity, or at consistent low-level activity? If it was a concentrated burst in the 1120s, we could interpret it as a result of settled government under Henry I, and as technically in some respects quite

---

[1] For the excavations and examination of the fabric, see Y. Froidevaux, 'L'église abbatiale de Lessay', *Congrès archéologique*, 124 (1966), pp. 70-82.

[2] *Gallia christiana*, 11, cols 268, 270.

[3] See the interpolation by Robert of Torigny in William of Jumièges, *Gesta Normannorum ducum*, ed. J. Marx, Société de l'Histoire de Normandie (Rouen, 1914), p. 313.

[4] J. Thirion, 'La cathédrale de Bayeux', *Congrès archéologique*, 122 (1974), pp. 246-50, opts for *c.* 1120; L. Serbat, 'La cathédrale de Bayeux', *Congrès archéologique*, 75 (1908), p. 146, opts for *c.* 1163-5.

[5] M. Baylé, *La Trinité de Caen* (Paris, 1979), pp. 138-42; D. Kahn, *Canterbury Cathedral and its Romanesque Sculpture* (London, 1991), pp. 117-23.

advanced. If it was in the 1150s, it might reflect settled government under Henry II, but would be architecturally very conservative. The thirty years difference in date would materially affect our interpretation of architectural development within twelfth-century Normandy, and how we should relate that development to English architecture.

In spite of these caveats, I think we can say with some certainty that the distribution of building over the century is different in rhythm from that in England. The great period of building in Normandy was from *c.* 1020 to about the time of the Conqueror's death. After that there were few new projects. Even the Caen activity, whatever its date, consisted in finishing or altering existing large-scale buildings, and building small ones. The handful of large-scale new projects – Lessay, Boscherville, and Evreux Cathedral – are disappointing. Their designs are cramped, reduced versions of their grand galleried predecessors, with mere roofspace openings at the middle level; and their details are often alarmingly coarse in execution. In mitigation, it must be said that both Lessay and Boscherville were baronial rather than ducal or royal foundations.

In England, the great projects naturally postdate the Conquest – apart from the Confessor's Westminster – and only really gather momentum at the turn of the century, just as energy, or money, or interest seemed to falter in the duchy. It was not that there was no need to build in the duchy. Henry I's control of it was gained, and to a large extent maintained, by war, and there was much destruction and forced rebuilding of churches. Henry's rebuilding of Evreux, though, is hardly a distinguished piece of royal patronage. Bayeux Cathedral was damaged in 1105, and it has been suggested that the spandrel decorations in the nave are part of the rebuilding to repair that damage. But even those art historians who assume this, and thus date the spandrels much earlier than they have usually been dated, are reluctant to put them before 1120, which would mean that Bayeux Cathedral stood for fifteen years in a severely damaged state.[6] Whatever its date, it was in no way a complete rebuilding. The response to damage, even serious damage, was often patchy repair work rather than rebuilding. Exactly what happened at Bayeux is unclear, but we know from Arnulf of Lisieux's letters that he was only able to reconstruct his cathedral, damaged in 1144, some thirty years later.[7] Whether the relative paucity of building, its slow rate and mediocre quality in the first half of the twelfth century should be ascribed to the frequent instability, unrest and warfare that bedevilled the duchy after the Conqueror's death is unclear. Certainly building activity seems to have picked up again, both in quantity and quality, around 1160, maintaining this impetus for another hundred years or so. When this new life came, much of it was centred on Rouen and Upper Normandy, and much

[6] Thirion, 'La cathédrale de Bayeux', pp. 246-50.

[7] *The Letters of Arnulf of Lisieux*, ed. F. Barlow, Camden Society, 3rd series, 61 (London, 1939), pp. xlvii-viii.

of it stemmed from, or was related to, the initiative taken in that area by the Empress and Henry II, at Le Valasse, Mortemer, Petit Quevilly and, presumably, Notre-Dame du Pré at Rouen.[8]

In England, on the other hand, the rate and quality of building never faltered. Even the dangers and uncertainties of the Anarchy in the 1140s failed to halt it: indeed they were in many cases conducive to the undertaking of ambitious building projects.

In the first half of the twelfth century at least, English building was far more original and experimental than Norman. Plan types were elaborate and novel, with Roger of Salisbury's Old Sarum Cathedral, begun around 1125, setting a fashion for retrochoir designs that reached its apogee around and after 1200. The late eleventh-century Cluniac houses of Lewes and Bermondsey boasted double eastern transepts, as did Prior Ernulf's choir at Canterbury around the turn of the century. St Augustine's at Canterbury sported a late eleventh-century rotunda, and English architects showed a continuing interest in centralised plans for churches which had reason to ape the Holy Sepulchre in Jerusalem, such as St John at Clerkenwell, of *c.* 1160; and for chapter houses, starting with Worcester around 1130. There were some startling experiments with west fronts, notably the west transept designs of Lincoln, Peterborough and Ely; and the complex ground plans of major English churches were often mirrored by a silhouette bristling with towers. The high ribbed vaults of the choir at Durham, supported by buttressing walls, represented a major structural breakthrough; and the constructional advantages of the rib appealed to many English workshops, at Gloucester, Peterborough and Lincoln for instance. The choir and transepts of Peterborough were experimental in wall structure, with superimposed passages running along the length of the wall. This experiment was not fully developed in England; but increasingly open passageways at clerestory level encouraged a reversion to wooden roofing in the second half of the century. In the western marches architects toyed, at Tewkesbury and Pershore, with four-level elevations, while Gloucester, Tewkesbury and Shrewsbury initiated a local obsession with elevations dominated by massive columnar piers. Reading Abbey, begun by Henry I in 1121, seems to have been behind a related English obsession with giant order designs.[9] Indeed most things about this architecture are gigantic: it spreads on the ground; it towers into the sky; its aim is maximum mass and scale. It tries to make you feel small, especially if you are an Anglo-Saxon. It was elaborate too. Its effects were richly patterned and exotic. The East Anglian abbeys

---

[8] See L. Grant, 'The Architecture of the Early Savignacs and Cistercians in Normandy', *A-NS*, 10 (1988), pp. 111-143; eadem, 'The Architectural Patronage of Henry II', *Cahiers de civilisation médiévale*, forthcoming.

[9] For the foundation of Reading see *Reading Abbey Cartularies*, ed. B.R. Kemp, Camden Society, 4th series, 31 (London, 1986), i, pp. 15-18. For the dates of the building campaigns, see F. Henry and G. Zarnecki, 'Romanesque Arches Decorated with Human and Animal Heads', *Journal of the British Archaeological Association*, 3rd series, 21 (1958), esp. p. 27.

played sophisticated variations on the theme of the composite pier. Columns and shafts were carved with surface patterns, or faceted into octagonal forms. Shafts were often detached, and from the 1140s were often cut from coloured marble-like stone – Tournai marble at Faversham, blue lias at Glastonbury, real Roman onyx on monastic building at mid century Canterbury. The desire to pattern piers is apparent as early as Lanfranc's work at Canterbury. By the early twelfth century the chevron was becoming ubiquitous, and by the 1120s, at Reading or Sarum, the decorative impulse verged on the obsessive.[10]

Against this powerful and vibrant if unsubtle architecture, twelfth century Normandy makes a pale showing. There was not the slightest interest in retrochoirs, in eastern or western transepts, in centralised plans, in massive west fronts, or even in a multiplicity of towers. The giant order was only attempted around 1200 at Rouen, but it belongs to a very different tradition from the Reading type.[11] Round piers were generally confined to unpretentious buildings. The standard Norman pier type for a major building remained the composite pier, much as at eleventh-century Saint-Etienne at Caen, though the introduction of sexpartite vaulting into the Bessin leads to a revival of alternation between composite and columnar piers in some small churches. There is no evidence of patterned shafting, octagonal shafting, of marble or marble-like stone, nor indeed much of detached shafting. Shafts in Normandy are coursed with the wall.[12]

Not only was England more original and inventive than Normandy in the twelfth century, it was also more open to outside influence. This is not the paradox it seems. English architects, masons and patrons had a voracious

[10] The best overview of English Romanesque architecture of the twelfth century remains P. Kidson in P. Kidson, P. Murray and P. Thompson, *A History of English Architecture* (London, 1962), but see also R. Gem, 'English Romanesque Architecture', in *English Romanesque Art, 1066-1200* (Arts Council, London, 1984), pp. 27-40. Otherwise the literature is mainly a matter of specialist studies of single buildings, patrons or problems. See especially, for this paragraph, B. Cherry, 'Romanesque Architecture in Eastern England', *Journal of the British Archaeological Association*, 131 (1978), pp. 1-29; R. Stalley, 'A Twelfth-Century Patron of Architecture: A Study of the Buildings Erected by Roger, Bishop of Salisbury, 1102-1139', *Journal of the British Archaeological Association*, 3rd series, 34 (1971), pp. 62-83; L. Hoey, 'Pier Form and Vertical Wall Articulation in English Romanesque Architecture', *Journal of the Society of Architectural Historians*, 48 (1989), pp. 258-83; A. Borg, 'The Development of Chevron Ornament', *Journal of the British Archaeological Association*, 3rd series, 30 (1967), pp. 122-40; N. Stratford, 'Notes on the Norman Chapterhouse at Worcester', *Medieval Art and Architecture at Worcester Cathedral, BAACT*, 1 (1978), pp. 51-70. See also the various articles quoted throughout these footnotes; and the many relevant articles, some of which are quoted here, in successive volumes of BAACT.

[11] L. Grant, 'The Cathedral of Rouen, 1200 – *c*. 1240', *Medieval Art and Architecture at Rouen and the Seine Valley*, ed. J. Stratford, *BAACT*, 12 (1993), pp. 60-68.

[12] For twelfth-century Romanesque architecture in Normandy, see L. Musset, *La Normandie romane*, 2 vols (La Pierre qui Vire, 1967 and 1974): for Gothic architecture in twelfth-century Normandy, L. Grant, 'Gothic Arthitecture in Normandy, *c*. 1150-*c*.1250' (unpublished Ph.D. thesis, University of London, 1987).

appetite for new fashions, but they rapidly made them their own. Rhenish, Flemish/Picard and Italian influences were pervasive, and were to an extent traditional. They were present as artistic undercurrents ready to be given architectural form before the Normans arrived. The immensity of English crypts, the many-towered silhouette, and the distinctive English development of the cushion and scallop capital were borrowed from the Rhineland;[13] presumably the incoming Normans found the scale of imperial building attractive. Italy, home of the popes, and of those mythical heroes, the Romans, exerted a continual fascination, surfacing, for instance, in Bishop Alexander's frieze at Lincoln;[14] while Eadmer's description of Prior Ernulf's choir at Canterbury – richly painted, with a wooden roof above slender columns – is more suggestive of a Roman basilica than of a church in the Caen tradition.[15] The relationship with the Flemish/Picard seaboard was of long-standing, but seems to have tightened under Stephen, who had married the heiress to Boulogne. It was Stephen and his brother Bishop Henry who were responsible for introducing lavish coloured marble effects, and in particular black Tournai stone, from this area into England.[16] The complex shafting and pier forms of English Gothic, often keeled, fasciculated and usually detached – clearly emerged from the repertoire of sea-board Picardy and Flanders.[17]

Ecclesiastical connections brought Burgundian influence. England, unlike Normandy, crawled with Cluniacs. Cluniac or affiliated houses, such as Lewes, Bermondsey and Reading, had, like Cluny III, double eastern transepts. Most Cluniac abbeys were conspicuously lavish in decoration, though there was no exclusively Cluniac 'style'.[18] The broken arches at Malmesbury, together with several decorative features, have been ascribed to the Cluniac background of Abbot Peter Moraunt, who had them built.[19] Hard on the heels of the Cluniacs

[13] See the essay by E. Fernie in this volume, above pp. 105-16.

[14] G. Zarnecki, *Romanesque Lincoln: The Sculpture of the Cathedral* (Lincoln, 1988), pp. 38-40.

[15] R. Willis, *The Architectural History of Canterbury Cathedral* (London, 1845), pp. 17, 33.

[16] G. Zarnecki, 'Romanesque Sculpture: Introduction', in *English Romanesque Art, 1066-1200* (London, 1984), p. 148; and idem, 'Henry of Blois as a Patron of Sculpture', *Art and Patronage in the English Romanesque*, ed. S. Macready and F.H. Thompson, Society of Antiquaries, Occasional Papers, new series, 8 (1986), pp. 159-172.

[17] See L. Grant, 'Gothic Architecture in Southern England and the French Connection in the Early Thirteenth Century', *Thirteenth-Century England*, 3, ed. P. Coss and S. Lloyd (Wood-bridge, 1991), pp. 117-118; C. Wilson, 'The Cistercians as "Missionaries of Gothic" in Northern England', *Cistercian Art and Architecture in the British Isles*, ed. C. Norton and D. Park (Cambridge, 1986), esp. pp. 91-99, 101-5; P. Fergusson, *Architecture of Solitude: Cistercian Abbeys in Twelfth-Century England* (Princeton, 1984), pp. 81-82.

[18] R.B. Lockett, 'A Catalogue of Romanesque Sculpture from the Cluniac Houses in England', *Journal of the British Archaeological Association*, 3rd series, 34 (1971), pp. 43-61.

[19] C. Wilson, 'The Sources of the Late Twelfth-Century Work at Worcester Cathedral', *Medieval Art and Architecture at Worcester Cathedral, BAACT*, 1 (1978), p. 82.

came the Cistercians, and English daughter houses maintained close relationships with the founder houses of the order in Burgundy. St Bernard despatched the Burgundian architect Geoffroi d'Ainai to direct the building of the first church and abbey at Fountains, and a Burgundian skeleton is still evident in the transverse barrel vaults in the aisles of the present nave of the second church.[20] Besides Burgundy became the unhappy English churchman's favourite refuge from an English king. Whether, like Henry of Blois, one accepted Cluniac, or like Becket, Cistercian hospitality, one was well placed for good access to the emperor, the pope or the king of France.

Ligerian influence has been detected too. Zarnecki has ascribed decorative features, particularly beakhead, in the cloister of Henry I's foundation at Reading to the impact of the marriage of Matilda and Geoffrey of Anjou.[21] He relates Reading cloister to the cloister of St Aubin at Angers, and predicates a key role for Matilda in this, though presumably the last thing she would have wanted in her father's mausoleum was a cloister that reminded her of her unloved spouse. Her marriage was a second stage in an Anglo-Angevin alliance. Henry had already married his only legitimate son, who drowned in the White Ship disaster, to Matilda of Anjou, so Angevin influence may have been active at Reading from the start. Reading does indeed seem to be the point at which Angevin beakhead entered the English repertoire. Buildings from the middle Loire and its hinterland – like Loudun, or Saint-Père at Chartres – seem to have provided the background for the column-dominated English elevation type, and for the related giant order. Extant examples in France reach the Perche at Nogent-le-Rotrou, and it is arguable that the type had penetrated the southern Norman marches. Certainly it emerged in the western marches in England, in an area dominated by, and in buildings connected with, families like the Bellêmes, the fitz Osberns, and the counts of Perche, who originated from the southern borders of the duchy.[22] When Abbot Suger set the pace in the Ile de France, with a revolutionary and rather Italianate west front and portal design, finished in 1140, those great English patron-bishops Henry of Blois and Alexander of Lincoln, rushed to emulate. Bishop Henry's very Saint-Denis-like shafts come from his palace at Wolvesey; but it is clear from William of Malmesbury's *De antiquitate Glastoniensis ecclesiae*, that the Abbey of Glastonbury, under Henry's abbacy, saw itself as very much the English equal of Saint-Denis in antiquity and sanctity.[23]

---

[20] Fergusson, *Architecture of Solitude*, pp. 36, 39.

[21] F. Henry and G. Zarnecki, 'Romanesque Arches Decorated with Human and Animal Heads', *Journal of the British Archaeological Association*, 3rd series, 21 (1958), pp. 11-12, 20-24.

[22] R. Halsey, 'Tewkesbury Abbey: Some Recent Observations', *Medieval Art and Architecture at Gloucester and Tewkesbury, BAACT*, 7 (1985), pp. 25-27.

[23] William of Malmesbury, *De antiquitate Glastoniensis ecclesiae*, in *Adami de Domerham Historia de rebus gestis Glastoniensibus*, ed. T. Hearne, 2 vols (Oxford, 1727), 2, p. 15. For bishops Henry and Alexander's attempt to emulate Suger, see G. Zarnecki, 'Henry of Blois', pp. 160-62, and idem, *Romanesque Lincoln*, pp. 16-19, 32-35.

This artistic piracy was not indiscriminate. What appealed was the very grand, the overwhelming, the decoratively complex, and the very latest. English patrons could afford to consume conspicuously, and they had the confidence to ignore the risk of being thought emperors with no clothes.

Nor was the architectural traffic all one way. The English contribution to the emergence of Gothic in the Ile de France was vital. The rib vault, the flying buttress in embryonic form as a buttressing wall beneath the gallery roof, and the voided wall with superimposed passages were all developed from English experiments.[24]

Twelfth-century Normandy did not swirl, as did England, in the full current of European artistic exchange, but seemed becalmed in its own backwater. Architecturally it was remarkably closed in on itself, contrasting not only with twelfth-century England, but also with early eleventh-century Normandy. There was minor penetration of Ligerian idioms along the southern marches: Verneuil-sur-Avre recalls Saint-Père at Chartres; the square domical vaults of the refectory at Savigny recall Le Mans. But that is about as far as it goes. The situation did not materially alter when western France was politically united under Henry II. There is no sign in Normandy of the distinctive keeled fasciculated shaft forms of early Gothic in the Picard/Flemish seaboard: and this is odd because Normandy is separated from Ponthieu in Northern Picardy only by the River Bresle; and because these were precisely the pier forms, from precisely the area, which were so important in the generation of English Gothic.[25] Indeed for much of the twelfth century, Ponthieu was held by the Norman family of the counts of Sées. William II Talvas, in particular, was an active patron of church building, particularly of the reformed Orders, in both areas.[26] Sadly none of the buildings he commissioned have survived, so we have no way of knowing whether his patronage encouraged architectural affinities between his two counties. Throughout the century, it seems that when Normandy did adopt features emanating from eastern France or the Empire, like the scallop capital, or the *remois* passage at Saint-Etienne at Caen in the 1180s, it did so through the intermediary of England.[27] Unlike England, Cluniacs were conspicuous by their absence.[28] The Cistercians arrived rather late, probably because Normandy had its own indigenous reformed order, the Savignacs, who merged with the Cistercians in 1147. When the Cistercians as

[24] J. Bony, *French Gothic Architecture of the Twelfth and Thirteenth Centuries* (Berkeley, CA, 1983), pp. 7-27.

[25] Grant, 'Gothic Architecture in Southern England', passim.

[26] *Recueil des actes des comtes de Ponthieu, 1026-1279*, ed. C. Brunel (Paris, 1930), eg. p. 43, no. xvii; pp. 44-5, no. xxvii; p. 47, no. xxviii.

[27] For scallop capitals see Baylé, *La Trinité de Caen*, pp. 130-31; for Saint-Etienne, L. Grant, 'The Choir of Saint-Etienne at Caen', *Medieval Architecture and its Intellectual Context: Studies in Honour of Peter Kidson*, ed. E. Fernie and P. Crossley (London, 1990), pp. 113-25.

[28] *Chartes du prieuré de Longueville*, ed. P. Le Cacheux, Société de l'histoire de Normandie (Rouen and Paris, 1934) p. viii.

such became established in the duchy, in the 1150s, and very much under the protection of the Empress and Henry II, there was nothing Burgundian about their buildings.[29]

To this architectural autism there is one consistent exception. The Seine, with its tributaries of Eure and Oise, linked Upper Normandy in a tight riverine nexus with the French Vexin and the heart of the Ile de France. Evreux Cathedral, with its composite piers and compartmentalised rectangular bays, articulated in the expectation of ribbed vaulting; with its cramped middle level and thin upper wall, belongs to a type of building developing across the Oise, Vexin and Evrecin in the 1120s and 30s, represented by Saint-Etienne at Beauvais and the narthex at Saint-Denis. Evreux seems to stand early in this sequence. It is possible that the rib vaulting is the Norman and the thin wall the French contribution at Evreux. But in fact most early twelfth-century building in Upper Normandy was thin-walled, and it may be that the tradition of Jumièges rather than French influence was the determining factor. Certainly it seems that Upper Norman expertise with ribbed vaulting constituted a major element in the emergence of Ile de France Gothic. All the Upper Norman vault experiments – at Evreux, Jumièges chapter house, Saint-Paul at Rouen – involved quadripartite vaults over more or less rectangular bays, as did the earliest Ile de France examples. It may be significant that what would become the distinctive Parisian Gothic rib profile, an angle between two rolls, is typical of these early Upper Norman vaults. Certainly many of the early Gothic ribs in the Oise are associated with the sort of heavy chevron decoration so typical of Anglo-Norman building – as for instance at Saint-Denis. The problem here is that while heavy chevron is ubiquitous in Lower Normandy it is far less frequent in the Upper Norman quadripartite vault group, in which geometric decoration is apt to be rather restrained.

But Upper Normandy did not keep the Gothic initiative. As Gothic emerged throughout the duchy, what was not indigenous came from the Parisis. The portal and the lopped corner nave arcade abaci of Arnulf of Lisieux's cathedral, the most overtly French work in the duchy, reveal its debt to Mantes and Paris. The choir of Saint-Etienne at Caen draws its basic design from Saint-Denis, enhanced with more fashionable window and pier types from Notre Dame.[30] The choir of Cistercian Mortemer, begun in 1174 by Henry II, reveals its debt to Saint-Denis in its undulating chapel plan.[31] Fécamp, too, begun in 1168 by Abbot Henry de Sully, nephew of Henry of Blois, was initially planned to have a full double ambulatory after the manner of Saint-Denis. The arch between the outer north aisle and the northern radiating chapel was originally open: the capitals cornice continues through it, and the blocking wall is but a thin piece of rubble (Plates 7 and 8). Otherwise, Fécamp epitomises the inward-looking nature of twelfth-century architecture

---

[29] Grant, 'Early Savignacs and Cistercians', pp. 111-43.
[30] Eadem, 'Saint-Etienne at Caen', pp. 113-25.
[31] Eadem, 'Architectural Patronage of Henry II'.

in Normandy. Its design harks back, it seems to me quite self-consciously, to its splendid Norman predecessors of a century earlier, with full lantern tower, stair turrets flanking the apse, and the revival of the clerestory passage and grand vaulted gallery. It seems to have struck a chord in the duchy, establishing the accepted elevation for all Gothic buildings of pretension for the next fifty years.[32]

There were, of course, links between Normandy and England. The duchy does play its part in a couple of the more advanced English architectural games of the early twelfth century. The superimposed passages in the apses at La Trinité at Caen and at Cerisy la Forêt lie behind the wall structure at Peterborough, begun in 1114. I say 'lie behind', accepting oft-repeated datings: but the sole indication of a date for the apse campaign at La Trinité is the resemblance of some of its capitals to the crypt capitals at Canterbury of around 1100;[33] and there is no evidence for dating the apse of Cerisy at all, though it is generally assumed to be late eleventh century.

The whole question of rib vaults in England and Normandy is an old chestnut, but it remains a hot one.[34] I incline to the view that the late eleventh-century date for the rib vaults as Lessay is unlikely, and that rib vaulting really emerged in England rather than Normandy, with the choir vaults at Durham, around 1100. The Durham aisle vaults, approximating to a square in plan, were quadripartite: the choir vaults themselves were sexpartite over two bays, which gave them a stable, basically square form, with an extra cross rib for support in the middle. Most other English high vaults are lost, so we do not really know how they developed. English architects also experimented around 1100, at Gloucester and Chichester, for instance, with rib-vaulted apses.[35] Norman architects continued and refined these experiments over the next two decades. The Upper Norman examples, all of which feature quadripartite vaulting, developed an expertise in covering squarish bays, as at Jumièges chapter house, which was then extended to the intrinsically less stable rectangle at Evreux. The profiles on the apse ribs – the only early ribs in the church,– link Boscherville with this group. Boscherville and Evreux are our two buildings with a *terminus a quo*, and it seems reasonable to cluster this Upper Norman group around them, spanning perhaps a decade either side of 1120. Lessay's vaults are also quadripartite over distinctly rectangular bays, and on these grounds alone one might expect them to be later rather than

[32] Eadem, 'Gothic Architecture in Normandy', pp. 66-69.

[33] Baylé, *La Trinité de Caen*, p. 120.

[34] J. Bilson, 'Durham Cathedral: The Chronology of its Vaults', *Archaeological Journal*, 79 (1922), pp. 101-60; J. Bony, 'Le projet premier de Durham: voûtement partiel ou voûtement total?', *Urbanisme et architecture (en honneur de Pierre Lavedan)*, (Paris, 1954), pp. 41-49; idem, 'Diagonality and Centrality in Early Rib-Vaulted Architecture', *Gesta*, 15 (1976), pp. 15-25; J. James, 'The Rib Vaults of Durham Cathedral', ibid., 22 (1983), pp. 135-45; Y. Froidevaux, 'L'église abbatiale de Lessay', *Congrès archéologique*, 124 (1966), pp. 70-82.

[35] C. Wilson, 'Abbot Serlo's Church at Gloucester, 1089-1100', *Medieval Art and Architecture at Gloucester and Tewkesbury, BAACT*, 7 (1985), pp. 52-83.

earlier in the sequence of vaulting experiments. But Lower Norman vaulting was generally dominated by the Caen sexpartite vault. Both Saint-Etienne and La Trinité naves were revaulted in the twelfth century; Saint-Etienne with a true, La Trinité with a false, sexpartite vault. Their sexpartite form reveals that, however belatedly, and perhaps with some lost intermediary, they derive from the choir vaults at Durham. The dates of the Caen vaults have been much disputed. I am going to suggest the 1120s for the Saint-Etienne vaults, comparing a capital from the upper levels of Saint-Etienne (Plate 9) with one from that rare object in Normandy, a dated building, in this case Falaise Castle, rebuilt by Henry I in 1123,[36] (Plate 10) and with a Caen stone capital from an English building of the 1120s – Henry I's Reading abbey cloister.[37] (Plate 11) It is generally agreed that the Trinité vault is later; and it seems to me to be by a very different workshop. I accept Kahn's argument that the Trinité workshop was active at Canterbury in the 1150s,[38] and would like to suggest that they were working at Caen in the previous decade, when the city and its hinterland were generally under the firm control of Robert of Gloucester and his family.[39]

The progeny of the Caen vaults was mainly local, though they had some impact in Upper Normandy, where the transept vaults of Montivilliers of, needless to say, indeterminate date, contain a false rib, and thus relate in structure, as well as rib profile, to the false sexpartite ribs at La Trinité. But it was the rectangular, quadripartite vault type of Evreux, supported by a clearly articulated system of shafts rising from composite piers, which pointed the way forward towards Gothic developments in the duchy. Once they had been introduced to the rib vault, Norman architects seemed much more attached to it than their English counterparts who had invented it. Perhaps this is because, between 1100 and 1130 – the vital decades in the development of the rib vault – the likeliness of fire damage, friendly or otherwise, as a result of war, was significantly greater in Normandy than in England. Only in very settled circumstances, as at Ernulf's Canterbury, could one afford that combustible luxury, a painted wooden ceiling.

In my discussion of vaulting, I noted a Caen workshop at Canterbury in the mid century, and compared capitals from Saint-Etienne at Caen and Falaise with work at Reading. It is clear that Caen and its environs, unlike Upper Normandy, did maintain a consistent interchange with England, owing to the unrivalled quality and transportability of Caen stone. But shipments of Caen stone did not always guarantee the dispersal of Caennois architectural precepts. Ernulf's choir at Canterbury is built in Caen stone; but architecturally it has nothing to do with Normandy. The connections, as might be expected

---

[36] Robert de Torigny, *Chronica*, in *Chronicles of the Reigns of Stephen, Henry II and Richard I*, ed. R. Howlett, Rolls Series (London, 1889) iv, pp. 106-7.

[37] See above note 9 and for the date of the cloister, Henry and Zarnecki, 'Romanesque Arches', pp. 20-24.

[38] Kahn, *Canterbury Cathedral*, pp. 117-23.

[39] C.H. Haskins, *Norman Institutions* (Cambridge, MA, 1918), p. 129.

where shipment of stone is concerned, are apt to be decorative rather than structural. Canterbury consistently shipped Caen stone, because there was no good stone locally, and sculptural relationships between Canterbury and Caen emerge again and again. Maylis Baylé has compared La Trinité apse capitals to Canterbury crypt. Deborah Kahn has identified the Trinité vault team as the rude mechanicals working on campaigns connected with the installation of the waterworks at Canterbury. The west bay triforium figures at Evreux are strikingly close to Canterbury choir screen figures of *c.* 1180.[40] (Plates 12 and 13)

But it does not seem that a decorative repertoire arrived in England with the Caen stone. English centres, especially Canterbury and then Reading, played a key role in the development of the overloaded decorative quality of later English Romanesque. They imported high-quality Caen stone to make this sort of complex cutting possible, but the designs were developed in England. In England, the impact of Reading can be felt clearly in buildings associated with the court circle of Henry I, such as Old Sarum, Lewes, Lincoln and the works associated with Henry of Blois. I am tempted to suggest that the same is true in Normandy. I have compared capitals at Henry I's Falaise Castle, and Reading Abbey, with one from Saint-Etienne at Caen. One might speculate that Henry took a more than passing interest in the vaulting of the church which housed the Norman regalia and William the Conqueror's tomb,[41] and that his son, Robert of Gloucester, lord of Caen, may have felt it worthwhile to complete the sister church of La Trinité in which William's wife Matilda lay buried. Two of the smaller Bessin churches which are closely associated with the La Trinité revamping and vaulting are Creully and the priory of Saint-Gabriel. Creully is the parish church at the gates of Robert of Gloucester's principal Norman castle: Saint-Gabriel was very much under the control of Robert and his family.[42] Was Robert of Gloucester investing in Caen as the Angevin capital of Normandy, in the early 1140s, when Rouen was apt to support Stephen?

One of the very few Upper Norman buildings to share this decorative quality is Boscherville. Its portal has palmette capitals reminiscent of Reading, and a sort of skeletal beakhead. (Plate 14) The patron, William de Tancarville, was Henry's chamberlain in the duchy. The spandrel decorations at Bayeux Cathedral should also, I think, be put in this English-inspired court context. (Plate 15) It too features beakhead, which both in type and in its hard, dried-

---

[40] Baylé, *La Trinité de Caen*, p. 120; Kahn, *Canterbury Cathedral*, pp. 117-23. The Evreux west bay triforium is quite unlike any other sculpture in the cathedral or the city. It seems reasonable to suppose that it is by sculptors from Caen. It anticipates in a striking manner the spandrel sculpture in the cloister at Mont Saint-Michel, which, unlike the rest of the building, is in Caen stone.

[41] For the regalia at Caen, see B. English, 'William the Conqueror and the Anglo-Norman Succession', *Historical Research*, 64 (1991), pp. 232-36.

[42] For the Gloucesters' connection with Saint-Gabriel, see *Gallia christiana*, 11, col. 361; R.B. Patterson, *Earldom of Gloucester Charters* (Oxford, 1973), pp. 75-78, no. 70 and n.

out quality compares particularly well with the latest work produced for Roger of Salisbury at Old Sarum (Plate 16) and for Roger's nephew, Bishop Alexander at Lincoln in the early 1140s (Plate 17). The new bishop of Bayeux in 1142 was Philippe d'Harcourt. He had just spent the last couple of years attempting to succeed Roger as bishop of Salisbury, and one might suggest that, like Alexander of Lincoln, he found his sculptors at Sarum.[43]

Such architectural relationships as existed between kingdom and duchy in the twelfth century depended on two factors: on the use of Caen stone, which occasionally meant that masons came too; and on the whims and preferences of specific patrons. In both cases, links were apt to be decorative rather than structural. But a century is a long time. Did the nature of the relationship shift within it?

Under Henry I, there is enough evidence to suggest that Henry and his immediate circle liked their Norman buildings to be at least superficially quite like the lavish constructions they knew in England. Count Henry of Eu, for instance, insisted on importing from England marble shafts for the cloister of his foundation at Foucarmont, to achieve the desired English polish.[44] But when, under Henry II and the Empress, building activity quickened around 1160, it was focused on Upper Normandy, and there was nothing remotely English about it. It continued trends in vaulting and articulation that had been established in the duchy by 1130. It looked to the Parisis for that extra fashionable edge, but was otherwise often self-consciously, archaically Norman. The fundamental cultural alignments of England with north-east France and Flanders, and Normandy with the Seine/Oise nexus meant that England and Normandy depended on and interacted with significantly different Gothic sources. The Anarchy reinforced this architectural drift. It split families, even at the highest social levels, into branches which were fundamentally Norman and those which were fundamentally English:[45] while Stephen's own connections introduced a stronger and more specific Flemish/Boulonnais influence to England. The changed relationship between kingdom and duchy is written in stone at Boscherville. When William I de Tancarville wanted a smart new church in the 1120s, he commissioned a reflection of Henry I's buildings at Reading and Caen. When his grandson William II wanted a smart new chapter house around 1160, he imported sculptors from the Ile de France.[46]

---

[43] For Philippe d'Harcourt's career see *Antiquus cartularius ecclesiae Baiocensis*, ed. V. Bourrienne, Société de l'Histoire de Normandie (Rouen and Paris, 1902), i, pp. liv-lx. For the links between Old Sarum and Lincoln, see Henry and Zarnecki, 'Romanesque Arches', pp. 22-23, and Stalley, 'Roger, Bishop of Salisbury', pp. 71-76.

[44] *Chronique des comtes d'Eu*, in *Recueil des historiens des Gaules et de la France*, ed. M. Bouquet et al. (Paris, 1869-1904), xxiii, pp. 439-48, though this is a late, fourteenth-century source. See Grant, 'Early Savignacs and Cistercians', p. 132 and n. 52.

[45] See, for instance, D. Crouch, *The Beaumont Twins: The Roots and Branches of Power in the Twelfth Century* (Cambridge, 1986), esp. pp. 50-57.

[46] K. Morrison, 'The Figural Capitals of the Chapter House of Saint-Georges de Boscherville', *Medieval Art and Architecture at Rouen and the Seine Valley*, ed. J. Stratford, *BAACT*, 12 (1993), pp. 46-50.

10

The Effect of the Conquest of 1066 on Monasticism in Normandy: The Abbeys of the Risle Valley

Véronique Gazeau

The subject of this essay is the four baronial abbeys situated in the lower part of the Risle valley.[1] The abbeys concerned are Le Bec, founded in 1034-35 by Herluin, a poor knight who was a member of the household of Count Gilbert of Brionne and who also became the community's first abbot; Saint-Pierre des Préaux, founded in the same year by Humphrey de Vieilles, ancestor of the Beaumont-Meulan-Leicester family; Notre-Dame and Saint-Léger des Préaux, a nunnery founded by the same Humphrey and his wife between 1040 and 1050; and Notre-Dame of Grestain, founded in 1050 by Herluin, the husband of Herleva, the Conqueror's mother. The distance between the northernmost and the southernmost of the two abbeys, Grestain and Le Bec, is approximately 40 kilometres. Two of the four, Le Bec and Saint-Pierre des Préaux, were founded before William the Conqueror inherited the duchy of Normandy; the other two, during the period when the young duke was struggling to enforce his authority.

It is necessary at the outset to stress the relatively modest scale of all four of the initial foundations. Also that while three of them were set up by a single founding family, the fourth, Le Bec, owed its fortunes to the generosity of several families. Le Bec acquired a unique reputation because of its famous school. Grestain was notable because of the exceptional prestige of the family associated with its foundation and development. The two abbeys at Les Préaux possessed a special status because their founders were among the most eminent members of the Norman aristocracy. As we examine the problem of

---

[1] This essay is a synthesis of my own investigations into the patrimonies of the monasteries of the Risle valley. It also owes a great deal to the research of Marjorie Chibnall, Judith Green, Jennifer Ward, David Crouch and David Bates. I am grateful to David Bates for bringing his discovery of the *pancarte* of the abbey of Notre-Dame of Grestain to my attention; see further, D. Bates and V. Gazeau, 'L'abbaye de Grestain et la famille d'Herluin de Conteville', *Annales de Normandie*, 40 (1990), pp. 5-30. For the foundations of the abbeys: Le Bec, *Recueil des actes des ducs de Normandie de 911 à 1066*, ed. M. Fauroux (Caen, 1961), p. 31, no. 4; Saint-Pierre des Préaux, ibid., p. 30, no. 2; Saint-Léger des Préaux, *Neustria Pia*, ed. A. du Monstier (Rouen, 1663), p. 521; Grestain, Bates and Gazeau, 'L'abbaye de Grestain', p. 24.

the effect of the Conquest on these religious houses, we need to keep in mind the basic definition that monasteries are communities which draw recruits from various social and geographical origins and that the lives of their inmates are given over to individual and collective prayer. To support this role, they hold property which has usually been donated to them by the secular aristocracy and, in particular, by the families which had been responsible for their foundation. In this context, this essay will examine changes in the organisation of communal life; the recruitment of monks and nuns; liturgy; and the everyday existence of the inmates. It will also look at the attitudes taken after the battle of Hastings by the families whose interests had been most closely connected with the abbeys before the Conquest.

Sadly, the sources of information available for the histories of the individual abbeys differ in quality and quantity. In the case of Grestain, there is only the general confirmation of the abbey's properties contained in a *pancarte* of William the Conqueror.[2] Similarly, for Saint-Léger, there is also only a confirmation *pancarte* by William, to which additions were made after his death, and which was finally confirmed by Henry I.[3] In contrast, the cartulary of the abbey of Saint-Pierre des Préaux, which was copied out in 1227, provides a rich supply of information.[4] For Le Bec, in addition to late copies of the abbey's cartulary, there are also narrative sources such as the *vitae* of the abbots and the considerable correspondence of St Anselm.[5] For some aspects, I have made use of a further useful source, the cartulary of the collegiate church of La Trinité of Beaumont, founded in 1087-88 by Roger de Beaumont, the son of the founder of the two abbeys at Les Préaux. La Trinité is situated in the valley of the Risle, 20 kilometres upstream from Le Bec.[6]

For the purpose of this essay, I have deliberately taken the view that the effects of the Conquest ceased to be felt around the years 1100-1120. St Anselm died at Canterbury in 1109. By then, the third generation of the aristocratic families which had been responsible for establishing the abbeys was dying out, and all the major grants of property had been made. Those made subsequently were mostly smaller in size and value.

Earlier historians have listed the Norman monks who were sent across the Channel after the Conquest.[7] As far as the abbeys of the Risle valley are concerned, attention can be drawn to Arnost, a monk of Le Bec, who became bishop of Rochester in 1076; Gilbert Crispin from Le Bec, who became abbot

---

[2] Bates and Gazeau, 'L'abbaye de Grestain', pp. 24-30.

[3] *Neustria pia*, p. 525.

[4] AD Eure, H 711.

[5] BN, MSS lat. 12884 and 13905; 'Vita Herluini, auctore Gilberto Crispino', in J.-P. Migne, *Patrologiae Latinae completus cursus*, 251 vols (Paris, 1844-55), vol. cl, cols 698-714; *Sancti Anselmi Cantuariensis archiepiscopi opera omnia*, ed. F.S. Schmitt (Edinburgh, 1946), iii.

[6] *Cartulaire de l'église de la Sainte-Trinité de Beaumont-le-Roger*, ed. E. Deville (Paris, 1912).

[7] D. Knowles, C.N.L. Brooke and V. London, *The Heads of Religious Houses: England and Wales, 940-1216* (Cambridge, 1972), passim.

of Westminster in 1085; and a certain Richard who was promoted to the abbacy of St Werburgh of Chester in 1092-93. Richard, the son of Richard de Bienfaite, went to Ely. There were numerous monks from Le Bec in the communities at Chester and St Neots. The tradition continued into the twelfth century with, for example, Master Reginald, a monk of Grestain, who became prior and abbot of Walden. The quality of many of the monks who left the Risle valley for England appears to have been very high. This seems to be true especially of monks from Le Bec. The *Vita Herluini* indicates that the monk Henry from Le Bec, dean of Christ Church, Canterbury, and later abbot of Battle, was 'A tall and fertile tree . . . a man outstandingly well qualified in all the disciplines of ecclesiastical life'.[8] The monk Maurice, solicited by Lanfranc, despite Anselm's opposition, was of the same calibre.[9]

It is highly likely that the community at Le Bec, whose school was effectively a training-school for administrative positions in England, was impoverished both qualitatively and quantitatively by this movement of personnel. It should be noted that Anselm, whilst he was archbishop of Canterbury, complained of having to resolve problems caused by the bad behaviour of Norman monks, some of whom must have come from the Risle valley and from Le Bec itself.[10] Even bad monks crossed the Channel, and – certainly – some very good ones stayed behind in Normandy. The sources contain plenty of information about the high standard of the monks who remained in the abbeys in the Risle valley. Le Bec had always trained monks destined to pursue careers not only in Normandy but farther afield. Guitmond, for example, born near Evreux, entered Le Bec when he was quite young and was taught by Lanfranc; he became bishop of Aversa in southern Italy.[11] While Le Bec rapidly became a fertile recruiting-ground for the Anglo-Norman ecclesiastical hierarchy, further research is needed to prove whether the majority of its products were destined for England; this would require a wide-ranging study of the careers of ecclesiastics in Normandy and England.[12] Any weakening in quality may also have been compensated by a regular influx of monks from England; we know, for example, that Lanfranc at Canterbury sent English monks to Anselm for instruction at Le Bec.[13] Once trained, such individuals would most probably have returned to their native land. Some, however, certainly stayed in Normandy. We should note, for example, a certain *monacus de Anglia* who intervened in a mortgage contract made at Saint-Pierre des Préaux,[14] and that one Roger Abbadon left England to become a monk at Saint-Pierre-des-

[8] 'Vita Herluini', *Patrologia Latina*, vol. cl, col. 707.
[9] A. Porée, *Histoire de l'abbaye du Bec*, 2 vols (Evreux, 1901), i, p. 168.
[10] *Anselmi opera*, iii, ep. 96, 97.
[11] M. Gibson, *Lanfranc of Bec* (Oxford, 1978), p. 35.
[12] I am currently preparing a study of Norman abbots.
[13] *Anselmi opera*, iii, ep. 4, 14, 20, 33, 50, 59.
[14] AD Eure, H 711, fo. 109v, no. 326.

Préaux in the first half of the twelfth century.[15] Once such English monks were integrated into the communities on the Risle, their original nationality would probably no longer be identified in the sources. This suggests that there were more of them than are mentioned in the surviving documents. This pattern of recruitment, with England both giving and receiving, is linked to other aspects of the English contribution to the communal and liturgical life of the monasteries of the Risle valley.

We know that the scriptorium at Le Bec was not a very important one.[16] On occasions when Anselm required philosophical or liturgical works, he sought help directly from England. He wrote to Lanfranc for a copy of St Dunstan's Rule and he begged the monk Maurice to make efforts to send him a copy of Bede's *De temporibus*. He requested that this copy be as good as possible because it was to be used to correct the one held at Le Bec, which was defective.[17] It is probable that during his first visit to England Anselm acquired the key to St Neot's reliquary as well as a small fragment of one of the saint's bones, which he brought back to Le Bec.[18] The calendar of Le Bec included several English saints: St Neot, St Dunstan, St Augustine, St Edmund and St Etheldreda. The *coutumier* sets out precise arrangements for the celebration of St Neot's feast day.[19]

There can be no doubt that the intellectual and liturgical life of the Risle valley monasteries was significantly enriched by contacts with England. As is well known, considerable changes occurred in English monasticism after Lanfranc's arrival at Canterbury, or at any rate during the 1070s. The consequent English influence on the abbeys would appear to have been much stronger than is normally thought. This has been largely ignored by historians who have tended to be exclusively interested in the impact of the Normans on the church in England. It is a subject to which more research could be devoted.

There was also a notable English contribution to the economic well-being of the four monasteries. Numerous letters written by Anselm whilst prior at Le Bec are concerned with the abbey's needs; he wrote, for example, to Henry, prior of Christ Church, Canterbury, to thank him for the sum of money he had sent, with a reminder about his own anxieties about resources.[20] As soon as he had become abbot of Le Bec, Anselm went to England to visit the abbey's

---

[15] AD Eure, H 711, fo. 54v, no. 126.

[16] See P. Riché, 'La vie scolaire et la pédagogie au Bec au temps de Lanfranc et de Saint Anselm', in *Les mutations socio-culturelles au tournant des XIe-XIIe siècles*, Publications de la CNRS (Paris, 1984), p. 222.

[17] G. Nortier, *Les bibliothèques médiévales des abbayes bénédictines de Normandie* (Paris, 1971), p. 38.

[18] M. Chibnall, 'The Relations of Saint Anselm with the English Dependencies of the Abbey of Bec, 1079-1093', *Spicilegium Beccense*, i (1959), p. 525.

[19] The calendar of Le Bec is edited in Porée, *Histoire du Bec*, ii, pp. 579-91. For St Neot's feast-day, ibid., p. 309 n. 1.

[20] *Anselmi opera*, iii, ep. 58.

English estates and to obtain new sources of cash from them.[21] It is perhaps surprising that he should have turned to England when his monastery already held a large quantity of property in France, possessions which had recently been confirmed in 1077 by William the Conqueror and by the French king Philip I.[22] Yet, in two letters sent to Lanfranc, Anselm again mentions Le Bec's difficulties and that Lanfranc was helping to mitigate them, thanks to Canterbury's resources.[23] In 1088 Lanfranc convinced Anselm that he should borrow money from the Lombards.[24]

Le Bec's prestige does not appear to have suffered. The abbey was able to support its rapid rise to pre-eminence among the monasteries of Normandy, but possessions seem to have been slow to materialise after 1066, just as they had been at the beginning. In 1077 the monastery received the political support of the kings of both England and France. Even so, its range of obligations and its status meant that it had to have adequate funds at its disposal. It was a large community whose responsibilities included provision for young children and the poor and which was required to maintain the buildings for its school and to entertain the mighty. Its expansion had required three rebuildings. It is therefore easy to understand why Anselm turned for additional funds towards a kingdom which he knew to be prosperous. Furthermore, while the long *pancarte* in which William the Conqueror confirmed the abbey's possessions conveys an impression of considerable wealth, the widespread dispersal of its property must in reality have been a cause of confusion and difficulty. The churches, tithes and plots of arable land (whose size and value are difficult to measure), which formed the majority of its possessions, and which had been granted by the middle-ranking and lesser aristocracy who lived near the abbey, were not sufficient to ensure a reasonable life for the community. Donations located in England flooded into Le Bec's hands after 1079. Even before Anselm's departure for Canterbury in 1093, the abbey drew revenue from about ten English manors and possessed two priories in England; considerable resources which were far greater than those available to it on the Continent.[25] It is also worth noting that grants made in France directly to the abbey of Le Bec – as opposed to its French priories – significantly diminished after the confirmation of the great *pancarte* of 1077 and the arrival of the first grants from England.

The two abbeys of Les Préaux do not seem to have encountered the same economic difficulties as Le Bec, as the founding family had provided them with

---

[21] Chibnall, 'Relations', p. 521.

[22] See V. Gazeau, 'Le domaine continental du Bec, aristocratie et monachisme au temps d'Anselme', *Les mutations socio-culturelles au temps d'Anselme*, pp. 259-71. The *pancarte* of Le Bec is printed in Porée, *Histoire du Bec*, i, pp. 645-49. For Philip I's confirmation, *Recueil des actes de Philippe Ier roi de France (1059-1108)* (Paris, 1908), no. 90.

[23] *Anselmi opera*, iii, ep. 89, 90.

[24] Ibid., iii, ep. 124.

[25] Chibnall, 'Relations', i, p. 523.

considerable property.[26] This said, it should be recognised that the historian does not have at his disposal the same range of hagiographical and epistolary sources that exist for Le Bec. At the end of the 1070s, Saint-Pierre des Préaux was given numerous tithes in Dorset, Norfolk, Warwickshire, Oxfordshire and Berkshire.[27] It subsequently received two manors at Toft Monks in Norfolk and Warmington in Warwickshire.[28] The nunnery of Saint-Léger was endowed with the *villa* of Stour Provost in Dorset.[29] All these manors were granted before the end of the eleventh century. When Grestain's history is reexamined in the light of the recently discovered *pancarte*, it is clear that the abbey only really became securely established with the donations made in England before 1082 by Robert, count of Mortain.[30] These comprised several manors whose revenues must have been greatly superior to those given to the abbey in Normandy before 1066. In addition, Count Robert of Meulan's single gift of the manor of Eddington (Berks.) to the collegiate church of La Trinité of Beaumont, which his father had founded, was a substantial property in comparison with the church's continental possessions.[31] Given the size of the English properties which all the communities received, we can safely conclude that the conquest of England brought important resources to all of them in the second generation after their foundation.

How did English resources reach the valley of the Risle? English money, sterling, did not become widely current there. In the mortgage contract involving Saint-Pierre des Préaux, which has already been referred to, 8s. sterling were lent. But it should be noted that the sum was due to be repaid in the money of Rouen.[32] Count Robert I of Meulan granted £20 *anglice monete* to Saint-Pierre in 1087-90 and £8s 6s. 0d. to Saint-Léger from his Leicester exchequer.[33] His vassals granted several sums of money to the collegiate church of La Trinité of Beaumont which were to be taken out of their English income.[34] Lastly, in the *pancarte* of Grestain, the *pincerna* of the Countess Matilda of Mortain promised an annual sum of £15 *Anglorum nummorum* to the abbey at her death in 1082.[35] The first example excepted, it can be presumed that the money was exchanged into the currency in use in the valley of the Risle before the amounts in question were handed over to the monasteries.

[26] See V. Gazeau, 'Le domaine continental de l'abbaye de Notre-Dame et Saint-Léger des Préaux au XIe siècle', *Cahiers des Annales de Normandie*, 22 (1988), pp. 165-83; eadem, 'Le temporel de l'abbaye de Saint-Pierre des Préaux au XIe siècle', *Recueil d'études en hommage à Lucien Musset*, in *Cahiers des Annales de Normandie*, 23 (1990), pp. 237-53.
[27] AD Eure, H 711, fo. 145v, no. 468.
[28] AD Eure, H 711, fo. 146r, no. 470 and fo. 3r, no. 1.
[29] *Neustria pia*, p. 524.
[30] Bates and Gazeau, 'L'abbaye de Grestain', p. 23.
[31] *Cartulaire de Beaumont-le-Roger*, p. 7, no. iii.
[32] See note 14 above.
[33] AD Eure, H 711, fo. 127r, no. 395bis; *Neustria pia*, p. 524.
[34] *Cartulaire de Beaumont-le-Roger*, p. 7, no. iii.
[35] Bates and Gazeau, 'L'abbaye de Grestain', p. 29.

Grestain possessed a house in London and Count Robert I of Meulan gave a house in Pont-Audemer to his business representative, Roger of Southampton, at which money was exchanged for the benefit of the two monasteries at Les Préaux.[36] It is certain, however, that the treasuries of the four monasteries contained sterling despite the scarcity of references in the sources, even if it did not replace Norman money in general circulation. The abbeys indeed benefited remarkably from the Conquest, entailing a break with the practice whereby they drew the main part of their resources from Normandy. In some cases it was the Conquest which rescued them from financial difficulties. We would very much like to know how far their economic situation had changed by the end of the period under consideration. It is notable that in 1112-13 Robert I of Meulan granted the manor of Kislingbury to the monks of Le Bec to provide for their kitchen.[37] This suggests that the food supply was still a problem for the community and that some difficulties still existed.

It is notable that William the Conqueror's interest in the abbeys of the Risle valley apparently declined after he became king. He had favoured Le Bec and Saint-Pierre des Préaux quite generously before 1066.[38] After that date, while he granted a general confirmation of their possessions to Saint-Léger des Préaux, Le Bec and Notre-Dame of Grestain between 1077 and 1082, he gave only the manor of Penton Grafton in Hampshire to Grestain and land at Watlington in Oxfordshire to Saint-Pierre des Préaux.[39] The other communities received nothing from him, not even in Normandy, a state of affairs which contrasts markedly with his generosity to the two abbeys at Caen.[40] Among the four Risle valley communities, Grestain's treatment after 1066 was slightly different. This must have been because the abbey had been founded by his step-father and his half-brother. William's grant, which was not an especially generous one, was the least that he could do.

In contrast to the treatment they received from William, Notre-Dame of Grestain and Saint-Léger des Préaux were not neglected by their traditional aristocratic benefactors after 1066. The bulk of the grants which contributed to Grestain's substantial endowment in England came from Herluin de Conteville's son and successor, Count Robert of Mortain, with support from Robert's father-in-law, Roger de Montgomery. The *pancarte* states that Roger transferred to Grestain the property in England which he had given to his daughter Matilda (Robert of Mortain's wife) on her death in 1082.[41] Apart from the king and the *pincerna* of the countess of Mortain, Grestain had no

---

[36] Cartulaire de la léproserie de Saint-Gilles de Pont-Audemer, Rouen, BM, MS Y200, fo. 9r.

[37] BN, MS lat. 13905, p. 42.

[38] *Recueil des actes des ducs de Normandie*, nos 98, 178, 179, 189 (for Le Bec); nos 89, 97, 121 (for Saint-Pierre).

[39] Bates and Gazeau, 'L'abbaye de Grestain', p. 25; AD Eure, H 711, fo. 145v, no. 468.

[40] See *Les actes de Guillaume le Conquérant et de la reine Mathilde pour les abbayes caennaises* (Caen, 1967), passim.

[41] Bates and Gazeau, 'L'abbaye de Grestain', p. 29.

other benefactors in England. The situation of Saint-Léger des Préaux was similar, but requires some explanation. From the beginning its property was composed of two sorts of donation. The first were dowries given by heads of families at the moment when young girls or women entered the convent. In this case they had no reason to expand their grant, especially as many of the postulants were originally from places far from the nunnery.[42] It is therefore entirely to be expected that the post-1066 benefactors did not include anyone who had supported a nun's entry to the community in this way. The second type of donation consisted of grants made by the founding family, whose members continued to give support after 1066. Roger de Beaumont granted Stour Provost in Dorset to the nuns. His son Robert I of Meulan gave them an annual income from his Leicester exchequer, a grant which was in fact his only gift to the abbey.[43] In similar fashion, Robert made only one donation to the collegiate church of La Trinité at Beaumont (the manor of Eddington). With the exception of a few of the count's vassals, who also made English grants to La Trinité, no other families made gifts to the canons of Beaumont.[44] The three communities discussed therefore have one central feature in common: all illustrate a strictly familial pattern of patronage which left no room for Anglo-Norman lineages which were not related to the founders.

Saint-Pierre des Préaux had been patronised by the founding family and its vassals, and also by several other Norman families before 1066. After the battle of Hastings, it received grants in England from its founders, but not from any of the others. Two new benefactors appeared from families which had become established in England. These were Ernulf de Hesdin and the sheriff of Yorkshire, Hugh fitz Baldric, who donated respectively a church at Newbury in Berkshire; and tithes at Stratfield in Hampshire and at Shaw in Berkshire.[45] Despite these gifts, the abbey's history was otherwise similar to the family type of monastery. Only Roger de Beaumont and his sons, Robert of Meulan-Leicester and Hugh of Warwick, the king and the two men referred to above gave property in England to the abbey of Saint-Pierre des Préaux.[46]

Matters are inevitably different and more complex in the case of Le Bec which from the start had managed to gain support from a great many Norman families. Together with Herluin and his relatives, his lord Count Gilbert of Brionne (who was also a cousin of the Conqueror's father, duke Robert the Magnificent) and Gilbert's sons, its pre-1066 benefactors included the Giroies, the Crispins, the Beaumonts and their vassals, William fitz Osbern, the count of Eu, Hugh de Gournai and Hugh de Bolbec, who was a vassal of Walter

---

[42] Gazeau, 'Le domaine de Saint-Léger', p. 171.

[43] *Neustria pia*, p. 524.

[44] See note 34 above.

[45] AD Eure, H 711, fo. 145v, no. 468.

[46] Roger de Beaumont and his sons, AD Eure, H 711, fo. 145v, no. 468; Count Robert of Meulan, AD Eure, H 711, fos 127r, 146r, 146r-v, nos 395bis, 470, 471; Earl Henry of Warwick, AD Eure H 711, fo. 3r, no. 1; William the Conqueror, AD Eure H 711, fo. 145v, no. 468.

Giffard.[47] Several members of these families became monks at Le Bec. After 1066 William fitz Osbern and his descendants made no donations in England. However, his son William de Breteuil, who inherited his father's Norman lands, entered Le Bec and died there.[48] Walter Giffard granted a manor at Blackenham in Suffolk, in a sense taking on from where his vassal had left off.[49] All the other pre-1066 benefactors or their descendants made grants to Le Bec from their new English estates. Two different attitudes are discernible among them. There were firstly those who made contributions in both Normandy and England, such as the Giroie-Grandmesnil family, the Beaumont-Meulan-Leicester family, the counts of Eu and the Gournai and Crispin families.[50] In the case of the Crispins, only one branch, Milo Crispin's, made a grant in England; the rest of the family held nothing there and could only continue to favour Le Bec in Normandy. Secondly, there were the Clares, the descendants of Gilbert of Brionne, who are notable because their gifts were made exclusively from England. These comprised two priories and several manors, all given during the time of Anselm's abbacy.[51]

Several families which had not traditionally taken an interest in Le Bec started to do so after 1066. Two groups can again be distinguished. Firstly, there were Earl Hugh of Chester, Count William of Mortain and Ernulf de Hesdin, who donated only English property to Le Bec. Secondly, there were the Montfort, Envermeu and Tosny families, who displayed their generosity on both sides of the Channel.[52] The Tosny family had never endowed the abbeys in the Risle valley, because of their preoccupation with their own foundation at Conches and because they were long-standing enemies of the Beaumonts. They abandoned their reservations in 1085 and presented Le Bec

---

[47] *Recueil des actes des ducs de Normandie*, p. 32, no. 8; p. 33, nos 16, 17, 19; nos 98, 180, 181; Porée, *Histoire du Bec*, i, pp. 645-49.

[48] BN, MS lat. 12884, fo. 105v.

[49] Porée, *Histoire du Bec*, i, p. 451.

[50] Hugh de Grandmesnil: 'ut res ipsius monasterii per Novum Mercatum sine exactione transeant quantum ad eum pertinebat', Porée, *Histoire du Bec*, i, p. 648; between 1086 and 1098 he gave the manor and church of Monxton (Hants.), M. Chibnall, 'The English Possessions of Bec in the Time of Anselm', *Les mutations socio-culturelles au temps d'Anselme*, p. 276. Henry, count of Eu, founded the priory of Saint-Martin-du-Bosc in 1106 and gave it his lands at Hooe (Sussex), BN, MS lat. 12884, fo. 124r; Chibnall, 'English Possessions', p. 277. Hugh I de Gournay gave his *dominium* of Bosc-Guérard (BN, MS lat. 13905, fo. 115r) and added tithes in some Essex manors; his son Gerard granted the manor and church of Lessingham in Norfolk, Chibnall, 'English Possessions', p. 277. The 1077 *pancarte* contains many gifts by the Crispins (Porée, *Histoire du Bec*, i, pp. 647-48); Milo Crispin gave the manor and church of Swyncombe in Oxfordshire and the tithe of most of his demesnes in the extensive honour of Wallingford, Chibnall, 'English Possessions', p. 276.

[51] M. Morgan [Chibnall], *The English Lands of the Abbey of Bec* (Oxford, 1946), p. 11.

[52] Hugh, earl of Chester, gave Atherstone (Warwickshire), Chibnall 'English Possessions', p. 276. Count William of Mortain gave 'terram que vocatur Prestituna que est in rupe de Pevenseia', BN, MS lat. 12884, fo. 265r. Ernulf de Hesdin gave the manor of Ruislip in Middlesex with the church, Chibnall, 'English Possessions', p. 276.

with an important grant in Normandy and later a manor at East Wretham in Norfolk.[53] The Montfort and the Envermeu families both founded a priory in Normandy and made grants to their foundations from both sides of the Channel.[54]

The abbey of Le Bec therefore remained the focus of the patronage of a large number of families after 1066. In addition, and as a result of the Conquest, there was a notable influx of resources from England to support its priories. It would also seem that the benefactor families felt obliged to clarify their endowment policies after 1066. At the time of Le Bec's foundation, the Brionne and Beaumont families, whose possessions were closely intermingled with those of Le Bec, were continually trying to outdo each other's influence there. Ousted from the valley of the Risle before the Conquest, but solidly established in England after 1066, the Clares (the descendants of Gilbert of Brionne) showed themselves eager to regain their place among the aristocratic benefactors of Le Bec. As early as 1079, Richard of Clare founded Le Bec's first English priory at St Neots.[55] While the Clares acquired a multiplicity of interests in England, the Beaumonts were conspicuously absent there. Roger de Beaumont possessed little land in England and made grants only to the two abbeys at Les Préaux. Earl Henry of Warwick likewise preferred to patronise Saint-Pierre des Préaux.[56] Robert I of Meulan only belatedly took an interest in Le Bec in 1112-13.[57] This consistent neglect by members of a family which had formerly been a generous patron must to an extent be linked to the well-known hostility which existed between Robert of Meulan and Anselm; above all it must be a consequence of the fact that the Beaumont-Meulan family did not acquire important lands and positions in England until the end of the eleventh century.

Robert of Meulan's resentment at this state of affairs is illustrated by two events. In 1090 Duke Robert Curthose confiscated the castle of Brionne, which was at the time held by Robert of Meulan, in order to give it to Robert, son of Baldwin de Meules, the grandson of Gilbert de Brionne and the cousin of Gilbert of Clare.[58] During the same year Gilbert granted the collegiate church of St John the Baptist in the castle of Clare to Le Bec, with the stipulation that it should be made into a priory.[59] Once Robert of Meulan had regained the castle of Brionne he became eager to restore his family's prominence among the benefactors of Le Bec. To do so, he shifted his

[53] Ralph de Tosny: BN, MS lat. 13905, fo. 95r; Chibnall, 'English Possessions', p. 276.

[54] Hugh de Montfort founded the priory of Saint-Philbert at Saint-Philbert-sur-Risle in 1097 and Robert de Montfort gave it the church of Saltwood (Kent), Porée, *Histoire du Bec*, i, p. 407; Chibnall, 'English Possessions', p. 277. Hugh d'Envermeu founded the priory of Saint-Laurent d'Envermeu and gave it the manor of Wilsford (Lincs.), BN, MS lat. 10056, fo. 1r; Chibnall, 'English Possessions', p. 277.

[55] See note 51 above.

[56] See note 46 above.

[57] See note 37 above.

[58] Orderic, iv, pp. 204-13.

[59] Morgan [Chibnall] *English Lands*, p. 11.

attention to his lands in the Ile-de-France, confirming in 1095 the possessions of Le Bec's priory of Saint-Martin-la-Garenne, and in 1095-98 transforming the collegiate church of Meulan into a priory of Le Bec.[60] He thereby discovered the basis from which to compete effectively with the Clares. His two French priories seem almost to be rivals of the Clares' two English priories. Like the Clares, he was operating beyond the borders of Normandy and establishing himself as a patron of priories and, in a certain sense, as a founder.

I am going to conclude this section on aristocratic patronage by noting that while the great majority of families made grants in England only to a single abbey, the Beaumont-Meulan-Leicester family made them to three of the four communities, omitting only Grestain from the list of monasteries which they favoured. This wide-ranging patronage probably reflects their political importance within the Risle valley. Otherwise only the counts of Mortain and the post-1066 newcomer Ernulf de Hesdin endowed two abbeys: both counts Robert and William of Mortain made generous grants to their own foundation of Grestain, and Count William was a patron of Le Bec. Ernulf de Hesdin was a benefactor of both Saint-Pierre des Préaux and Le Bec.[61] It should also be noted that no English religious house received any possessions in the valley of the Risle after 1066.

When aristocratic patronage is set in the wider context of the effects of the Conquest on the abbeys of the Risle valley, the overwhelming temptation is to argue for continuity. Grestain and the two Préaux abbeys remained pre-eminently the family monasteries which they had been before 1066. The Brionne-Clare family, whose contribution to the beginnings of Le Bec had been an indispensable one, renewed its patronage as soon as possible, albeit by transferring its generosity to English soil. Le Bec also remained more than ever at the confluence of many families' interests. In particular, it should be noted that Robert of Meulan's resort to patronage from his lands in the Ile-de-France occurred indirectly as a result of the Conquest, which gave him very few lands in England. It is also possible that, having succeeded his uncle, Hugh de Meulan, in the French county, Robert was simply continuing the policy towards the abbeys of the Risle valley initiated by Hugh.[62]

[60] L.A. Gatin, *Un village, Saint-Martin-la-Garenne* (Paris, 1900), pp. 233-34; E. Houth, *Recueil des chartes de Saint-Nicaise de Meulan* (Paris, 1924), pp. 1-2.

[61] Robert of Mortain was a benefactor of Saint-Pierre, but only in Normandy. For Ernulf de Hesdin, see E. Cownie, 'The Unusual Fate of St Peter's Abbey, Gloucester, 1066-1135: An Illustration of Religious Patronage in Anglo-Norman England', below, p. 147.

[62] Count Hugh of Meulan gave his demesne of Tessancourt near Meulan in 1069, *Recueil des actes de Philippe Ier*, no. 47. According to Philip I's confirmation charter of 1077, he had also given the collegiate church of Saint-Nicaise at Meulan, ibid., no. 90. In 1078, before he became a monk at Le Bec, Hugh gave Saint-Pierre des Préaux 'transitum navium vel bachorum nostrorum transeuntium iuxta castrum suum Mellent', AD Eure, H 711, fo. 132v, no. 415.

It is difficult to be absolutely precise about the effect which the Norman Conquest of England had on the abbeys of the Risle valley. There can be no doubt that the monasteries there were spiritually enriched by the human, cultural and liturgical contributions which came from the other side of the Channel. It is undeniable that there was an opening up towards England: Anselm's insistence on obtaining books from England is somewhat surprising; the real need for books referred to in his correspondence does, however, place the matter beyond doubt. If continuity means persisting in the state of deprivation which Le Bec endured at the time of its foundation, then the Conquest resulted in a salutary change. It is justifiable to think in terms of a real material crisis which was overcome by means of revenues taken from English manors. The same is true of Grestain, which was poorly endowed by its founder. The two monasteries at Les Préaux were better provided for by the Beaumont family but, like the others, they received English donations from 1078-80. It should also be noted that the first abbots of Saint-Pierre des Préaux and Le Bec both died in 1078 and that the royal confirmation *pancartes* were granted at the end of the 1070s or at the beginning of the 1080s. Those of Le Bec and Saint-Léger, as well as the unfinished *pancarte* from Saint-Pierre, list only the continental donations. They mark the point at which it is possible to see a break in the abbeys' histories, since from then on donations flowed in from England. Less than fifteen years after the Conquest the four monasteries of the Risle valley had established themselves in England; indeed, their livelihood in considerable measure depended on it.

In expanding out of its local setting, monasticism in the valley of the Risle nonetheless retained its traditional character. It was after all the families which had always favoured the four abbeys that managed their English estates in their favour. These families assured a basic continuity. Anselm knew very well what he was doing when he organised the commemoration of Richard and Rohais of Clare after their deaths with a solemnity which equalled that of ceremonies held for members of the ducal family.[63] It is tempting to say that the history of the abbeys of the valley of the Risle valley was one of continuity over the 1066 divide, but that the continuity concerned was very different from that which we would be describing if the Conquest of England had not taken place.

---

[63] *Consuetudines Beccenses*, Corpus consuetudinum monasticarum, ed. M.-P. Dickson, ii (Sigeburg, 1967), p. 216.

11

Gloucester Abbey, 1066-1135: An Illustration of Religious Patronage in Anglo-Norman England

Emma Cownie

On 27 March 1085 whilst supervising the building of the new church of St Guthlac, Hereford, Walter de Lacy fell from the scaffolding to his untimely death.[1] Walter's body was then transported twenty-four miles for burial in the chapter house of St Peter's abbey, Gloucester.[2] Following this, Emmelina, his wife, gave to the same church five hides of land in Duntisbourne Abbots, Gloucestershire, *pro redemptione animae viri sui.*[3]

Walter was the largest tenant-in-chief in Gloucestershire and Herefordshire and he had already shown his preference for St Peter's, Gloucester, five years earlier when his seven year old son and name-sake Walter entered that house as a monk.[4] The choice of Gloucester for Walter's patronage and final resting place instead of a Norman house is very interesting. Yet it is precisely this sort of relationship between the existing Old English monasteries and the Anglo-Norman aristocracy which has been largely neglected in the study of post-Conquest patronage in this period.

In 1962 Professor Donald Matthew published his eminent work *The Norman Monasteries and their English Possessions.*[5] In this work he asserted that the reason why the lords of the Conquest did not found large monasteries in England was because they preferred to give lands to their own Norman houses. He stated that this was because they 'continued to regard Normandy as their own land . . . not until the families began to identify themselves with their new

---

[1] An earlier version of this paper was presented to the Early Medieval Seminar at the Institute of Historical Research, London in November 1991. I would like to thank my supervisor, Dr David Bates, for his advice, support and endless patience. Thanks are also due for the helpful comments of the various participants of the 1992 Reading Conference, in particular, Dr Marjorie Chibnall, Dr Jennifer Ward, Ms Kathleen Thompson and Ms Véronique Gazeau.

[2] W.E. Wightman, *The Lacy Family in England and Normandy, 1066-1194* (Oxford, 1966), p. 168.

[3] *Historia et cartularium monasterii Sancti Petri Gloucestriae*, ed. W.H. Hart, Rolls Series, 3 vols (London, 1863-67), i, p. 73.

[4] DB, i, fos 184a-185b, 167d-168a; *Historia*, i, p. 92; *Regesta regum Anglo-Normannorum, 1066-1154*, ed. H.W.C. Davis et al., 4 vols (Oxford, 1913-68), i, no. 225.

[5] D. Matthew, *The Norman Monasteries and their English Possessions* (Oxford, 1962).

homes in England did they foster English monasteries'. Matthew goes on to remark that, 'this process of losing touch with Normandy is hardly noticeable before the death of Henry I'.[6] This assertion has subsequently been repeated so often by other scholars that it has become something of a cliché.[7] Le Patourel offered a different perspective in his now controversial *The Norman Empire*, observing that when the Normans did found monasteries in England during the early years after Hastings, these were often put under the direction of, or actually colonised from, monasteries in France.[8] The number of priories subject to continental houses, founded in the period 1066-1100, was double the number of those dependent on English houses.[9] Le Patourel was keen to emphasise the importance of these continental priories as strong cross-Channel ties. He went on to point out that after the 'Conquest generation' (meaning presumably the generation alive up until the turn of the century), the Anglo-Norman barons put more of their wealth into religious institutions they were founding in England than those founded by their fathers and grandfathers in Normandy, 'yet', Le Patourel remarked, 'Norman houses continued to receive support from England'.[10]

I do not intend to attempt to revise Matthew's thesis as far as it concerns the experience of Norman houses; that is beyond the scope of this essay. I intend to travel in rather a different direction and point out that the overall picture is more subtle than Matthew and Le Patourel thought. Their assumptions not only disregard the question of the position of the existing English monasteries after the Conquest but Matthew also overlooks the surge of 'new' foundations in England which took place during Henry I's life time. Other scholars, such as David Walker, Jennifer Ward, Judith Green and Brian Golding, have displayed more sensitivity to the general situation.[11] Green has alluded to the complex nature of patronage as 'gifts were made to English monasteries, sometimes by the same men who endowed continental houses'. Golding has also shown that the majority of the Anglo-Normans, 80 per cent, chose to be buried in England, not on the Continent.[12] Well before the death of Henry I

---

[6] Ibid., p. 28.

[7] For example B.D. Hill, *English Cistercian Monasteries and their Patrons in the Twelfth Century* (Urbana, IL, 1968), p. 36, states that 'the men who settled in England in 1066 retained their loyalties to the family monasteries in the duchy of Normandy . . . but the magnates of Stephen's reign were probably beginning to regard themselves as English barons'.

[8] J. Le Patourel, *The Norman Empire* (Oxford, 1976), p. 38.

[9] F. Barlow, *The English Church, 1066-1154* (London, 1979), p. 184.

[10] Ibid., p. 333.

[11] D. Walker, *The Norman Conquerors* (Swansea, 1977), pp. 83-84; J.C. Ward, 'Fashions in Monastic Endowment: The Foundations of the Clare Family, 1066-1314', *Journal of Ecclesiastical History*, 32 (1981), p. 437; J.A. Green, 'Unity and Disunity in the Anglo-Norman State', *Historical Research*, 63 (1989), p. 131; B. Golding, 'Anglo-Norman Knightly Burials', *The Ideals and Practice of Medieval Knighthood*, ed. C. Harper-Bill and R. Harvey (Woodbridge, 1986), pp. 35-48.

[12] Golding, 'Anglo-Norman Knightly Burials', pp. 35-48.

the Normans were choosing not only to be buried in English daughter houses of Norman foundations but also in houses which obviously had no connection with Normandy such as Gloucester, Bury St Edmunds, Abingdon, Westminster, Belvoir and Colchester.[13] Unfortunately, Golding does not break down these figures for this seventy-year period. It is therefore unclear whether this pattern is constant or irregular over the years.

The evidence for the study of St Peter's history in this period is relatively abundant. There is a shortish chronicle which I shall refer to as the *Historia* and an extensive index in three fifteenth-century manuscripts. Professor Christopher Brooke worked on this material over thirty years ago and demonstrated that, where they can be verified, the documents are reliable.[14] There are also numerous charters, only a few of which are regarded as suspect. Even these dubious charters contain authentic information which can be used to supplement the picture which has already been drawn.[15]

Gloucester abbey's experience of the Conquest years was unlike the difficulties that many, but by no means all, of the English abbeys underwent. William the Conqueror had already shown an interest in Gloucester, before the royal court celebrated Christmas there in 1080.[16] The author of the *Historia* maintains that the Conqueror's influence was used to Gloucester's advantage over some of the lands disputed with the archbishop of York. When Abbot Serlo recovered the lost estates of Frocester and Coln St Aldwyn, in Gloucestershire, the *Historia* states it was achieved 'with the help of King William'.[17] The *Historia* also records that William had granted land at Nympsfield, Gloucestershire, to Gloucester's English abbot, Wulfstan, who subsequently died on pilgrimage to Jerusalem in 1072.[18] Wulfstan's death gave William the opportunity to appoint the talented and energetic Serlo (1072-1104), who had been a monk at Mont Saint-Michel, as abbot in the same year.[19] Other benefits were

[13] Ibid., p. 47.

[14] C.N.L. Brooke, 'St Peter of Gloucester and St Cadoc of Llancarfan', *Celt and Saxon: Studies in the Early British Border*, ed. N.K. Chadwick, (Cambridge, 1963), pp. 258-332; reprinted in C.N.L. Brooke, *The Church and the Welsh Border* (Woodbridge, 1986), pp. 50-94; D. Bates, 'The Building of a Great Church: The Abbey of St Peter's, Gloucester, and its Early Norman Benefactors', *Transactions of the Bristol and Gloucestershire Archaeological Society*, 104 (1984), pp. 129-32. Bates has suggested that the *Historia*'s dates may often not be accurate but the conflicting dates of the examples quoted, as he indicates, conflict only with dates supplied by forged charters.

[15] *Regesta*, i, no. 379a, printed in *Regesta*, ii, p. 410. This *pancarta* appears to be based on one or two originals from William Rufus's reign, to which at least one grant from Henry I's reign has been added. For some remarks on this charter see Brooke, 'St Peter and St Cadoc', *Celt and Saxon*, p. 270.

[16] Simeon of Durham, *Opera omnia*, ed. T. Arnold, Rolls Series, 2 vols (London, 1882-85), ii, p. 211.

[17] *Historia*, i, p. 11.

[18] Ibid., i, pp. 101, 9; DB, i, fo. 163a, the only Domesday Book reference to Nympsfield, Gloucestershire, is to three hides held there by William the Conqueror.

[19] *Historia*, i, p. 10.

also forthcoming from the Conqueror. Lands at Barnwood, in Gloucester-shire, in Brampton Abbott's, in Herefordshire, and the church of St Peter, Norwich, were all gifts from William.[20] The gift of the church of St Peter in Norwich, gave Gloucester one of its earliest interests outside Gloucestershire and Herefordshire.[21] It also proved to be the precursor of numerous small grants in East Anglia, which were given in the time of William Rufus.

The revitalising of this particular Anglo-Saxon house had numerous practi-cal advantages for William I and his sons. In particular, Gloucester, which was a thriving urban centre, was located at a very important crossing-point of the River Severn into Wales. Gloucester's position made it an effective centre from which defensive or offensive action against the Welsh could be launched, as Harold had done in 1055.[22] The Normans, likewise, found Gloucester invaluable for defence, communications and, not least of all, for hunting. Edward the Confessor sometimes held his court at Gloucester and hunted in the forest of Dean.[23]

William was always keen to emphasise the legitimacy of his claim to the English throne and it became increasingly important to stress the continuity in the government of the realm from Edward's reign to William's; thus Harold's brief reign was consigned to legal oblivion.[24] One aspect of this policy has been most recently illustrated by Martin Biddle.[25] Biddle has demonstrated that one of the forms that this policy took was the crown-wearing ceremonies at Old English palaces at various seasonal festivals; at Westminster, Winchester and Gloucester. Although William the Conqueror and William Rufus both main-tained the crown wearing festivities enough to suggest conformity to the 'traditional' pattern, Henry I only used this device in the early years of his reign. In fact Henry I never actually celebrated Christmas at Gloucester and after 1110 even the propaganda was dropped. Gloucester's wealth was meagre in comparison with that of the abbeys at two other crown-wearing locations, Westminster and Winchester. In 1086 their possessions were each worth six times those of Gloucester's.[26] Patronage of St Peter's, initially encouraged by William's generous example, was most likely directed at emphasising his commitment to maintaining and advancing this tangible link with his Anglo-

[20] Ibid., i, pp. 101, 65, 67, 102.

[21] *Historia*, i, pp. 93, 386-87. Linkenholt, in Hampshire, was given by Ernulf de Hesdin in 1081.

[22] *The Anglo-Saxon Chronicle*, ed. D. Whitelock et al. (London, 1961), p. 131.

[23] F. Barlow, *Edward the Confessor* (London, 1970), p. 205.

[24] For the evolution of this theory see G. Garnett, 'Coronation and Propaganda: Some Implications of the Norman Claim to the Throne of England in 1066', *Transactions of the Royal Historical Society*, 5th series, 36 (1986), pp. 91-116.

[25] M. Biddle, 'Seasonal Festivals and Residence: Winchester, Westminster and Gloucester in the Tenth to Twelfth Centuries', *A-NS*, 8 (1987), pp. 51-72.

[26] D. Knowles, *The Monastic Order* (Cambridge, 1966), pp. 702-3. Knowles calculated that the Domesday lands of Westminster Abbey were worth £583 in 1086 and those of Winchester, Old Minster, were worth £600.

Saxon predecessors. Although its origins were English, Gloucester's wealth and subsequent influence were very much a Norman creation.

The new lords in Gloucestershire and Herefordshire were imbued with a tradition of patronising Benedictine monasteries. Gloucester, safely under the rule of the Norman Serlo, was an acceptable recipient for their grants. Patronage of Gloucester was one means of not only anchoring but also stabilising the position of the new aristocracy and their followers in the locality. By 1086 Serlo managed to secure the patronage of Gloucestershire's wealthiest three lay magnates; the king, Walter de Lacy and his widow Emmelina, and Ernulf de Hesdin.[27] Walter and Ernulf were strictly speaking important magnates with local interests: Ernulf held lands in thirteen Domesday counties worth over £270 and Walter's were worth £325 in all.[28] Within the first generation after the Conquest, Serlo's efforts to attract grants had promoted Gloucester from obscurity to a position of relative significance within the locality. By 1086 Gloucester's modest wealth had already exceeded that of Winchcombe Abbey, Gloucester's geographically closest monastic rival. Wealthier rivals, with more splendid traditions and saints' relics, such as Evesham and Malmesbury, were sufficiently far away to enable Gloucester to take advantage of the generous inclinations of local lords like the Lacys.

The nature of the numerous grants that Gloucester Abbey received in the reign of William Rufus indicate not only continuing royal concern with Gloucester, but also the extension of this interest to members of the royal court. In 1093, when William Rufus was gravely ill at Gloucester, his belief that he was dying prompted (amongst other actions) his gift of the church of St Gwynllyw, in Newport.[29] Besides this he gave land at Chelworth and Rudford, both in Gloucestershire, and all the sturgeon caught in the royal fishery on the River Severn.[30] Like his father, William appears to have sided with Serlo against the archbishop of York in the matter of some disputed estates. In 1095 on Easter Sunday, Thomas, archbishop of York, formally returned these lands, although the dispute was not finally ended until the abbacy of Hamelin (1148-79).[31]

In the reign of William Rufus Norman penetration into Wales began to make significant headway.[32] The Wales that the Normans invaded did not contain

---

[27] *Historia*, i, pp. 65, 67, 73, 85, 89, 92, 93, 101, 102, 374-75, 386.

[28] For an assessment of the value of Ernulf de Hesdin's Domesday holdings see K. Cooke, 'Donors and Daughters: Shaftesbury Abbey's Benefactors, Endowments and Nuns, *c*. 1086-1130', *A-NS*, 12 (1990), p. 34; for the holdings of the Lacy family see C.P. Lewis, 'The Norman Settlement of Herefordshire Under William I', *A-NS*, 7 (1985), p. 202.

[29] *Historia*, i, p. 102, for this grant and Gloucester's subsequent dispute with Robert, earl of Gloucester, see J.K. Knight, 'St Tatheus of Caerwent', *The Monmouthshire Antiquary*, 3 (1970-71), pp. 34-35.

[30] *Historia*, i, pp. 68, 239, 109, 115, 293; *Regesta*, i, no. 445.

[31] *Historia*, i, p. 11.

[32] For the Anglo-Normans in Wales see D. Walker, 'The Norman Settlement of Wales', *A-NS*, 1 (1979), pp. 131-43; R.R. Davies, *The Age of Conquest: Wales, 1063-1415* (Oxford, 1991).

any foundations of a recognisable continental type. Therefore there was 'little hope that Norman generosity might be transferred to local monasteries'.[33] Gloucester's location on the frontier with Wales meant that it was one of the first in line for the fruits of the Norman conquest of South Wales. Bernard de Neufmarché and Robert fitz Haimo both gave generous grants of land, tithes and churches in Wales to Gloucester in Rufus's reign.[34] The grant to Gloucester of several ancient Welsh houses, such as Llancarfan, prompted Brooke to suggest that the abbot of Gloucester was 'evidently looked upon as the man to organise the resurrection of monastic life in the Welsh Church'.[35] Other abbeys, including Shrewsbury and Tewkesbury, which were also relatively close to the Welsh border, received lavish endowments of land and tithes which had been held by Welsh churches.[36]

In the course of Serlo's abbacy and the reign of William Rufus, Gloucester attracted gifts from men who were important on both a local and national level. Serlo's monastery had gained a reputation for strict observance of the Rule and Anglo-Normans quickly regarded Gloucester as a suitable place for themselves and their sons to enter as monks.[37] The royal court that sporadically visited Gloucester brought plenty of prestigious benefactors, who otherwise had no obvious connection with the locality, to St Peter's. This was particularly evident in William Rufus's reign as there are over twenty of these men, such as Hugh de Port, the sheriff of Hampshire; Roger Bigod, the sheriff of Norfolk and Suffolk; Odo fitz Gamelin, a Devonshire tenant-in-chief; Ranulf Peverel of Hatfield Peverel, in Essex; William d'Aubigny *Brito*, the royal justice; and Robert and Nigel d'Oilly, the royal constables. The court visited Westminster and Winchester far more frequently than it ever did Gloucester, yet neither of those two abbeys received gifts on anything like the same scale as Gloucester. Familiarity with a monastery was clearly not the only factor which prompted grants. Other forms of encouragement, either from the king or the Lacy family, must have been major ingredients in the decision making process.

Christopher Harper-Bill has pointed out that 'the support of a particular house was frequently the expression of corporate solidarity within a feudal grouping'.[38] In William Rufus's reign the Lacy tenants copied their lords' generosity and also patronised Gloucester abbey. The work of Richard

---

[33] D. Walker, *The Norman Conquerors*, p. 85.

[34] *Historia*, i, pp. 64, 80, 93, 122, 314, 315; iii, p. 5; *Regesta*, i, no. 300.

[35] C.N.L. Brooke, 'The Archbishops of St David's, Llandaff and Caerleon-on-Usk', *Studies in the Early British Church*, ed. N. Chadwick (Cambridge, 1958), p. 223.

[36] Davies, *The Age of Conquest*, pp. 180-81.

[37] *The Letters of Lanfranc, Archbishop of Canterbury*, ed. H. Clover and M. Gibson (Oxford, 1979), p. 168. Entrants to Gloucester included Walter de Lacy's son Walter in 1080, Roger of Berkeley in 1091, Hugh de Port in 1096 and Richard fitz Nigel's two sons in 1126; *Historia*, i, pp. 92, 93, 112, 118.

[38] C. Harper-Bill, 'The Piety of the Anglo-Norman Knightly Class', *A-NS*, 2 (1980), p. 67.

Mortimer and Jennifer Ward on the tenants of the honor of Clare, and of David Crouch on the honors of Kenilworth and Breteuil, has highlighted other instances of this aspect of religious patronage.[39] This occurrence of tenants imitating their lords' religious patronage in England was relatively common, but usually only on an honorial basis and then the house concerned was a 'new' institution founded by the overlord's family, such as Lewes, Eye and Bridlington. Although not unknown, such a pattern of gift-giving was not usual for English abbeys. In the few English houses in which this phenomenon did occur, its extent was limited, with only a handful of tenants following their overlord.[40] In the case of Gloucester Abbey, this occurrence was relatively extensive. The Herefordshire tenants of Walter de Lacy included Robert de Baskerville, Walter of Lyonshall and William Devereux, who gave tithes and land in Gloucestershire and Herefordshire.[41] Walter did not give exclusively to Gloucester Abbey and his tenants followed suit. In 1100 Gilbert de Eskecot gave land in Duntisbourne Abbots, Gloucestershire, specifically 'for the soul of his lord Walter de Lacy'.[42] Gilbert also gave a hide at Cuple, in Herefordshire, to the church of St Guthlac's, Hereford, where his nephew had become a monk.[43]

The tenants of Roger Bigod also followed their overlord's example, but they are highly unusual in that they did not hold their lands locally but in East Anglia. William Courson, Ralph fitz Walter, Thurstan fitz Guy and John fitz Richard gave Gloucester tithes from at least seven manors in Norfolk.[44] Sir Frank Stenton showed how the Bigod tenants had joined their overlord in the harassment of St Benet of Holme in Norfolk, and again in the endowment of his new Cluniac establishment at Thetford.[45] These numerous grants to a

---

[39] R. Mortimer, 'Land and Service: The Tenants of the Honour of Clare', *A-NS*, 8 (1986), pp. 177-97; J.C. Ward, 'The Place of the Honour in Twelfth-Century Society: The Honour of Clare, 1066-1217', *Proceedings of the Suffolk Institute of Archaeology and Natural History*, 35 (1983), pp. 191-202; D. Crouch, 'Strategies of Lordship in Angevin England and the Career of William Marshal', *The Ideals and Practice of Medieval Knighthood*, 2, ed. C. Harper-Bill and R. Harvey (Woodbridge, 1988), pp. 1-25.

[40] For example the tenants of Odo, bishop of Bayeux, and William d'Aubigny *pincerna* were benefactors of Rochester Cathedral priory, see H. Tsurushima, 'The Fraternity of Rochester Cathedral Priory About 1100', *A-NS*, 14 (1992), pp. 313-37.

[41] *Historia*, i, pp. 81, 118; *Regesta*, i, no. 379a.

[42] *Historia*, i, p. 73.

[43] D. Walker, 'The "Honours" of the Earls of Hereford in the Twelfth Century', *Transactions of the Bristol and Gloucestershire Archaeological Society*, 79 (1960), p. 186.

[44] *Historia*, i, pp. 92, 79, 114; Robert Courson, Ralph fitz Walter and Thurstan fitz Guy were Domesday tenants of Roger Bigod in Norfolk and Suffolk; John fitz Richard, was a tenant-in-chief in Norfolk as well as tenant of Ely and St Benet of Holme in Norfolk; DB, ii, fos 265b-266a, 214a, 217a-b.

[45] F.M. Stenton, 'St Benet of Holme and the Norman Conquest', *EHR*, 37 (1922), pp. 225-35; W. Dugdale, *Monasticon anglicanum*, ed. J. Caley, H. Ellis and B. Bandinel, 6 vols in 8 parts (London, 1817-30), v, pp. 143, 149; Ralph fitz Walter, with his wife Matilda, arranged to be buried at Thetford and were benefactors, as was William de Courson.

monastery on the other side of the country could not have served the 'usual' purpose of tying tenants to the lordship as those to Thetford did. One explanation is that these men may well have travelled in Roger Bigod's entourage and therefore have come into direct contact with St Peter's and Serlo.[46]

Henry I's attitude towards Gloucester and Abbot Serlo was initially favourable. In 1101 he granted Maisemore, Gloucestershire, *ad victum monachorum* to Serlo.[47] After Serlo's death in 1104, Henry issued at least two, and possibly four, confirmation charters to the abbey.[48] For whatever reason, Serlo's successor, Peter, failed to entice gifts from Henry I and it was not until the abbacies of William Godeman (1113-30) and Walter de Lacy (1130-39) that royal grants resumed. These were grants of rights and tithes as well as land at Hartpury and Ruddle (or Rodle), Gloucestershire – to pay for a light to be burnt for the salvation of the soul of Robert Curthose, who had been incarcerated for so many years in Cardiff Castle. In 1134 Robert finally died and his body was brought for burial in Gloucester's chapter house.[49] This was the closest St Peter's came to becoming a royal mausoleum until the windfall of Edward II's burial there almost 200 years later.

The multi-layered pattern of endowment that had been established in the time of William Rufus and Serlo continued in Henry I's time. Grants from men with interests in Wales such as Winebald de Ballon, Hugh fitz Norman and Gilbert fitz Richard continued to be made.[50] The continuing importance of Wales is demonstrated by fact that in the 1130s, or later, the nucleus of a collection known as the *Vitae sanctorum Wallensium* was compiled at Gloucester.[51] Royal officials were also making fewer grants, but there were some from Thomas de Saint-Jean and Hugh Bigod.[52] The wealthier and more influential of the locally important families, however, were now choosing to establish their own foundations such as Llanthony *Prima*, Tewkesbury, and Llanthony *Secunda*. Robert fitz Haimo's foundation at Tewkesbury attracted grants from at least two men who were benefactors of Gloucester, Robert of Baskerville and Winebald de Ballon.[53] Although such families as the Lacys and the sheriffs of Gloucester continued to make donations and, more and more often, confirmations, gifts from their tenants were reduced to a trickle.

---

[46] Dr Chibnall has suggested that these grants of tithes were given in return for the grant of fraternity, as they were at Rochester Cathedral priory (personal communication).

[47] *Historia*, i, p. 99-100; *Regesta*, ii, no. 554.

[48] Ibid., ii, nos 673, 678, 1005, 1006.

[49] *Historia*, i, 72, 74, 78, 90, 110-11, 115; ii, 134, 174, 220.

[50] Ibid., i, pp. 61, 77, 91, 106, 116, 124, 285; ii, pp. 73-76; for Gilbert fitz Richard's grant see Ward, 'Fashions in Monastic Endowment', pp. 438-39.

[51] K. Hughes, 'British Museum MS Cotton Vespasian A. xiv (*Vitae sanctorum Wallensium*): Its Purpose and Provenance', *Studies in the Early British Church*, ed. N. Chadwick (Cambridge, 1958), pp. 183-200.

[52] *Historia,* i, pp. 78. 109, 119.

[53] Dugdale, *Monasticon*, ii, pp. 65, 66, no. iii.

Patronage from Walter de Lacy's family had not ended with Walter's death. Walter's son, Hugh de Lacy, confirmed and added to his father's gifts in the last years of Serlo's abbacy but, from the end of the first decade of the twelfth century, his interest was diverted to his own foundation of Llanthony *Prima*.[54] Walter de Lacy's younger son, Walter, became Gloucester's abbot in 1130, when links between the abbey and his family were re-emphasised. Sybil de Lacy, Hugh's niece, to whom the bulk of his lands had descended in about 1121, granted lands to her uncle, the abbot of Gloucester.[55] Sibyl also made grants to another Lacy concern, the church of St Guthlac, in Hereford. This had been merged with the church of St Peter, Hereford, and both given to Gloucester in 1101 by Hugh de Lacy.[56] Sibyl's husband, Payn fitz John, the royal justice, was a benefactor of both Llanthony *Prima* and Gloucester Abbey, where his father and brother had already given gifts, and in which place he was buried in 1137.[57]

The sheriffs of Gloucester also made grants regularly, but not exclusively, to Gloucester throughout this period: Roger des Pîtres, his wife Adeliza, his son Walter of Gloucester, Durand, his brother, and Durand's son, Roger of Gloucester all in their time gave grants and confirmed each other's gifts.[58] However, like the Lacy family, in the twelfth century, the sheriffs of Gloucester founded their own religious house. Established on the outskirts of Gloucester in 1136, the Augustinian priory of Llanthony *Secunda*, was another rival for gifts from men who had previously given to Gloucester.[59] In the eyes of the Gloucester monks this Augustinian house 'poached' grants from local families, many of whose representatives had previously given to St Peter's. Robert, earl of Gloucester, Hugh de Lacy, Payn fitz John, Ralph de Baskerville, Walter the constable and Miles of Gloucester, who had founded Llanthony *Secunda*, had all previously been connected with Gloucester. The tension over benefactors is illustrated by the long-running row between Gloucester and Llanthony over where Miles's body was to be buried after his death in 1143.[60]

The endowment of Gloucester was not constant throughout this period nor was the status of the benefactors. There were roughly one hundred donations over seventy years. Taking into account the different lengths of the three kings'

[54] *Historia*, i, pp. 84, 100, 109, 123, 326; ii, 92-3.

[55] Walker, 'The "Honours" of the Earls of Hereford', p. 188.

[56] A. Binns, *Dedications of Monastic Houses in England and Wales, 1066-1216* (Woodbridge, 1989), p. 75.

[57] F.G. Cowley, *The Monastic Order in South Wales. 1066-1349* (Cardiff, 1977), p. 30; *Historia*, i, p. 114; *Regesta*, i, no. 379a; *CP*, xii, pt ii, p. 270.

[58] *Historia*, i, pp. 69, 112, 118, 235, 81; *Regesta*, ii, no. 1041; *Historia*, i, pp. 58, 69; DB, i, fo. 181a: *Historia*, i, p. 118.

[59] Walker, 'Earls of Hereford', pp. 174-75, 182-83, 186; Dugdale, *Monasticon*, vi, p. 137, no. iv.

[60] For this dispute, which was only finally settled in the last decade of the twelfth century, see D. Walker, 'A Register of the Churches of the Monastery of St Peter's, Gloucester', *An Ecclesiastical Miscellany* (Gateshead, 1976), pp. 18-19.

reigns, it is evident that during Rufus's reign, when over a third of the grants were made, that grants were being made at a tremendous rate. It was also Rufus's reign which witnessed a shift in the status of Gloucester's donors. Before 1087 endowments came largely from men with strong links with Gloucestershire, like Walter de Lacy, Roger of Berkeley and Durand of Gloucester.[61] The next thirteen years saw gifts of more distant property from both royal officials, their tenants and from local tenants. This pattern continued through Henry's reign albeit with less intensity.

The author of the *Historia* casts Abbot Serlo as the hero responsible for the renewed wealth and influence of Gloucester. Orderic Vitalis described Serlo as being 'of good reputation and even better life' and also communicates something of the respect William Rufus evidently had for the abbot, placing the compliment that 'he is a good abbot and a sensible old man' in Rufus's mouth.[62] Although probably authentic, there is most likely an element of exaggeration about the *Historia*'s remarks about the dilapidated state of the abbey, as Serlo found it in 1072, discovering only two adult monks and eight boys.[63] By the time of Serlo's death in 1104 the community had supposedly grown to one hundred souls. The very size of the new abbey church begun under his direction supports the claim of one hundred souls and indicates a certain degree of confidence in the abbey's future revenue. Furthermore, Serlo was responsible for placing the abbey's administration on a more businesslike footing with the swift introduction of the office of the cellarer.[64] The author of the *Historia* asserts that, under Serlo's direction, Odo the cellarer's efforts produced a substantial increase in the amount of the abbey's lands and possessions. Analysis of the information recorded in Domesday Book demonstrates that Serlo's and Odo's skills extended to estate management. The same lands that were worth only £29 in 1066, yielded £67 in 1086.[65] This doubling in value was the 'exception rather than the rule' for Gloucestershire estate values in these years. David Walker has estimated that out of 300 of Gloucestershire's 363 estates, just over a third remained the same value, just under half dropped in value, 'often [by] substantial proportions', and only a fifth rose in value.[66] The value of all the lands Serlo acquired is uncertain and does not take account of lands in Wales or income from the numerous tithes and churches granted to Gloucester. Calculating the value of estates granted after the magic date of 1086 is very difficult. Those newly-acquired estates, for which figures can be obtained from Domesday, total £71 8s. 0d. The real figure, however, must have been much higher. By 1104 Gloucester's estates had risen in value to over

---

[61] *Historia*, i, pp. 92, 112; DB, i, fo. 181a.

[62] Orderic, iv, pp. 83, 87.

[63] *Historia*, i, p. 10.

[64] In 1077 the abbey's first cellarer, Odo, became a monk of the abbey, ibid., i, p. 11.

[65] My own figures using the Phillimore edition of Domesday Book.

[66] D. Walker, 'Gloucester and Gloucestershire in Domesday Book', *Transactions of the Bristol and Gloucestershire Archaeological Society*, 94 (1976), p. 116.

£138, in other words to over five times what they had been worth in 1066. On paper the achievements of Serlo look very impressive and the frequency of grants do seem to have decreased somewhat after Serlo's death. While William Godeman's and Walter de Lacy's abbacies witnessed a resumption in the numbers of grants, by 1135 Gloucester was still nowhere near as wealthy as the very prosperous English houses such as Glastonbury, Ely or Bury St Edmunds but its wealth must have compared well with the post-Conquest foundations such as Battle, Lewes and Reading.

The patronage that St Peter's, Gloucester received in this period was never guaranteed and could, and did, fluctuate in its distribution and value. Although the experience of Gloucester Abbey was remarkable, there are certain elements which have parallels in the history of other English houses. Kathleen Cooke has examined a list of benefactors of Shaftesbury Abbey who gave gifts in the period *c.* 1086-1121.[67] She concludes that, very soon after the Conquest, Shaftesbury was supported by the new Norman landowners who held estates close to the abbey, and that those families who sent their daughters to the abbey were 'not members of the richest barons in post-Conquest England'.[68] Like Gloucester, this house received support from neighbouring Anglo-Norman landholders, dating from at least the first years of William Rufus's reign, if not earlier. However, Cooke points out that, 'it seems that these families made no further endowments to the abbey other than the dowries provided when their daughters entered'.[69] Evidently grants made to nunneries did not tie families in the same way as those given to a monastery tended to. Unlike Gloucester, Shaftesbury attracted donations from only one man of national importance, Ernulf de Hesdin.[70] Situated over fifty miles from Gloucester, Shaftesbury shared at least two other donors with St Peter's, Gloucester.[71]

In her work on the estates of Westminster Abbey, Barbara Harvey asserted that as none of the Norman kings chose to be buried there 'the springs of royal generosity' were covered until the thirteenth century.[72] Emma Mason's more recent work on the benefactors of Westminster Abbey has given more detailed elaboration to this theory. Mason describes William the Conqueror's grants to Westminster merely as 'perfunctory response[s] towards requests for judicial support, of a kind which he would have extended to any of his major abbeys'.[73] As Edward the Confessor had chosen Westminster as his mausoleum he had given generously. William's interests lay elsewhere at Caen. Westminster

---

[67] Cooke, 'Donors and Daughters', pp. 29-45.

[68] Ibid., p. 34.

[69] Ibid., p. 36.

[70] Ibid., pp. 32, 35.

[71] These were Ernulf de Hesdin, Roger of Berkeley and Odo fitz Gamelin.

[72] B. Harvey, *Westminster Abbey and its Estates in the Middle Ages* (Oxford, 1977), p. 28.

[73] E. Mason, 'Westminster Abbey and the Monarchy between the Reigns of William I and John (1066-1216)', *Journal of Ecclesiastical History*, 41 (1990), p. 208.

therefore did not occupy the same place in the Norman king's heart but nevertheless royal association was maintained with Edward the Confessor's favourite foundation. Westminster, like Gloucester, was the scene of crown-wearing at religious festivals and from 1066 onwards royal coronations, thus royal links were evidently conscientiously maintained. William the Conqueror's charters also show a care for detail in his dealings with Westminster which is far from being perfunctory.

Emma Mason also suggests that since William the Conqueror 'did not associate the interests of his dynasty with Westminster his barons and *curiales* had no incentive to make gifts associated with his'.[74] Westminster did not receive gifts on the scale that Gloucester did but, as this essay shows, Gloucester is near to being unique. Westminster did receive patronage from one of the realm's richest barons, Geoffrey de Mandeville.[75] Geoffrey founded Hurley Priory, Berkshire, in the reign of the Conqueror as a cell of Westminster and expressed the wish to be buried at Westminster where his first wife Athelaise was already buried.[76] The burial of Queen Matilda brought gifts from her brother David, earl of Huntingdon, soon to become king of Scotland.[77] The house was also supported by local men like Robert fitz Wymarc who supposedly had been present at the Confessor's death-bed and was the sheriff of Essex, Wulfric the moneyer of Henry I and the not so local William fitz Nigel, constable of Chester, who was also a benefactor of Gloucester, as well as Geoffrey, probably the illegitimate son of Eustace, count of Boulogne.[78] Westminster Abbey was clearly not ignored by the local Anglo-Norman baronage.

Abingdon Abbey's experience during this period was, in its way, as exceptional as Gloucester's. It was not until the reign of Henry I or rather the abbacy of Faritius that Abingdon received donations on anything like the scale that St Peter's did. In the early years of the Conquest the new neighbouring barons were more inclined to steal from the abbey than give to it. The one reason for this was that Abingdon had been actively involved in resistance against the Norman invaders. Ely, likewise, felt the cold wind of prejudice in the eleventh century for its part in Hereward's revolt against the Normans.[79] After a promising recovery under the Abingdon's first Norman abbot, Rainbald (1084-97), a three-year vacancy under the administration of Prior Modbert saw substantial losses in the number of the abbey's estates. The appointment of an

[74] E. Mason, 'The Donors of Westminster Abbey Charters: *c.* 1066-1240', *Medieval Prosopography*, 8 (1987), p. 28.

[75] Ibid., p. 33.

[76] Binns, *Dedications*, p. 76.

[77] *Regesta regum Scottorum*, i, *The Acts of Malcolm IV King of Scots 1153-65*, ed G.W.S. Barrow (Edinburgh, 1960), no. 6.

[78] *Regesta*, i, nos 202, 417: ii, nos 1178, 1882.

[79] For Ely's part in Hereward's revolt see C. Hart, 'Hereward the Wake', *Proceedings of the Cambridge Antiquarian Society*, 65 (1974), pp. 31-33.

Italian, Faritius, as abbot in 1100, was a calculated attempt by Henry I to restore Abingdon to prosperity, as he was apparently considered 'more useful to them than anyone else'.[80] During his seventeen-year abbacy, Faritius secured the return of many of the lands lost during the vacancy and the abbey also witnessed an explosion in the number of donations received.[81] A large measure of Faritius's success lay in the fact that he was the trusted physician of Henry I and Queen Matilda.[82] Not only was Faritius a very able abbot but his appointment, as Henry I's favoured man, was the stamp of approval for Abingdon from Henry I. Faritius's association with the king and the court brought Abingdon many donations from royal officials, usually with local connections, like Robert d'Oilly and the wife of Roger d'Ivry, both of whom were also benefactors of Gloucester.[83] Faritius's professional skills also attracted patronage from further afield, from patients and their families such as Miles Crispin, Aubrey de Vere and Robert fitz Haimo.[84] Many of the ties established during Faritius's abbacy were weakened by the four-year vacancy which followed his death in 1117. Donations only resumed with the appointment of Vincent in 1121 but by now they were few in number.

I have one last comparison to make. The experience of the cathedral priory of Rochester bears more than a passing resemblance to that of Gloucester in these years. Rochester was dissimilar from Gloucester in that it was a bishopric not an abbey, and that it had been given a monastic chapter in the Conqueror's reign.[85] Yet it should be remembered that Gloucester was practically a Norman refoundation itself. Rochester received gifts, mostly of tithes, from several men associated with the royal court, such Roger Bigod, Gilbert fitz Richard, Hugh and Henry de Port, whose families were also benefactors of Gloucester.[86] These men along with others like Eudo *dapifer*, William d'Aubigny *pincerna* and Haimo *dapifer*, Robert fitz Haimo's brother, were all royal officials.[87] The *Vita Gundulfi* also depicts Bishop Gundulph as a regular at Henry I's court and his part in the construction of the Tower of London may have developed earlier relations with the royal court.[88]

---

[80] *Chronicon monasterii de Abingdon*, ed. J. Stevenson, Rolls Series (London, 1858), ii, p. 44.

[81] For Faritius's recoveries see ibid., ii, pp. 65, 74, 126, 128, 129, 130, 131-35, 138, 288.

[82] Ibid., ii, pp. 44-46.

[83] Ibid., ii, pp. 12, 284, 72-74.

[84] Ibid., ii, pp. 55-56, 59, 60, 62, 97.

[85] For Rochester see A.M. Oakley, 'The Cathedral Priory of St Andrew, Rochester', *Archaeologia Cantiana*, 91 (1975), pp. 47-60; M. Ruud, 'Monks in the World: The Case of Gundulf of Rochester', *A-NS*, 11 (1989), pp. 245-60; A.F. Brown, 'The Lands and Tenants of the Bishopric and Cathedral Priory of St Andrew, Rochester' (unpublished Ph.D. thesis, University of London, 1974).

[86] *Textus Roffensis*, ed. P.H. Sawyer, Early English Manuscripts in Facsimile (Copenhagen, 1962), fos 182r-v, 182r, 185v, 198v; *Regesta*, i, no. 450; Gilbert fitz Richard's grant was of property which had been disputed with the priory.

[87] Ibid., fos 184v, 188v, 181v; *Regesta*, i, no. 451.

[88] Ruud, 'Monks in the World', pp. 249-53.

As the experience of Gloucester Abbey is so unusual, in many ways, it is not the best example for illustrating the wider conclusions I have reached about the patronage of the English church after 1066. However, I think that the experience of Gloucester and the other abbeys discussed demonstrates that the interpretation offered by Donald Matthew is both incomplete and too sweeping. When it comes to monastic patronage, amongst other things, the continental newcomers should not be treated as one homogeneous block of people, with the same backgrounds and interests. Admittedly, many families continued to maintain close connections with the Norman foundations which had been associated with them and their ancestors throughout this period. Yet, unlike the counts of Mortain and the Beaumont family, many families who settled in England after 1066 did not possess their own continental foundations or have existing ties with such foundations. The Clares only amplified their existing connections with Le Bec after 1066 had brought them new wealth.[89] Many other families also owed their fortune to the Conquest, and in the reign of William the Conqueror small numbers of these newcomers chose not only to patronise certain English houses, such as Bury St Edmunds, St Albans and St Augustine's, Canterbury, but also to found a small number of priories which were dependent on these English abbeys such as Belvoir, in Leicestershire, which was a cell of St Albans.[90] Many of the same Anglo-Normans, often involved with royal government, can be found patronising the existing English houses in increasing numbers by the time of William Rufus's reign.[91] Plenty of men were quick to found their own establishments. Many of these decisions concerning patronage were probably influenced by the necessity to find a means of bolstering colonisation in a locality or satisfying an overlord's desire to secure his tenants' loyalty, rather than such sentiments as regarding England or Normandy as home.

Le Patourel's analysis of monastic patronage emphasises the Normans' continuing interest in Norman houses alongside the new monasteries they were founding in England. This evaluation neglects the English foundations in these years. His argument that the progress of 'the Norman Conquest, domination and colonisation was a 'continuous and consistent process' has this same flaw in it.[92] If monastic patronage was part of colonisation, as it was, colonisation could not have been an even process because patronage certainly was not. The history of Abingdon Abbey proves just that. This essay suggests that, even if Le Patourel's model of colonisation can still be used, it is certainly insufficient in the form which he expressed it. One weakness of his approach was his excessive concentration on the great cross-Channel families. Current

---

[89] Ward, 'Fashions in Monastic Endowments', pp. 427-51.

[90] Bins, *Dedications*, p. 63.

[91] Ward, 'Fashions in Monastic Endowment', p. 437, Ward has suggested that, around the year 1100, there was a change in baronial attitudes, which resulted in more grants being made to English houses.

[92] Le Patourel, *Norman Empire*, p. 27.

orthodoxy represented by Green, Golding and Walker, although generally more sensitive to the situation in England, is insufficiently detailed to show the incredible complexity of the situation. Patronage was never uniform in its distribution between institutions or consistently given. In at least two of the examples I have quoted in this essay, royal interest was decisive in the continued well-being of English houses, as undoubtedly were the abilities of the individual abbots concerned. Apart from the two notable exceptions of Geoffrey de Mandeville and Alan Rufus of Brittany, both of whom had limited territorial interests in Normandy, the richest men of the realm had little to do with the English monasteries. Men like William of Warenne and Roger of Montgomery were far more interested in founding and being buried in their own foundations. The most constant support for the English houses commonly came from the strata of local Anglo-Normans, landholders and royal officials, often with local interests. The treatment England received after the conquest at the hands of the Normans was not uniform exploitation 'for the benefit of Normans and Normandy', as David Bates has suggested.[93] In reality, even in the reign of the Conqueror, there was a second undercurrent of Normans involved in the exploitation of England for the spiritual welfare of Norman individuals and their families. Without this the tremendous post-Conquest success of English houses like Bury St Edmunds, St Albans, Abingdon and Gloucester would have been inconceivable.

---

[93] D. Bates, 'Normandy and England after 1066', *EHR*, 104 (1989), p. 870.

12

Savigny and England

Béatrice Poulle

The foundation of the abbey of Savigny took place within the general context of the large movement of monastic renewal which was a feature of the late eleventh and early twelfth centuries, and which included the creation, among others, of new orders such as the Cistercians and, within the Plantagenet lands, the Grandmontines and the Fontevrauldines.[1] Savigny's founder was St Vitalis who was, at different times, a hermit in the forests of Maine and Fougères and an itinerant preacher. St Vitalis' life was a turbulent one during which his spiritual life was shaped as much by poverty and prophecy, as by a personal commitment to asceticism. It has many similarities with the lives of other hermit preachers who were Vitalis' contemporaries and neighbours, and with whom he was in any case in contact, including Robert d'Arbrissel, the founder of Fontevrault, and Bernard, the founder of Thiron.[2]

A hermit at Mortain in 1093, and afterwards at Dompierre, St Vitalis did not set up his community definitively at Savigny until 1112, when the forest was given to him by Ralph de Fougères. The new abbey was located in Normandy but close to the territories of Maine and Brittany. St Vitalis died soon afterwards in 1119. The rapid growth of the Savignac Order began during the abbacy of his successor, Geoffrey, a remarkable period of expansion during which thirty-one daughter-houses were established during thirty-five years. The foundation of Savigny was an attempt at monastic renewal parallel to, contemporary with, and very similar to Cîteaux; spirituality, monastic customs and organisation reveal many common features.[3] For this reason, Serlo, the fourth abbot of Savigny, was able to solve a number of the Order's internal difficulties through merger with the Cistercians. I shall return to these problems later in this essay. The year of the merger, 1147, must be regarded as an

---

[1] For Savigny's history, see Dom Claude Auvry, *Histoire de la congrégation de Savigny*, published by Auguste Laveille, Société de l'Histoire de Normandie (Rouen and Paris, 1896).

[2] 'Vita Beati Vitalis', ed. E.P. Sauvage in *Analecta bollandiana*, 1 (1882), pp. 355-410. See also the translation of a Dutch thesis, Jaap von Moolenbroek, *Vital l'ermite, prédicateur itinérant, fondateur de l'abbaye normande de Savigny*, in *Revue de l'Avranchin*, 68 (1991), pp. 1-395.

[3] On comparisons between the Savignacs and the Cistercians, see the Ecole des Chartes thesis by Jacqueline Buhot, *L'abbaye de Savigny au diocèse d'Avranches des origines à la fin du XIIe siècle*, with a summary in *Ecole Nationale des Chartes, positions des thèses* (1935), pp. 37-44.

important date in the abbey's history, since it changed from being the head of an independent monastic order into one of the numerous daughter-houses of Cîteaux. Savigny nonetheless retained traces of its former status for a long time afterwards.

Although the abbey buildings, which were sold at the Revolution and systematically demolished, have almost completely disappeared, except for some pieces of wall and the Romanesque door of the refectory, an impressive collection of charters survives, despite the vicissitudes and destruction of the last two centuries. The early thirteenth-century cartulary contained more than 680 charters, and the scholars who examined it during the nineteenth century – from Léopold Delisle to John Horace Round – were all agreed on its quality. It was burnt in the fire which destroyed the Archives at Saint-Lô in 1944, but there still exist four complete and three incomplete copies, as well as extracts, from which I am currently preparing an edition.[4] A copy of a second cartulary is preserved in the Archives of Mayenne.[5] Finally, despite the loss of some 2,000 files of documents at Saint-Lô in 1944, there are still over 1,500 original charters in existence,[6] of which a portion have been edited in my Ecole des Chartes thesis.[7]

This collection of documents is the starting-point for my attempt to establish the nature of Savigny's relations with England. It has been possible to add to Round's catalogue in a number of ways,[8] and to provide a more complete record of the textual history of the thirty-nine charters he mentioned, either because the originals have been rediscovered, or because he did not mention copies in the cartulary. A further thirty or so charters were not mentioned in Round's catalogue and are therefore not previously known. These include nineteen charters of Henry I, Matilda, Henry II and John, several papal bulls relating to Savigny's English daughter houses, charters of magnates who play an important role in England's history, like Richard du Hommet, or of important English magnates such as William de Mandeville, earl of Essex, as well as three charters concerned with Savigny's English possessions.

Savigny's landholdings in England were never very numerous or important in comparison with its lands in France. It must be pointed out that at the time of Savigny's foundation, in 1112, almost fifty years had passed since the

---

[4] *Liber cartarum domus Savigneii*, BN, MS nouv. acq. lat. 1022 (copy by Léopold Delisle); BN, MS. nouv. acq. lat. 2500; Caen, Musée des Beaux-Arts, collection Mancel, MS 302 (copy by Paul de Farcy), Caen, collection Mancel, MS 298 (copy by Charles de Gerville); Flers, BM (copy by Auguste Surville). For incomplete copies, BN, MS fr. 22, 325; Caen, collection Mancel, MS 302; AD Mayenne, MS 33. The reconstituted *Liber cartarum* is henceforth referred to as 'Cartulary'.

[5] AD Mayenne, MS 35.

[6] AN, L966-78; Rouen, BM, collection Leber 5636; AD Maine-et-Loire, 67 H1; as well as a number of charters dispersed elsewhere.

[7] Béatrice Poulle, *Le chartrier de l'abbaye de Savigny au diocèse d'Avranches: édition partielle (1202-1243) et comentaire*, thèse pour l'obtention du diplôme d'archiviste paléographe (1989); summary in *Ecole Nationale des Chartes, positions des thèses* (1989), pp. 167-71.

[8] J.H. Round, *Calendar of Documents Preserved in France* (London, 1899), pp. 287-308.

Norman Conquest of England and the consequent extension across the Channel of the lands of the Norman aristocracy. Out of the 680 charters in the early thirteenth-century cartulary, whose contents cover the entire twelfth century, only twenty-six are specifically concerned with English lands. Half of these twenty-six deal with the parish of Long Bennington (Lincs.).

The church of Long Bennington had been given to Savigny by Ralph II de Fougères, a descendant of the abbey's founder.[9] He held the church of his mother Olivia, who gave her assent to the grant in 1174.[10] Olivia's second husband, William de Saint-Jean, similarly abandoned all his rights in the church.[11] An agreement made between Savigny and the abbey of La Lucerne suggests that William de Saint-Jean and Olivia had originally planned to give the church of Long Bennington to La Lucerne.[12] Ralph's grant was successively confirmed by Conan IV, duke of Brittany and earl of Richmond, in 1166 in his position as Olivia's kinsman,[13] and by Henry II between 1172 and 1181.[14] Savigny's possession was also acknowledged in charters of Archbishop Baldwin of Canterbury in 1185[15] and of the bishop and chapter of Lincoln between 1189 and 1195.[16] It is also mentioned among the churches held by Savigny in several papal confirmations.[17] Two charters deal with a dispute about the tithes of the manor of Long Bennington between Savigny and the priory of Swavesey, a dependency of the abbey of Saint-Sergius and Saint-Bacchus of Angers.[18] Finally, in 1201, William de Fougères granted two silver marks in rent from his manor of Long Bennington.[19]

Another of Savigny's English possessions which features in several charters was the annual rent of £10 from land at Field Dalling (Norfolk) granted by

[9] AN, L968, no. 220; copy in 'Cartulary', *Capitula in diversis episcopatibus*, no. xix; Round, *Calendar*, no. 847.

[10] AN, L968, no. 216; 'Cartulary', *Capitula in diversis episcopatibus*, no. lv; Round, no. 849.

[11] AN, L968, nos 218, 221; 'Cartulary', *Capitula in diversis episcopatibus*, no. xx; Round, *Calendar*, no. 850.

[12] AN, L969, no. 217; 'Cartulary', *Capitula in episcopatu Abrincensi*, no. liv.

[13] 'Cartulary', *Capitula in diversis episcopatibus*, no. li; Round, *Calendar*, no. 848; C.T. Clay, ed., *Early Yorkshire Charters*, 9 vols (Wakefield, 1935-65), iv, *The Honour of Richmond*, pp. 68-69.

[14] AN, L968, no. 219; 'Cartulary', *Capitula in diversis episcopatibus*, no. liii; Round, *Calendar*, no. 851.

[15] AN, L968, no. 225; Round, no. 854.

[16] For the bishop's charter, AN L968, no. 224; 'Cartulary', *Capitula in diversis episcopatibus*, no. xli; Round, *Calendar*, no. 855. For the chapter's charter, AN, L968, no. 223; 'Cartulary', *Capitula in diversis episcopatibus*, no. xlvii; Round, *Calendar*, no. 856.

[17] For a bull of Lucius III, 'Cartulary', *Capitula privilegiorum Romanorum*, no. xxxvi; of Gregory VIII, ibid., no. xxviii; Alexander III, ibid., no. xlvii (Round, *Calendar*, no. 852).

[18] Charter of the abbot of Cîteaux, AN, L968, no. 227; 'Cartulary', *Capitula in diversis episcopatibus*, no. liv; Round, *Calendar*, no. 818. Notification by three papal judges-delegate, 'Cartulary', *Capitula in diversis episcopatibus*, no. lvi.

[19] AN, L968, no. 226; 'Cartulary', *Capitula in diversis episcopatibus*, no. lxxi; Round, *Calendar*, no. 857.

James de Saint-Hilaire in 1138,[20] and confirmed by his brother Peter de Saint-Hilaire.[21] This grant was confirmed in *c.* 1140 by King Stephen,[22] and later by Earl Roger de Clare (1151-73).[23] Savigny also held land in Ingleby (Yorks.) given in *c.* 1140 by Count Alan of Brittany,[24] a virgate near '*Ciriel*' given by Robert III, earl of Leicester, and his wife Petronilla, and confirmed by Henry II,[25] as well as a rent of £40 from the land of *Piria* (Potterspury, Northants.), which was given by Robert de Ferrières in *c.* 1140.[26] There were also two grants of rents from English estates.

It should be noted that all these grants of English property were made by individuals from among the high-ranking magnate families who received lands in England: namely, by Ralph de Fougères, the brother of Peter de Saint-Hilaire, Alan of Brittany and the earl of Leicester. By way of contrast, the donors of continental property came from a much wider social range, including great barons, lesser knights and vavassors. What seems to me to be equally important about the links which existed between Savigny and England is the care with which the abbey obtained exemption from all levies (such as tolls, etc.) on the movement of its goods, and had this privilege renewed by each successive English king. As early as 1112, that is, at the time of Savigny's foundation, Henry I ordered his *prepositi* and servants in England and Normandy and at the harbours on the sea coast to exempt the goods of the hermit Vitalis from all dues on their transportation.[27] Stephen granted the same privilege to Savigny.[28] Henry II confirmed it twice, one of his charters being addressed specifically to the *prepositi* of Southampton, Dover, Barfleur, Caen, Ouistreham and Dieppe, harbours situated on both sides of the Channel.[29] Richard I and John renewed the privilege at the start of their respective reigns.[30] It is also of interest to note that Savigny and its daughter house, the abbey of Aunay, shared a property on the sea coast at Portsmouth, their possession of which was confirmed by the prior of Southwick.[31]

---

[20] 'Cartulary', *Capitula in episcopatu Abrincensi*, no. ciii and *Capitula in diversis episcopatibus*, no. v; Round, *Calendar*, no. 801.

[21] 'Cartulary', *Capitula in episcopatu Abrincensi*, no. civ; *Capitula in diversis episcopatibus*, no. vi.

[22] Ibid., nos viii and xlii; Round, *Calendar*, no. 802; *Regesta regum Anglo-Normannorum*, iii, ed. R.H.C. Davis and H.A. Cronne (Oxford, 1968), no. 802.

[23] 'Cartulary', *Capitula in episcopatu Abrincensi*, no. cv; *Capitula in diversis episcopatibus*, no. vii; Round, *Calendar*, no. 803.

[24] AN, L969, no. 392; 'Cartulary', *Capitula cartarum in episcopatu Redonensi*, no. xvii; *In diversis episcopatibus*, no. xv; Round, *Calendar*, no. 805; *Early Yorkshire Charters*, iv, pp. 28-30.

[25] 'Cartulary', *Capitula in diversis episcopatibus*, no. xliii.

[26] 'Cartulary', *Capitula in diversis episcopatibus*, nos xxi and xlv; Round, *Calendar*, no. 806.

[27] 'Cartulary', *Capitula in diversis episcopatibus*, no. iv.

[28] Ibid., no. ix; Round, *Calendar*, no. 804a.

[29] AN, L966, no. 24; Round, *Calendar*, no. 825; 'Cartulary', *Capitula in diversis episcopatibus*, no. xxxvii.

[30] Ibid., nos lxi, lxix.

[31] Ibid., no xlviii; Round, *Calendar*, no. 842.

A charter which was not included in Round's *Calendar* allows us to examine contacts other than economic ones between Savigny and the British Isles.[32] At an unspecified date between 1179 and 1186, during the rule of Abbot Simon, a certain Simon de Cardiff gave the abbey an annual rent of 40 shillings sterling from his estate at *Topefeld* (Toppesfield, Essex?) to contribute to the monks' allowances on St Bernard's day. Simon made this grant because he had become a monk at Savigny in order to atone for his sins. The idea of crossing the Channel to become a monk at Savigny was therefore one which could be entertained during the twelfth century.

The case of Ewan, the third abbot of Savigny, is also important. He was a monk of Savigny who had been born at Avranches of English parents, and had become the first abbot of Furness in 1127, before returning to Savigny as abbot in 1139. Fifty years later, Abbot William, who was elected in 1187, was known as William of Dover, suggesting that he was a member of an originally Norman family which had established itself in England. The best-known English abbot of Savigny was undoubtedly Stephen of Lexington, an Englishman by birth who studied in Paris before becoming a monk at Stanley, the daughter house of a daughter house of Savigny, of which he was soon afterwards abbot, and who was elected abbot of Savigny in 1229. In his case an ecclesiastical career provided the opportunity to move across the Channel several times.[33]

I have omitted the other abbots of Savigny, either because they were of Norman origin or because we don't have information about them. If the biographical details of some abbots' lives are scarce, our knowledge of ordinary monks is inevitably even less specific. Several other charters like that relating to Simon de Cardiff which contain grants made by individuals who subsequently became monks exist in Savigny's archives, but none of them relate to Englishmen. Aside from cases where such charters survive, the information that we have about the monks is of the briefest kind, most often no more than a simple mention of a name in a list of witnesses. Among those whose names suggest an English origin in the twelfth century are William de Neath (Neath was a daughter house of Savigny in the diocese of Llandaff) and a William *Anglicus*,[34] and, in the thirteenth century, a Thomas *Anglicus* and another William *Anglicus*.[35] The eponym *Anglicus* is not, however, always a certain proof that its bearer was English.

It is also necessary to chart the foundation of Savigny's daughter houses in England. At the time of the merger with Cîteaux in 1147, Savigny was the head of an Order which consisted of thirty-one abbeys, of which twenty-four were daughter houses, five were grand-daughters, and one a great grand-daughter.

---

[32] 'Cartulary', *Capitula in episcopatu Baiocensi*, no. lxi.

[33] For information on the abbots, Auvry, *Histoire de la congrégation*, passim, where use was made of the surviving *Vitae*.

[34] Ibid., iii, p. 124.

[35] AN, L976, no. 1091; a charter of 1232 subsequently added to the 'Cartulary', which is no. 146 in Delisle's copy of the 'Cartulary'.

When subsequent foundations are taken into account, Savigny's family ultimately consisted of fifty abbeys.[36] Out of these fifty, only five were houses for women; in contrast to the houses for men, all these were on the Continent. Is the creation of the autonomous order of Sempringham the reason for the absence of houses of Savignac nuns in England?

The situation is very different when it comes to abbeys for monks. Out of the twenty-seven dependencies of Savigny founded before 1147, a little over half, namely fourteen, were in the British Isles, not only in England but also in Wales and Ireland.[37] The vast majority of the founders of these abbeys, and of the donors of property, were of continental origin, even if their origins were not always recent. This is true, for example, of Richard de Granville, a knight in the entourage of the earl of Gloucester, who founded Neath in 1130; of Baldwin de Reviers, the first earl of Devon, whose father was a Norman, who founded Quarr in 1132; of Rannulf Gernon who founded Basingwerk in 1133 and Calder in 1135; of William de Montfichet, whose father was the founder of Stratford in 1135; and so on. Two foundations are attributable to Stephen of Blois: Furness, which was founded in 1127 before he became king, and Buckfast in 1136 after his coronation. The latter's foundation charter is in the cartulary of Savigny.[38] The foundation of Coggeshall was due to Stephen's wife, Matilda of Boulogne. Only two foundations owed nothing to the Continent, and neither of these was strictly speaking in England: these were Rushen, founded in 1135 on the Isle of Man by Olaf Kleinig; and St Mary's, Dublin, whose foundation in *c.* 1139 is obscure, but is attributed to the Irish.

Savigny's archives also contain evidence of a failed English foundation. This is an undated charter of Aubrey Gernon who granted to Savigny three ploughlands at *Acheleia* (Oakley, Essex), the wood of *Wittriggeho* (unidentified), a mill, a fishery and a pond so that an abbey could be founded in honour of the Virgin Mary.[39] No known list of the daughter houses of Savigny mentions either a foundation at Oakley or one made by Aubrey Gernon. The charter probably refers to an attempt at a foundation which failed. This failure can probably be explained by a letter of Aubrey Gernon, which is also in the Savigny cartulary, which asks bishop Robert of London to protect the donation of the manor of Oakley against the claims of Aubrey's brother Rannulf.[40]

The foundation of Savigny's fourteen British daughter houses was, after the first expansion to Furness in 1127, spread throughout the 1130s, with an average rate of foundation of more than one abbey per year. On the other hand, no foundation took place between the establishment of the last English

[36] P. Leopoldus Janauschek, *Originum cisterciensium*, i (Vienna, 1877).

[37] Dom Léon Guilloreau, 'Les fondations anglaises de l'abbaye de Savigny', in *Revue Mabillon*, 5 (1909-10), pp. 290-335.

[38] 'Cartulary', *Capitula in diversis episcopatibus*, no. x; Round, *Calendar*, no. 800.

[39] AN, L967, no. 91; 'Cartulary', *Capitula in diversis episcopatibus*, no. xvi; Round, *Calendar*, no. 808.

[40] 'Cartulary', *Capitula in diversis episcopatibus*, no. xvii; Round, *Calendar*, no. 807.

daughter house at Coggeshall in 1140 and the merger with Cîteaux in 1147. On the Continent, the last daughter house of Savigny founded before 1147, La Vieuville, was established in 1140 at a place granted to Savigny in 1137. Although it is generally agreed that it was the difficulties which Savigny undoubtedly encountered in maintaining its authority over its English daughter houses which eventually caused the abbot of Savigny to amalgamate his order with the Cistercians, the absence of any foundations between 1140 and 1147 must be a further indication of the order's internal problems. A further explanation must be the difficulties caused during these years by the war between Stephen and the Empress Matilda.

The course of the conflict between Savigny and Furness can be partly followed thanks to a very interesting dossier of material preserved in Savigny's cartulary and at the Archives Nationales in Paris. Calder, a daughter house of Furness, had been devastated in 1137 during the war between King Stephen and the Scots.[41] When Furness refused to take in the monks who had been driven out of Calder, they embarked on several years of wandering and hardship before finally settling at Byland in 1143 as a result of the generosity of Roger de Mowbray. Given the poor reception which he and his monks had received at Furness, the former abbot of Calder asked the general chapter to permit the new community to be directly subject to Savigny. This was agreed but was not willingly accepted by Furness. A bull of Lucius II provisionally decided the affair.[42] Indeed Furness sent some other monks to reestablish the community at Calder.

The second episode in the conflict occurred in 1148, after the merger with Cîteaux. The abbot of Furness sought to profit from the merger in order to be released from Savigny's jurisdiction. The matter was assigned to two papal judges-delegate, the archbishop of Rouen and the bishop of Lisieux, who decided the dispute in Savigny's favour, after accepting as proof a charter of King Stephen and a bull of Eugenius III, both of which are in the cartulary.[43] The archbishop of York, in whose diocese Furness lay, was informed of the judgement.[44] Finally, in 1153, taking advantage of the election of a new abbot

---

[41] Auvry, *Histoire de la congrégation*, ii, pp. 366-68.

[42] See F.R. Swietek and T.M. Deneen, 'Pope Lucius II and Savigny', *Analecta cisterciensia*, 39 (1983), pp. 3-25.

[43] For Stephen's grant of the abbey of Furness to Savigny, 'Cartulary', *Capitula in diversis episcopatibus*, no. xi; *Regesta*, iii, no. 803; Round, *Calendar*, no. 804. For Eugenius III's bull which contains a list of the daughter houses which were obliged to accept Cistercian customs, *Capitula privilegiorum Romanorum*, no. ix.

[44] For the letter of the judges-delegate to the abbot and community of Furness, AN, L970, no. 531 and 'Cartulary', *Capitula in diversis episcopatibus*, no. xiii (Round, *Calendar*, no. 813); letter of the archbishop of Rouen to the monks of Furness, AN, L970, no. 530 and *Capitula in diversis episcopatibus*, no. xxiii (Round, *Calendar*, no. 814); letter of the archbishop of Rouen to the archbishop of York, AN, L970, nos 529, 532, and *Capitula in diversis episcopatibus*, no. xii (Round, *Calendar*, no. 815).

of Savigny, the abbot of Furness called into question the nature of Savigny's rights over the abbey of Byland as they had been established ten years previously by the general chapter of the Savignac order. The general chapter of Cîteaux gave the responsibility for the settlement of the dispute to Ailred of Rievaulx, who was given full powers to reach a verdict. After an inquest, he recognised that Byland was directly under Savigny's authority. The abbot of Furness submitted unconditionally.[45]

Savigny's problems with its English daughters had been the cause of the merger with Cîteaux. Savigny established only two more houses after 1147, and both of these were in France, in the dioceses of Bayeux and Le Mans.[46] The growth after 1147 of the Savignac family was predominantly the achievement of its daughter houses. If the Savignac Order before 1147 was in some respects an international one, it was because it had spread through the foundation of daughter houses directly subject to Savigny both in France and England. In contrast, Savigny's daughters, both French and English, expanded only on the side of the Channel on which they were established. An extreme example of this is supplied by the abbey of Combermere (Cheshire), in the diocese of Coventry, which established three daughter houses, likewise situated in the diocese of Coventry. The single exception is supplied by the abbey of Aunay, in the diocese of Bayeux, which established one of its two daughter houses in the diocese of Lincoln. The Savignac Order was therefore both French and English, but only because of Savigny itself, not thanks to its daughters. Its international role was confined to a relatively short period of time.

I want finally to examine the attitude of the English kings towards the abbey. As has already been pointed out in the discussion of exemption from payments on the transport of goods, Savigny benefited from constant royal protection. During the twelfth century Savigny was the recipient of forty-one royal charters, from the reign of Henry I to the reign of John. Among these were Henry I's confirmation of the foundation charter and Stephen's foundation of the two daughter houses of Furness and Buckfast, the exemptions from toll already mentioned, numerous confirmations of both specific and general grants, and finally a number of gifts made by the kings themselves.

With the exception of the two vineyards at Avranches which were given by Henry I,[47] all the grants made by the kings were located in the Passais, the region which was the last to be integrated into the duchy of Normandy, and which formed a sensitive frontier with Maine. This shows the trust which was placed in the abbey. Henry I's initial grant of Saint-Auvieu, Dompierre and la

---

[45] AN, L967, nos 130, 131; 'Cartulary', *Capitula in diversis episcopatibus*, no. xviii; Round, *Calendar*, no. 819.

[46] The abbeys of Barbery and Champagne.

[47] 'Cartulary', *Capitula in episcopatu Abrincensi*, no. vi.

Fresnouse[48] was subsequently rounded off by Henry II[49] and John. [50] However, despite the favour from which the abbey was able to benefit, there is a significant gap in the chronological sequence of royal charters, which occurs during the period from 1162 to 1170, exactly the years when Thomas Becket was given asylum by the Cistercian abbey of Pontigny. Henry II would certainly have made Savigny feel the impact of his resentment against the entire Cistercian Order. However, we know that the first meeting between papal legates and Henry's ambassadors responsible for bringing to an end the conflict caused by Thomas Becket's murder was held at Savigny, a meeting which led ultimately to the ceremony which took place at Avranches in 1172.[51]

One of Henry II's general confirmation charters for Savigny might have been obtained at the request of a monk of Savigny, St Haimo. According to the *vita* of this saintly monk, which was written by a monk of Savigny in around the year 1180,[52] St Haimo met Henry II on a number of occassions, in particular in Brittany in 1167, when St Haimo persuaded Henry not to attack the Bretons on the day of SS. Peter and Paul. According to the biographer, the successes which the king achieved later in the year showed him how sensible Haimo's advice was, and he therefore listened readily to him. Haimo also met Henry II at Barfleur, where the king confessed his sins to him and to Rotrou, the future archbishop of Rouen. Henry again confessed his sins to St Haimo at Domfront, where the saint was able to secure royal forgiveness for a knight who had plotted against Henry. The Empress Matilda also confessed to him on one occasion. The biographer recounts the saint's numerous visions. One of them, in which Henry II appeared, was interpreted as a sign announcing the friendship which was going to bind Henry and the saint. Henry's confession at Barfleur, and also Matilda's, were both preceded by a vision in which Haimo met the future penitent. The royal grants therefore represent in material terms the spiritual links which existed between the English king and Savigny.

The seizure of the duchy in 1204 of course influenced Savigny's links with England. All grants from England come to an end. During the first half of the thirteenth century only four charters out of more than 400 are concerned with England. Three of them, dating from 1219, deal with an annual payment which Savigny was obliged to make to a clerk named Thomas of *Tuifort* (orTifort), which it was agreed he need no longer pay.[53] The clerk promised to return the charter recording the original agreement to the abbey after his return to England. The other charter is an agreement between Savigny and one of its English daughter houses, Dieulacres.[54]

[48] 'Cartulary', *Capitula in episcopatu Cenomanensi*, no. i; Round, *Calendar*. no. 793.
[49] 'Cartulary', *Capitula in episcopatu Cenomanensi*, no. iv.
[50] Caen, Musée des Beaux-Arts, collection Mancel, MS 302, p. 421; Round, *Calendar*, no. 845.
[51] F.R. Swietek, 'King Henry II and Savigny', *Cîteaux, commentarii cistercienses*, 38 (1987), fasc. 1-2.
[52] 'Vita beati Hamonis', ed. E.P. Sauvage, *Analecta bollandiana*, 2 (1883), pp. 475-560.
[53] AN, L968, no. 222; L978, no. 1370; L966, no. 28bis.
[54] AN, L969, no. 424.

The role of the English kings as protectors and benefactors of Savigny was not taken over by the kings of France. There is a charter of 1205 in which the new count of Mortain installed by Philip Augustus, Rainald de Dammartin, confirmed the various grants made in the Passais by the English kings.[55] In this charter, Rainald de Dammartin portrayed himself as the successor of the Plantagenets. But his efforts were limited to a single charter. We have to wait until 1212, that is, eight years after the Conquest, for any charter of Philip Augustus in favour of Savigny.[56] Then it is a text in stereotypical form, by which Philip orders his *baillis* in Normandy to allow Savigny the rights and liberties it had enjoyed in the time of Henry II and Richard I. Identical charters were issued at the same time for the abbeys of Le Bec, Saint-André-en-Gouffern and Saint-Etienne of Caen. This is the only French royal charter in Savigny's archives from the whole of the first half of the thirteenth century. Savigny did indeed have an abbot of English origin in the middle of the thirteenth century, but this was Stephen of Lexington, the future abbot of Clairvaux. By this time, Savigny was no more than a stepping-stone in the ecclesiastical career of a great Cistercian.

[55] AN, L967, no. 141.

[56] *Recueil des actes de Philippe-Auguste*, ed. H.-F. Delaborde, J. Monicat et al, 4 vols (Paris, 1916-79), iii, no. 1249, pp. 371-72.

13

William Talvas, Count of Ponthieu, and the Politics of the Anglo-Norman Realm

Kathleen Thompson

When Robert, count of Alençon and Sées, changed his allegiance from King John to Philip Augustus in January 1203, it was, in the words of F.M. Powicke, 'the beginning of the end' for John's rule in Normandy.[1] Robert could control the services of over a hundred knights and his lands clustered around the important route through Argentan which joined Normandy to Le Mans and the southern Plantagenet domains.[2] His defection was, if not crucial, then at least highly significant, for it indicated the King of England's loss of support among the Norman aristocracy on whom his ancestors had relied so heavily for the continuance of the Anglo-Norman realm. Little detailed work has been done in English on the barons of twelfth-century Normandy, so there is no real explanation as to why certain families, who had served the dukes of Normandy over several generations, should have suddenly decided to throw in their lot with the French king.[3] It will be the argument of this essay that shifts in their attitudes can be detected during the course of the twelfth century and in particular during the lifetime of the generation represented by Robert's grandfather, William Talvas, count of Ponthieu.

William's paternal family had its roots at Montgommery in central Normandy, but had taken on an important position as marcher lords on the southern borders of Normandy through an advantageous marriage during the eleventh century. They had enjoyed some thirty-five years of landed influence in both England and Normandy before King Henry I had evicted William's father, Robert of Bellême, from England in 1102 and imprisoned him for life in

---

[1] I am very grateful to Dr Marjorie Chibnall and Dr David Crouch for their comments on an earlier draft of this essay. The quotation is taken from F.M. Powicke, *The Loss of Normandy 1189-1204* (Manchester, 1913), p. 234.

[2] *Red Book of the Exchequer*, ed. H. Hall, Rolls Series (London, 1897), ii, p. 626.

[3] D. Crouch, *The Beaumont Twins* (Cambridge, 1986); L. Musset, 'Aux origines d'une classe dirigeante: les Tosny, grands barons normands du Xe au XIII siècle', *Francia*, 5 (1978), pp. 45-80; idem, 'Quelques problèmes posés par l'annexion de la Normandie au domaine royal français', *La France de Philippe Auguste: le temps des mutations*, ed. R.-H. Bautier (Paris, 1982), pp. 291-307. For the most detailed work, Powicke, *Loss of Normandy*, appendix ii, 'The Division of the Norman Baronage', pp. 482-520.

1112, confiscating all of his Norman patrimony. Historians have, by and large, been reluctant to rescue the family from this low point. Dr. Chandler in her recent paper even goes so far as to suggest that this was the end of the Montgomery family. In fact the events of 1112 did not mean a complete eclipse, but marked the beginning of the family's emergence as exclusively French nobles.[4]

The author of the recovery in the family's affairs was Robert of Bellême's only legitimate son, William, a man whose career has been largely neglected in comparison with the interest shown in his immediate forbears.[5] Precise details of William's date of birth are not available, but when his father granted the family foundation of Saint-Leonard of Bellême to Marmoutier in 1092, he associated his brothers with the gift, so at that date they were probably his heirs and William's birth must therefore be tentatively dated to 1093 or later. He was the only child of what Orderic would have us believe was the extremely unsuccessful marriage between Robert of Bellême and Agnes, the heiress of the small, but strategically significant, county of Ponthieu on the north-eastern borders of Normandy.[6] The choice of his Christian name was perhaps surprising. There appear to have been no earlier Ponthevin counts called William and his father's family had not used the name for a generation. Its choice must therefore represent either a compliment to the king or perhaps more likely was a reference to Robert of Bellême's maternal grandfather, William Talvas, and his great-grandfather, William of Bellême. William, count of Ponthieu, never in fact described himself as Talvas (the shield), although both Orderic Vitalis and Robert of Torigni use this nickname, which was applied to his grandmother and great grandson, as well as to his great grandfather.[7]

William did not attest his father's acts in the late 1090s and early 1100s, although there were precedents within his family for childhood attestations. His appearance in his father's act given at Marmoutier in March 1106 therefore marks the beginning of his adult career.[8] The reference to *terra sua* in that act

[4] On the family background, J.F.A. Mason, 'Roger de Montgomery and his Sons (1067-1102)', *Transactions of the Royal Historical Society*, 5th series, 13 (1963), pp. 1-28; K. Thompson, 'The Norman Aristocracy before 1066: The Example of the Montgomerys', *Historical Research*, 60 (1987), pp. 251-63; eadem, 'Robert of Bellême reconsidered', *A-NS*, 13 (1991), pp. 263-86: G.H. White, 'The First House of Bellême', *Transactions of the Royal Historical Society*, 4th series, 22 (1940), pp. 67-99; J. Boussard, 'Le seigneurie de Bellême aux Xe et XIe siècles', *Mélanges d'histoire du moyen âge dediées á la mémoire de Louis Halphen* (Paris, 1951), pp. 43-54; K. Thompson, 'Family and Influence to the South of Normandy in the Eleventh Century: The Lordship of Bellême', *Journal of Medieval History*, 11 (1985), pp. 215-26; V. Chandler, 'The Last of the Montgomerys: Roger the Poitevin and Arnulf', *Historical Research*, 62 (1989), pp. 1-14.

[5] *L'art de vérifier les dates* (Paris, 1783-7), p. 688; *CP*, xi, p. 97; J. Le Patourel, *The Norman Empire* (Oxford, 1976), pp. 77-78.

[6] *Cartulaire de Marmoutier pour le Perche*, ed. P. Barret (Mortagne, 1894), no. 13. For his parents' marriage, Thompson, 'Robert of Bellême', pp. 268-69. On the comital family of Ponthieu, *Carmen de Hastingae Proelio of Guy Bishop of Amiens*, ed. C. Morton and H. Muntz (Oxford, 1972), pp. xxx-xxxii.

[7] White, 'First House of Bellême', p. 82.

[8] *Recueil des actes des comtes de Ponthieu*, ed. C. Brunel (Paris, 1930), no. 16.

implies that William had acquired control of some property by then and this was almost certainly his mother's inheritance of Ponthieu.[9] He seems not to have fought at Tinchebrai but can be found administering both Ponthevin and Norman estates before 1112.[10]

After the imprisonment of his father in November of that year, William assumed sole responsibility for the family's Norman lands. His position as acting head of the family is clearly indicated by his confirmation to the family foundation of Saint-Leonard at Bellême.[11] He was not to enjoy possession of his father's estates for long. Perhaps underestimating the extent of King Henry's hostility, William concentrated his own efforts on the defence of Ponthieu and left his ancestral home of Bellême in the hands of the local lords. It was a disastrous miscalculation for, when its castle fell to the king on 3 May, Bellême was lost to the family, never to be recovered, and all William's lands in Normandy were confiscated.[12]

William was then left in possession only of Ponthieu. The so-called 'Hyde chronicler', who seems extremely well-informed about events on the Norman borders in the 1110s, stresses William's energetic opposition to Henry. He clearly fostered links with Henry's enemies, in particular with his overlord, King Louis VI of France.[13] At some date shortly after 1112 William married Ella, daughter of the duke of Burgundy, who was the widow of a count of Toulouse, a cousin of the French king and niece of the future pope Calixtus II.[14] As well as a network of useful contacts the marriage brought William a

[9] His mother, Agnes, had probably just died for Robert dropped all use of the title count of Ponthieu, Thompson, 'Robert of Bellême', p. 277 n. 65. Agnes's last datable act was to recommend a cleric for preferment in 1102, *Recueil des historiens des Gaules et de la France* (Paris, 1738-1904), xv, p. 192.

[10] *Ponthieu*, ed. Brunel, no. 17; K. Thompson, 'Une acte supposée de Guillaume le Bâtard', *Annales de Normandie*, 34 (1984), pp. 411-12.

[11] *Ponthieu*, ed. Brunel, no. 18; Orderic specifically describes William Talvas defending Ponthieu, Orderic, vi, p. 182; Suger, *Vie de Louis VI le Gros*, ed. H. Wacquet (Paris, 1964), p. 110 for Ponthevins fighting against Henry.

[12] Orderic, vi, p. 182, for the fall of Bellême. The position of William's holdings in northern Maine is unclear, as no acts conclusively datable to this period survive, but it seems likely that Henry's new found friendship with Fulk of Anjou, *iure uxoris* count of Maine, who fought with Henry at the siege of Bellême, ensured forfeiture there too.

[13] *Liber de monasterii de Hyda*, ed. E. Edwards, Rolls Series (London, 1866), p. 308. William attested a charter in Louis's presence among his *proceres*, *Cartulaire-chronique du prieuré Saint-Georges d'Hesdin*, ed. R. Fossier (Paris, 1988), no. 181.

[14] Orderic, vi, p. 430; J. Richard, 'Sur les alliances familiales des ducs de Bourgogne aux xiie et xiiie siècles', *Annales de Bourgogne*, 30 (1958), pp. 37-46. Ella's first marriage had taken place in 1095, C. de Vic and D. Vaissete, *Histoire générale de Languedoc*, ed. A. de Mege (Toulouse, 1840-46), iii, no. 268, pp. 602-03. Dr Keats-Rohan suggests that Orderic may have confused Ella and her aunt of the same name, so that William did not in fact marry the count of Tripoli's widow, K. Keats-Rohan, 'The Prosopography of Post-Conquest England: Four Case Studies', *Medieval Prosopography*, 13 (1993), p. 41.

widely-travelled and capable wife, perhaps somewhat older then he, who seems to have adapted as readily to life in Ponthieu as to that in Toulouse or Tripoli, the centres of her first husband's power. William's Ponthevins are listed among King Louis's allies against Henry I in the conflicts of the late 1110s and a member of William's family, his uncle Arnulf, who had spent some time at the court of King Henry's rivals, the Plantagenet counts of Anjou, can be found in Alençon in 1118 at precisely the point when that town rose in rebellion against Henry. There is also some evidence of a revolt at much the same time among former tenants of William's family, which added to Henry's difficulties in central Normandy and which may well have been engineered by the family.[15] In June 1119 Henry relented and restored much of the Montgommery-Bellême patrimony to William.[16] The Anglo-Saxon Chronicle even makes a special note of the settlement between Henry and the count of Ponthieu.[17]

William's property after 1119 was by no means as extensive as that administered by his family before 1102, but it is clear that, as soon as it was expedient, William resorted to his old family technique of division of labour. Just as Roger of Montgommery had looked after his English estates personally in the 1080s and early 1090s, leaving the Norman and Manceau property in the hands of Robert of Bellême, so William of Ponthieu, after no more than ten years of running the family business, passed his interest in Ponthieu over to his son Guy.[18] It is unclear why William should have decided to turn his back on Ponthieu and to devote himself to the Norman patrimony at this particular stage. Possibly his departure had something to do with the events in Flanders in the late 1120s. There are indications that William had enjoyed good relations with the Flemish counts.[19] The influential Flemish dowager Clementia (Baldwin VII's mother) was the Countess Ella's aunt and her name had been given to William and Ella's eldest daughter. After the murder of Count Charles the

---

[15] Suger, *Vie*, pp. 188-90. On Arnulf at Alençon and the rebellion in the Hiémois, Orderic, vi, pp. 206, 214.

[16] Orderic, vi, p. 224.

[17] *Anglo-Saxon Chronicle*, ed. D. Whitelock et al. (London, 1961), p. 187.

[18] Robert of Torigni, *Interpolations in William of Jumièges, Gesta Normannorum ducum*, ed. J. Marx (Rouen and Paris, 1914), p. 322. Brunel in his introduction to *Ponthieu*, p. vi nn. 2 and 3, suggests no later than 17 October 1129. William and Ella cannot have been married much before the end of 1112 since her first husband died in Tripoli in April of that year, De Vic and Vaissete, *Languedoc*, iv, p. 24. Guy, who was given the name of his father's maternal grandfather, cannot therefore have been more than fifteen years old in 1129. C.W. Hollister and T. Keefe, 'The Making of the Angevin Empire', *Journal of British Studies*, 12 (1973), pp. 1-25, comment on a similar naming practice, that of the Empress Matilda naming her eldest son for her father. Eleanor of Aquitaine was to name her short-lived first-born son after her father William.

[19] He witnessed an act of Count Baldwin VII, F. Vercauteren, *Actes des comtes de Flandre, 1071-1128* (Brussels, 1938), no. 55 and Baldwin's attack on Normandy in 1118 fell back on Abbeville, *Liber Hyda*, p. 315.

Good in 1127, William may not have wished to become too closely connected with the new count of Flanders, Robert Curthose's son, William Clito, for fear of offending his Norman overlord, King Henry. An uncomfortable decision had already had to be made in 1124, when William, together with his brother-in-law, Hugh of Burgundy, and other great nobles, had sent troops to Reims to assist their suzerain King Louis against the Emperor Henry V, ally and son-in-law of King Henry of England. Although no conflict had ensued between William's two lords, a division of family interests along clearly definable Ponthevin and Norman lines might be considered highly desirable.[20]

Once Guy was established as ruler of Ponthieu, William's role there diminished with the passing years. He approved several of his son Guy's acts and seems particularly to have been involved in the period immediately before the Second Crusade, in which both Guy and William Talvas were to participate. Guy was to die at Ephesus.[21] In 1148-49 William wrote to his grandson, the new count, John, and his daughter-in-law, the Countess Ida, strongly advising them, for the sake of Guy's salvation, to restore property to the priory of Abbeville, but the tone of the letter is that of a request rather than an order and implies perhaps a genuine concern for the eternal well-being of a dead son rather than the demands of the head of a family who has real authority.[22]

Judging from his later acts, William regained all his father's Norman property which lay in a compact bloc stretching from the upper reaches of the River Dives around Montgaroult, Vignats and Juvigny, through Sées and Alençon southwards to Neufchâtel, and other properties south of the forest of Perseigne in northern Maine. There were outliers of the old family heartland in the hills around Montgommery itself, estates near Troarn and property in the Cotentin.[23] Bellême itself was not returned, remaining in the hands of Henry's son-in-law, Rotrou, count of Perche.[24] Henry also withheld control of the fortresses, the custody of which had made William's father such a powerful figure in southern Normandy at the turn of the twelfth century.[25]

Almost immediately William seems to have entered upon a series of tidying exercises. In 1127 he granted to the abbey of Saint-Sauveur-le-Vicomte, a house never before patronised by his family, land in the modern *département* of Manche and also gave to Montebourg tithes in the Cotentin.[26] An act in

---

[20] Suger, *Vie*, p. 224.

[21] *Ponthieu*, ed. Brunel, nos 26, 33, 38.

[22] Ibid., no. 47.

[23] In contrast to the 'shreds of patrimony' described by J. Boussard, *Le gouvernement d'Henri II Plantagenêt* (Paris, 1956), p. 92.

[24] *Cartulaire Marmoutier Perche*, ed. Barret, no. 21 for Rotrou in Bellême.

[25] Orderic, vi, p. 224: Thompson, 'Robert of Bellême', p. 273.

[26] *Ponthieu*, ed. Brunel, nos. 19, 22 bis. The tithe of Saint-Germain-de-Tournebut was a confirmation of a gift which his ancestors had once made 'quam antecessores mei ipsi . . . olim dederunt'. Since William scrupulously mentions both sets of grandparents by name in his Saint-Sauveur-le-Vicomte act, this argues that the original donation was of some antiquity since he cannot put a name to his ancestors. The property may have been in the family as a result of a marriage in the tenth or eleventh century, Thompson, 'Montgomerys', pp. 251-56.

favour of Lessay covering possessions in the Manche is also likely to date from this period of consolidation, when William appears to have been rationalising his holdings and disposing of property not lying along the Almenêches/Sées/ Alençon axis.[27] But although William's lands in Normandy were restored in 1119, there is no evidence that he was received into royal favour. Only three records show him even in the presence of King Henry. In addition to legal proceedings in front of the king at Falaise in 1129, William witnessed two of Henry's acts at Rouen, one in November 1128, the other in the autumn of 1130.[28] Unlike his father, who had succeeded his father and grandfather in the office of ducal *vicomte*, William held no official position.[29] Relations between William and King Henry therefore appear to have been cool. Orderic makes it clear that William was only allowed to return to Normandy on sufferance, as a result of Angevin pressure.[30]

William may indeed have favoured the traditional alignment of his Bellême ancestors with the counts of Anjou, or perhaps simply recognised the rising star of Count Geoffrey Plantagenet and his wife, the Empress.[31] The siege and destruction by Geoffrey in 1135 of Beaumont-sur-Sarthe, which lay immediately to the south of William's lands, made certain his support for the Angevins.[32] Robert of Torigni says that William was the cause of the friction in 1135 between the Empress and her father.[33] Orderic, however, speaks only of Geoffrey's demanding castles which were owed as part of Matilda's marriage settlement.[34] William's loyalty to Henry was clearly less than whole-hearted and it may well be that custody of the castles within his honour, which he had been denied since his restoration in 1119, was the price he demanded from Geoffrey for his support of Matilda's claim to succeed her father. During 1135 William was repeatedly summoned to the king's court, but the fate of his father, Robert of Bellême, had made William perfectly aware of the risks involved in visiting Henry and he declined the invitation. Instead, in September of that year, he retired to his northern Manceau estates under the protection of Geoffrey of Anjou. Henry promptly repossessed William's Norman estates and enlarged the moats of Argentan, strengthening its defences in anticipation of an attack by his daughter and son-in-law.[35] He placed the castles of Alençon and Almenêches in the hands of Guignan Algason, one of his 'new men' and the holder of the office which had

[27] *Ponthieu*, ed. Brunel, no. 73.
[28] *Regesta regum Anglo-Normannorum*, ii, ed. C. Johnson and H.A. Cronne (Oxford, 1956), nos. 1553, 1570, 1680.
[29] For William's father, Thompson, 'Montgomerys', p. 260. On his father, C.H. Haskins, *Norman Institutions* (Cambridge, MA, 1918), p. 105.
[30] Orderic, vi, p. 224.
[31] For the earlier Bellême/Anjou connections, Thompson, 'Family and Influence', pp. 222-23.
[32] Orderic, vi, p. 444.
[33] Robert of Torigni, *Chronique*, ed. L. Delisle, 2 vols (Rouen, 1872-73), i, p. 200.
[34] Orderic, vi, p. 444.
[35] Ibid., p. 446.

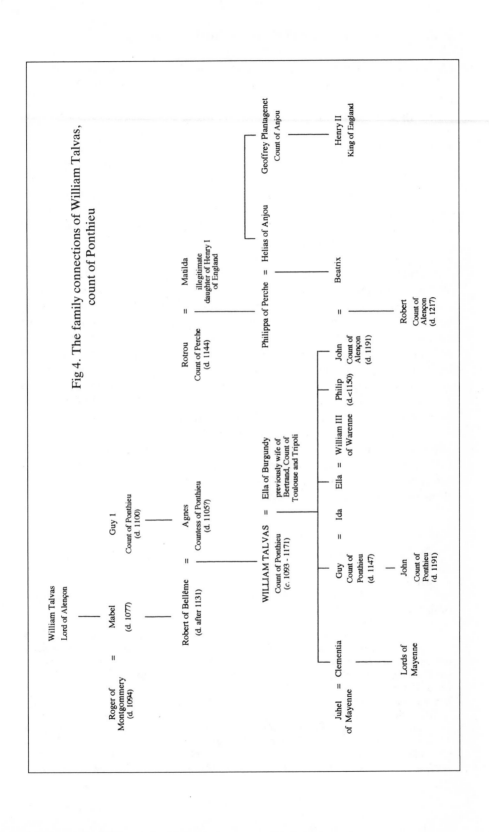

Fig 4. The family connections of William Talvas, count of Ponthieu

traditionally been a perquisite of William's family, *vicomte* of the Hiémois.[36]

In the event Henry did not go to war with his daughter. On his deathbed in late November 1135 he revoked the forfeitures he had enacted, allowing exiles to return and the disinherited to recover their ancestral estates, so it would have been possible for William Talvas to return to his lands lawfully.[37] However, he seems at this period to have been closely associated with his Angevin overlord and he remained with him. The Empress Matilda arrived in Normandy alone, in the first week of December, to take possession of her dowry castles of Argentan, Exmes and Domfront, which were readily surrendered to her by Guignan Algason.[38] Her husband, Geoffrey, followed with an army, accompanied by William Talvas and they were received by the men of Sées and other castellans from Talvas's honour. Robert of Torigni says that all property which Henry had taken before his death was restored to William Talvas at this point, together presumably with the much sought after castles.[39] William's son-in-law, Juhel of Mayenne, was entrusted with three castles on the Manceau border. With a bridgehead into Normandy secured, Geoffrey was set to pursue his wife's claim.[40] Unfortunately, he was temporarily distracted from the task by a rebellion in Anjou and it was left to William to defend this Angevin salient. While the Empress Matilda awaited the birth of her third son, safe behind Henry's new defences at Argentan, William repelled an attempt by supporters of King Stephen to retake Exmes in the summer of 1136.[41] William's support for the Angevin cause was clear-cut and probably prompted the anathema on his lands pronounced by the bishop of Sées in 1136 – the Norman churchmen almost universally supported the anointed king, Stephen. When Geoffrey returned to the Norman front in late September of that year William Talvas fought alongside him, but the Angevin army encountered stiff opposition in a particularly brutal campaign which saw some of William's tenants fighting on the other side. Geoffrey soon retreated.[42]

[36] On Henry's use of patronage, C.W. Hollister, 'Henry I and the Anglo-Norman magnates', *A-NS*, 2 (1980), pp. 101-02.

[37] Orderic, vi, p. 448.

[38] M. Chibnall, *The Empress Matilda, Queen Consort, Queen Mother, Lady of the English* (Oxford, 1991), pp. 66-67.

[39] Torigni, *Chronique*, i, p. 200.

[40] Ibid., i, p. 199. For Juhel's marriage to Clementia of Alençon, Robert of Torigni, *Interpolations*, p. 322. This must be dated around 1125 at approximately the period when William began to concentrate on his Norman lands, since in July 1128 Juhel, Clementia and their eldest son, Geoffrey, ratified an act in favour of Mont Saint-Michel, *Cartulaire de Saint-Michel de l'Abbayette*, ed. A. Bertrand de Broussillon (Paris, 1894), no. 10. Juhel had ceded Ambrières and Gorron to Henry I, *Book of Fees*, ed. H.C. Maxwell Lyte (London, 1920), p. 97.

[41] Orderic, vi, p. 462.

[42] Ibid., vi, p. 474 shows Engelram of Courtomer and Robert of Médavy in action against the Angevins. An act in favour of Saint-Martin of Sées by Engelram's tenant Robert Brito was approved by William Talvas, *Livre blanc de Saint-Martin de Sées* (Bibliothèque de l'Evêché de Sées) fo. 124v. Robert of Médavy was probably a relative of Hugh of Médavy, see below, note 59.

Thereafter William disappears from the narratives. Geoffrey's campaigns during the late 1130s into central Normandy were mounted through William's lands along the Le Mans/Alençon/Sées/Argentan corridor into Normandy.[43] Orderic describes the ravaging of the Hiémois and the protection money paid to the count of Anjou by local monks, but William's property, lying for the most part safely behind the Angevin lines, probably remained untouched.[44] His continued commitment to the Angevin cause is indicated by the marriage between his son, John, and Count Geoffrey's niece, Beatrix.[45] The marriage of his daughter, Ella, to William III of Warenne, the bulk of whose lands lay in England and who was to be a consistent supporter of King Stephen, may indicate that William felt that some access to Stephen's party was necessary. Although William and his other son-in-law, Juhel of Mayenne, had been the mainstay of Count Geoffrey's first advance into Normandy, William may well have sought to keep his options open in the apparent stalemate between 1137 and 1140, when the Angevins made very little headway.[46]

After 1137, having regained his lands and his castles, William appears to have withdrawn from active involvement in Norman ducal politics; he witnessed only two acts of his ally Geoffrey Plantagenet as duke of Normandy.[47] Possibly influenced by the interdict of 1136, he seems to have become preoccupied with his religious life, and in particular with his two foundations of Saint-André-en-Gouffern and Notre-Dame de Perseigne, respectively Savignac and Cistercian houses whose foundation charters both date from the middle 1140s.[48]

Perseigne was clearly the house which commanded most of William's affections. He and most of his family were buried there in preference to his grandfather's Benedictine house at Sées or the Montgommery family foundation at Troarn where his grandmother, Mabel, lay.[49] William's father-in-law, Eudes Borel, duke of Burgundy, had been an early patron of the Cistercian

---

[43] For other raids into Normandy along this route: D.C. Douglas, *William the Conqueror* (London, 1964), p. 72, for events leading to the battle of Varaville; *ASC*, ed. Whitelock, p. 171 for King Philip of France's attack on Argentan in support of Robert Curthose in 1094; Orderic, vi, pp. 466-74, 482-86, 514-16, 526-28, 546-50 for Geoffrey of Anjou's campaigns into Normandy.

[44] Ibid., vi, p. 482.

[45] For John's marriage, *L'art de vérifier les dates*, p. 688. In the early 1130s Beatrix's mother, Philippa, and her husband, Helias of Anjou, were probably regarded as the heirs of Philippa's father, the count of Perche, *Cartulaire de l'abbaye de la Sainte-Trinité de Tiron*, ed. L. Merlet (Chartres, 1883), i, no. xxxiii.

[46] William III of Warenne, the half-brother of Waleran, count of Meulan, had been born in *c.* 1119, *Early Yorkshire Charters*, viii, ed. C.T. Clay (Leeds, 1949), p. 2.

[47] *Regesta regum Anglo-Normannorum*, iii, ed. H.A. Cronne and R.H.C. Davis (Oxford, 1968), nos. 407, 747.

[48] *Ponthieu*, ed. Brunel, nos. 27, 32. Torigni, *Chronique*, i, p. 238 for a contemporary building boom.

[49] *Cartulaire de l'abbaye cistercienne de Perseigne*, ed. G. Fleury (Mamers, 1880), pp. cii-ciii. For Mabel at Troarn, Orderic, iii, p. 134-38.

Order so it is possible that Ella influenced her husband.[50] Alternatively it may simply have been a reflection of contemporary interests. In 1139 their eldest son Guy had founded a Cistercian house in Ponthieu at Valloires and there may even have been family rivalry at stake.[51]

In Saint-André-en-Gouffern William patronised the native Norman Order, again making generous provision for the house within his forest of Gouffern. While William gave the land for the establishment of the house, many of the endowments were made by local people often in quite small units, two acres here, a meadow there. William confirmed all these benefactions, but the impression is very much that of a house sponsored by its neighbours which the local magnate acknowledged and protected, rather than of the great lordly foundation which Perseigne clearly was.[52] It may also be significant that the forest of Gouffern was the location of the Plantagenet foundation of Silli-en-Gouffern. It is possible that William was anxious not to outdo his important neighbours.

In addition to his two major foundations William appears to have supported virtually every worthy ecclesiastical cause of the mid twelfth century. He granted property to the Templars, the canons of Sainte-Barbe-en-Auge and the priory of La Chaise Dieu;[53] customs and free passage at Alençon to Saint-Etienne of Caen;[54] a general confirmation to Saint-Evroult;[55] several confirmations to both Sées and Troarn and the tithe of a mill to Thiron.[56] He also confirmed benefactions to Almenêches, Cerisy, Lessay, Savigny, Sées, Saint-Vincent at Le Mans and the Hospitallers, all of which had been made by his followers.[57]

From among those followers it is possible to discern several who might

[50] Orderic, iv, p. 322.

[51] *Ponthieu*, ed. Brunel, no. 26.

[52] Ibid., no. 27, cf. remarks on patronage of the Cistercians by the dukes of Burgundy, C. Bouchard, *Sword, Miter, and Cloister: Nobility and the Church in Burgundy, 980-1198* (Ithaca, NY, 1987), pp. 132-33.

[53] S. Lowenfeld, 'Documents relatifs à la croisade de Guillaume comte de Ponthieu', *Archives de l'Orient Latin* (Paris, 1881-84), ii, pp. 251-55; *Ponthieu*, ed. Brunel, no. 57; AD Eure, H 1437, p. 11. I am grateful to Daniel Power for drawing my attention to this notice of an unpublished act of William, count of Ponthieu.

[54] *Recueil des actes de Henri II*, ed. L. Delisle and E. Berger (Paris, 1909-27), i, p. 278.

[55] *Ponthieu*, ed. Brunel, no. 74.

[56] For Sées: ibid., nos. 31, 45; for Troarn: no. 41; for Thiron: *Cartulaire de Tiron*, ed. Merlet, ii, p. 154.

[57] For Almenêches: L. Musset, 'Les premiers temps de l'abbaye d'Almenêches des origines au XIIe siècle', *L'abbaye d'Almenêches-Argentan et Sainte-Opportune*, ed. Y. Chaussy (Paris, 1970), p. 36; for Cerisy: *Recueil des actes des ducs de Normandie*, ed. M. Fauroux (Caen, 1961), no. 168, *Ponthieu*, ed. Brunel, no. 30 bis; for Lessay: *Pontieu*, ed. Brunel, no. 73; for Savigny: *Actes Henri II*, i, p. 186; for Sées: *Ponthieu*, ed. Brunel, nos. 45, 54; for Troarn: *Ponthieu*, ed. Brunel, nos 44, 42, 41; for Le Mans: *Cartulaire de l'abbaye de Saint-Vincent du Mans*, ed. R. Charles and S. Menjot d'Elbenne (Le Mans, 1886), no. 841; for Hospitallers: *Cartulaire générale des Hospitalliers de Saint-Jean de Jerusalem*, ed. J. Delaville le Roulx (Paris, 1906), i, p. 126.

reasonably be described as honorial barons and to fill out some of their careers with other material. Most important among them was the Médavy family. Hugh of Médavy, who was *dapifer* in the 1120s, had served with William's father, Robert of Bellême,[58] and was succeeded in the count's service by his sons, Payn and Gervase, who witness respectively thirteen and eight of William's acts and some of his son John's.[59] Médavy lies between Argentan and Sées, close to the Montgommery stronghold of Almenêches. It seems reasonable to see in the family middle-ranking barons who worked closely with the local magnate and found the relationship a rewarding one. From the lords of Bailleul William enjoyed a similar family tradition of loyalty. Rainald of Bailleul had been Roger of Shrewsbury's sheriff in Shropshire in 1086 and had married Earl Roger's niece, Amieria, widow of his predecessor as sheriff, Warin. It was he or his son of the same name who defied Henry I in 1119 in the months before Henry was eventually obliged to restore William Talvas's Norman property.[60]

Another family's links with William's went back three generations. A Pantulf had witnessed the earliest surviving Montgommery family act, dating from the 1030s, and Orderic describes the often stormy relations between the two families.[61] William Pantulf was, for example, suspected of the murder of William Talvas's grandmother, Mabel, and was responsible for the success of King Henry's campaign against Robert of Bellême in Shropshire in 1102.[62] It therefore is perhaps surprising to find Pantulfs in attendance on William Talvas.[63] Their lands appear to have been widespread and the implication seems to be that they were significant barons in their own right. They were attracted to William's family as the most important local magnates, but did not follow them as wholeheartedly as smaller fish. The lords of Montgommery for their part would have found the Pantulfs too independent perhaps for comfort, but too important to be ignored.

Four other associates of William may be usefully considered together as they raise some interesting questions about twelfth century Normandy. Three of these men appear in William's presence as witnesses either of the count's acts

[58] *Ponthieu*, ed. Brunel, no. 22 bis; Orderic, vi, p. 178.

[59] For Payn, *Ponthieu*, ed. Brunel, nos 30 bis, 57, 27, 76-78, 84, 22 bis, 20, 44, 42, 41; *Cartulaire de Saint-Vincent du Mans*, ed. Charles and Menjot d'Elbenne, no. 841; for Gervase, *Ponthieu*, ed. Brunel, nos 77-79, 84, 80, 45, 41-42.

[60] *Domesday Book* (London, 1783-1816), i, fo. 254r; Orderic, vi, p. 214.

[61] Orderic, iii, pp. 154-64.

[62] R. Eyton, *Antiquities of Shropshire* (London, 1854-60), ix, pp,. 157ff; C.W. Hollister, 'The Campaign of 1102 against Robert of Bellême', *Studies in Medieval History Presented to R. Allen Brown*, ed. C. Harper-Bill, C.J. Holdsworth and J.L. Nelson (Woodbridge, 1989), pp. 193-202.

[63] *Troarn*, ed. Sauvage, p. 28 (1149-71). William confirmed William Pantulf's benefactions to Saint-Evroult at the request of his grandson and Philip Pantulf made further gifts in William's presence, *Ponthieu*, ed. Brunel, no. 74.

or his son's and clearly belong to a burgeoning group of ducal administrators. Herbert, son of Bernard of Argentan, was later to farm the forest of Gouffern for the king. He went on to become an official in the ducal treasury at Caen.[64] Durand *prepositus* must surely be the bailiff whose joint account for Alençon is recorded in the 1180 Norman exchequer roll, while Robert of Neuville is described in an act of Henry Plantagenet as 'custodian of my forest of Argentan'.[65] In Herbert, Durand and Robert we can glimpse the kind of men who were being recruited as ducal officials during the mid twelfth century, but the best example from this group is William Tanetin. He came from another family with a history of links with the Montgommerys. In 1092 one Roger Tanetin had given property, which he held of earl Roger of Montgommery, to the Montgommery family foundation at Troarn. William Tanetin himself endowed Talvas's foundation of Gouffern in its very early days.[66] In the late 1120s William Tanetin replaced Hugh of Médavy as *dapifer* to the count. By the middle 1130s he was also a royal justice and, together with the bishop of Lisieux, presided over the hearing in which William Talvas himself was involved.[67] The implication is that there was now an alternative career available to a go-ahead middle-ranking baron beyond being drawn into the orbit and service of the local magnate. Where William Talvas's father and grandfather had been *vicomtes* or ducal agents, William himself held no such position and the office of justice, which was becoming increasingly important in the localities, was held by men of lower social standing.[68]

Of William's own officials some five chaplains are mentioned by name, by far the most frequent being Serlo, who attested eight acts and probably served longest.[69] Unlike the acts of his grandson the Ponthevin Count John, in which a notary first makes an appearance in the middle 1150s,[70] William's acts mention only one *clericus* and scribes, who would have staffed a writing office, never appear. Given the nature of some of William's surviving acts – letters addressed to the bishop of Sées and to his grandson and a grant of property to

[64] *Magni rotuli scaccarii Normanniae*, ed. T. Stapleton (London, 1840) i, p. 17; Powicke, *Loss of Normandy*, p. 278. Herbert's son Ralph witnessed an act of William Talvas's son John, AD Calvados, H 6511(3).

[65] *Livre Blanc de Sées*, fo. 124v; *Magni rotuli scaccarii Normanniae*, ed. Stapleton, i, pp. 18-20; *Troarn*, ed. Sauvage, p. 28; *Actes Henri II*, ed. Delisle and Berger, i, p. 12.

[66] *Calendar of Documents preserved in France*, ed. J.H. Round (London, 1899), no. 467; *Ponthieu*, ed. Brunel, nos 24 bis.

[67] *Ponthieu*, ed. Brunel, no. 19; Haskins, *Norman Institutions*, p. 98.

[68] Haskins, *Norman Institutions*, p. 95.

[69] *Ponthieu*, ed. Brunel, nos 30 bis, 22, 27, 77, 84, 20; *Cartulaire de Saint-Vincent du Mans*, ed. Charles and Menjot d'Elbenne, no. 841; *Livre Blanc de Sées*, fo. 124v.

[70] *Ponthieu*, ed. Brunel, p. lxvii.

two illegitimate sons, for example – it is highly unlikely that they can have been drafted elsewhere than the comital household.[71]

William's foresters are well represented in his acts: two are mentioned by name and the custodians of his forest of Almenêches are the recipients of a writ.[72] William seems to have been anxious to encourage the exploitation of the woods which must have covered a considerable part of his lands in the watershed between the valleys of the Orne and the Sarthe.[73] Most of William's benefactions were either tracts of forest or exemptions from tolls and customary dues. Grants of land as such were rare and seem to be confined to small units. The other major component of his largesse was rights of justice, which he lavished on Perseigne in particular, but also on Sées and Saint-Evroult. Only two references to William's court can be detected, however, in marked contrast to the wealth of material surviving from his father and grandfather's courts.[74] The picture which emerges is that of a great feudal magnate. William's wealth was based on land and the traditional sources of revenue available to him, such as exemptions, mills and justice, and he was supported by his ability to rely on the services of a honorial baronage.

Towards the end of his long life there are indications that William was beginning to withdraw from the running of his property, relying more and more on his son John, to whom he was to leave the Norman lands. Several acts of John, the son of Count William, survive from the 1150/60s and, although William served on a jury of barons as late as 1157, it is John who is briefly mentioned in Robert of Torigni's work for 1151.[75] In the campaigns of the early 1150s, when the Angevins sought to retain their hold on Normandy and to stave off the French king's attacks, William and his son seem to have slipped into the traditional role of their ancestors as marcher lords, when they faced raids from the Perche where the king's brother was established as stepfather of the young count.

William continued throughout his life to call himself count of Ponthieu, but his son was rather more equivocal about his status, sometimes describing himself as Count John, but more often than not referring to himself as John, son of Count William of Ponthieu, even after his father had died.[76] Contemporary writers were equally uncertain. John was count of Ponthieu to Benedict

[71] Ibid., nos. 29, 47, 83.

[72] Ibid., nos 22 bis, 79, 57.

[73] Forest revenue is discussed in J.A. Green, 'Unity and Disunity in the Anglo-Norman State', *Historical Research*, 62 (1989), pp. 126-27.

[74] *Ponthieu*, ed. Brunel, no. 80; *Cartulaire de Saint-Vincent du Mans*, ed. Charles and Menjot d'Elbenne, no. 619.

[75] For John's acts, *Perseigne*, ed. Fleury, no 3 (before 1156), no. 6 (before 1161); *Actes Henri II*, ed. Delisle and Berger, i, p. 203; *Cartulaire Saint-Vincent du Mans*, ed. Charles and Menjot d'Elbenne, no. 633; *Troarn*, ed. Sauvage, p. 27; *Cartulaire des abbayes de Saint-Pierre de la Couture et de Saint-Pierre de Solesmes* (Le Mans, 1881), no. 101; Torigni, *Chronique*, ii, p. 254.

[76] *Perseigne*, ed. Fleury, nos 343, 346.

of Peterborough, count of the Sonnois to Ralph of Diceto and simply Count John to the compilers of the 1172 inquest.[77] The dignity of count, which later members of the family assumed, reflected the personal standing of William as count of Ponthieu, rather than being a ducal creation such as that of Eu, Mortain or Evreux.[78] A county emerged because there was a count and a comital family in the region. In many ways this was analagous to the French experience and it is perhaps significant that William's world was essentially French.[79] Apart from his foray to the Holy Land, he can be found only in the castle of Alençon, at Sées, at Neufchâtel and by implication in Ponthieu. His preoccupations were not Anglo-Norman, as had been those of his father, his grandfather and his rulers, the dukes of Normandy.

There are two highlights in William's long and apparently unremarkable period as head of his family: the restoration of his Norman property in 1119; and his wholehearted commitment to the Plantagenets in 1135. His other activities suggest a certain caution; and even the location of his architectural patronage bespeaks discretion.[80] He apparently decided to exploit the traditional relationship of his Bellême ancestors with the counts of Anjou at the expense of his relationship with the duke of Normandy who was also king of England. In 1119 this paid off and he regained his Norman property. When that property was threatened in 1135, William again backed his Angevin lord, though reopening channels of communication with the English king while there was still a chance that Stephen might after all retain his hold on Normandy. William clearly therefore identified his interest as lying in Normandy. He appears never to have made any attempt to recover the English lands of his father and grandfather.[81]

[77] Benedict of Peterborough, *Gesta regis Henrici Secundi*, ed. W. Stubbs, Rolls Series (London, 1867), i, p. 45; Ralph of Diceto, *Opera historica*, Rolls Series (London, 1876), i, p. 371; *Red Book*, ed. Hall, ii, p. 626.

[78] In Philip Augustus's Register A the family appear among the dukes and counts of the King of France, *Recueil des historiens de la France*, xxiii, p. 682. Later family titles: 'Comte d'Alencon', *Catalogue des actes de Philippe Auguste*, ed. L. Delisle (Paris, 1856), nos 892, 936, 1223, 1342. Torigni, *Chronique*, i, p. 360 describes William as 'comes Sagiensis'; *Cartulaire normand de Philippe Auguste, Louis VIII, Saint Louis et Philippe le Hardi*, ed. L. Delisle, Mémoires de la Société des Antiquaires de Normandie, 2nd series, vi (Rouen, 1852), no. 1126, describes Robert III as 'Roberti quondam comitis de Alenceon'; *Perseigne*, ed. Fleury, pp. 13, 17 describes John I and Robert III respectively as 'comes Alenconis'; Robert III is described as count of Sées in royal records, *Rotuli Normanniae in turri Londinensi asservati* (Record commission, 1835), pp. 52, 66, 70, 71, 73, 75, 78.

[79] A.W. Lewis, 'Fourteen Charters of Robert I of Dreux, 1152-1188', *Traditio*, 41 (1985), pp. 156-57.

[80] I am grateful to Dr Lindy Grant for her comments on the scale of William's architectural patronage.

[81] There is only one somewhat dubious reference to English property in William's acts, *Ponthieu*, ed. Brunel, no. 31. The act which confirms Sées' possessions in the kingdoms of England and France granted by William's grandfather, Roger, survives only in a seventeeth-century copy and may represent a later formulation of an oral confirmation by William. It is accepted by Brunel as

continued

After Geoffrey Plantagenet's seizure of Normandy in 1144 William had at last an overlord of his choice. In a period of apparent contentment he issued foundation charters for his two major religious houses and participated in the Second Crusade, emulating the crusading traditions of his wife's family. But the unforeseen union of Normandy with the wider lands of Henry II in 1152 and Henry's acquisition of England in 1154 again challenged William's position. He was no longer the chief supporter and mainstay of an Angevin domination of Normandy. He was not even a border magnate balancing between his Norman and Angevin lords and looking for sweeteners from both. His property lay in the centre of what had become a continental empire where the interests of his new lord, Henry II, did not necessarily coincide with his own. In 1167 the new facts of political life were demonstrated when William, his son John and his grandson John, count of Ponthieu, were forced by Henry to surrender the strongholds of Alençon and La Roche Mabille, whose tenure had been the price of William's support for the Angevins in 1135.[82] By the end of his life in 1171 William's carefully thought out strategy had to some extent misfired. Henry II, like his grandfather before him, was an energetic ruler while William was merely one lord in his large dominions with little access to the perquisites of office which had made service in a similar empire attractive to his grandfather, Roger of Montgommery, in the previous century. In wholeheartedly supporting his Angevin overlord's design on the duchy of Normandy against the claims of a king/duke, William had inadvertently destroyed his own bargaining power as a border lord.

Yet William's career was far from being unsuccessful. He had consolidated his family's hold on their Norman property so that there was no further royal attempt at dispossession, even after John of Alençon's involvement in the Young King's rebellion of 1173.[83] Meanwhile the marriages of William's children and grandchildren established a network of contacts which allied his descendants to their neighbours.[84] Thenceforward the counts of Alençon were to be Franco-Norman in outlook and it would be only a generation before

genuine and so suggests a perception by William of the political realities of an English kingdom and French kingdom, in which lay a *comitatus de Alenconio*.

[82] Torigni, *Chronique*, i, p. 360. This policy probably provoked Count John into refusing to allow Henry's ally Matthew of Boulogne to cross Ponthieu in order to assist Henry in Brittany, ibid., ii, pp. 7-8.

[83] Benedict, *Gesta Henrici Secundi*, ed. Stubbs, i, p. 45.

[84] Robert III of Alençon's first wife was the Breton, Joanna of La Guerche, and his sisters married the Norman lords Robert fitz Erneis and William Malet. Descendants of William Talvas's daughter, Clementia, married the lord of Sablé and, naming patterns would suggest, the lord of Fougères. The lords of Mayenne continued to be closely associated with the counts of Alençon, *Perseigne*, ed. Fleury, nos 348 (probably late 1180s), 346 (1188), AD Calvados H 6511(6) (probably late 1180s), H 6511(9) (1171 x 91). By 31 January 1203, less than a month after the defection of his cousin Robert of Alençon, Juhel of Mayenne had joined King John's enemies, *Rotuli Normanniae*, p. 72. For Robert among the nobility of the Norman/Manceau borders, *Catalogue Philippe Auguste*, ed. Delisle, no. 1223 (July 1210).

Count Robert III realised that he occupied a position on the borders of the Plantagenet lands remarkably similar to that of his Bellême ancestors and of William Talvas. Robert III's position differed only in that he stood poised, not between a king/duke and the count of Anjou, but between a king/duke (who was also count of Anjou) and the Capetian king of France.

Jaques Boussard claims that Henry I reduced the Montgommery-Bellême family to silence, but it was by no means the silence of weakness. Unlike the Mortain family who were entirely replaced by Henry's nominees after 1106, the Montgommery-Bellême family had their boltholes in Ponthieu and northern Maine and William withdrew there and regrouped in 1112 and 1135. Henry I was ultimately unable to dislodge the family from Normandy and his grandson sought only to limit their power rather than destroy them. Just as William's decision to support the Angevins had unforeseen consequences in promoting the growth of a Plantagenet 'Empire' under Henry II, so Henry I's destruction of the cross-Channel commitment of William Talvas's family ultimately had a disastrous outcome for his descendant, King John. In confining the count of Alençon and Sées to one side of the Channel, Henry I created a Norman family of considerable resources and potential influence. With such clearly defined interests and no commitment outside the duchy, it is perhaps no surprise that William's grandson should see no further gain in the cross-Channel connection with England and was prepared to accept a new French overlord.

14

Normandy and England in 1180: The Pipe Roll Evidence

Vincent Moss

In recent years the use of pipe roll material as the focus for major historical studies has produced some very fruitful results. Judith Green's study of the English roll of 1129-30 led to important reconsiderations of both the structure of English administration and the political balance of forces vis-à-vis Henry I and his barons.[1] It also provided a decisive contribution to the rather vexed debate concerning the rise of 'new men' into governmental circles. From a rather different angle, Robert Stacey has used pipe roll material to produce an outstanding study of the economic resources of Henry III, providing a detailed consideration of the administrative structure of royal government.[2] T.K. Keefe, on the other hand, has utilised pipe roll evidence to produce perhaps the most important reconsideration of the relationship of the Angevin kings with their barons since J.C. Holt's *The Northerners*.[3] Where pipe roll material has not been the central focus of a historical work it is increasingly becoming a significant, even a necessary, ingredient: hence David Carpenter in his study of the minority of Henry III has used such material to reveal how weak royal government actually was during this transitional period.[4]

Given the generalised utilisation of pipe roll material in recent times, it may well be argued that a sober and nuanced consideration of the precise limitations of this type of evidence is overdue. However, given the relative underutilisation of this source, this is probably somewhat premature. Historians are still testing the pipe roll as an instrument to answer almost any and every question. Its precise limitations are not immediately apparent. A few words concerning its distinct strengths and weaknesses as a source will need to be stated.

Charters are, in a sense, the codification of social relations. They are normally highly specific and limited to a localised geographical area. Pipe rolls, on the contrary, are about government. They are unitary texts, not simply a

---

[1] J.A. Green, *The Government of England under Henry I* (Cambridge, 1986).

[2] R.C. Stacey, *Politics, Policy and Finance under Henry III, 1216-1245* (Oxford, 1987).

[3] T.K. Keefe, *Feudal Assessment and Community under Henry II and his Sons* (Los Angeles and Berkeley, 1983). See also, J.C. Holt, *The Northerners* (Oxford, 1961).

[4] D.A. Carpenter, *The Minority of Henry III* (London, 1990).

haphazard list of debts. They reflect the interrelated totality of royal administration. In fact they need a certain critical mass of such administration in order to come into being. Precisely because they are a direct product of government, they reflect and register changes in administration far more effectively than other sources. Indeed, the flexibility in pipe roll structure, evolving new forms of recording and organising information often itself gives us a unique insight into twelfth-century government. This kind of information was only infrequently recorded by the chroniclers while charters, given their specific nature, only occasionally reveal innovation in government. The major weaknesses of the pipe roll as a source stem precisely from these strengths. Government was still a relatively puny instrument in the twelfth century. Society was still intensely localised. The very unitary picture presented by the rolls often conveys a false and misleading impression of the relationship of state to society. The severe limitations of government is not a lesson that is immediately apparent from an examination of pipe roll material.

This essay will focus on the Norman roll of 1180 compared with the English roll of the same year. So far, the Norman rolls have not been the subject of a major historical study. Stapleton provided a useful if somewhat quirky and now outdated introduction to the English publication of the rolls in the 1840s.[5] Delisle made some telling and interesting comments, mainly of a social and economic nature.[6] Haskins touched on this material but the emphasis of *Norman Institutions* lies elsewhere.[7] Packard revealed a series of important supplementary texts relating to the Norman pipe rolls and made some important comments of a legal nature based on pipe roll evidence.[8] But he never utilised pipe roll evidence as a whole to produce generalised statements concerning Norman society and government. Later studies have attempted to utilise the rolls as evidence for the reasons behind the fall of Normandy. With the writings of Holt and Gillingham pipe roll evidence has taken on a new guise, that of a measure of fiscal strength between opposing powers.[9] Whilst this debate has led to a reconsideration of the later Norman rolls, albeit as purely quantitative measurements, the earlier rolls have received almost no serious attention. The one important exception to this was Powicke's *The Loss of Normandy*.[10] Whilst Powicke is best remembered for the later sections of this work, especially the consideration of the financial strain imposed upon

[5] T. Stapleton, ed., *Magni rotuli scaccarii Normanniae sub regibus Anglie*, i (London, 1840).

[6] L. Delisle, 'Des revenues publics en Normandie au douzième siècle', *Bibliothèque de l'Ecole des Chartes*, 10 (1848-49), pp. 173-210; 11 (1849-50), pp. 400-51; 13 (1851-52), pp. 105-35.

[7] C.H. Haskins, *Norman Institutions* (1918; repr. New York, 1960).

[8] S.R. Packard, 'Miscellaneous Records of the Norman Exchequer', Smith College Studies in History, 12 (1927). Also S.R. Packard, 'Normandy under Richard and John' (unpublished dissertation, Widener Library, Harvard University, 1927).

[9] J.C. Holt, 'The Loss of Normandy and Royal Finance', *War and Government in the Middle Ages*, ed. J. Gillingham and J.C. Holt (Woodbridge, 1984), pp. 92-106. See also J.C. Holt, 'The End of the Anglo-Norman Realm', *Proceedings of the British Academy*, 61 (1975), pp. 223-65; J. Gillingham, *The Angevin Empire* (London, 1984), pp. 71-73.

[10] F.M. Powicke, *The Loss of Normandy* (2nd edn, Manchester, 1961), pp. 36-78.

Normandy by castle-building, the earlier part, with its discussion of Norman administrative structure, does use early pipe roll material extensively. Even so, the limitations of the work are evident. It still comes as something of a shock, even in a relatively neglected field, to find that the totals of not a single category of income have been calculated for the rolls of 1180 and 1184.

A further problem, which highlights the necessarily tentative and initial nature of this essay, relates to the uneven character of Norman historiography. The amount of material devoted to the study of medieval Normandy is considerable. The problem, however, is that it is almost all clustered within a very specific time span. Starting from the formation of the principality, it reaches a peak in the reign of William the Conqueror, only to retreat into a very thin and sometimes murky trickle by the end of Stephen's reign. As a result, the classic Norman historians such as Delisle and Musset have relatively little to say about the 1180s. Haskins devoted just one, though useful, chapter to the reign of Henry II.[11] The new wave of Norman historians, such as Bates, Crouch and Green, though doing much to highlight crucial distinctions between England and Normandy before 1154, have yet to concern themselves extensively with the later period.[12] Indeed, except for the debate concerning the fall of Normandy the cupboard of historical research is somewhat bare. The situation is, in some ways, summed up by the most recent biography of Henry II, by W.L. Warren, a book which is far more informative about what were peripheral areas of the Angevin Empire, such as Scotland and Ireland, than it is about Normandy.[13] Yet Normandy, based on almost any analysis of the topic, was at the very heart of the Angevin Empire.

The year 1180 was by no means typical. It belonged to a period of relative peace before the onset of large scale Anglo-French warfare. In 1176 Richard of Ilchester had been, at the very least, involved in a major reorganisation of the Norman exchequer. Judith Green has suggested that this was nothing less than the refoundation of a fully functional Norman exchequer, citing the abundant evidence in the 1180 roll for the importance of the year 1176 to back up her case.[14] There are, however, some problems with this argument. The incomplete roll of 1180 is an impressive and detailed text. After the accession of Henry II as king of England it was eight years before the English exchequer produced a text which is comparable in terms of length and detail. To measure

---

[11] Haskins, *Norman Institutions*, pp. 156-95.

[12] Clearly, there are some exceptions to this general picture, e.g. D. Crouch, *William Marshal: Court, Career and Chivalry in the Angevin Empire, 1147-1219* (London and New York, 1990); L. Musset, 'Quelques problèmes posés par l'annexion de la Normandie au domaine royal français', *La France de Philippe Auguste: le temps des mutations*, ed. R.-H. Bautier (Paris, 1982), pp. 291-311.

[13] W.L. Warren, *Henry II* (1973, reprinted, London, 1991)

[14] 'It is not inconceivable that only from 1176 was there a fully restored exchequer in Normandy, meeting each year to hear the accounts of financial agents', J.A. Green, 'Unity and Disunity in the Anglo-Norman State', *Historical Research*, 62 (1989), pp. 122-23, with the quotation at p. 122.

exactly how much of the 1180 roll is missing is impossible. But an estimate based on areas present in the later Norman rolls but absent in 1180 suggests that as much as 30 per cent could well be missing. If this is so it is ten years before an English roll reached a comparable length.

It must also be remembered that England exceeded Normandy in both size and population.[15] English rolls are bigger than their Norman counterparts in each comparable year. The very size and detail of the 1180 roll makes a refoundation year as early as 1176 somewhat questionable. It could be argued that developed localised forms of Norman administration made a much greater rapidity of pipe roll development possible. But the 1180 roll shows no trace of such regional diversity in terms of organisation, accounting or recording methods. There should be some trace of these things if the roll were formed in 1176. For these reasons the case for a refoundation date of 1176, whilst tempting because of the arrival of Richard of Ilchester, is problematic. It might be more prudent to locate such an event in the 1160s, when Henry first turned to the question of Norman government, despite the absence of detailed supplementary evidence from the chronicles.[16]

The income of the 1180 Norman roll is far smaller than that of 1195 and 1198. To make use of J.C. Holt's terms, receipts combined with expenditure totalled 26,898 *livres angevins* compared with 88,191 *livres angevins* in 1195 and 175,922 *livres angevins* in 1198.[17] Furthermore, there is no evidence of large-scale infusions of English money to finance Norman expenditure. The first serious evidence for this is to be found in the roll of 1184.[18] By 1195 this infusion had become systematic.[19] The roll of 1180 dates from a time when Normandy was not under significant financial and military strain.

There are, however, definite advantages for an Anglo-Norman comparison in this year. The king was not present in England or Normandy for any real length of time during this year. The problem of the king's presence on one side or other of the Channel, stimulating income demand and thus distorting comparison, is thus avoided. Even more importantly, the vexed question of income paid into the chamber and not recorded on the roll is, as Richardson and Sayles pointed out, not a problem in 1180, given the absence of the monarch.[20] Little can be deduced from the rolls concerning the functioning of

---

[15] Gillingham, *Angevin Empire*, p.41.

[16] I will discuss this problem in my forthcoming thesis, 'Normandy and the Angevin Empire: A Study of the Evidence of the Norman Pipe Rolls', to be submitted for the degree of Ph.D. in the University of Wales. Given the complexity of the calculations on which this and other statements are based, I have preferred not to burden the footnotes of this essay with statistics which will be treated fully elsewhere.

[17] Holt, 'Loss of Normandy'; idem, 'The End of the Anglo-Norman Realm', passim.

[18] Moss, 'Norman Pipe Rolls'.

[19] Holt, 'Loss of Normandy'; idem, 'The End of the Anglo-Norman Realm' passim.

[20] H.G. Richardson and G.O. Sayles, *The Governance of Mediaeval England from the Conquest to Magna Carta* (Edinburgh, 1963), p. 232.

the English and Norman exchequers. The *Dialogue of the Exchequer* stresses that very significant differences in organisation did exist.[21] The 1195 roll records payments to two clerks of the Norman exchequer,[22] officials who are not mentioned in the *Dialogue*'s list of the treasury household. There is also evidence for a far more important role for local treasuries in Norman fiscal organisation.[23] The crucial texts for the analysis of the function of the Norman exchequer are, however, the *Extractus memorandorum*. These, together with an extant of a chamber roll, were published by Packard in the 1920s and, with the honourable exception of Strayer, ignored ever since.[24] An evaluation of these highly important, if oblique, texts will be the subject of another essay. An initial appraisal of this evidence strongly suggests that the *Dialogue*'s stress on difference is very much a correct and apt description.

In terms of layout the English and Norman rolls are very similar. One important difference concerns the sum of money owed for a farm which, as Haskins has pointed out, is recorded on the Norman rolls whilst in England it has to be calculated by elementary arithmetic. He also noted that the English rolls tend to supply more background information concerning fiscal payments.[25] The most important distinction in terms of social content has, however, to date not been addressed. Nearly a third of the farms recorded on the Norman roll were farmed by more than one farmer.[26] This practice was very rare in an English context. In 1180 there are just two examples and they appear in the entirely explicable circumstance of the combination of two English county farms.[27] In fact, there are three examples on this roll of a farmer accounting for two combined county farms: a practice which never occurred in a Norman context.[28] This tends to suggest that slightly wider circles were involved in administration in Normandy than in England. The case is reinforced when we note that twelve of these seventeen multiple farms were farmed by two or more farmers.[29] Having made these distinctions, it would be churlish to deny the broad similarity of farm and accounting methods employed by both sets of rolls.

---

[21] 'verum in pluribus et pene maioribus', Richard Fitz Nigel, *Dialogus de scaccario*, ed. and trans. C. Johnson, with corrections by F.E.L. Carter and D.E. Greenaway (Oxford, 1983), p. 14.

[22] Stapleton, ed., *Magni rotuli*, i, p. 225.

[23] Moss, 'Norman Pipe Rolls'.

[24] Packard, 'Miscellaneous Records of the Norman Exchequer'; J.R. Strayer, *The Administration of Normandy under Saint Louis* (Cambridge, 1932), pp. 6-11.

[25] Haskins, *Norman Institutions*, pp. 176-77.

[26] Seventeen of the sixty-one Norman farms were farmed by more than one farmer. For a complete list of all Norman farms and a detailed discussion see Moss, 'Norman Pipe Rolls'.

[27] J.H. Round, ed., *Magnus rotulus pipae de anno vicesimo septimo regis Henrici Secundi, 1180-1181* (London, 1909), pp. 101, 156.

[28] Ibid., pp. 10, 80 and 121.

[29] For the five farms with two farmers, see Stapleton, ed., *Magni rotuli*, i, pp. 29, 39, 70 and 85. For the twelve farms with more than two farmers see ibid, pp. 8, 9, 18, 28, 29, 38, 68, 75 and 82.

In analysing the content of the rolls, two types of measurement will be used, those of quality and quantity. The former consists of category types such as farm income, justice, feudal income and other types of royal or ducal income. Judith Green chose to combine land and farm income on the grounds that both stemmed from land held by the king.[30] I have chosen not to do so since, as is evident from the returns of the Norman rolls, farm income would include revenue from tolls, fairs and mills as well as pleas.[31] It is likely, however, that a significant, if unquantifiable, proportion of farm income was a product of agricultural production. Land income accounted separately from that of the farm only, represents a (perhaps) small proportion of total land income. Wardships, reliefs and scutage are to be treated separately from revenue such as *bernagium* and other royal rights. Finally, justice will have a relatively narrow definition, comprising basically all payments for amercements, agreements and access to right accounted for separately on the roll.

Four terms of quantitative analysis will be utilised. Potential income, total amount owed, actual income (the amount paid in) and expenditure are generally self-explanatory. What is not, and requires some discussion, is what I have called the yield ratio. This is actual income plus expenditure divided by potential income (what is owed) as expressed by a percentage. The advantage of this is that when we are dealing with income that the exchequer expects to receive, by using this formula we can measure the relative fiscal effectiveness of the different exchequers. However, it is clear that there were debts that the exchequer did not want to collect from barons held high in royal favour, and even large debts held as an insurance policy over potentially disloyal magnates.[32] The use of this yield rate therefore requires some care. Yet, even when it tells us nothing of consequence about effectiveness, it can help us to indicate examples of deliberate non-collection. Thus, on the English roll of 1180, payments for the 'goodwill of the king' total £1,601 sterling with only £108 paid and no expenditure.[33] This realises a very low yield ratio of 6 per cent. As it happens, there is no Norman equivalent to this income source – an issue to be considered later – but while the fiscal significance of this income is minimal, its political importance as a resource should not be underrated. The yield ratio works best as a measurement of direct income from royal or ducal farms, lands, wardships and regalian rights, or the collection of income made up of very small payments owed by a large number of people, where the incentive is on the exchequers to collect income. Even here, there were occasionally problems: a royal favourite like Robert de Stuteville could owe two years' income for the farm of Lillebonne (as it happens this was paid off in 1180),[34]

[30] Green, *Government of England under Henry I*, p. 55.
[31] Stapleton, ed., *Magni rotuli*, i, pp. 9, 17, 18, 27, 28, 30, 38, 40, 50, 58, 70, 73, 90, 97 and 104.
[32] A point stressed by Keefe, *Feudal Assessments*, pp. 122-40.
[33] Considerations of space prevent me from presenting detailed statistical arguments here. The data will be fully presented in Moss, 'Norman Pipe Rolls'.
[34] Stapleton, ed., *Magni rotuli*, i, p. 68.

but by and large the yield ratio is a useful tool of analysis for these kinds of income.

It must be said, especially in an essay which will stress difference, that there are considerable areas of broad similarity between England and Normandy as regards revenue sources. In both territories in 1180 farm income accounted for the majority of actual income combined with expenditure. In both areas the farm yield ratio is over 70 per cent.[35] While the number of wardships in each area was different, the right was exercised with fiscal vigour on both sides of the Channel. There is also a very rough equivalence of income from forest and separately accounted for land on the two rolls.

There are important areas of difference within this broad similarity. It seems very likely that, as Powicke has suggested, the Norman aid of the *vicomte* which, unlike the English aid, was a kind of land tax, was generally accounted for inside the Norman farm.[36] The evidence is very sketchy but it is more than possible that mill tolls, bakeries and fairs made up a higher proportion of the Norman farm compared with its English counterpart.[37] There were distinct types of Norman farm, known as *vicomte* and *prepositura* whose functions were very different. For Powicke at least, *vicomte* farms held a monopoly on justice whereas *prepositura* were far more based on land.[38] This is a distinction of far more significance than, for example, that between English county and borough farms. It can also be argued that the process of recovery by Henry II of land lost under the reign of Stephen found different fiscal forms in England and Normandy. In the latter, recovered land was reabsorbed into the farm. In England this land was accounted for separately in the roll.[39] Thus, the similarity between land separately accounted for in terms of income in both territories may well be more apparent than real.

Whatever formal similarity there may have been in forest income, the type of revenue and the administration of that income was very different. There was no Norman equivalent to the complex English forest eyre system analysed by Young.[40] At most, there is some evidence of a very local enquiry in Normandy in the 1195 roll concerning forest income.[41] English forest income tended to be about infringement of royal right. Norman forest income tended to concern the sale of forest produce. In Normandy, unlike England, there was the fiscally highly effective farm and a unique Norman revenue form *regardum*, which was partly drawn from the forests.[42] While forest income was important in Normandy and in England, its forms and methods of organisation were very

[35] Moss, 'Norman Pipe Rolls'.
[36] Powicke, *The Loss of Normandy*, pp. 47-48.
[37] Moss, 'Norman Pipe Rolls'.
[38] Powicke, *The Loss of Normandy*, pp. 77-78.
[39] Warren, *Henry II*, pp. 273-78.
[40] C.R. Young, *The Royal Forests of Medieval England* (Leicester, 1979), pp. 18-60.
[41] Stapleton, ed., *Magni rotuli*, i, p. 144. Also see Moss, 'Norman Pipe Rolls'.
[42] On *regardum*, see Moss, 'Norman Pipe Rolls'.

different. Despite these important qualifications, it would be foolish to deny the broad similarity of fiscal returns for farm, forest and wardship in England and Normandy.

Difference can be located at two levels. Firstly, at the level of income category. That is, a type of income in one territory with no equivalent in the other or, at least, only a partial and inexact counterpart. Secondly, major difference in terms of fiscal quantity or yield for common income forms in both territories.

Perhaps the best place to begin is with England. Besides payments for the king's benevolence, which we have already noted, there were also revenue forms of an interrelated character: payments for dealings with the king's enemies and fines for failing to swear fealty or do homage to the monarch. These again were politically important but, from a fiscal viewpoint, insignificant. The most financially important source with no Norman counterpart was that of regalian right.[43] Responsible for roughly 10 per cent of actual income plus expenditure it had a yield ratio of 98 per cent. The *murdrum* fine, a product of the Conquest, was a unique and by English standards a fiscally effective income form. Finally, there was an assortment of rights concerning lead, a payment for the granting of a charter and a series of other odds and ends not found in Normandy. The social terrain of most of these rights is relatively clear. They revolve around the special status of the king of the English, whose royal status generated a series of special rights not enjoyed by a duke even if, as in this case, the duke happened to be a king. This is not to say that kingship necessarily generated such power. It is to say that kingship could do this in the right social context in a way that dukedom could not.

The special rights enjoyed by the Norman dukes occupied a very different kind of political space. *Bernagium* was paid partly in money and partly in kind for the upkeep of the duke's hunting dogs.[44] *Regardum*, as noted above, was a type of fiscal payment levied on the duke's forest, but which also extended into other domains. *Vinum super venditum*, which finds an inexact and pale reflection in the English rolls, is a fiscal source based on the extensive wine trade conducted in Normandy.[45] *Crassus piscis* concerned ducal rights to whales found around the Norman coast.[46] The fiscal significance of these rights was not substantial. The actual income plus expenditure figure worked out at £1,028 5s 10d *livres angevins*: only 3.8 per cent of the total roll figure; though some small allowance must be made for *bernagium* payments in kind, which cannot always be converted into a fiscal form.

[43] For an impressive study of these rights see M. Howell, *Regalian Right in Medieval England* (London, 1962), pp. 32-48.

[44] D. Bates, *Normandy before 1066* (London and New York, 1982), p. 153.

[45] Moss, 'Norman Pipe Rolls'.

[46] L. Musset, 'Quelques notes sur les baleiniers normands du Xe au XIIe siècle', *Revue d'histoire économique et sociale*, 42 (1964), pp. 147-61.

There were, however, two Norman fiscal sources of a substantial character not directly recorded on the roll. One that has already been mentioned was the Norman *vicomte* aid. The other was the *fouage*, a household-based tax for financing the production of new coinage.[47] There are references to the *fouage* in the 1184 and 1195 rolls but little in 1180. Finally, there were the rights of the Norman duke over his harbours which may find some reflection in the 1195 roll.[48]

All these rights were public in character. They were rights over things and only consequentially over people. The production of money, the wine trade, land tax, harbours and forests have a curiously modern ring. In reality, as Musset and David Bates have pointed out, revenue sources such as *crassus piscis*, *bernagium*, and the *vicomte*'s aid have Carolingian roots.[49] What is more interesting is that this type of power should enjoy an extension with the development of *vinum super venditum* and *regardum*: terms which have no early ducal, Viking or Carolingian origin. All these rights are not quasi-feudal or even magnate-specific. Indeed, if Powicke is right the great lords were exempt from *vicomte*'s aid.[50]

This diffused series of public rights over strategic resources can be contrasted with the specific rights of the kings of England. In England, the special powers of the king enmeshed the great men in a web of special obligation to the monarch. In Normandy, a far less developed dukedom was buttressed by extensive Carolingian-style public rights. It is interesting to note, in this respect, the absence of *vis et voluntas* statements on the Norman rolls. Jolliffe's picture of the strong Angevin monarchy, so impressive when it comes to England, finds little reflection in the Norman rolls.[51]

Few issues have excited the English medieval historian as much as the legal reforms of Henry II. Milsom has argued that they set in motion a dynamic which crucially undermined the whole system of baronial justice.[52] Coss has argued that they triggered a defensive reaction which should be described as 'bastard feudalism'.[53] The major impact of these developments took place in the thirteenth rather than the twelfth century. The point, however, is that this process has drawn English-speaking historians to the study and, indeed, praise

---

[47] T.N. Bisson, *Conservation of Coinage* (Oxford, 1979), pp. 14-29.

[48] L. Musset, 'Les ports en Normandie du XIe au XIIIe siècle', *Autour du pouvoir ducal normand, Xe-XIIe siècle* ed., L. Musset et al. (Caen, 1985), pp. 113-28. It is just possible that a fine on the 1195 Roll for permission to carry grain outside Normandy is a reflection of this right. On the other hand, there is no *transmarine* formula. See Stapleton, ed., *Magni rotuli*, i, p. 171.

[49] Bates, *Normandy before 1066*, pp. 147-88. Also useful is L. Musset, 'Que peut-on savoir de la fiscalité publique en Normandie à l'époque ducale?', *Revue historique de droit français et étranger*, 4th series, 38 (1960), pp. 483-84.

[50] Powicke, *The Loss of Normandy*, pp. 47-48.

[51] J.E.A. Jolliffe, *Angevin Kingship* (London, 1955).

[52] S.F.C. Milsom, *The Legal Framework of English Feudalism* (Cambridge, 1976).

[53] P.R. Coss, 'Bastard Feudalism Revised', *Past and Present*, 125, (1989).

of these developments at the expense of any extensive examination of Normandy. No one has attempted a quantitative fiscal comparison of the two justice systems. The results are surprising. In England payments for amercements, agreements and access to right amount to £9,277 owed, with £1,496 paid, expressed in pounds of England. Converted to *livres angevins* this becomes £37,108 owed with £5,984 paid in. In Normandy £5,933 10s. 7d. *livres angevins* are owed, with £2,409 15s. 6d. *livres angevins* paid in, whilst expenditure was £119 19s.8d. *livres angevins*.[54]

The yield ratio in England works out at 16.1 per cent. In Normandy this ratio is 42.6 per cent. It should be stressed that the high Norman yield is not to be explained by English royal favour to barons with large debts. Large justice debts were rare on both rolls. Moreover, these were very often paid back at the same rate as smaller debts. The vast majority of justice income was, in any case, made up of small debts. The basic difference, as any scan through the Norman roll of 1180 illustrates, was that in Normandy there was a practice of paying debts for justice at a rate of 100 per cent or 50 per cent. In England this repayment was often at 33 per cent. It is true that the general yield of the Norman roll as a whole, at 61 per cent, is higher than the 49.9 per cent of England. But this does not explain a 42 per cent to 16 per cent yield ratio difference. The reasons for this require more detailed research. The regional diversity of Norman justice income, heavily concentrated in Falaise, Argentan, Caen, and Dieppe, all towns whose earlier development is generally associated with Duke Richard II in the early eleventh century, may well be crucial to any explanation. The effectiveness of Norman justice is a surprising and significant contrast to that of England.

Lastly, a few comments at a macro-economic level. English income and expenditure was just under three and a half times greater than that of Normandy. Interestingly, expenditure in 1180 as a proportion of income was only slightly higher in Normandy: 40 per cent, as against 36 per cent in England. At the heart of English revenue and expenditure lay the farm, the wardship and regalian rights. These three accounted for more than four-fifths of actual income and expenditure. In Normandy the situation was rather more diffused: farms and wardships account for only 62 per cent of the total. Part of this can be explained by the absence of Norman 'regalian rights'. But part of the reason lay with the high yield of Norman justice and, to a lesser extent, the unique public rights of the Norman dukes.

Two different feudal social formations thus emerge from this essay. In England there was a powerful monarchical structure, armed with a series of distinct royal rights, backed up by ruthless and effective exploitation of regalian rights, farms and wardships. Normandy was far more paradoxical. On the one hand there existed a political structure that was in some senses underdeveloped, based on ducal not royal power. On the other, a high-yield

[54] Moss, 'Norman Pipe Rolls'.

justice system, supported by a unique combination of public rights and situated in an economy which, in terms of commodity circulation, was relatively advanced.[55] It may well be that, in the long term, the ducal character of government was a crucial weakness. In 1180 this was by no means apparent. At the accession of Philip Augustus the chronicler Conan of Lausanne estimated that Philip had an income of 19,000 *livres parisis* which, converted to *livres angevins*, is almost exactly equal to that of Normandy. The difficulties with Conan's figure have, however, been highlighted by Baldwin.[56] This seems much too low, and may well refer to the *prévôt* farms only of the Capetian monarchy. Even if this is so, the potential farm income of Normandy works out at 12,488 *livres parisis*, or 65 per cent of the Capetian figure. Normandy in 1180 seemed very much a going concern. The omens, despite later developments, looked good.

[55] A somewhat surprising unanimity exists amongst Norman historians upon this issue. The most recent contribution, which contains perhaps the greatest quantitative assemblage of evidence for the circulation of money and commodities in eleventh-century Normandy, is E.Z. Tabuteau, *Transfers of Property in Eleventh-Century Norman Law* (London and Chapel Hill, NC, 1988), pp. 1-142.

[56] J.W. Baldwin, *The Government of Philip Augustus: Foundations of French Royal Power in the Middle Ages* (London, 1986), p. 54.

15

England, Normandy and the Beginnings of the Hundred Years War, 1259-1360

W.M. Ormrod

The seizure of Normandy by Philip Augustus in 1204 and the formal renunciation of Angevin claims to that region by Henry III in 1259 are usually seen to have marked the effective end of Plantagenet ambitions towards the duchy. Attention thereafter shifted to the south and to the maintenance of English rule in Aquitaine. It was the successive seizures of this province in 1294, 1324 and 1337 that provoked the series of Anglo-French hostilities and 'caused' the Hundred Years War. While Edward III's title to the throne of France, formally enunciated in 1340, allowed him the opportunity to intervene in the affairs of Normandy, the king was quick to compromise his claims in return for the sovereign control of Aquitaine apparently achieved in 1360. Consequently, Henry V's conquest and occupation of the duchy, far from being a continuation of the policy of his more recent ancestors, marked a radically new departure in English strategy and a fundamentally new phase in the Hundred Years War.

The present essay does not seek to challenge the consensual view of the peripheral role played by Normandy in Anglo-French relations during the thirteenth and fourteenth centuries. To do so, indeed, would be to run directly counter to an historical tradition that stretches back to the time of Henry V himself.[1] Even the copious archives of the medieval English state are largely silent on the matter: the only aspects of Anglo-Norman relations that are at all well documented in the 'lost' period between 1259 and 1337 are the fate of the former cross-Channel estates, the history of the dependent houses of Norman monasteries (the so-called alien priories), and the enduring but often acrimonious relationship between English and Norman merchants.[2] But precisely

---

[1] For historical justifications of Henry V's claims in Normandy see A. Curry below, pp. 243-47. I am grateful to Dr Curry and to Prof. M.C.E. Jones and Dr A. Ayton for comments on an earlier version of this essay; the errors that remain are my own.

[2] E.g., F.M. Powicke, *The Loss of Normandy, 1189-1204* (2nd edn, Manchester, 1961), appendix ii; A. McHardy, 'The Effects of War on the Church: The Case of the Alien Priories in the Fourteenth Century', in M. Jones and M. Vale, ed., *England and her Neighbours, 1066-1453: Essays in Honour of Pierre Chaplais* (London, 1989), pp. 277-92; G.P. Cuttino, *English Diplomatic Administration, 1259-1339* (2nd edn, Oxford, 1971), pp. 62-87.

because of the inner complexities of these subjects, there has been virtually no attempt to draw together the other scattered material on Anglo-Norman relations between the treaties of Paris and Brétigny and to suggest how that subject fits into the larger context of the origins and early phases of the Hundred Years War. This essay is intended as a first step towards that synthesis.

For Sir Maurice Powicke and a whole generation of English constitutional historians, the loss of Normandy was not only inevitable but also beneficial, in the sense that it relieved the Plantagenets of the troublesome distraction created by a major colony and allowed the kingdom of England to develop its rightful role as an insular sovereign state.[3] More recently, however, both English and French historians have come to realise that this was not exactly the way the situation was seen during the thirteenth century.[4] To begin with, the seizure of the duchy, depending as it did on the right of a feudal suzerain to confiscate the lands of a contumacious vassal, may have been legitimate in the short term, but could not in itself provide a basis for permanent occupation.[5] It was the contrasting political and financial circumstances of Louis IX and Henry III, rather than any assumptions about the Capetians' natural right to rule the duchy, that forced the Plantagenets to abandon their claims not only to Normandy but also to Anjou, Maine and Touraine in 1259. Furthermore, it is vital to remember that Normandy remained a distinct political unit throughout the thirteenth and fourteenth centuries, attached to the French crown but not to the kingdom and jealously protecting its distinct legal and administrative traditions against the intrusive policies of the late Capetian and early Valois kings.[6] That the Norman barons caught up in the provincial leagues of 1314-15 should have reacted to what they saw as the undue attentions of the French monarchy by harking back to a mythic golden age of 'English' rule may seem unlikely. But from the Plantagenet perspective, the disaffection of leading noblemen within an important province of the French crown was obviously useful in strategic, diplomatic and propaganda terms. A member of the English royal administration writing to Edward I in 1304 on the attempts of Philip the Fair to impose taxation within the duchy found it quite natural to define the Normans' claims to immunity in terms of the 'usages and customs'

[3] Powicke, *Loss of Normandy*, pp. 280-307.
[4] Recent thinking on the subject is summarised by J.C. Holt, 'The End of the Anglo-Norman Realm', *Proceedings of the British Academy*, 61 (1975), pp. 223-65; and L. Musset, 'Quelques problèmes posés par l'annexation de la Normandie au domaine royal français', in R.-H. Bautier, ed., *La France de Philippe Auguste: Le temps des mutations* (Paris, 1982), pp. 291-307.
[5] J. Le Patourel, *Feudal Empires: Norman and Plantagenet* (London, 1984), chapter XI, pp. 37-38.
[6] J.R. Strayer, *The Administration of Normandy under St Louis* (Cambridge, Mass., 1932); C.T. Wood, 'Regnum Franciae: A Problem in Capetian Administrative Usage', *Traditio*, 23 (1967), pp. 117-47.

that they had enjoyed 'in the time of the kings of England'.[7] On the eve of the Hundred Years War a copy of Louis X's *Charte aux Normands* of 1315 was actually in circulation among the councillors of Edward III.[8] These scattered snippets of evidence make it at least possible to argue that for a long time after 1259 the Plantagenets and their agents continued to speculate on ways in which the French monarchy's hold over the duchy might be undermined and even challenged as and when a suitable opportunity arose.

That opportunity did not present itself for nearly eighty years. Despite the Lord Edward's protest over the renunciation of Normandy in 1259, there is no indication that his accession to the throne in 1272 marked any revival of English claims to the duchy.[9] The Capetian apologist Guillaume Guiart accused Edward of planning to conquer Normandy during the Anglo-French hostilities of the 1290s, but his fanciful interpretation of the war proves no more reliable than that of the gossip-mongering English chroniclers who saw it as a consequence of Edward's thwarted lust for the sister of Philip the Fair.[10] If the war of 1294-98 has any significance for Anglo-Norman relations, it is only in respect of the more limited issues arising from maritime disputes. The full ramifications of this subject are far too complex to be dealt with in detail here, but a brief review may help to illustrate the general direction of English policy towards Normandy in the half century before the Hundred Years War.[11]

To understand the Plantagenets' policy towards the resolution of disputes at sea, it is important to appreciate the difference between suits concerning their Gascon subjects on the one hand and their English subjects on the other. The subordinate status imposed on the duchy of Aquitaine under the terms of the treaty of Paris meant that maritime conflicts between Gascons and Normans were fraught with jurisdictional problems: as Edward I found to his cost in 1293-94, the Capetians could always use the failure of the Plantagenet regime to provide satisfaction in such cases as a pretext for confiscating Aquitaine.[12] When quarrels broke out between English and Norman shipping, however, the three Edwards found themselves on rather surer ground. Here they could

---

[7] PRO, SC 1/21/192.

[8] PRO, C 47/28/5, no. 44.

[9] P. Chaplais, *Essays in Medieval Diplomacy and Administration* (London, 1981), ch. I, p. 244. Edward made further protests over Normandy in 1273 (ibid., ch. III, p. 18), but according to the *Flores historiarum*, ed H.R. Luard (London, 1890), iii, p. 52, he renounced his claim to Normandy on receiving the county of Ponthieu in 1279.

[10] M. Vale, *The Angevin Legacy and the Hundred Years War, 1250-1340* (Oxford, 1990), pp. 183, 193; M. Prestwich, *Edward I* (London, 1988), p. 380.

[11] For important general discussions see Chaplais, *Essays*, ch. IX; F.L. Cheyette, 'The Sovereign and the Pirates, 1332', *Speculum*, 45 (1970), pp. 51-54.

[12] Prestwich, *Edward I*, pp. 376-81. In 1316 there was another serious dispute between the men of Bayonne and Normandy which might easily have provoked a further confiscation: T. Rymer, *Foedera* (Record Commission edn, 3 vols in 6, II, ii, p. 299; *CPR, 1313-17*, p. 557. A similar conflict was in discussion on the eve of the war of 1324-25: *The War of Saint-Sardos (1323-1325)*, ed. P. Chaplais, Camden Society, 3rd series, 87 (1954), nos 9, 13, 14, 17.

negotiate as equals: indeed, should the French monarchy fail to act, the Plantagenets could invoke their historical claim to sovereignty of the seas and claim a superior jurisdiction over maritime cases.[13] The difficulties encountered by the late Capetian and early Valois kings when they tried to interfere in the distinctive legal traditions of Normandy gave the Plantagenet regime the pretext for an increasingly ruthless policy of reprisals.[14] From the beginning of Edward III's reign, the crown was frequently sanctioning seizures of goods as compensation to aggrieved English merchants,[15] even issuing general orders for the arrest of all Norman and other French shipping threatening English seafarers both in the Channel and on the Atlantic seaboard.[16]

What made this policy all the more urgent was the growing realisation that, in the event of full-scale war between the two kingdoms, a hostile French fleet operating out of Normandy might provide a major threat to English security. Preparations had already been made against this eventuality in the 1290s and the 1320s and were taken up by Edward III on a regular basis after the coastal raids of 1336-38.[17] The threat from hostile shipping did not of course come solely from Normandy. But the writs issued by the English chancery after 1338 tended to follow a standard formula which referred to the gathering of enemy fleets in Normandy manned in part or whole by Normans.[18] Under these circumstances, it is hardly surprising that the likes of Lawrence Minot should have seen the battle of Sluys of 1340 specifically as an engagement between the English and the Normans.[19] The discovery and promulgation in 1346 of a text of Philip VI's celebrated scheme of 1339 for a new 'Norman Conquest' of England[20] confirmed a point that the English political and mercantile community had already known for a long time: that the Normans, quite simply, were not to be trusted.[21]

---

[13] Chaplais, *Essays*, ch. IX, pp. 270-71.

[14] In November 1327 Charles IV had to admit that he could not help English merchants wishing to bring charges of robbery in Norman courts: PRO, SC 1/55/104. Nor did the appointment of the future John II as duke of Normandy in 1332 make matters any easier: see *CCR, 1333-37*, pp. 507-8, 620.

[15] See, e.g., the case of Elias Stubton of Lincoln: *CCR, 1327-30*, pp. 175, 203, 301, 313, 321-22, 337-38, 428, 432, 440, 446, 450-51, 471; *CCR, 1333-37*, p. 634. For further cases at the time of the outbreak of war in 1337-38, see *CCR, 1337-39*, pp. 6, 43-45, 53, 306, 455-56.

[16] *CCR, 1327-30*, pp. 298, 397-98; PRO, SC 1/34/175.

[17] Prestwich, *Edward I*, pp. 383-84; Rymer, *Foedera*, II, i, pp. 562, 573; J. Sumption, *The Hundred Years War: Trial by Battle* (London, 1990), pp. 155-68.

[18] See, e.g., *Treaty Rolls, ii, 1337-39* (London, 1972), nos 844-45, 909, 911; Rymer, *Foedera*, II, ii, p. 1133; PRO, C 76/17, m. 35d.

[19] *Political Poems and Songs Relating to English History*, ed. T. Wright (London, 1859-61), i, pp. 70-72.

[20] Adam Murimuth, *Continuatio chronicarum*, ed. E.M. Thompson (London, 1889), pp. 205-12.

[21] M. Bennett, 'Stereotype Normans in Old French Vernacular Literature', *A-NS*, 9 (1987), p. 41 and n. 41.

The most substantial body of material on Anglo-Norman relations between the 1290s and the 1330s indicates a growing antipathy between two peoples once united under a single ruler and divided by a narrow sea. That is not to say that there were no continued expressions of amity. The English aristocracy still had a good deal more in common both culturally and politically with their counterparts in northern France than they did with the nobility of the remaining Plantagenet possessions in Aquitaine.[22] Despite the almost complete elimination of the cross-Channel estates in the generation after 1204, the rather more relaxed atmosphere that obtained in Anglo-French relations during the early decades of the fourteenth century actually allowed one of the most important Norman families, the Briennes, counts of Eu, to reestablish a landed interest for themselves in England and Ireland.[23] Even after the outbreak of the Hundred Years War, there were plenty of Norman clerics and merchants who continued to reside, under royal protection, in the kingdom of England.[24] But the English intervention in the duchy during the early stages of the Hundred Years War was certainly not carried through on a wave of mutual nostalgia for the old Norman Empire. Once the war had begun the Normans were quickly identified as the particular enemies of the English who, it was hoped, would one day quake before the Plantagenet forces of conquest.[25]

How, then, did the growing hostility exhibited by the English towards the Normans come to be channelled into the full-scale war that emerged in the middle decades of the fourteenth century? The answer, as John Le Patourel taught, lay in the development of Edward III's 'provincial strategy', the scheme by which Edward set himself up as a pretender to the kingdom of France and a natural rallying-point for everyone with a grievance against the Valois regime.[26] Emerging first in Flanders in 1340 and employed to stunning effect in Brittany after 1341, this scheme was of necessity a pragmatic one, responding more to the internal politics of the French principalities than to any grand master-plan. Le Patourel himself emphasised this opportunism with specific reference to Normandy, denying that Edward III's two interventions in the duchy – in 1345-46 and 1356-57 – were anything more than an attempt to deflect Philip VI's forces away from the other theatres of war in the south and

---

[22] Vale, *Angevin Legacy*, pp. 9-47.

[23] *CP*, v, pp. 171-73. These lands were permanently forfeited after the outbreak of war in 1337, and the count received compensation from Philip VI: R. Cazelles, *La société politique et la crise de la royauté sous Philippe de Valois* (Paris, 1958), p. 138 n. 11. The count later offered Edward III the county of Guînes in satisfaction of the huge ransom charged after his capture in 1346. This seems to have been a matter of desperate negotiation rather than sympathy for the English cause, and resulted in Brienne's execution on his return to France. See S.H. Cuttler, *The Law of Treason and Treason Trials in Later Medieval France* (Cambridge, 1981), p. 154.

[24] E.g., *CPR, 1348-50*, pp. 149, 407.

[25] *Political Poems and Songs*, i, pp. 55, 77, 155; J. Barnie, *War in Medieval Society: Social Values and the Hundred Years War, 1337-99* (London, 1974), pp. 14-15, 49.

[26] Le Patourel, *Feudal Empires*, ch. XII, p. 179-89.

the west.[27] Le Patourel's pupils and successors have kept faith with this interpretation,[28] and very little attention has been given to the possibility that Normandy may also have had a place in Edward III's developing plans for territorial expansion in France. The remainder of this essay attempts to set the war in Normandy within that wider framework and to assess the arguments for and against the idea that Edward entertained similar ambitions to those actually achieved by Henry V.

In order to appreciate Edward III's objectives in Normandy, it is necessary to contrast the circumstances that surrounded his two interventions in the duchy. Despite some superficial similarities, and the appearance of some key characters in both episodes, they were otherwise quite different and distinct. When Godfrey Harcourt, lord of Saint-Sauveur-le-Vicomte, did homage to Edward as king of France in June 1345,[29] the English made no direct offer of assistance in the private war that Harcourt and his supporters were fighting against the ducal administration. Harcourt's defection was no more significant than that of the many other members of French chivalry to whom Edward III was actively appealing throughout the spring and summer of 1345.[30] The major force that disembarked at Saint-Vaast la Hougue under Edward's leadership in 1346 was therefore intended not as an army of Normandy but as part of a still larger strategy directed against the forces of Philip VI.[31] While those who fought on this campaign later referred to it as the *viage de Normandie*,[32] and certainly developed an abiding interest in the ransoms and plunder to be had from such a wealthy province,[33] there is little to suggest that Edward himself entertained any coherent ambitions towards the duchy at this point.[34] Despite

---

[27] Ibid., ch. XII, pp. 182-84; J. Le Patourel, 'Normandy', *Dictionary of the Middle Ages*, ed. J.R. Strayer (New York, 1982-89), ix, p. 169.

[28] E.g., M. Jones, 'Relations with France, 1337-1399', in Jones and Vale, ed., *England and her Neighbours*, pp. 251-52.

[29] Rymer, *Foedera*, III, i, p. 44. For full details of this episode see L. Delisle, *Histoire du château et des sires de Saint-Sauveur-le-Vicomte* (Valognes, 1867), pp. 56-58; Cazelles, *Société politique sous Philippe de Valois*, pp. 136-40; J. Tricard, 'Jean, duc de Normandie et héritier de France, un double échec', *Annales de Normandie*, 29 (1979), pp. 30-32.

[30] Rymer, *Foedera*, III, i, pp. 35, 45.

[31] I favour the traditional interpretation, but it should be noted that Sumption, *Hundred Years War*, pp. 532-33, has recently argued that Edward planned to occupy the duchy in 1346.

[32] PRO, SC 1/39/180, 187, 192; SC 1/40/111, 128, 143, 211; SC 1/41/2, 39.

[33] The many newsletters sent back from the campaign suggest that the wealth of the province became proverbial in England after 1346: for full references see K.A. Fowler, 'News from the Front: Letters and Despatches of the Fourteenth Century', *Guerre et société en France, en Angleterre et en Bourgogne XIVe-XVe siècle*, ed. P. Contamine, C. Giry- Deloison and M.H. Keen (Lille, 1991), pp. 63-92. The comments of Jean le Bel on the wealth of Normandy provided a basis for the speech later concocted by Froissart in which Geoffrey Harcourt is supposed to have enticed Edward into the duchy: *Chronique de Jean le Bel*, ed. J. Viard and E. Déprez (Paris, 1904-05), ii, pp. 70, 76; *Chroniques de Froissart*, ed. S. Luce, G. Raynaud, L. and A. Mirot (Paris, 1869-1975), iii, pp. 131, 357.

[34] The defection of Harcourt back into the French camp at the end of 1346 would certainly have put an end to any notion of an English occupation: Delisle, *Saint-Sauveur*, pp. 66-68.

the obvious advantages of disembarking under Harcourt's protection in the Cotentin, at least one of the English noblemen in this army thought that the Normandy landing had been forced on the king by bad weather.[35] The campaign of 1346-47 may have had some of its greatest successes in the duchy – above all in the spectacular sack of Caen – but it certainly did not make Edward III duke of Normandy.

Up to 1347, Edward III's approach to the internal affairs of Normandy was no different from that adopted towards some of the other more politically divided provinces of France. There are signs that the triumphant progress through the duchy in 1346 had sufficient impact in England to encourage a popular idea that the king might make a serious bid for Normandy itself. A number of unofficial sources dating from shortly after 1347 argued that Edward had a two-fold claim to the former Angevin possessions in northern France, not only in his capacity as self-styled king of France but also, perhaps more significantly, as the descendant of William the Conqueror.[36] The king's response to such ideas is difficult to judge.[37] In 1353 it was reported before the great council that Edward had offered to give up his claims to Normandy if the French crown could prove that it had a legitimate claim to the duchy.[38] This is often seen as an example of Edward's willingness to renounce his more fanciful claims in return for the real concessions that he sought in Aquitaine, but it could also be interpreted as a real challenge to the legality of the earlier Capetian annexation of Normandy. If one takes the latter view, it is possible to argue that the very absence of references to Normandy in the subsequent draft treaty of Guînes of 1354 signified an English determination to maintain at least a residual claim to the duchy, and indeed to Anjou, Maine and Touraine and to the contested suzerainty of Brittany and Flanders.[39] Consequently it may be

[35] Murimuth, *Continuatio chronicarum*, p. 200; Sumption, *Hundred Years War*, pp. 497-98.

[36] *Political Poems and Songs*, i, pp. 35, 153, 155. For the dates of composition of the texts from which the latter two references are drawn, see A.G. Rigg, 'John of Bridlington's *Prophecy*: A New Look', *Speculum*, 63 (1988), pp. 596-613.

[37] English propaganda directed specifically at the Normans is generally lacking, and it is not certain whether Edward ever explicitly played on his rights as the descendant of William the Conqueror. He does not seem to have made capital out of a fact brought to the attention of his government more than once in the 1330s that the king of England continued to rule the Channel Islands in his capacity as duke of Normandy: J.H. Le Patourel, *The Medieval Administration of the Channel Islands, 1199-1399* (London, 1937), pp. 29, 37. It may be that, like Henry V after him, Edward III preferred to leave it to the Normans to decide whether he claimed the duchy through his 'English' or his 'French' ancestry: C.T. Allmand, *Lancastrian Normandy, 1415-1450* (Oxford, 1983), pp. 122-26. The allusion to his rights in the record of the homage of Godfrey Harcourt in 1345 was suitably ambiguous: 'Et si Dieu nous donit grace de recoverir nostre heritage en Normandie . . .': Rymer, *Foedera*, III, i, p. 44. Nothing seems to have been made of Edward's patrilineal claims during the peace negotiations at Avignon in 1344: see *Froissart*, xviii, pp. 256-72.

[38] *Rot. Parl.*, ii, p. 252.

[39] F. Bock, 'Some New Documents Illustrating the Early History of the Hundred Years War (1353-1356)', *Bulletin of the John Rylands Library*, 15 (1931), pp. 91-93, as interpreted by Le Patourel, *Feudal Empires*, ch. XII, p. 177; G.P. Cuttino, *English Medieval Diplomacy* (Bloomington, IN, 1985), p. 89.

here, in the euphoric atmosphere following the great victories of 1346-47, that we see the first and as yet hesitant signs of what was later to develop into a clear and consistent policy of promoting the Plantagenets' dynastic claims to the duchy of Normandy.

The complicating factor in this policy, and the reason why it was not in fact taken up by Edward at this point, was the intervention of his cousin, Charles, king of Navarre, in Anglo-French diplomacy. Whether or not Charles the Bad, as the grandson of Louis X, had a better claim than Edward III to be the legitimate Capetian contender for the throne of France,[40] he was certainly the natural pretender to the duchy of Normandy. As count of Evreux and Mortain, Charles enjoyed an important landed base within the duchy and an extensive network of supporters among the Norman baronage. His alliance with John II in February 1354 increased his holdings considerably, making him lord of virtually half the duchy, including most of the Cotentin.[41] During the *rapprochement* between the English and the Navarrese later in 1354, Edward III freely accepted that Charles was more likely to succeed in Normandy and offered him the duchy, together with other extensive lands throughout northern France, in return for his military assistance and his formal recognition of Edward as the legitimate king of France.[42] For the moment, then, Charles had compromised Edward's ambitions towards Normandy and apparently forced the English to return to their policy of using dynastic claims as a bargaining counter in the negotiations over the future of Aquitaine.[43]

The situation only changed with the unexpected arrest of Charles of Navarre by John II in the spring of 1356. This episode forms one of the most colourful set-pieces in the Hundred Years War and has been repeatedly and dramatically

[40] The jurisitic arguments are summarised by Le Patourel, *Feudal Empires*, ch. XII, pp. 173-75. See also the comments of D. Sutherland reported in J.B. Henneman, *Royal Taxation in Fourteenth Century France: The Captivity and Death of John II, 1356-1370* (Philadelphia, 1976), p. 87 n. 15.

[41] D.F. Secousse, *Mémoires pour servir à l'histoire de Charles II, roi de Navarre et comte d'Evreux* (Paris, 1755-58), ii, pp. 33-36; R. Cazelles, *Société politique, noblesse et couronne sous Jean le Bon et Charles V* (Geneva, 1982), pp. 85-90.

[42] BL, MS Cotton, Caligula D. III, no. 61, printed in R. Delachenal, 'Premières négociations de Charles le Mauvais avec les Anglais (1354-1355)', *Bibliothèque de l'Ecole des Chartes*, 61 (1900), pp. 280-82. K. Fowler, *The King's Lieutenant: Henry of Grosmont, First Duke of Lancaster, 1310-1361* (London, 1969), pp. 141-43, suggested that this undated document preceded the treaty of Mantes, but I am more inclined to follow the general line of Delachenal's argument and place it late in 1354, or possibly early in 1355; that is, after both the treaty of Mantes and the draft treaty of Guînes. See also R. Delachenal, *Histoire de Charles V* (Paris, 1909-31), i, pp. 87-91; Le Patourel, *Feudal Empires*, ch. XII, p. 177; Cazelles, *Société politique sous Jean le Bon*, p. 168; P. Jugie, 'L'activité diplomatique du Cardinal Gui de Boulogne en France au milieu du XIVe siècle', *Bibliothèque de l'Ecole des Chartes*, 145 (1987), pp. 119-23.

[43] By the end of 1354, indeed, the crown was prepared to make specific promises of the renunciation of Normandy in order to secure a *bone pees* with the French: Bock, 'New Documents', pp. 94-96; P. Chaplais, *English Medieval Diplomatic Practice*, pt I (London, 1982), i, pp. 189-91.

retold over the centuries.[44] For present purposes, it is necessary only to emphasise the scale of the political reaction that resulted within the duchy: this time it was not only Godfrey Harcourt but also Philip of Navarre, count of Longueville and brother of Charles the Bad, who appealed to Edward III for assistance in the military enterprise they proposed to mount against the tyrant of France. When they performed homage to Edward, both these men explicitly recognised the latter's rights not only to the kingdom of France but also, quite separately, to the duchy of Normandy.[45] Thus began a brief period during which certain public instruments emanating from the English chancery in reference to the duchy carried the unusual and highly significant royal style 'king of France and duke of Normandy'.[46] It has usually and not unnaturally been assumed that this represented a deliberate appeal to provincial sensibilities, a clever way in which to increase the already considerable support for a combined Anglo-Navarrese operation intended to drive out the hostile forces of Valois centralism.[47] Another interpretation is possible. It may be that Edward III was deliberately seeking to make capital out of the temporary removal of Charles of Navarre by asserting his ancient patrilineal right to the duchy of Normandy and thus challenging the competing dynastic claims of both the Valois and the Navarrese.

The successful campaign led by the duke of Lancaster through Normandy in the summer of 1356 appeared to confirm the fact that Philip of Navarre and his allies could only hold out against the French crown with direct military support from the English.[48] Edward was therefore in a powerful bargaining position when it came to drawing up the formal indentures of homage with the Norman rebels. A neglected series of memoranda associated with the homage of Philip of Navarre allows a particularly valuable glimpse of the way in which the two sides saw the impending alliance.[49] Philip was principally interested in obtaining the release of his brother, securing Edward's support for Charles's territorial claims in Champagne and Brie, and extracting a firm promise that he and his

---

[44] A. Coville, *Les états de Normandie: leur origines et leur développement au XIVe siècle* (Paris, 1894), pp. 74-81; Delachenal, *Charles V*, i, pp. 134-57; Cuttler, *Law of Treason*, pp. 160-62.

[45] Rymer, *Foedera*, III, i, pp. 332, 340.

[46] J. Le Patourel, 'Edouard III, "roi de France et duc de Normandie" ', *Révue historique du droit français et étranger*, 4th series, 31 (1953), pp. 317-18.

[47] Le Patourel, *Feudal Empires*, ch. XII, pp. 182-84.

[48] Fowler, *King's Lieutenant*, pp. 147-53.

[49] BL, MS Cotton, Caligula D.III, nos 43-53. Several of these documents were printed by Kervyn de Lettenhove, but he confused their chronological order. He conflated two separate documents in *Froissart*, xviii, pp. 398-401: the first (BL, MS Cotton, Caligula D.III, no. 43), which ends in the printed version at line 9 on p. 399, seems in fact to represent proposals put forward by Philip during the drafting of the indenture of Sept. 1356, and answered, point by point, in BL, MS Cotton, Caligula D.III, no. 53, printed by Kervyn de Lettenhove on pp. 380-81. This material was not used by Delachenal, *Charles V*, i, pp. 168-70. The final form of the indenture is PRO, E 30/72, printed in Rymer, *Foedera*, III, i, p. 340 and enrolled in *CCR, 1354-60*, p. 333.

supporters would be allowed to keep all the conquests they made in Normandy. This wider strategy could be pursued quite satisfactorily by recognising Edward as king of France alone, and it was this title that was specified in the draft indenture. Subsequently, the wording of Philip's oath of homage was changed to accommodate Edward's newly-assumed double title.[50] Since the indenture was being made with the brother and lieutenant of the king of Navarre, it seems likely that Edward was now following a particularly subtle strategy, at once appeasing and mobilising the Navarrese party within the duchy while at the same time undermining the diplomatic and political pretensions of its temporarily incapacitated leader, Charles the Bad.

The news of the Black Prince's victory at Poitiers at the end of September 1356 can only have confirmed Edward in his new ambition. Ultimately, the capture of John II at Poitiers was to compromise the English position in Normandy by calling a halt to the war and creating a new scale of priorities in Anglo-French diplomacy. Through the winter of 1356-57, however, Edward's attitude towards Normandy remained unchanged. A force of at least 100 men at arms and 130 mounted archers was dispatched to the duchy at the king's expense.[51] The Plantagenet administration set up under the direction of Peter Pigache, lord of Turqueville, symbolised Edward's altogether novel policy of exercising direct political influence within the duchy.[52] Despite the appointment of Philip of Navarre as his lieutenant in Normandy in October 1356,[53] Edward clearly had no intention of allowing the military and political establishment there to pass completely under the control of the Navarrese. When Godfrey Harcourt died in action at the end of 1356, his lands were immediately taken into the king's hands and placed in the custody not of a Norman baron but of an English royal agent, Simon Newenton.[54] Philip took strong exception to this, but in the resulting correspondence with the English crown he was sharply rebuffed and reminded of the obedience he owed to the king-duke through his recent oath of liege homage.[55] At the same time, Edward further undermined Philip's position by ordering that all lands within the *bailliage* of Cotentin confiscated from Valois supporters should be reserved to

---

[50] During the negotiations, it was stated that 'le dit Monsieur Phelippe feroit au roy homage come a roy de France en recognoisant le droit quil a au royaume de France' (BL, MS Cotton, Caligula D.III, no. 43). In the draft indenture (ibid., no. 50), the wording of the oath of homage itself is not given, but it is only an interlineation in the preamble that specifies that it was to be rendered 'come a roi de France et duc de Normandie'. The draft also omits two clauses found in the finished indenture relating to rights to lands in Normandy, and is undated.

[51] PRO, E 403/382, mm. 5, 7, 9, 12, 17.

[52] Rymer, *Foedera*, III, i, p. 333; K. Fowler, 'Les finances et la discipline dans les armées anglaises en France au XIVe siècle', *Les Cahiers Vernonnais*, 4 (1964), pp. 72-73.

[53] Rymer, *Foedera*, III, i, p. 342.

[54] Ibid., p. 346; Delisle, *Saint-Sauveur*, pp. 111-12 and nn. Harcourt had made over his lands to Edward III by a deed dated 18 July 1356: *CPR, 1354-58*, p. 477.

[55] BL, MS Cotton, Caligula D.III, nos 54, 56. The latter is printed and dated in Chaplais, *English Medieval Diplomatic Practice*, pt 1, i, pp. 75-76.

him.[56] This, as was later pointed out, went directly against the terms of Philip's indenture.[57] Nevertheless, Edward continued to make grants to English captains of castles and lordships in Lower Normandy, sometimes enjoying a third of the profits of the ransoms that were then extorted from the dependent communities in the duchy.[58]

Nor did the release of Charles of Navarre from prison late in 1357 substantially alter Edward's policy of direct intervention in the duchy.[59] For some time, Charles was preoccupied with the Jacquerie and the attempt to recover his ancestral rights in Champagne. Consequently, Edward III continued to maintain his position with regard to Normandy throughout the intense diplomatic negotiations both with the dauphin and with Charles the Bad in 1358-59.[60] Charles's defection to the Valois cause in July 1359 has often been seen as a serious blow to the Plantagenets both in Normandy and elsewhere.[61] In many ways the real victim was Philip of Navarre, who found himself outmanoeuvred by his own brother and locked into an increasingly anomalous alliance with the English. The appointment of Sir Thomas Holand as joint lieutenant of Normandy in October 1359 was a further indication of the extent to which Philip's original aims had been overtaken by the military priorities and diplomatic objectives of his English ally.[62]

If Edward III was indeed making serious claims to Normandy after 1356, it is obviously important to ascertain the extent to which such pretensions were

---

[56] Rymer, *Foedera*, III, i, pp. 345-46.

[57] PRO, C 76/35, m. 14.

[58] Rymer, *Foedera*, III, i, pp. 363, 383; PRO, C 76/38, m. 7; T.F. Tout, *Chapters in the Administrative History of Mediaeval England* (Manchester, 1920-33), iv, p. 250 and n. 5; G.L. Harriss, *King, Parliament and Public Finance in Medieval England to 1369* (Oxford, 1975), p. 501 and n. 3.

[59] For Charles's mixed reception in Normandy after his release see Delachenal, *Charles V*, i, pp. 332-35; G. Bois, *The Crisis of Feudalism: Economy and Society in Eastern Normandy, c. 1300-1550* (Cambridge, 1984), pp. 295-96.

[60] For the Anglo-French negotiations surrounding the two draft treaties of London of 1358 and 1359 I follow Le Patourel, *Feudal Empires*, ch. XIII. The English response to the agenda of 1 August 1358 for an Anglo-Navarrese alliance, which is printed, but misdated, in Rymer, *Foedera*, III, i, p. 228 (see E. Déprez, 'Une conférence Anglo-Navarraise en 1358', *Révue historique*, 99 (1908), pp. 34-39), differed significantly from that indicated in the proposals of 1354 in that it reserved the question of Normandy to a discussion between Edward and Charles. It should be remembered that Charles was in a desperate situation at this point; it is therefore possible to interpret this prevarication over Normandy as a deliberate refusal on the English side to return to the concessions of 1354. See S. Luce, 'Négociations des Anglais avec le roi de Navarre pendant la révolution parisienne de 1358', *Mémoires de la société de l'histoire de Paris et de l'Ile de France*, 1 (1875), pp. 113-31; Delachenal, *Charles V*, ii, pp. 2-7; Henneman, *Captivity of John II*, pp. 87-88.

[61] Le Patourel, *Feudal Empires*, ch. XII, p. 189. Cf. Delachenal, *Charles V*, ii, pp. 79-80, who argued that Edward had already determined to marginalise Charles of Navarre before this defection took place.

[62] Rymer, *Foedera*, III, ii, pp. 452-53. For Holand's career in Normandy before this point see *CP*, vii, p. 152. To this list should be added his appointment as keeper of Barfleur on 6 Oct. 1359: PRO, C 76/38, m. 7.

justified and supported by the military situation in the duchy. Unfortunately, the nature of the war in Normandy makes it very difficult to trace its exact course. In March 1357 an Anglo-French truce was established at Bordeaux pending talks on the release of John II.[63] The war that continued to rage in northern France between 1357 and 1359 was therefore an unofficial affair without formal backing from the English government. Although an information system continued to function after 1357,[64] it is doubtful that the domestic administration could have made very much of the disjointed snippets of information emerging from the duchy. While the Anglo-Navarrese were numerous enough to wreak havoc on the non-combatant population particularly of Lower Normandy, they clearly lacked both the local coordination and the relief forces from England that would have been necessary to mount a major campaign of conquest: there was to be no sack of Caen, let alone a fall of Rouen, during this particular phase of the Hundred Years War. Indeed, given that almost all the major towns outside the Cotentin remained loyal to the Valois cause between 1356 and 1360, it is easy to assume that the military operations in Normandy were of little strategic value. On closer inspection there are at least some indications that the activities of the Anglo-Navarrese forces in the duchy did provide some basis for the aggressive diplomatic posture taken up by Edward III between 1356 and 1359.[65]

Following Lancaster's campaign of 1356, the initial stages of the war in Normandy comprised a series of raids out of the English and Navarrese strongholds in the Cotentin and the Evrecin. The locations of the castles and fortified churches taken in these operations may suggest some degree of planning: certainly the numerous positions captured in the region between Bayeux and Caen must have impeded the defensive measures mounted by these two principal Valois strongholds in Lower Normandy. It must be stressed that a large number of these initial conquests were retaken by the French in 1357-58, some by negotiation and others by force. Despite this, the occupying forces still seem to have had the upper hand: they held an apparently unassailable grip on the Cotentin, and had managed to build up and maintain control over a string of important fortresses in the south of the duchy stretching from Avranches, Mortain, Tinchebray, Messei and Domfront in the west to La Ferté Frênel, Orbec, Beaumont le Roger, Le Neubourg and Evreux in the east. The virtual cessation of royal taxation in Lower Normandy during 1357 and 1358 is but one striking example of the almost complete administrative and economic breakdown that had resulted from the ravages of the free companies

---

[63] Rymer, *Foedera*, III, i, pp. 348-51.

[64] PRO, E 403/384, mm. 10, 11, 16; E 403/388, mm. 29, 30; E 403/392, m. 15; E 403/394, mm. 8, 9, 11, 17, 18, 19, 28, 29, 34; E 403/396, m. 25; E 101/313/31, 36, 37, 38.

[65] The following account derives largely from S. Luce, *Histoire de Bertrand du Guesclin et de son époque: la jeunesse de Bertrand* (Paris, 1876), pp. 231-84, 459-509. See also Delisle, *Saint-Sauveur*, pp. 84-118; H. Denifle, *La Guerre de Cent Ans et la désolation des églises, monastères & hôpitaux en France* (Paris, 1899), ii, pp. 295-310; Delachenal, *Charles V*, i, pp. 159-87.

in this area.[66] In 1358-59 the Anglo-Navarrese turned their attention to Upper Normandy, temporarily establishing themselves in a number of fortresses in the centre and extreme north east of the duchy, including Normanville, Saint-Denis le Thiboult, Aumale and Château sur Epte. There are signs that the dispersion of the companies across much of northern France in this period weakened the hold on Normandy, where the citizens of Rouen began to take a more active role in coordinating pro-Valois operations and re-establishing some sense of administrative order.[67] But there were few signs that the Anglo-Navarrese could be wrenched from their positions in the Cotentin and the south. Moreover, the occupation of fortresses on the outskirts of Saint-Lô and Argentan, the ransoming of Dreux, and the investiture of two strategically important positions at Honfleur and Roches d'Orival, all in 1359, must certainly have caused the French continued concern for the security of the duchy. It is no surprise that the Valois government, when appraised of Edward's invasion plans in 1359, speculated that the English army might choose to land in Normandy.[68]

In the event, the invasion force landed at Calais and marched for Reims, leaving the English forces in Normandy, now under the direction of the earl of Warwick,[69] to devise a diversionary strategy of their own. There are strong suggestions that the English government signally failed to understand the true nature of the fighting in the official war that resumed in Normandy during 1359-60: the obsessive efforts of the Westminster administration to trace £5 worth of onions and garlic that had not been properly accounted for by the keeper of victuals in the newly-established English garrison at Honfleur suggests a scale of priorities completely divorced from the realities and hazards of war.[70] Those hazards were indeed considerable: a number of English landholders were killed in Normandy during the period immediately before the treaty of Brétigny, and Sir Thomas Holand, restored to the lieutenancy of the duchy in September 1360, died there two months later.[71] Not that such personal tragedies proved a general disincentive: indeed, Normandy seems to have continued to attract large numbers of English soldiers up to, and indeed beyond, the establishment of peace in 1360.[72] The war within the duchy had turned into precisely the sort of operation that careerist soldiers wanted: an

---

[66] Henneman, *Captivity of John II*, pp. 39-40, 51; Bois, *Crisis of Feudalism*, pp. 295-97.

[67] Henneman, *Captivity of John II*, pp. 99-100, 101, 107.

[68] Delachenal, *Charles V*, ii, p. 149 n. 4.

[69] Fowler, 'Les finances et la discipline', p. 72. Warwick was paid for 120 men at arms and 120 archers between 20 Sept. 1359 and 18 May 1360, and 81 men at arms and 100 archers between 25 May and 29 Sept. 1360: PRO, E 101/393/11, fos 79v, 87r. I owe these references to Dr Ayton.

[70] PRO, C 76/40, m. 7; *CCR, 1360-64*, pp. 83-84, 186.

[71] *CPR, 1354-58*, p. 381; *CCR, 1360-64*, pp. 184-85; *CIPM*, x, nos 473, 539, 551, 557: *CP*, vii, p. 153. In Oct. 1360 Holand received wages and regard for sixty men at arms and 140 archers then serving with him in Normandy: PRO, E 403/402, m. 1.

[72] See in particular the comments of Sir Thomas Gray, *Scalacronica*, ed. J. Stevenson (Edinburgh, 1836), pp. 177-78.

opportunity to escape the command structures, discipline and profit-sharing that were associated with the receipt of wages from the crown and to indulge in a unrestrained orgy of looting and pillaging.[73] The enormous ransoms charged for the release of Anglo-Navarrese positions, both before and after the treaty of Brétigny, are testimony to the huge profits of war that were made by the likes of Robert Knolles, Otes Holand, Thomas Uvedale, Thomas Fogg, James Pipe and the many other English captains who fought in Normandy and other parts of northern France during the late 1350s.[74] Nor should it be forgotten that this was precisely the kind of war that the English political community itself tended to favour: a war that demanded no large outlay of public funds and which would pay for itself many times over in the plunder and bullion stripped from the king's enemies and shipped home by loyal, if self-serving, soldiers.

This analysis has suggested that Edward III's assumption of the title of duke of Normandy in 1356 marked the start of a consistent and not wholly unrealistic policy pursued over the following three years and intended to bring about the restoration of the duchy, along with the other former Angevin dominions in northern France, to the English crown. Far from causing controversy at home, this approach appealed directly to a number of significant groupings in the English political and military elite and was more likely to provoke criticism if it were ever to be abandoned.[75] Given this argument, it is obviously of key importance to explain why Edward III subsequently offered to renounce his claims to Normandy at Brétigny in May 1360. For Le Patourel, the crucial answer lay in the failure of the winter campaign of 1359-60.[76] Undoubtedly, Edward must have been frustrated by his failure to enter the city of Reims and have himself crowned king of France. It is also possible that the campaign gave Edward a first-hand impression of the formless, not to say chaotic, way in which his provincial strategy had been operating since the truce of Bordeaux and persuaded him that the military situation was simply inadequate to effect the diplomatic strategy that he had developed over the previous three years. The real key to Edward's apparent volte-face at Brétigny lies in the alterations made to the treaty when it was presented for ratification at Calais in the autumn of 1360. Someone – and the chances are that it was Edward himself – insisted that the renunciation clauses, requiring him to give up his claims to the throne of France and the northern territories – were taken out of the main text

---

[73] D. Hay, 'The Division of the Spoils of War in Fourteenth-Century England', *Transactions of the Royal Historical Society*, 5th series, 4 (1954), p. 104.

[74] Delachenal, *Charles V*, ii, pp. 22-24, 31-40, 312-13; G.F. Beltz, *Memorials of the Order of the Garter* (London, 1841), pp. 84-85; Fowler, *King's Lieutenant*, p. 280, n. 50; Luce, *Bertrand du Guesclin*, pp. 290-91.

[75] For later English criticism of the renunciations demanded by the treaty of Brétigny see W.M. Ormrod, *The Reign of Edward III: Crown and Political Society in England, 1327-1377* (London, 1990), p. 217 n. 21.

[76] Le Patourel, *Feudal Empires*, ch. XIII, p. 32.

of the treaty and set aside for fulfilment at a later date.[77] Quite what Edward intended to achieve by this manoeuvre remains uncertain, for in many respects he proved faithful to the Brétigny settlement: he immediately stopped using the title of king of France and went to some lengths to ensure that his continued contacts with Brittany, Flanders and Normandy should not jeopardise the peace.[78] On the other hand, the formal reservation of Edward's rights in these areas provided the most effective means of guaranteeing the transfer of the southern territories that were to make up the newly enlarged duchy of Aquitaine, and was therefore to provide an important negotiating position when the transfers failed to take effect and the war reopened in 1369. In this sense at least, Normandy can be said to have remained vital to English interests in the 1360s.

The duchy was to play very little part in the new phase of the Hundred Years War that began in 1369. Such a rapid collapse of English interests in the duchy is explicable in a number of different ways. It has been suggested, for example, that Edward's primary motivation in delaying the required renunciations lay in his continued determination to carve out continental appanages for the cadet branches of his large family.[79] If Normandy had any place in such a scheme, it is clear from earlier English and French practice that the duchy would be reserved for the king or his eldest son.[80] Given the Black Prince's preoccupation with the administration of Aquitaine after 1362 and the rapid deterioration of his health after the reopening of the war in 1369, it is easy to see why the Plantagenets' interests in Normandy were not maintained during the years after the Treaty of Calais.

The military situation in the duchy was highly unlikely to provide a basis for renewed English ambitions. On the eve of the Brétigny agreement, the Anglo-Navarrese still held a substantial number of positions within the duchy, but the terms of the peace required the handing over to the French of most of the principal fortresses stretching in an arc from Husson and Tinchebray to Le Neubourg and Roches d'Orival.[81] In addition, both the English and the Navarrese evacuated a number of strongholds not specified in the treaty: the most striking English examples are those of the coastal positions at Barfleur and Graffart in the Cotentin. The reason why both the obligatory and voluntary evacuations were carried through with relative ease and speed lies in the large ransoms that the Anglo-Navarrese captains were able to extort as the

---

[77] 'Some Documents Regarding the Fulfilment and Interpretation of the Treaty of Brétigny 1361-1369', ed. P. Chaplais, *Camden Miscellany, xix*, Camden Society, 3rd series, 80 (1952), p. 7; Le Patourel, *Feudal Empires*, ch. XIII, pp. 38-39.

[78] M. Jones, *Ducal Brittany, 1364-1399* (Oxford, 1970), p. 15 and n. 3.

[79] W.M. Ormrod, 'Edward III and his Family', *Journal of British Studies*, 26 (1987), pp. 408-16.

[80] J. Le Patourel, *The Norman Empire* (Oxford, 1976), pp. 179-90; J. Gillingham, *The Angevin Empire* (London, 1984), pp. 29-33; P.S. Lewis, *Later Medieval France: The Polity* (London, 1968), p. 96 and n. 1.

[81] Rymer, *Foedera*, III, i, pp. 536, 546-47.

price of their departure.[82] Once again, the substantial independence enjoyed by the English forces operating in Normandy meant that the profit motive prevailed over other possible strategic implications. By the end of 1361 the only official English presence left in Normandy was at Saint-Sauveur, whose fortress and lordship had been specifically reserved to Edward III in the 1360 treaties. This was hardly an adequate base from which to mount a full-scale onslaught on the duchy, and it is significant that under its new keeper, Sir John Chandos, Saint-Sauveur became not so much a military stronghold as the centre of an administrative system created specifically to organise the evacuation of the northern French fortresses and to receive the ransom payments already falling due for the release of King John II.[83]

It was the position of Charles the Bad which once again prevented the continuation of English claims in Normandy after 1360. The treaties of Brétigny and Calais had the effect of releasing Philip of Navarre from the English alliance; as a result, any vestiges of a combined Anglo-Navarrese operation fell apart, and Philip actually assisted in the Valois campaign to rid the duchy of the free companies.[84] If he wished to retain an interest in Normandy, Edward had either to find a new power-base that would support him as a claimant to the duchy or to retreat from the diplomatic position of the late 1350s and give support to Charles of Navarre as and when the latter chose to defect once more from the Valois cause. When this second option presented itself in 1363-64, there are some signs that both Edward and the Black Prince encouraged the freebooting English soldiers still operating in Normandy to give assistance to the Navarrese.[85] It is also apparent that they were not prepared to jeopardise the Anglo-French peace either by providing official backing for Charles or, indeed, by reviving their own dynastic claims to the duchy.[86] Normandy, which had once seemed to offer such great prospects to the English monarchy, had simply ceased to be a viable part of the surviving Plantagenet nexus in northern France.

Consequently, by the time the Anglo-French war reopened in 1369, Edward III's earlier ambitions in the duchy were already largely forgotten.[87] The English crown became somewhat careless even of its established rights in the duchy: the controversial surrender of Saint-Sauveur to the French in 1375 was particularly criticised as an example of military and diplomatic mismanagement during the Good Parliament of 1376.[88] The government of Richard II

---

[82] Henneman, *Captivity of John II*, pp. 217-19.

[83] Rymer, *Foedera*, III, i, pp. 491, 516, 555; III, ii, pp. 678; PRO, E 403/403, m. 14; E 101/28/10; 'The Ransom of John II, King of France, 1360-1370', ed D.M. Broome, *Camden Miscellany, xiv*, Camden Society, 3rd series, 37 (1926), esp. pp. 28-29.

[84] Delachenal, *Charles V*, ii, pp. 257-58.

[85] Henneman, *Captivity of John II*, pp. 230-33; Luce, *Bertrand du Guesclin*, pp. 408-10.

[86] Rymer, *Foedera*, III, ii, pp. 754-55.

[87] For John of Gaunt's brief foray into Normandy in 1369, see A. Goodman, *John of Gaunt: The Exercise of Princely Power in Fourteenth-Century Europe* (London, 1992), pp. 229-32.

[88] G. Holmes, *The Good Parliament* (Oxford, 1975), pp. 37-46, 131-33.

came to consider Normandy only in the context of its newly-evolving 'barbican policy', the attempt to create a ring of garrisons around the French coast from Calais to Bayonne, with a single Norman base at the former Navarrese stronghold of Cherbourg.[89] This policy was itself an attempt to respond to the loss of English supremacy at sea and the continued rumours of French, and sometimes specifically Norman, plans for the invasion of southern England. By the 1380s Anglo-Norman relations can therefore be said to have come full circle and returned very much to the situation on the eve of the Hundred Years War. Edward III's claim to be the true and rightful duke of Normandy may not have been completely forgotten in courtly and diplomatic circles,[90] but in the dying decades of the fourteenth century it can hardly have seemed more than a fanciful posture, an expression of personal vanity and dynastic piety taken up at a moment of supreme confidence in the reign of England's greatest warrior king. No one in England surely can have contemplated that they would shortly have a ruler who would make that fancy a reality and, in the process, outrank even the glorious Edward in the late medieval hierarchy of royal heroes.

---

[89] Jones, *Ducal Brittany*, p. 84.
[90] For the brief revival of claims to the Angevin Empire in 1395, see J.J.N. Palmer, *England, France and Christendom, 1377-99* (London, 1972), pp. 169-71, 256-57.

16

The Norman 'Nation' and the French 'Nation' in the Fourteenth and Fifteenth Centuries

Philippe Contamine

The history of national sentiment has recently benefited from, both in France and as far as France is concerned, a notable revival of interest.[1] This is closely linked to the favour which the study of *mentalités* currently enjoys but it also arises out of the contemporary situation where the future of nations within Europe is more debated than ever before. The most significant problem arising in this context is the notion that down the centuries even to the present day, French national identity has competed, and indeed still competes, with identities which, without prejudging their nature, can be called regional. As a result, when looking at any given period it seems appropriate to scrutinise such provincial identities in the same way as national identity or, in other words, to weigh the strength, vitality and political role of the differing 'national' sentiments which have been able to coexist within the geographical boundaries of France.

Within this area, there are nations (*nationes*) and peoples (*gentes*) who can legitimately claim much greater antiquity than the Norman nation and the Normans. Without going back as far as Julius Caesar and his *Gallic Wars*, let us merely open the so-called *History of the Franks*, of Gregory of Tours where under various headings we see in action alongside the Franks, the Angevins, the Auvergnats (or Alvernes), the Baïocasses, the Basques, the Blésois, the Burgundians, the Bretons, the Champenois, the Limousins, the Nantais, the Parisians, the Poitevins, the Toulousains, the Tourangeaux. From the same perspective it has been possible to hail the emergence of Aquitaine and the Aquitainians in the Merovingian era as the 'naissance d'une région'.[2] It is true that some of the other peoples, or rather the other names, subsequently

---

[1] See, in particular, *Les lieux de mémoire*, ed. P. Nora, ii, *La nation*, *, **, *** (Paris, 1986) and for the medieval period C. Beaune, *Naissance de la nation France* (Paris, 1985).

[2] M. Rouche, *L'Aquitaine des Wisigoths aux Arabes, 418-781: naissance d'une région* (Paris, 1979); J. Lejeune, *Liège et son pays: naissance d'une patrie (XVIIIe-XIVe siècle)* (Liège, 1948), provides a good example, although for a later period, of a study concentrating on a more limited area.

disappeared, for example the Neustrians of whom the Normans of the middle ages considered themselves to be the successors.[3]

A few years ago, Professor Michael Jones wrote a fundamental article entitled '*Mon Pais et ma Nation*: Breton Identity in the Fourteenth Century'.[4] In order to evoke Breton national sentiment, which grew stronger as events unfolded reaching its apogee during the second half of the fifteenth century,[5] he was able to use all kinds of sources, particularly historical and literary, as well as all kinds of arguments relating especially to institutions. It would probably be difficult to assemble an equally rich, coherent and diverse body of material for Normandy and the Normans in the later middle ages. Nevertheless, we can concede that Normandy was certainly one of the most strongly established *pays* (*patriae*),[6] and that the Normans formed one of the nations and peoples whose identity appears extremely vigorous in the context of the rather nebulous French identity of the period. The Normans are, for example, quite often mentioned in the narrative texts of the fourteenth century as clearly distinct from the French. Jean Le Bel pointed out the drowning at the battle of L'Ecluse in 1340 of 'Francoys, Normans, Gascons, Bretons, Genevoys'.[7] The *Chronique parisienne anonyme* distinguishes the knights 'de Normandie, de France comme d'Engleterre' confronting the Scots.[8] And again, in the *Chronique normande du XIVe siècle*: 'En ce temps que celle guerre fut en Gascoingne, s'assemblerent François en Normandie et entrerent en mer. Et les mena le conte de Guines et Robert Bertran et estoient six mille hommes de France et de Normandie.'[9] In 1358, 1359 and 1360 'the Navarrais, the Germans, the Normans and the men of other nations assembled by companies in many parts of France'.[10] And in Froissart:

[3] *Chronique rimée de Philippe Mouskes*, ed. Baron de Reiffenberg, ii (Brussels, 1838), p. 37, lines 13,028-30: 'Et puis s'enallerent a Ruem/ Et destruisent toute Neustrie,/ Quen nous apielons Normandie.'

[4] First printed in *War, Literature and Politics in the Late Middle Ages*, ed. C.T. Allmand (Liverpool, 1976), pp. 144-68, and reprinted in M. Jones, *The Creation of Brittany: A Late Medieval State* (London and Ronceverte, 1988), pp. 283-307.

[5] See several of the contributions in *1491, La Bretagne, terre d'Europe: Colloque international, Brest, 2-4 octobre 1991*, ed. J. Kerhervé and T. Daniel (Brest and Quimper, 1992).

[6] The word *patrie* did not in fact appear in the French language until the sixteenth century.

[7] Jean Le Bel, *Chronique*, ed. J. Viard and E. Déprez, i (Paris, 1904), p. 179. See also Froissart, *Chroniques* ed. Kervyn de Lettenhove, iii (Brussels, 1867), p. 211, referring also to the battle of L'Ecluse: 'Par avant li François ne fissent point trop grant compte de ces Normans.'

[8] 'Chronique parisienne anonyme de 1316 à 1339 précédée à la chronique dite de Guillaume de Nangis (1206-1316)', ed. A. Hellot, *Mémoires de la Société de Paris et de l'Ile-de-France*, 11 (1884), p. 75.

[9] *Chronique normande de XIVe siècle*, ed. A. and E. Molinier (Paris, 1882), p. 38.

[10] 'Navarri, Almanni, Normanni et (homines) aliorum nationum in multis locis Francie per societates congregati'; *Chronographia regum Francorum*, ed. H. Moranvillé, ii, *1328-1380* (Paris, 1893), p. 286.

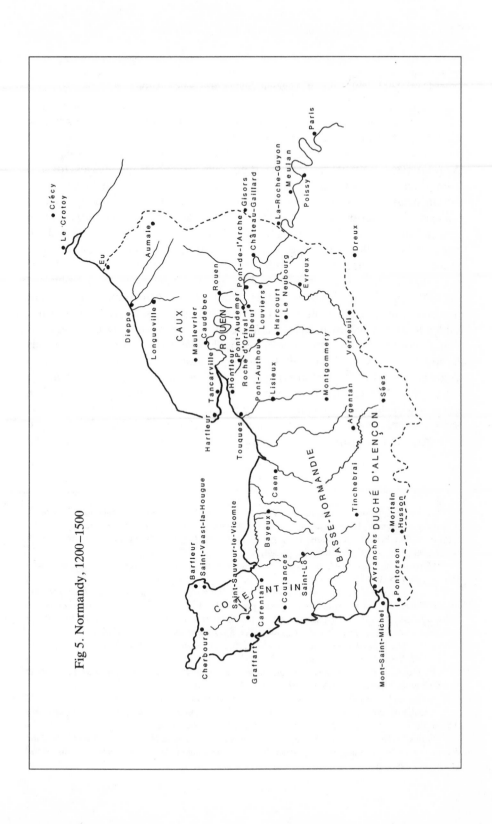

Fig 5. Normandy, 1200–1500

Ensi tinrent les gens le roy de France en celle saison iiii sieges en France, en Bretagne et en Normendie: li Normant devant Becherel, li Breton devant Brest et Derval et li Poitevin et li Angevin devant la Roche sur Ion.[11]

However, it is not unusual in texts of this period to find Normandy expressly cited as part of the kingdom of France.[12]

In any case, these Normans had their own law (the *Grand coutumier de Normandie*, c. 1250), as well as their own practices and usages for the administration of lands and for the organisation of lordships,[13] and also for the administrative framework of society (the *vicomtés*). In due course, particular traits of character were attributed to the Normans, namely ingenuity of mind and circumspection.[14] In taverns they were recognised by their accent and the peculiarities of their language. On occasion they were called 'traystres normans', 'villains normans'.[15] The aide of 1346 granted to Philip VI was accorded by the 'prelas, barons, nobles et communes pour ce assemblez et entre les autre ceuls desdiz estatz de la langue de Normandie'.[16] They were accused – but were they alone in this? – of having an excessive love of drink. Gilles le Muisit recalls in his *Annales* the fatal diversion of Louis X and his companions to the forest of Vincennes on 29 May 1316; it was warm and this happy band, overheated, fell to drinking 'comme les Normands avaient coutume de boire'.[17] The limits and extent of the duchy were well known: 'Ce dit pays de Normandie a six journees de long et quatre de large et y a six eveschiés et ung archevesque . . . et y a aussi C villes que villes et chasteaus sans ceux qui ont esté abatus et desmolis par la guerre.'[18] Normandy continued to enjoy an almost perfect coincidence between its ecclesiastical and feudal

[11] Froissart, *Chroniques*, viii, p. 260. When the same author speaks of 'li Franchois, li Normant, li Breton, li Pickart, li Bourghegnon et li compaignons estraignier ensamble', he seems to be admitting that French, Normans, Bretons, Picards and Burgundians are not strangers to each other (ibid., vii, p. 193; see also viii, p. 284).

[12] Christine de Pisan, *Le livre des fais et bonnes meurs du sage roy Charles V*, ed. S. Solente, i (Paris, 1936), p. 199.

[13] See the article 'Coutumiers de Normandie' in *Dictionnaire de lettres français: le moyen âge*, ed. G. Hasenohr and M. Zink (Paris, 1992), pp. 352-56; L. Delisle, *Etudes sur la condition de la classe agricole et l'état de l'agriculture en Normandie au moyen âge* (Evreux, 1851); A. Plaisse, *La baronnie de Neuborg: essai d'histoire agraire, économique et sociale* (Paris, 1961).

[14] Jehan Masselin, *Journal des états généraux de France tenus à Tours en 1484 sous le règne de Charles VIII*, ed. A. Bernier (Paris, 1835), p. 632.

[15] B. Guenée, *Politique et histoire au moyen âge: recueil d'articles sur l'histoire politique et l'historiographie médiévale (1956-1981)* (Paris, 1981), p. 187.

[16] Cited in H. Prentout, *Les états provinciaux de Normandie*, i (Caen, 1925), p. 37.

[17] 'Sicut Normanni bibere consueverunt', *Chronique et annales de Giles le Muisit, abbé de Saint-Martin de Tournai (1272-1352)*, ed. H. Lemaître (Paris, 1905), p. 90.

[18] Gilles Le Bouvier, dit le Héraut Berry, 'Le recouvrement de Normandie', *Narratives of the Expulsion of the English from Normandy*, MCCCCXLIX-MCCCL, ed. J. Stevenson, Rolls Series (London, 1863), p. 369.

frontiers, as well as a reputation for economic and demographic abundance at least before the onset of plague and war.[19]

Although far from unknown, the following fifteenth-century texts may be mentioned here. One of them, undoubtedly idealised but more precise than one might at first sight think, is taken from the *Livre de la description des pays* which Gilles Le Bouvier wrote towards 1450:

> Puis y est le païs de Normandie, qui est bonne duché, puissant et riche et est tres bon païs de blez et de bestial blanc et rouge et foison de belles forestz et petites rivieres et grant foison de pommes et poires, dont l'on fait le citre et le poiré, dont le peuple boit pour ce qu'il n'y croist point de vin, combien qu'il en vient assez par mer, et par la riviere de Saine. En ce païs font de moult bons draps, et grant foison, et est ce païs de grant revenue au prince.[20] En ce païs a sept cités, c'est assavoir Rouen, archevesché, Cee, Avranches, Coustances, Baïeux, Lisieux, Evreux. Les deux meilleurs villes dudit païs sont Rouen et Caen. Et y a plusieurs contes, hommes du duc. Premierement la conté d'Alençon, qui est de present duché, la conté de Harecourt, la conté d'Evreux, la conté d'Aumalle, la conté d'Eu, la conté de Tancarville, la conté de Longueville, la conté de Maulevrier, la conté de Mortain et la conté de Montgommery, qui sont dix contés. En ce païs a grant noblesse et de grans seigneurs et barons et y a grant foison de bons marchans, par mer et par terre, et sont les populaires de grant peine, et fors laboureurs, hommes et femmes. Et sont honnestes gens de vesture et de mesnaige et sont grans buveurs en leurs festimens et grans chieres se font a boire.[21]

The second text, clearly of the same period and equally idealised, owes its existence to the pen of the Norman 'patriot' Robert Blondel, in the chapter entitled *Descripcio Normannie situs et morum Normannorum* of his *Reductio Normannie*.

> Normandy was formerly called Neustria by our ancestors because of its natural fertility. Today it takes its name, properly speaking, from the Normans who, sailing from Norway and fighting under Duke Rollo, gained by their feats of arms the coast lands of the Gallic sea and finally ended up in possession of the whole province to its furthest boundaries, an area to which they gave the name Normandy. It is bounded by the Breton ocean to the west, France to the south and the sea to the north. It is a land which is very fertile, with luxuriant and abundant pasture for sheep, and fruitful forests and meadows filled with a variety of wild animals and birds. It is rich in rivers and sea ports, filled to overflowing with fruit-bearing trees, endowed with notable towns and provided with many strongholds. Its metropolitan see is Rouen, a mighty town by virtue of its ancient population and its wealth, situated on the river which is called Seine. Its people

---

[19] 'Le meilleur païs, plus rice, plus cras et mieulx pourveus de tous biens qui fust ou monde', Froissart, *Chroniques*, iv, p. 384.

[20] It is worth noting that the Héraut Berry used this term and not that of the king. This also applies to the usage of the term duke in the rest of the text, because at the time he was writing there was no duke of Normandy.

[21] *Le livre de la description des pays*, ed. E.T. Hamy (Paris, 1908), pp. 47-48.

are numerous, strong, warlike, civilised in their habits, measured in their speech and dutiful in their affections. They are of a pacific nature, patient in their endeavours, shrewd in the art of making themselves rich, devoted to divine worship, loyal in the payment of tithes, obedient to prelates and cherishing even unto death their sovereign lord.[22]

There follows an entirely predictable elaboration on the oppression suffered by the Normans for thirty-two years at the hands of their most cruel enemy (i.e. the English) and on their liberation effected by Charles VII.

The third text refers to another well-known characteristic of the Normans; their liking for legal actions and for chicanery. The Norman Thomas Basin noted in his *Histoire de Louis XI* the existence in this 'province' (*provincia*) of a multitude of (secular) lawyers, who never ceased

> to incite the inhabitants to judicial processes and conflicts, to which they had never before been disposed. They encourage the people to such judicial actions because they themselves draw from this public plague their own chief sustenance and support. Thus by their trickery they exhaust and bleed dry all that remained to the people after the payment of taxes and public renders. Ignoring all civilised practices and all principles of divine and human law, they rely only on the few customs and usages which often they twist into the worst and most pernicious abuses, and which they never cease to model or remodel, corrupting them by blameworthy interpretations in order to make them conform to the self-interest which is their constant objective. So they take control of virtually the whole government of the *patria*, to the extent that there is no prelate or nobleman, no matter how powerful, who does not find himself compelled to submit to them and to fear them. They are so closely united and bound together that to meddle with one is to attack them all. They hold under their sway all the courts of justice of the land. When the public meetings of the Estates occur,[23] they alone, rather than the whole country, decide what suits them almost at will and thus bring discussion to an end.[24]

---

[22] 'Normania a priscis patribus Neustria rerum naturalium ubertate condam appellata fuit, et diebus hodiernis a propriis Normanis nomen sortita est, qui navigio vecti de Nourvegia, sub Rolone duce militantes, littus occeani Gallici armis obtinuerunt, qui tandem provinciam totam in circitu possidentes, eam Normanniam vocarent. Habet autem occeanum Britanicum ad eurum et sinum maris ad occidentem, Galliam ad meridiem et occeanum ad aquilonem. Est enim ejus gleba frugum uberrima, piguis agris, pastura pecorum opima, nemoribus et pratis fecunda, ferarum et volatilium varietate referta, fluminibus et portubus marinis locuples, fructiferis aboribus consita, urbibus insignibus decorata et prevalidis opidis munita; cujus metropolis existit Rothomagum, urbs antiqua populo et diviciis potens, super fluvium sita qui Sequana dicitur. Cujus gens est populosa, fortis et bellicosa, urbana in habitu, modesta in affatu, pia in affectu, pacifica in convictu, laboris patiens, opum augendarum industria sagax, circa divinum cultum devota, decimarum solutione fidelis, prelatis obsequens, et in vite extremum supremi principis amantissima.' *Oeuvres de Robert Blondel: historien normand du XVe siècle*, ed. A. Héron, ii (Rouen, 1891), pp. 53-54.

[23] An obvious allusion to the estates of Normandy.

[24] *Histoire de Louis XI*, ed. and trans. C. Samaran, i (Paris, 1963), pp. 55-57.

From whence derived Basin's opposition as a man of the church to the *charte aux Normans* which he calls elsewhere, through a play on words, the 'chartre aux Normands'.[25]

Of course, the solidarity of the Normans expressed itself particularly outside Normandy. Note, for instance, from the thirteenth century onwards the existence of a Norman nation (*veneranda natio*) at the university of Paris alongside the French, Picard and English nations. Just like the other nations, the Norman nation brought together with a *procurator* in overall charge the students and the masters of the faculty of arts, as well as some masters in other faculties who had graduated in arts. It is remarkable that all the members of this Norman nation were from the province of Rouen. As a result it was, in theory at least, the most homogeneous of all four nations.[26]

Just as a rich Breton historiography was in existence at the end of the middle ages,[27] so likewise there was a Norman historiography, scarcely less flourishing, whose 'jewel in the crown' was without doubt the *Croniques de Normandie*.[28] Here is the appropriate place to mention the loan of a copy of this work which the *échevins* of Rouen made in December 1465 to the comte de Harcourt. The manuscript, which still exists,[29] was passed on to the brother of Louis XI, Charles, at that time duke of Normandy; the latter ordered a public reading of the passage which related how Louis IV of Outremer had to acknowledge, whether he liked it or not, the right of the son of William Longsword (Longespee) to the peaceful possession of his heritage.[30]

The well-known rivalry, particularly in the economic sphere, between Paris and Rouen was sustained by, and in its turn encouraged, Norman identity.[31] In late medieval rolls of arms the armorial of Normandy features regularly, proof in its own way of the unity of the Norman nobility.[32]

Let us come now to the more strictly political dimensions of the problem. To what extent did Norman identity and solidarity interact in the political sphere, in particular with relations to the French monarchy? One point must be stressed at the outset. For more than a century the Capetian kings took care not to detach Normandy from their demesne in order to grant it as an appanage to one of their sons. Anjou, Maine, Poitou, the counties of Artois, Valois, Alençon, La Marche and several other fiefs were alienated from the crown,

[25] Thomas Basin, *Apologie ou plaidoyer pour moi-même*, ed. and trans. C. Samaran and G. De Groër (Paris, 1974), pp. 238, 264.

[26] Although there were Bretons from the province of Tours present within it.

[27] J. Kerhervé, 'Aux origines du sentiment national: les chroniqueurs bretons de la fin du moyen âge', *Bulletin de la Société Archéologique du Finistère*, 108 (1980), pp. 165-206.

[28] *Les croniques de Normandie, 1223-1453*, ed. A. Hellot (Rouen, 1881).

[29] BN, MS fr. 2623.

[30] B. Guenée, *Entre l'église et l'état: quatre vies de prélats français à la fin du moyen âge* (Paris, 1987), p. 396.

[31] M. Mollat, *Le commerce maritime normand à la fin du moyen âge: étude d'histoire économique et sociale* (Paris, 1952); J. Favier, *Paris au XVe siècle, 1380-1500*, (Paris, 1974).

[32] M. Popoff, *Marches d'armes*, ii, *Normandie* (Paris, 1985).

but never Normandy, because of the geographical significance of the duchy, its financial revenues and human resources. Normandy found itself deprived of a prince around whom national sentiment might have strengthened, developed or gravitated. It has often been said that national sentiment at the end of the middle ages was most emphatically love of the homeland, but equally it was love of the prince and thus took the form of a sense of dynasty. Yet the opposite is also true: no dynasty, no national sentiment. The rule is proved, for example, by the county of Toulouse after 1271, and the county of Champagne after 1284. No one bore the title 'duke of Normandy' except between 1332 and 1364[33] and at the end of 1465.[34] Thereafter, we have to wait until the reign of Louis XVI to find the reappearance of a duke of Normandy in the person of the second son of the king, the future Louis XVII.

Despite all the links which tied it to England, the ease with which Normandy accepted the domination of the kings of France is remarkable. Of course the latter on the whole respected the special nature of their conquest, particularly in terms of its institutions. Significantly, it was in Poitou that Henry III chanced his arm. There was no Norman Taillebourg, despite appeals sent to the Plantagenet king during this period. Signs of tension between the Capetians and the Normans did exist but they were sporadic.[35] Even so, there may have been a desire to disarm the Normans and their province. On 15 December 1346 Philip VI of Valois authorised Yon, sire de Garencières to 'recloure et refermer' with walls and ditches the 'ville et chastiaus' of Baudemont, so that the inhabitants could find refuge there. In fact the order goes on to say that the *pays* of Normandy

a este moult desole et desgarniz par noz anemis en ceste presente annee[36] de chasteaux et de forteresses en traison de ce que, après la conqueste faite dudit païs par noz devanciers . . . il fu ordené que toutes les forteresses dudit païs seroient abatues se n'estoient celles qu'il retindrent pour le demaine de la duché de Normandie laquelle des lors il annexerent et adjousterent a la couronne de France.[37]

All the same, the work of the Norman, Pierre Dubois, champion of the royal cause, argues in favour of Normandy accepting without difficulty attachment to the crown of France, just as the support which Philip the Fair found in the 'légistes' of the south, such as Guillaume de Nogaret and Guillaume de

---

[33] J. Tricard, 'Jean, duc de Normandie et héritier de France; un double échec?', *Annales de Normandie*, 29 (1980), pp. 23-44.

[34] H. Stein, *Charles de France, frère de Louis XI* (Paris, 1919).

[35] J. Favier, 'La Normandie royale', *Histoire de Normandie*, ed. M. de Boüard (Toulouse, 1970), pp. 195-217.

[36] An allusion to the campaign of Edward III.

[37] Cited in C. Goldmann, 'Les Garencières-Le Baveux: vie et mort d'un lignage de la moyenne noblesse normande (XIIIe-XVe siècles)' (unpublished doctoral thesis, University of Paris IV, 1991), iii, pp. 56-58.

Plaisians, bears witness to an important stage in the integration into the kingdom of the *pays de langue d'oc*.[38]

To find the first great political manifestation, that is, the first major demonstration of Norman distinctiveness, we must go back to the end of the reign of Philip IV (le Bel) and to the reign of his son Louis X (le Hutin) into the well-known setting of what are called 'baronial alliances' or 'provincial lea-gues' – taking provinces to be as many elements as together exactly made up the kingdom of France. It is not anachronistic to suggest that a similar geographical conception of such issues – what we might call the dialogue between the centre and the periphery or, in other words, the problem of decentralisation – applied in the fourteenth century.[39] This can be proved by a passage in the *Chronique rimée* of Geoffrey de Paris concerning the movement of 1314-15;

> En cel temps, en cele saison
> Dont je fais ja raison,
> Les barons de France assemblerent:
> et tous ensemble s'accorderent
> Et de France et de Picardie,
> Aveques celz de Normendie,
> Et de Borgoingne et de Champaingne,
> D'Anjou, de Poito, de Bretaingne,
> De Chartrain, du Perche, du Mainne,
> Celz d'Auvergne et celz de Gascoingne
> Et de tout le royaume de France.[40]

In the same vein, the *Chronique des quatre premiers Valois* refers specifically to the 'provinces' of the kingdom in a passage relating to political assemblies which marked the accession of Charles VI (1380): the *ambaxadeurs* of the king and of Louis, duc d'Anjou, came to Rouen to explain that for the defence of the kingdom it would be necessary to maintain 8,000 men-at-arms. The answer was

> que la province de Normandie feroit comme les autres provinces. Et fut prinse journee au jeudi avant Noel. Et la a Paris furent faits plusieurs parlemens de

[38] See the article 'Dubois, Pierre' in *Lexikon des Mittelalters*, iii (Munich aand Zurich, 1986), col. 1433-34.

[39] P.S. Lewis, 'The Centre, the Periphery and Power Distribution in Later Medieval France', *The Crown and Local Community in England and France in the Fifteenth Century*, ed. J.R.L. Highfield and R. Jeffs (Gloucester, 1981), pp. 33-50.

[40] Cited in P. Contamine, 'De la puissance aux privilèges: doléances de la noblesse française aux XIVe et XVe siècles', *La noblesse au moyen âge, XIe-XVe siècles: essais à la mémoire de Robert Boutruche*, ed. P. Contamine (Paris, 1976), p. 243.

toutes les provinces du royaume de France, ou furent prelas, nobles et gens des bonnes villes de toutes les provinces dudit royaume pour avoir adviz ensemble.[41]

I shall not linger here over the content of the three charters granted to the Normans by Louis X, in both Latin and French, on 19 March 1315 and again in July of the same year.[42] In retrospect, the important thing to note is that whilst several charters of this type rapidly sank into obscurity,[43] the 'charte aux Normands' (*Carta Normannorum* – that *Magna Carta* of Norman liberties, if the comparison is not presumptuous), entrusted for safe-keeping to the cathedral chapter of Rouen, enjoyed an unusually extended longevity. Various stages of its existence are worth recalling here.

There was no confirmation by the later Capetians nor by Philip of Valois at his accession. But according to the *Chronique des quatre premiers Valois* on several occasions in 1337 (no doubt this should read 1339) meetings of prelates, barons, nobles and bourgeois of the *bonnes villes* of Normandy were held at Pont-Audemer thanks to a royal initiative with a view to keeping 'les libertés et franchises du païs'. They ended by granting to the king and his son John, duke of Normandy, 'une grant somme de pecune, par ainsi que le roy et le duc les maintiendroient en leurs libertés et franchises, selon ce que la charte des Normans le contient. La somme fut levee et le roy et le duc jurerent ce tenir et garder fermement'.[44] In fact, the charter was confirmed by Philip VI and his son John, duke of Normandy, count of Anjou and Maine in March 1339, in terms which it is important to elucidate. In this confirmation in Latin, the king made reference to a unanimous devotion shown in his favour by the 'barons, knights and other nobles, citizens, inhabitants and people' of Normandy against his enemies and those of his kingdom.

He made reference to the oppressions and excesses committed by his men 'against the *registrum Normanniae* and against the franchises, liberties and

---

[41] *Chronique des quatre premiers Valois, 1327-1393*, ed. S. Luce (Paris, 1862), p. 293. A study in the sources of the fourteenth and fifteenth centuries of the word *province* (beyond its meaning in the ecclesiastical sphere) being used to designate a certain part of the kingdom of France, along with the words *pays* and *région*, would no doubt be revealing. The expression *états provinciaux* to describe the estates proper to a certain fief or region appeared only in 1576, referring specifically to the 'congregation et assemblée des Estatz provinciaux de Normandie' (see the article 'Etats provinciaux' by N. Bulst in the *Lexikon des Mittelalters*, iv (1989), col. 51). See also G. Dupont-Ferrier, 'Sur l'emploi du mot "province", notamment dans le langage administratif de l'ancienne France', *Revue historique* (1929), 160, pp. 241-67; 161, pp. 278-303.

[42] The original is preserved in the Archives Départmentales de la Seine Maritime, G 3692. The *trésor des chartes* and the *chambre des comptes* of the king of France possessed in their registers an official copy of it; A. Artonne, *Le mouvement de 1314 et les chartes provinciales de 1315* (Paris, 1912), pp. 150-51.

[43] This was not the case with the so-called charter to the Languedociens, confirmed by Philip VI (1328), Charles V (1368), Charles VII (1446) and Louis XI (1463) (Artonne, *Mouvement*, p. 155). Without having demanded confirmation, the dukes of Brittany kept their charter of 1315 amongst their archives in their *trésor* (M. Jones, 'The Capetians and Brittany', *Bulletin of the Institute of Historical Research*, 63 (1990), pp. 1-16.

[44] *Chronique des quatre premiers Valois*, pp. 8-9.

worthy usages anciently observed in this *pays*, in infraction of their charters, privileges and royal letters', notably those conceded by Louis X. The charter therefore appears as the central plank of something much more wide-ranging.[45] But according to the *Chronique des quatre premiers Valois* Godfrey de Harcourt went to Rouen in 1356 to pay homage to Charles, duke of Normandy. He carried from the cathedral of Notre-Dame

> la charte aux Normans ou sont contenus les privileges de Normendie. Laquelle charte il apporta sur sa teste par devant le duc et dit oyant tous: 'Mon seigneur naturel, vecy la charte des Normans. En la fourme qu'il est contenu dedens, s'il le vous plaist a jurer et tenir, je suis tout prest de vous faire hommage'. Sur ces paroles, le conseil du duc de Normendie voulust veoir et avoir la dicte chartre. Et monseigneur Godefroy respondi que la dite charte il avoit promis rendre et restablir presentement en la dicte eglise et qu'il lui porteroit. Mais se copie ou *vidimus* en voulloient, bien le pourroient avoir.[46]

There the matter rested, and Godfrey de Harcourt departed with his charter without paying homage. There is no confirmation by Charles V, but Charles VI confirmed it on 25 January 1381; on 1 April of the same year the parlement registered the 'privileges, franchises et libertez octroiees par nos predecesseurs rois de France a nos bien amez les habitants de nostre païs de Normandie'.[47] John, duke of Bedford, regent of the kingdom of France, also confirmed it on 16 November 1423 in the name of Henry VI.[48]

On 31 December 1450, only a few days after the solemn entry of Charles VII, the canons of the cathedral church of Rouen authorised their dean to communicate to the estates of Normandy the original manuscripts of the charter in order to make one or more *vidimus*. A Norman delegation was later sent to the king, then in Touraine, to 'obtenir dudit seigneur la confirmation entierement de ladicte chartre'. A document of 1452 makes reference to the 'quatre principaulx requestes deliberees par les Etats de Normandie a requerir au roy pour le bien de ce pays de Normandie, c'est assavoir la confirmation de la charte aux Normands, la chambre des comptes et des generaulx de Rouen, le seel du roy audit lieu de Rouen et l'Université en la ville de Caen'. The negotiation dragged on. In April 1458 Charles VII, tired of war, finally confirmed the charter, even adding that in accordance with past practice no tax should be raised without the consent of the men of the three estates of the duchy, unless 'l'evidente utilité ou la necesité urgente' demanded it .[49] Louis XI confirmed the charter on 4 January 1462.[50]Later on, although it was barely mentioned during the meeting of the estates general at Tours in 1484,[51] it was

---

[45] *Ordonnances des rois de France*, vi (Paris, 1741), p. 549.
[46] *Chronique des quatre premiers Valois*, p. 34.
[47] *Ordonnances des rois*, vi, p. 549.
[48] Artonne, *Mouvement*, p. 151.
[49] H. Prentout, *Etats provinciaux*, i, p. 158.
[50] Artonne, *Mouvement*, p. 152.
[51] Masselin, *Journal*, p. 634.

confirmed by Charles VIII on 27 April 1485, by Louis XII on 30 September and 2 October 1508, by Francis I in 1517, by Henry II in 1550 and lastly by Henry III in April 1579.[52]

But if subsequent kings of France thought that they could limit the charter by disregarding it, it was not completely forgotten. The estates of Normandy demanded it should be respected in 1583, 1585 and 1595.[53] The *Nu-Pieds* drew inspiration from it in 1639; 'Si vous ne conservez pas votre charte, Normands, vous n'avez pas de coeur.'[54] The decades which preceded the French Revolution witnessed several references to it, such as in the remonstrances made to Louis XV by the parlement of Rouen in 1760 and again at the time of the suppression of the parlements in 1771: the *Manifeste aux Normands* considered the *pacte* proclaimed by the charter of 1315 broken to such an extent that if the king persisted, the estates would have to be summoned. The *Lettre de la noblesse normande* to the king amalgamated two articles of different origins: only the first of these was found in the document of 1315, namely the declaration that 'les causes du duché doivent être jugés par l'Echiquier du duché sans être préalablement consentie par les gens des trois Etats du duché'.[55] In 1787 the parlement of Rouen, after having recalled the services rendered by the Normans to the monarchy, took care in its turn to raise the article whereby 'les princes déclarent qu'ils ne pourront, eux ni leurs successeurs, lever aucuns impôts sur les biens et les personnes sans utilité évidente et une urgente nécessité et par la convention et assemblée des gens des trois Etats'.[56] The *cahiers de doléances* of 1789 drawn up by the clergy of Caen and Alençon, as well as by the clergy and nobility of the bailliages of Coutances, Rouen and Evreux, did refer to the *charte aux Normands*. The *cahiers* of the third estate of the city of Rouen put it this way: 'Que les députés demanderont aux prochains Etats généraux la confirmation de la charte normande et le maintien des privilèges qu'elle assure à la province', and those of the Third Estate of Saint-Gervais-lès-Rouen: 'Que les Etats provinciaux luy soyent rendus et que la charte normande reprenne sa première vigueur, non obstant toutes lois antécédentes et atténuatives qui auraient pu être surprises.' Or again, in the *cahier* of Darnetal, 'Que cette charte soit traduite correctement et fidèlement et qu'elle soit lue tous les ans à la rentrée tant du Parlement que des sièges royaux et seigneuriaux de la province, pour y être gardé de point en point et exécutee suivant sa forme et teneur'.[57] Naturally the events of the

[52] A. Floquet, 'La charte aux Normands', *Bibliothèque de l'Ecole des Chartes*, 4 (1842), pp. 421; Prentout, *Etats provinciaux*, i.

[53] C. de Beaurepaire, *Cahiers des états de Normandie sous le règne de Henri III*, i and ii (Rouen, 1887-88).

[54] M. Foisil, *La révolte des Nu-pieds et les révoltes normandes de 1639* (Paris, 1970), p. 189.

[55] Prentout, *Etats provinciaux*, p. 379.

[56] Ibid., p. 386.

[57] M. Bouloiseau, *Cahiers de doléances du tiers état du bailliage de Rouen pour les états généraux de 1789*, i and ii (Paris, 1960), see in the general index, ii, p. 493 under *Charte normande*.

Revolution, and in particular the *fête de la fédération* which occured on 14 July 1790 at the Champ de Mars – the act which founded France of the *nouveau régime* – consigned to the dustbin of history this famous document. Since the end of the middle ages the *charte* had been copied many times, most notably as an appendix to the numerous manuscripts of the *Coutume de Normandie*. It had made a significant contribution to the fostering and strengthening of the identity of a *pays*.

Can we deduce from all of this that the legal and institutional existence of such a Norman identity constituted for the crown of France a major, indeed mortal, danger? The problem here is knowing whether there was a common political attitude on the part of the Normans which might have led them under certain circumstances to wish to detach themselves *en masse* from the cause of the kings of France.

Even before the beginning of the Anglo-French conflict Philip of Valois, doubtless in order to ensure his own place on the throne of France, insisted on granting the title of duke of Normandy to his eldest son, John. This was a clever move, involving fairly limited risks, it seemed, insofar as the title had lain for a long while in abeyance. Confronted, indeed affronted by Edward III, Philip of Valois had to make concessions and to accept compromises in order to obtain the military and financial support of the Normans. Initially there was no indication whatsoever that the Normans would prove less loyal than the other subjects of the king. The decisive turning-point came in 1339. This is revealed by a document dated at the Bois de Vincennes on 23 March 1339. This was in effect both a treaty, promise and an agreement. A good fifty or so of the great Norman lords led by Raoul, count of Eu, constable of France, Jean, count of Harcourt (a fairly recent elevation!), Robert Bertrand, sire de Bricquebec, marshal of France, and Godfrey de Harcourt – taking note of the affection shown by the king towards Normans of all degrees whose privileges he had just indicated his willingness to confirm, and acting in the name of the nobles, citizens, inhabitants of the towns and of the common people of Normandy (the prelates, we note, were not involved) – undertook to cross to England under the command of the duke of Normandy. This was to be with 4,000 men-at-arms of good standing (a figure made up of 160 knights banneret, 640 knights bachelor, and 3,200 esquires) and 40,000 *sergents de pied*. The last figure was subsequently lowered by royal concession to 20,000. Of this 20,000 there were supposed to be 5,000 crossbowmen. The duke was to have a certain number of the 4,000 men-at-arms in order to form his own *bataille* but this was not to include either the *chevetaines* or their *bataille*. Put another way, the *bataille* of Raoul d'Eu, for example, was to remain both intact and separate. High wages were to be paid to all. The king guaranteed that he would see to the keeping of the sea in order to ensure the revictualling of the army. The expedition was to last for 100 days at the most. For the last fifteen days the wages would be paid by the duke. This offer was valid for 1339, 1340 and 1341. If the king needed the Normans for the defence of his kingdom, he could call off the enterprise and take them into his service at their own expense for eight weeks. At the same time they were exempted from other feudal services such as the *arrière-ban*. Once the privileges had been confirmed, sealed and announced, they were to be taken to Rouen for the first meeting of what was to become the estates of Normandy, and to be given to any interested party. If the service was not fulfilled the forfeit would be 300,000 *livres*. The division of booty was already being envisaged. What belonged to the king of England in his kingdom would devolve to the duke of Normandy; what was held by the nobles, barons and other secular lords would come to the churches, barons, nobles and *bonnes villes* of Normandy. (It seems that in this complete dispossession the English church was to be spared.) The potential enriching of the Norman church was even calculated as 30,000 pounds sterling of rent which was to be paid out by the king of France once he had become king of England. The Scots would be recompensed for what they had previously lost. But if peace with England was made before the project came to fruition, the Normans would still keep their privileges. They would simply have to serve with 2,000 men-at-arms at high wages for three months in the first war which the king subsequently waged.[58]

Although this was all rather idealistic, the contract was surely taken seriously and was long debated. Did the discussion lead to the creation of a significant link between the king and his duchy? In spite of everything it is not clear whether Philip de Valois wished to pursue it. Perhaps he had been badly advised. For different reasons – strategic, political, or perhaps both – the plan was not put into operation save in its earliest stages.[59] In searching for an explanation, should we accept what Pierre Cochon said later in the *Chronique normande*?[60] The Normans had granted to Philip VI, if he would confirm their charter, 100,000 *livres* for its sealing. Furthermore, they promised him, on risk of their property and inheritances, to fight at their own costs against the king of England if he landed in Brittany, Normandy or Picardy, to take him to the king of France dead or alive, or else to fight to the death. Philip VI might have been seduced by this bravado but Philip (actually Miles) de Noyers, representing the Burgundian party, advised the king not to commit himself in this way. If they succeeded, these simple vassals of the crown would become too impertinent, puffed up with pride, 'chefs de leur entente'; never again would they obey the king. Miles de Noyers recommended another way: to have recourse to common law, to summon the Normans as subjects and, in their company, to oppose the English king: 'Car vous pourres mieux soustenir le fais atout vostre forche et les Normans avec vous que eulz tous seulz. Et si en arés l'onnour et non pas les Normans.'

[58] Froissart, *Chroniques*, xviii, *Pièces justificatives, 1319-99* (Brussels, 1874), pp. 67-75.

[59] J. Sumption, *The Hundred Years War*, i, *Trial by Battle* (London and Boston, 1990), pp. 261-62.

[60] *Chronique Normande de Pierre Cochon*, ed. C. de Beaurepaire, (Rouen and Paris, 1870), pp. 57-58. Along the same lines, according to Froissart, the 'François', did not 'firent point trop grant compte' of the losses suffered by the Normans at L'Ecluse, *Chroniques*, iii, p. 211.

Although the Normans were in large numbers in the host gathered at Bouvines the next year, it is striking that we find them dispersed between several *batailles*, those of the constable, the marshals (of whom Robert Bertrand was one), of the count of Alençon, of the king of France (which was where the count of Harcourt served), and of Philip, king of Navarre, count of Evreux, Angoulême, Mortain and Longueville. We might have expected them to be all regrouped behind the duke of Normandy, but this was not the case.[61]

The invasion of Normandy by Edward III and the enormous damage which resulted must have changed opinions. Even so, right from the outset the Normans had been loyal in their response. When an emissary of the English king told the inhabitants of the Cotentin that Edward III 'ne venoit pas en ycellui païs pour le gaster mes pour en prendre la saisine', they responded quite simply by killing him.[62] Godfrey de Harcourt was far from being typical of the whole of Normandy.

In 1347 John, duke of Normandy, obtained from his father effective possession of his duchy. He made his joyful entry into Rouen and lost no time in summoning the estates, which granted a subsidy of 450,000 *livres tournois*. This was a considerable sum, although it is true that the value of money had been greatly debased by as much as a half or two-thirds since 1330. Each Norman parish was to maintain a man-at-arms for one year at a rate of six *sous parisis* per day but this money would come in the main from a tax of 3.3 per cent on sales of commodities. At the centre the levy was to be controlled by a representative of each of the three estates sitting at Rouen. There remains much doubt whether the whole of this quite massive sum, to be collected by such uncertain methods, could have been raised.[63]

Arising out of a meeting of the estates at Pont-Audemer there was a new subsidy on the sale of goods in 1351. This prompted a reaction at Rouen in August of the same year, a conspiracy 'par maniere de harelle et de takehan'. The chest of the collectors were overturned and twenty-three drapers were hanged. Over the next few years the subsidy was raised but not, one imagines, without resentment. In 1355 the levy of a hearth tax for three months on the populations of the *bailliages* of Rouen, Gisors and Caux ought in principle to have realised enough for the provision of 2,000 men-at-arms, with their rates of pay set at 40 *sous parisis* per day for a knight banneret, 20 *sous* for a knight bachelor and 10 *sous* for an esquire. As far as Lower Normandy (Basse Normandie – the expression starts to appear in this period) was concerned,

---

[61] BN, MSS nouvelles acquisitions françaises 9238-40. P. Contamine, *Guerre, état et société à la fin du moyen âge: études sur les armées des rois de France, 1337-1494* (Paris and La Haye 1972).

[62] AN, MS JJ 76, fo. 240v, no. 393.

[63] A. Colville, *Les états de Normandie, leurs origines et leur développement au XVIe siècle* Paris, 1894), pp. 60-61; J.B. Hennemann, *Royal Taxation in Fourteenth Century France: The Developing of War Financing, 1322-1356* (Princeton, 1971), p. 229; G. Bois, *Crise du féodalisme: économie rurale et démographie en Normandie orientale du début du XIVe siècle au milieu du XVIe siècle* (Paris, 1976), pp. 258-59.

each group of 100 hearths was to maintain one man-at-arms and one archer for a specified length of time. Finally, in May 1356 the Dauphin Charles, who had become duke of Normandy in fact as well as name, considered himself in a position to raise for three months an aide of 10 *sous tournois* per hearth per month.[64]

From this quick overview the impression emerges that, although the Normans bandied fine words and formal gestures and gave many a proof of their apparent generosity, they made a rather moderate financial effort, at least until 1355. Events unfolded as if, frankly, they felt no real concern for the lot of their king, even though they suffered the full thrust of repercussions of war with the English. Indeed we must question the yield of these indirect taxes given the economic crisis of the period.

If that is the case, shouldn't we ask whether Normandy was simply a liability for the French monarchy? We must admit, however, that other provinces and regions of Languedoc and Languedoïl did not show themselves to be markedly more generous. From this perspective the Normans were neither more nor less *bons français* than the other subjects of the king.

It is impossible to overlook the problems raised by the existence of the Navarrese party. Even in the eyes of contemporaries there was undoubtedly a powerful Navarrese party which, by virtue of the territorial endowment of Charles II of Navarre as count of Evreux and of Mortain, discovered Normandy to be the foundation of its power. This party did not owe its existence simply to the wily and charismatic personality of Charles, although the latter became all the more determined one he was persuaded of the legitimacy of his grievances against his father-in-law and later his brother-in-law. This party crystallised all kinds of discontents, which were fed even more by French military defeats than by the style of government of those who formed the entourage of John the Good. It seems that if to be Navarrese meant being a reformer, everyone was indeed a reformer to a greater or lesser extent, save perhaps the masters of the kingdom – a mere handful. The true Navarrese party comprised a rather restricted number of loyal followers, incapable of controlling a province of any size beyond the personal domains of Charles of Navarre. In short, the Navarrese party should not be confused with Normandy nor Normandy with the Navarrese party. Even at the height of the crisis or crises, Normandy never drifted completely into the camp which opposed the king of France. Despite his blunders, the king always kept many supporters. During these years we are faced with a Norman society which was torn apart and divided in political terms. Such divisions and rifts can equally be found elsewhere. Conversely, even at the heart of his rule in Paris, King John had his detractors and opponents. It should be noted that when enumerating the groups of protagonists the *Chronique des quatre premiers Valois* regularly distinguishes between the Navarrese, Picards and Normans. Undoubtedly

---

[64] Bois, *Crise du féodalisme*, pp. 263-64.

Normans might find themselves alongside Navarrese, but they remained distinct. According to Pierre Cochon, the king of Navarre 'promist as Normans que, se ilz vouilloient obeir a luy et qu'il fust duc il s' obligeoit a les garder tous et contre tous et a [les] tenir en leurs franchises et libertez en la maniere que les tenoit le bon roy saint Loys'. A certain number of barons and knights accepted this written proposition, demonstrating their adherence by affixing their seals to it. The towns of Evreux, Caen and Bayeux were solicited for support, but declared that they would only add their seals after Rouen. The Norman capital refused to do so.[65]

The setting up by Charles V of an onerous system of impositions within the limits of the Languedoïl – a system which did not respect the special place of Normandy – aroused definite discontent, but such discontent was expressed on a national scale. Although at Rouen there was 'la Harelle', which spread to other towns in Normandy, there was also a revolt at Paris, the so-called Maillets' upheaval. There can be no doubt that during the 1370s Normandy developed, or even gained for the first time, both the position and reputation as the milch-cow of royal finances. The *charte aux normands* was shown to be totally useless in guaranteeing special financial privileges for the duchy. Indeed it is tempting to say that the very opposite was the case.

The division of opinion expressed in Normandy during the time of the king of Navarre resurfaced later during the quarrel of the Armagnacs and Burgundians. Indeed Burgundian sympathies were so strong that the province, taken as a whole, could pass for Burgundian. This did not prevent a significant number of the Norman nobility from adhering to Charles VII during the English invasion. Whatever one thinks about the English presence or occupation, Normandy should not be considered a subjugated province. This was despite the able and judicious policy of Bedford who not only sought to reestablish order and a feeling of prosperity but also took pains to consult the estates before all tax demands (which, incidentally, were heavy) and to dangle before the Normans the carrot of a sort of 'home rule'.[66]

At the end of these thirty-two years of tribulations, Norman identity certainly existed but in markedly different ways. On the one hand the Normans, or some of them, glorified in the fact of having been and continuing

---

[65] *Chronique normande*, pp. 81-82.

[66] L. Puiseux, 'Des insurrections populaires en Normandie pendant l'occupation anglaise au XVe siècle', *Mémoires de la Société des Antiquaires de Normandie*, 2nd series, 9 (1851); G. Lefèvre-Pontalis, 'Episodes de l'invasion anglaise: La guerre de partisans dans la Haute-Normandie, 1424-1429, *Bibliothèque de l'Ecole des Chartes*, 54-57 (1893- 96); 97 (1936); B.J.H. Rowe, 'The Estates of Normandy under the Duke of Bedford, 1422-1435', *EHR*, 46 (1931); idem, 'John, Duke of Bedford and the Norman "Brigands" ', *EHR*, 47 (1932); R. Jouet, *La résistance à l'occupation anglaise en Normandie, 1418-1450* (Caen, 1969); C.T. Allmand, *Lancastrian Normandy 1415-1450; The History of a Medieval Occupation* (Oxford, 1983); D. Goulay, 'La résistance à l'occupation anglaise en Haute-Normandie (1435-1444)', *Annales de Normandie*, 36 (1986), pp. 37-55, 91-104; M.R. Evans, 'Brigandage and Resistance in Lancastrian Normandy: A Study of the Remission Evidence', *Reading Medieval Studies*, 18 (1992), pp. 103-35.

to be more French than the French. That is clearly visible in several passages where Thomas Basin praises the peasants of the Pays de Caux for their steadfast love of their natural lord. 'These simple people, cultivators of the soil, had a strong sense of justice and obligation. They were moved by a passionate zeal and an habitual love for the kingdom and for the king of France as their ancient and natural lord.'[67] These remarks correspond with certain passages of Jean Masselin, who wanted to demonstrate that all parts of Normandy had not maintained the same stance.

> The people of the Pays de Caux who had always remained completely faithful to the king of France and who had never fallen under the sway of the enemy, save when compelled by the force of arms, groaned under the intolerable yoke of English domination. Having continually resisted it as much as they could, they conceived a glorious enterprise, trying by taking up arms to become once more the subjects of the king of France.[68]
>
> The fidelity of such men was not only sincere but also distinctive since rather than renouncing obedience to their natural master and their true king, they preferred to put themselves in danger by following the orders of a tyrant and usurper and by submitting to the yoke of a barbarian prince. They still have this consolation and glory: within this kingdom you will find no other nation [*natio*] which for the sake of the king's quarrel had made such strong resistance to the fury of the enemy armies. Without wishing to be disparaging, we can state that every other region which was attacked either rushed to surrender to its own impetuosity and to the evils of the time rather than to expose itself to mortal danger, or else supported the royal party in such a way that it itself remained unscathed. If the Pays de Caux should be pitied because of the terrible atrocities it suffered, it should also have special praise and favour because the cause of this horrific disaster was its own fidelity and courage. Only it carried the palm of constant loyalty and bravery.[69]

These attitudes can be dated by the passion with which they are expressed and also by their bombastic tone: they are the genuine product of war with the English.

The Normans had not surrendered in any way their liberties and privileges. Thomas Basin again shows clearly how they had returned to their allegiance to the French king with the precise hope of recovering 'these ancient and fine liberties, rights and franchises which their ancestors had known before the misfortunes of war'.[70] These proved to be idle thoughts. To some extent, the Normans should be counted as amongst those whose hopes were not fulfilled after the war either under Charles VII or, to an even greater degree, under Louis XI.

The attitude of the Normans during the War of the Public Weal vacillated wildly. In the early stages the Normans came in force to assist Paris when it was

---

[67] T. Basin, *Histoire de Charles VII*, i (Paris, 1933), p. 220. See also p. 225, where he sings the praises of 'those people particularly devoted to the king of France'.

[68] *Jean Masselin*, pp. 560-61.

[69] Ibid., pp. 568-69.

[70] T. Basin, *Histoire de Charles VII*, p. 217.

encircled.[71] Later, once peace had been made, these self-same Normans (whom one could hardly reproach in this case for being more royalist than the king) welcomed with enthusiasm their new duke, Charles of France. On the occasion of his enthronement in the cathedral of Rouen on Sunday 1 December 1465, the latter took care to take an oath on the Holy Gospels to respect the liberties of the church, nobility and communes, to observe the laws and customs of Normandy and, of course, the *charte aux Normands*.[72] The congregation responded with shouts of 'Rou, Rou, Rou'.[73] Even if we are struck by the ease with which Louis XI recovered Normandy in the early days of 1466, even if we should not underestimate the decision of the estates in 1468 to refuse forever any alienation of Normandy, it is certain that the Normans experienced a real feeling of frustration. Commynes, as ever, puts it well: 'A tousjours bien semblé aux Normands et faict encores[74] que si grand duchié comme la leur requiert bien un duc.'[75] This power vacuum was not filled by the existence from the fifteenth century (initially during the period of English control) of either a *lieutenant général et gouverneur*, or a *grand sénéchal* or a hereditary *maréchal* of Normandy.[76]

The least that can be said is that by the end of the fifteenth century Normandy was by no means the weakest point in the French political system – a system which was increasingly being consolidated. Indeed we can go further. Despite strong Norman identity and despite the *Charte aux Normands* there must be doubt whether the duchy had constituted the most vulnerable part of France even in the time of Philip of Valois and of John the Good. In fact, France began to split up between 1340 and 1360, following dynastic and military events which were for the most part unexpected. Loyalties which had seemed totally unshakable began to falter and to weaken, both in Normandy and elsewhere. Without doubt, the Normans could have then quite simply left the French polity had they wanted to. But this was not their way of looking at things: what they clung to was the preservation of freedom of action and of control of their own affairs, and also the desire for a return to a monarchical system ideally seen as complaisant, unobtrusive, and remote.

Victorious though it was, the Valois monarchy of the late fifteenth century nevertheless knew how to keep up appearances and how not to offend people's sensibilities. The solemn breaking of the ducal ring in 1468 was balanced by the decision of Charles VIII on 28 June 1491 whereby he made Louis of Orléans his

---

[71] *Journal de Jean de Roue connu sous le nom de Chronique scandaleuse, 1469-1483*, i (Paris, 1894), pp. 80-81, 92-93.

[72] Stein, *Charles de France*, p. 146.

[73] Floquet, 'Charte aux Normands'.

[74] Commynes was writing around 1490-91.

[75] Philippe de Commynes, *Mémoires* ed. B. de Mendrot, i, *1464-1477* (Paris, 1901), p. 85.

[76] G. Dupont-Ferrier, *Gallia regia*, iv (Paris, 1954), pp. 245-50, 253-60, 262-64. One such official, Louis de Brezé, comte de Maulévrier, was described as 'mareschal heredital, grand seneschal et refformateur general des païs et duché de Normandie' (ibid., p. 262).

'lieutenant général et gouverneur' of Normandy. In the act of appointment, the king said that Normandy 'est fructueuse et l'un des pays qu'il aime le mieux après son royaume', and that it was 'le premier fleuron et l'ainée fille de son royaume'. In order, therefore, to bring about the marriage of this beloved daughter, the king 'la bailla au sieur d'Orléans pour ce qu'il est le premier après le roi'.[77] It should be stressed that the duke of Orléans was at this stage not only the heir presumptive to the crown but also the brother-in-law of the king. This act, replete with symbolic significance, can be seen as a worthy complement of the king's marriage to Duchess Anne of Brittany which had been celebrated in the château of Langeais several months previously.

[77] Archives Communales de Rouen, cited by Prentout, *Etats provinciaux*, i, p. 223. Already the Dauphin Louis (the future Louis XI) had desired to obtain from his father – through the mediation of the estates of Normandy who had formulated the request – the government of Normandy (Basin, *Apologie*, p. 13).

17

Lancastrian Normandy: The Jewel in the Crown?

Anne E. Curry

Aficionados of Paul Scott and of television drama will instantly recognise the allusion in my title.[1] Unlike British India in the 1940s – Scott's 'jewel in the crown' – Lancastrian Normandy has not yet had the (mis)fortune to be the subject of a mini-series. Nor, as far as I am aware, has it provided the grist for any novelist's mill. There can be no doubt, however, that Normandy's significance was much stressed in both royal documentation and popular literature during the first half of the fifteenth century, and has continued to be emphasised by historians ever since. But nowhere, I think, has Normandy been called specifically 'a jewel in the crown'. Even if we were to come across this appellation, we would immediately be faced with a problem. Of which crown was it a jewel – Henry V's actual English crown, or, his merely titular French crown? More precisely, did he invade Normandy in 1415 and again in 1417 in pursuit of his supposed ducal rights as the descendant of William the Conqueror and of successive king/dukes? Was it his intention to revive the ancient links between the duchy and the kingdom of England by becoming ruler of both? This is a possibility which historians have already noted, and which forms the principal subject of this essay.[2] Or did Henry's invasion follow a more recent although by now well-established tradition, namely the claim which Edward III and his successors had laid to the crown of France itself? Did Henry V seize Normandy because it was part of royal Valois France? This last interpretation does not, of course, require Henry to have been hell-bent upon winning the French crown from the moment of his first invasion. Until the last

---

[1] P. Scott, *The Jewel in the Crown* (London, 1966). A drama series based upon the whole of his *Raj Quartet* was produced by Granada Television in 1984. I would like to take this opportunity to express my gratitude to Christopher Allmand and David Bates for their helpful comments on this essay.

[2] C.T. Allmand, *Lancastrian Normandy: The History of a Medieval Occupation, 1415-1450* (Oxford, 1983), pp. 122-26, and *Henry V* (London, 1992), pp. 185-88. See also G.L. Harriss' suggestion, *Henry V: The Practice of Kingship* (Oxford, 1985), p. 29, that the York Minster screen, probably designed in 1421 but not fully executed until after Henry V's death, 'may have been designed to celebrate and symbolize the recovery of Normandy, the ancient heritage of the English crown, which was held by all kings on the north of the archway until lost by John, the last represented, and was only repossessed by the last king on the south side, Henry V'.

months of 1419, Henry's principal aim was most likely to force the French to cede Normandy to him in full sovereignty. That is to say, he wanted to remove the duchy from the control of the king of France and to rule it as part of his own crown. But we are brought back to the problem of which crown.

This is a more important question than might appear at first sight for it raises some fundamental issues about English intentions in France from 1360 onwards. By the treaty of Brétigny, Edward III effectively gave up his claim to the French throne in return for fully sovereign ownership of the Calais march and of a reconstituted Plantagenet Aquitaine. These areas were thus, in English eyes at least, no longer part of the kingdom of France, but belonged to the English crown – a position maintained even after the resumption of war in 1369.[3] Although the promise of this French crown was won by Henry V in the Troyes settlement of 1420, and his son was subsequently crowned king in Paris in 1431, what remained under effective English control at Calais and in Gascony continued to be seen not as part of the Lancastrian crown of France but as 'pays subgiet au royaume d'Angleterre'.[4] In this respect they paralleled Wales and Ireland, territories which were not, in theory, part of the kingdom of England yet were inseparable from it.[5]

We have sailed away from Normandy somewhat, but now we must return to Henry V's ambitions there to see how they compare with policies towards these other territories. Negotiations during the second campaign suggest that he wanted Normandy in full sovereignty in addition to the fulfilment of the terms of the treaty of Brétigny and a marriage to Catherine.[6] Had the French agreed – and there are signs that they were moving towards agreement in the summer of 1419 – then we must surely assume that Normandy would have joined the rest of the territories appendant to Henry's English crown even if he had seen fit to retain the title king of France. There was, of course, no such settlement. The changing complexion of French politics after the murder of the duke of Burgundy on 10 September 1419 obliged Henry's acceptance as heir

---

[3] As recently as 1411 the people of Gascony had successfully petitioned to be considered not as aliens but as the true subjects of the king of England, and thus be enabled to hold property in England (*Rot Parl*, iii, pp. 656-57). If we are to accept the text of a letter which Walsingham cites as written by Henry of Monmouth to his father in the next year, we can see Aquitaine described as a heritage and right of the English crown, and annexed to that crown, *The St Albans Chronicle, 1406-1420*, ed. V.H. Galbraith (Oxford, 1937), p. 65.

[4] Triers of Gascon petitions, for instance, continued to be appointed in the English parliament even after Henry VI became king of France. When restrictions on the recruitment of foreign soldiers were imposed in Lancastrian Normandy during the 1430s, men from 'pays subgiet au royaume d'Angleterre' were placed on a par with those of the 'nascion d'Angleterre', A.E. Curry, 'The Nationality of Men-at-Arms Serving in English Armies in Normandy and the *Pays de Conquête*, 1415-1450: A Preliminary Study', *Reading Medieval Studies*, 18 (1992), pp. 141, 155-56.

[5] See R.A. Griffiths, 'The English Realm and Dominions and the King's Subjects in the Later Middle Ages', *Aspects of Late Medieval Government and Society: Essays Presented to J.R. Lander*, ed. J.G. Rowe (Toronto, 1986), pp. 83-105.

[6] Allmand, *Henry V*, p. 132.

and regent to the French throne, terms enshrined in the treaty of Troyes of May 1420.[7] This was a very different settlement from that which he had been close to effecting in the summer of 1419. Or was it? In one interesting respect it came remarkably close. Clause 18 of the treaty implicitly allowed Henry to keep the duchy of Normandy for life in what was effectively full sovereignty, for it merely said that at Henry's accession to the French throne, 'la duchié de Normandie et les autres et chascun lieux par lui conquis ou royaume de France seront soubz la jurisdiction, obeissance et monarchie de la couronne de France'. Thus the treaty confirmed Normandy as part of the kingdom of France and not as a special possession of the kings of England, a significant departure from Henry's stance hitherto. By implication, the lack of any mention of Calais and Gascony in the treaty can be interpreted as confirming these areas as part of the lands of the English crown by virtue of the Brétigny settlement. Put another way, Henry continued to hold these areas as king of England, whilst he held Normandy as heir of France. The omission of specific reference to Henry's full sovereignty in Normandy may have been deliberate in order to avoid any suspicion that the duchy was being taken out of France. The treaty left Normandy in Henry's hands in much the same fashion as when Capetian and Valois kings had created appanages for their cadet lines in earlier centuries. Indeed when John Hardyng wrote of the treaty, admittedly about twenty years on, he added to his mention of Henry's heirship and regency of France the following: 'And Normandy and Guyan as *appent* remayn should to hym and his heyres, Kynges of England evermore and to theyrs.'[8] One might even have expected Henry now to call himself 'duke of Normandy', for had not the eldest son of both Philip VI and John II held the title and the duchy whilst heirs apparent to the French throne, with the duchy returning to royal control at their accession to the French throne, much as it was intended to do in the case of Henry V? Yet Henry did not use the title 'duke of Normandy' after the treaty of Troyes, perhaps because he wanted to emphasise a major change in his stance. No longer did he seek to dismember France and to annex part of it to his English crown. He now wished to appear as the legitimate heir to the whole of Charles VI's French crown, Normandy included. Presumably he also wished to emphasise that he was no mere duke, but king-elect. One of the most intriguing things is that he *had* used the title duke of Normandy between 1417 and 1419, as will shortly be revealed.

There can be no doubt that the treaty of Troyes treated Normandy in rather awkward fashion by leaving it in Henry's hands in an ill-defined manner. Further awkwardness came when Henry VI inherited the French crown at the

---

[7] For the text of the treaty see E. Cosneau, *Les grands traités de la Guerre de Cent Ans* (Paris, 1889), pp. 100-15.

[8] *The Chronicle of John Hardyng*, ed. H. Ellis (London, 1812l repr. New York, 1974), p. 379. The emphasis is mine. For the dating of the work see A. Gransden, *Historical Writing in England*, ii, *c. 1307 to the Early Sixteenth Century* (London, 1982), pp. 276-77.

death of Charles VI. The duke of Bedford was reluctant to allow Normandy to be reabsorbed into France as the treaty laid down, yet he was obliged to abide by its terms. The necessary administrative moves were made, but the level of reintegration was never total. The Burgundians were therefore basically correct when they claimed in 1435 that Normandy had not been fully reunited with the crown of France 'car elle est gouvernee separement en fait de justice et de recepte de finances et en tous estas separement du royaulme et de la couronne comme il se faisoit au temps du roy d'Angleterre'.[9] What I would like to stress here is the last line 'comme il se faisoit au temps du roy d'Angleterre', emphasising the special status of Normandy from 1420 to 1422.[10] Even after the accession of Henry VI to both crowns, Normandy continued to be seen by the English as rather special, all the more so when Paris was lost in 1436. Wherever one looks, whether in official documents or in literary works of the reign of Henry VI, the stress was on English interests in 'Normandy and France', not merely in France.[11] In English consciousness the special emphasis placed upon Normandy by Henry V's glorious conquests was never lost, persisting even after its loss in expressions of retrospective appreciation of the kudos which its tenure had engendered. As William of Worcester emphasised in his *Boke of Noblesse*, Henry had 'wanne the said Duchie of Normandie first and after the kingdom of France'.[12] Bale's *Chronicle* named the provinces which the English lost in 1449-50 as Normandy, Anjou and Maine 'which hadde be the old enheritaunce and right evermore and tyme out of mynd of the kynges of England'.[13] One can also point to some amusing examples of historical 'chinese whispers'. Capgrave's *Liber de illustribus Henricis* (c. 1446-47) had Henry die at Rouen, a mistake which found its way into later historical prints.[14] And an early sixteenth-century poet, basing his

---

[9] A Bossuat, 'Le Parlement de Paris pendant l'occupation anglaise', *Revue Historique*, 229 (1963), p. 35 n. 1. On the question of integration after 1422, see Allmand, *Lancastrian Normandy*, pp. 128-51. The case between Jean de Gaucourt and Sir John Handford, *English Suits before the Parlement of Paris, 1420-1436*, ed. C.T. Allmand and C.A.J. Armstrong, Camden Society, 4th series, 26 (London, 1982), provides a useful example of the problematic relationship of Normandy with the rest of France after the treaty of Troyes.

[10] See also W.T. Waugh, 'The Administration of Normandy, 1420-22', *Essays in Medieval History Presented to T.F. Tout*, ed. A.G. Little and F.M. Powicke (Manchester, 1929), pp. 345-59; Allmand, *Henry V*, ch. 9.

[11] See, for instance, *The Brut or the Chronicles of England*, EETS, original series, 131, ed. F.W.D. Brie, 2 vols (London, 1906), e.g. ii, pp. 471, 503. A similar terminology is found in official documentation, such as in the impeachment of Suffolk in 1450 (*Rot Parl*, v, pp. 177–82).

[12] *The Boke of Noblesse*, ed. J.G. Nichols, Roxburghe Club (London, 1860), pp. 40-41, cited in C.T. Allmand, 'Henry V the Soldier and the War in France' in *Henry V: The Practice of Kingship*, ed. G.L. Harriss (Oxford, 1985), p. 133 n. 31.

[13] *Six Town Chronicles*, ed. R. Flenley (Oxford, 1911), p. 128, with dating and authorship discussed in Gransden, *Historical Writing*, ii, p. 233.

[14] Edited by F.C. Hingeston, Rolls Series (London, 1858), p. 123. The error is seen on a print in Barnard's *New, Impartial and Complete History of England* (London, 1790).

work on Lydgate's celebration of Agincourt, misinterpreted the latter's allu-
sion to Henry's demand for all that belonged to King Edward to mean Edward
I, thus making Henry desyr 'his heritage for to have, /That is Gascony and
Gien and Normandy . . . /all that belonged to the first Edwarde'.[15]

What we must examine is how this emphasis on Normandy developed in the
first place and what debt it owes to a late medieval understanding of the past
status of Normandy, even if equally garbled as that of the poet. Why was
Normandy seen as the jewel in the Lancastrian crown, whether of the English
or French crown or, after 1422, perhaps of both? The duchy's administrative
status changed over time. From 1417 to 1420 it was a conquest, with various
forms of justification being used for its tenure. From 1420 to 1422 it was a
quasi-appanage of France ruled by an English king as heir to the French
throne. From 1422 it was part of Henry VI's kingdom of France. Its changing
status had an impact upon the way it was viewed by English rulers and their
subjects, remembering that this last term must be taken to include Normans as
well as English. This is a vast topic and there is scarcely space here to review all
its aspects. I intend therefore to concentrate on the question of how the
English perceived Normandy in an attempt to explain both their conquest and
their subsequent tenure of the area. Only English sources are cited here,
although there are interesting references to the issue in French and Burgundian chronicles which merit discussion in another essay. The essay is weighted
in favour of the reign of Henry V because the most significant event must
surely be his initial decision to invade. All else follows from this.

Why Normandy? Various explanations have been put forward, ranging from
military considerations to an appeal to supposed Norman separatism, and
provoking grandiose statements on Normandy as *le lien naturel* between the
kingdoms of France and England.[16] The strategic explanation is simple. In
terms of troop movements and victualling, Normandy was more accessible than
Gascony and more fertile than the Calais march. Besides, the English already
held lands in these areas. Henry V wanted to make a dramatic impact by
attacking Valois France head on: Normandy was one of the Valois heartlands
and a major source of demesne and tax revenue, as he was soon to discover.[17]
French political problems made the time ripe for a decisive blow, as Henry
knew from recent English dabbling. A document arising out of negotiations in
1410-11 may indicate that an invasion of France through Normandy was
already being considered: English ambassadors objected to the inclusion of the
duchy in a truce 'car ils navroient par ou entrer ou royaume de France se le

---

[15] N.H. Nicolas, *History of the Battle of Agincourt* (London, 1833), p. 302 for Lydgate,
appendix, p. 69 for later poem.

[16] As expressed by J. Favier in *Histoire de la Normandie*, ed. M. de Bouard (Toulouse, 1970), p.
225.

[17] M. Rey, *Le domaine du roi et les finances extraordinaires sous Charles VI, 1388-1413* (Paris,
1965), pp. 44, 81-89.

pays de Normandie y estoit compris, car par le texte des treues particulieres nul ne peut entrer par pays estant en treues en pays non estant en treues pour faire guerre'.[18] In 1412 Henry's brother Clarence even led a successful *chevauchée* through Lower Normandy. Appreciation of the value of Normandy as a point of entry into France was thus present before Henry V's accession. On his initiative it fulfilled a second purpose, that of a secure military base to fall back on and from which to launch attacks on Paris and the heartlands of the French monarchy. Calais might have served as both point of entry and base, but its potential was limited at this juncture: although it is unlikely that a deal was ever struck with the Burgundians before the end of 1419, the English may have eschewed thoughts of an invasion via Calais for fear of alienating the duke and thus damaging important trade links with his Flemish lands. Of course by 1436 everyone in England hated the Flemish, but one suspects that at the beginning of the century it was the Normans who were unpopular. Trade connections did exist but by no means on the same scale or to the same value as with Burgundian lands.[19] In the chronicles of earlier wars Englishmen could read of the Normans as a long-term enemy, involved in coastal raids and providing a good proportion of the French fleet at Sluys.[20] They had been behind many of the recent 'piratical' attacks on English shipping and on the south coast, such as at Portland in 1404 (and indeed again in 1416).[21] In response there had been semi-official English raids into the coastlands of the Pays de Caux in 1403, 1410 (when Fécamp was targeted) and in 1413.[22] There was considerable sense in establishing an English base at Harfleur to provide security for shipping. The question of the defence of the sea had been much discussed in the first two years of Henry's reign and, as Bishop Beaufort declared at the opening of parliament of March 1416, Harfleur had been 'ab olim infectissime nobis' before its capture.[23] Henry V had no renegade Norman in his camp in the way that Edward II had been encouraged by the support of Godfrey de Harcourt, and no reason to believe that the Normans would rush to accept him. It remained a manner of considerable concern to Henry that few of the Norman nobility and gentry accepted his rule, for he realised that this was 'a thing which causeth the people

[18] Bod Lib, MS French b3, fo. 1r.

[19] See the comments of Walsingham in his *Historia Anglicana, 1272-1422*, ed. H.T. Riley, Rolls Series (London, 1863-64), ii, p. 110, on the trading benefits for the Normans in particular if a truce were agreed (1384). This comment is omitted in his *Ypodigma Neustriae*, ed. H.T. Riley, Rolls Series (London, 1876), although the truce is mentioned, p. 338.

[20] See, for example, *Historia Anglicana*, i, p. 227 (1340), 287 (1346), 366 (1378); ii, p. 135 (1385).

[21] Rymer, *Foedera* (Third Edition, The Hague, 1739-45), IV, i, p. 66; *Gesta Henrici Quinti*, ed. F. Taylor and J.S. Roskell (Oxford, 1975), p. 136 n. 1. On the earlier use of Harfleur see C.J. Ford, 'Piracy or Policy? The Crisis in the Channel, 1400-1403', *Transactions of the Royal Historical Society*, 5th series, 29 (1979), pp. 67, 71, 77.

[22] Bouard, *Histoire de la Normandie*, p. 227.

[23] *Rot Parl*, iv, pp. 4, 6, 15.

to be ful unstable', and he was well aware that his incessant waging of war in Normandy could cause amongst the people 'a general grouching and so a disobeissance'.[24] There can be no escape from the fact that on both his campaigns he went well-armed. He did not expect the conquest of Normandy to be an easy task.

The Normans were French, loyal subjects of the French king, and as such the enemy. They did resist as far as it was in their power to do so, only surrendering when appeals to their accepted Valois royal master had gone unheeded. We should not be misled, perhaps, by the supposed cosiness which later developed between English and Norman in Lancastrian Normandy. Henry V may have ended his life a francophile, but he did not enter France as one. The propaganda which he used to raise support in England for his campaigns was blatantly anti-French and did not distinguish between Norman and French. He invaded in 1415 and in 1417 on a tide of patriotic fervour, as is demonstrated by uses to which 'English' saints were put. Prayers before Harfleur invoked the Virgin and St George as the protectors of the crown of England, asked them to 'deliver from the swords of the French our king and his people', and banners of St George were placed on the town at its capture.[25] Elmham has Henry invoking SS. George and Edward the Confessor before the battle of Agincourt, and also the Virgin on behalf of England, her dower.[26] By the time the Lambeth MS 6 version of the *Brut* was written in the later fifteenth century, the myth had arisen that at Agincourt Frenchmen saw St George hovering in the air over the host of English, assisting them in their fight.[27] On a more mundane level, Henry sought to expel some of the Harfleurais and to people his town with English on a colonial model. The Normans may have wept over Henry's corpse in 1422 – according to Walsingham both Paris and Rouen offered large sums for the privilege of burying Henry – but they had other reasons for sorrow at his actions in 1415.[28]

Was there an remembrance of past ducal link with Normandy when Henry first set foot in it in 1415? Is there any evidence that Henry or indeed anyone else was trying to create the notion of a link to justify this invasion? Several problems arise in trying to answer these questions. The first campaign is difficult to interpret because its events may not have been in keeping with Henry's original intentions. He may have planned to conquer more than merely Harfleur. The indentures for the campaign, for service in Gascony or

---

[24] *Proceedings and Ordinances of the Privy Council of England*, ed. N.H. Nicolas (London, 1834), ii, p. 351, probably dated to 1419.

[25] *Gesta Henrici Quinti*, pp. 66-67, 54-55.

[26] 'Liber Metricus' in *Memorials of Henry the Fifth King of England*, ed. C.A. Cole, Rolls Series (London, 1858), p. 121. Several sources stress the fact that the defeat of the French fleet off Harfleur in 1416 and the signing of the treaty of Canterbury with the Emperor Sigismund both occurred on the Feast of the Assumption.

[27] *Brut*, ii, p. 596.

[28] *Historia Anglicana*, ii, p. 345.

France, envisaged an absence of twelve months. In the event, his soldiers served for less than four and no further conquests were made. On the other hand, we may be seduced by the happenings of the 1417 campaign into thinking that Henry was already determined to conquer Normandy in 1415 when in reality he was not yet so clear-sighted. It is true that a fully sovereign Normandy had been included as a demand of the first embassy of August 1414, but so too were all other lands to which the English king could possibly lay claim. There is no evidence that Normandy held any special significance for Henry at this stage in his reign. Indeed the duchy was dropped from his demands in March 1415, which were essentially for restoration of the Brétigny terms, but it was reinstated along with all the other areas of his first asking when war was about to break out. In terms of tenable justifications for war, especially ones that would stand international scrutiny, there was little mileage in a specific claim to Normandy. The right of the English kings to Normandy had been abandoned on two occasions, in the treaty of Paris in 1259, and again in the treaty of Brétigny. The contention over Brétigny had dominated Anglo-French relations thenceforward, yet Henry V's predecessors seem to have been satisfied with a settlement based upon it. Only in 1395 had Richard II added Normandy, Maine and Anjou to his demands but this can be dismissed as deliberate raising of the stakes to persuade the French to accept a marriage and long truce.[29] Although, as we have seen, an invasion of France through Normandy may have been envisaged under Henry IV, there is no proof that the latter had specific ambitions regarding Normandy or the other erstwhile Plantagenet lands outside Aquitaine. Henry V certainly knew of the Brétigny terms, and presumably of those of 1259 also. It could be claimed that neither treaty was valid since the French had not kept their terms. This notion may lie behind frequent references to perfidy of the French, yet these were always couched in unspecific terms, and probably deliberately so, for Henry's only tenable claim to Normandy was by virtue of his supposed title to the French throne.

A major problem in examining official documentation concerning Henry's policy towards France is indeed the frequent vagueness therein employed. There is no specific mention of special rights to the Norman duchy in either parliamentary or conciliar documents concerning the first expedition. The stress is on 'the recovrir and reintegration of the olde rights of your corone as wel as for you rightways heritage'.[30] On occasion the last notion was expanded by mention that this inheritance had been long withheld 'es temps de ses progenitours et predecesseurs Rois d'Engleterre'.[31] This was delightfully vague. It could apply to Henry's rights to the French crown as the descendant

---

[29] J.J.N. Palmer, *England, France and Christendom, 1377-99* (London, 1972), p. 170.

[30] *Proceedings and Ordinances*, ed. Nicolas, ii, p. 140; see also privy council deliberations of April 1415, ii, p. 155.

[31] *Rot Parl*, iv, p. 34.

of Edward III, but equally to his claim to a fully sovereign Aquitaine. It could also cover a claim to the other Plantagenet lands, Normandy included. Yet there is no unequivocal evidence that Henry sought to stress his ancestral claim to Normandy on the first campaign. He does not seem to have used the term 'ducatus noster', although he did call Harfleur 'villa nostra', but this was entirely compatible with a claim to the French throne.[32] In the opening speech of the November 1415 parliament, Harfleur was specifically stated to be 'es parties de France', and Henry's march from thence to Calais was described as being 'parmi le coeur de France'.[33] In the parliament of October 1416, it was noted that he had gone 'es parties de France' and taken the town of Harfleur 'la principall claeve de France', before fighting at Agincourt 'en le terre de France'.[34] In 1416 Henry may still have been toying with accepting a settlement based upon Brétigny with the addition of an outpost at Harfleur similar to Calais. The last-mentioned parliament continued to stress in vague terms his desire to have restitution of 'les droictures de sa coronne d'Engleterre par de la mer'.

Whether the man in the street or even the English intellectual had given much thought to a specific Norman heritage is equally difficult to fathom: so many of the sources which have come down to us are written with hindsight. A mid fifteenth-century version of the *Brut*, for example, claims that at a great council of the second year of the reign 'it was tretit and spoken of his title that he had to Normandy, Gascony and Gyan which was his enheritaunce of right', yet as we have seen the council records themselves are much less specific.[35] Even the *Gesta*, a valuable source for the first campaign, was compiled in the knowledge that Agincourt had been won and Harfleur retained in English hands. It emphasised throughout the triumph of Henry as English king (the author only names him as king of both England and France when citing cries in the London procession) and of his English people against the perfidious French. On the whole the *Gesta* is rather vague as to the nature of Henry's right to intervene in France, but makes one interesting statement on the notion of the ducal inheritance in connection with the first campaign: 'transfretare disposuit in Normanniam pro ducatu suo Normannie primitus recuperando qui est sui iuris plenarie a tempore Willelmi primi conquestoris quamvis modo sicut a multis retro temporibus contra deum et omnem justiticiam Gallorum violencia sic detentus'.[36] Henry later tells the Harfleurais that it was their

---

[32] In a letter to London of 22 September 1415 cited in full in J. Delpit, *Collection générale des documents français qui se trouvent en Angleterre* (Paris, 1847), i, pp. 216-17.

[33] *Rot Parl*, iv, p. 62.

[34] Ibid., iv, p. 94. There was apparently no real notion of a Ponthieu heritage either, for Agincourt lay within this county which had come to the English crown in 1279.

[35] *Brut*, ii, p. 552, *Proceedings and Ordinances*, ed. Nicolas, ii, pp. 140, 150.

[36] *Gesta Henrici Quinti*, pp. 16-17. Attention must be drawn to the use of the word *plenarie*. This was reminiscent of the offer made to Henry IV by the Armagnac leaders in 1412 of the duchy of Aquitaine to be held 'integre et in tam plena libertate sicut aliquis praedecessor seu praedecessor suus unquam possidebat', Rymer, *Foedera* (third edn), IV, ii, pp. 12-13. This treaty of Bourges/London also mentions that the duchy belonged to Henry 'jure haereditario et successione

continued

duty to restore 'villam illam, nobilem portionem hereditariam corone sue Anglie et ducatus sui Normannie'.[37] Elsewhere, however, the stress is on the rights of the crown of England: when Harfleur is threatened by the French in 1416, the earl of Dorset calls upon divine aid 'pro defensione sua et justicia corone Anglie'.[38] Yet the *Gesta* ends with a prayer that the two swords of France and England should return to the rightful government of a single ruler, implying that Henry was aiming for the French crown itself.[39] We should not expect the chronicler to be any more precise than official documentation. It is also highly likely that the *Gesta* was completed after the second campaign had been launched, in the knowledge that Henry was now blatantly claiming to be the rightful duke of Normandy and specifically naming Normandy as part of the rightful heritage of the English crown.

When this notion first arose is difficult, if not impossible, to know. Henry may have known that Edward III had used the title after Poitiers. He may always have had a sense of his Norman legacy. After all he was constantly reminded in official documentation that he was 'Henry, fifth since the conquest'. Others may have reminded him of the Norman link. In a poem on the death of Henry IV composed early in the reign, Thomas Elmham, one of Henry V's chaplains, stressed the Norman as well as the English pedigree of the late king.[40] In another poem, also written soon after Henry's accession, Elmham had urged the king to war.[41] Throughout his *Liber metricus*, which ends at the Easter following the capture of Falaise (1418), there is a stress on the ducal legacy of Henry. On the siege of Harfleur Elmham writes, 'hinc ea quae proprii juris sunt atque ducatus/ Portio Neustralis, fraude retenta darent'.[42] Before he commences his account of the second campaign he has three chapters on the king's claims in France. The order of these is significant; Normandy comes first, followed by Aquitaine, then the French crown itself.[43] The couplet on Normandy is worth citing in full: 'En! Rex Henricus Normannica colla terens est/ Jure Patrum spectat patria tota sibi'.

---

continued

naturali'. A few lines after the passage cited, the *Gesta* mentions that Henry V had ordered this treaty to be copied out. It may be that the author was conflating attitudes to Aquitaine and to Normandy, but what he is certainly implying is that Henry's aims in 1415 were limited rather than focusing on the French crown. See also his remarks, on pp. 14-15, on French refusals to accept a peace: 'enormi lesione corone Anglie et exhaeredacione perpetua eiusdem *in certis de nobilissimis porcionibus nostris in regno illo*'.

[37] *Gesta Henrici Quinti*, pp. 34-35.

[38] Ibid., pp. 116-17.

[39] Ibid., pp. 180-81.

[40] 'Claruit Henricus rex, regum germine natus, Anglus, Normannus, cum sit uterque parens . . . Anglia, Francia, Neustria, parte patris referuntur, nobilius reliquis stirps sua clara viret', *Political Poems and Songs Relating to English History*, ii, ed. T. Wright, Rolls Series (London, 1861), pp. 122-23.

[41] Ibid., p. 118.

[42] *Memorials of Henry the Fifth*, p. 109.

[43] Ibid., pp. 153-54.

Elmham's *Liber metricus* was not completed until at least six months into the second campaign, so that he, like the author of the *Gesta*, knew that Henry was now stressing his Norman legacy with some vigour. Although it is now thought unlikely that Elmham wrote the *Gesta*,[44] it is interesting to speculate that the idea of resurrecting the ducal past may have come from Elmham, or else that Henry may have used him to investigate its viability. Other writers were quick to seize upon the notion, although their works too were completed after the second campaign was well underway. Perhaps the most famous, yet also the most problematic, is Walsingham's *Ypodigma Neustriae*, which is usually dated to 1419. In some ways it forms the most explicit statement of Henry's Norman inheritance, tracing it back not merely to William the Conqueror but to the first attacks on the area by the Danes, preceding even the appearance of Rollo, whom Walsingham mistakenly considers to have been created duke of Normandy.[45] Such was its purpose, but as a work it falls rather short of its aim. It is particularly disappointing on Henry V's conquest of Normandy, providing a short account little different from those provided in the *Historia Anglicana* and the *St Albans Chronicle*, yet omitting the crucial siege of Rouen. None of Walsingham's accounts make anything of a special claim to Normandy. He does not even stress its status as a duchy, expressing Henry's victories in the second campaign as being won 'in provincia Normannorum'.[46] In all three works he includes the story of a monk of the abbey of Saint-Etienne at Caen who came to the duke of Clarence at the time of the siege, imploring him to spare the abbey's destruction on the grounds that Clarence was descended from the line of kings who had founded and supported the abbey.[47] We shall return to the treatment of the Norman abbeys later, but here two points are worthy of mention. The first is that, if one reads on, it is clear that the monk's request fell on deaf ears. Once the English realised that the abbey precinct offered an excellent emplacement for their guns to be trained onto the town, they did not hesitate to use the facility, although admittedly it seems that little damage was inflicted upon the abbey itself. Secondly, the story is reminiscent of others found in later chronicles. We could, of course, accept all such stories as proof that a strong sense of Norman heritage existed right from the start. But they can also be interpreted as showing that this sense developed as a result of English success in Normandy rather than being a major consideration at the outset. Walsingham goes on to mention the bravery of Sir Edmund Springhouse who met his death at the assault on Caen. Twenty or so years later, a version of the *Brut* developed this tale by claiming that such was Springhouse's valour that the king commanded him 'to be beryd in the abbey

[44] *Gesta Henrici Quinti*, introduction, pp. xix-xxiii.

[45] *Ypodigma Neustriae*, ed. H.T. Riley, Rolls Series (London, 1876). See p. 15 for the naming of Rollo as duke.

[46] *Historia Anglicana*, ii, p. 329.

[47] Ibid., p. 323; *St Albans Chronicle*, p. 112; *Ypodigma*, p. 479.

of Caen fast by William Conqueroure'.[48] Further research may prove the truth of the *Brut*'s version, but it has the ring of popular mythology about it.

Similar reservations can be expressed about another reference in a version of the *Brut*. Those besieged in Rouen in 1418-19 asked for a 'gentill' knight to hear their complaint. When they ascertained that his name was Sir Gilbert Umfraville, 'they thankid God and oure Lady that they had mette with hyme, for he was of the old blode of that contre of Normandy'.[49] It is another good story, and one which brings us to consider a further reference of interest in another *Brut* recension, BL, MS Harley 53, written after 1436.[50] This manuscript contains an account of Henry's campaigns, but of greater interest is the section on William the Conqueror. After his victory of 1066, 'ich worthy knight of Normaundy that was there laft a scochon of his armes with his name peyntet in a place of the batail clepit Southope, which was clepit the painted chamber, in remembrance of their honour and worship for ever'. To cut a long story short, the chamber fell down and the paintings were lost. Luckily for posterity, an esquire of the abbot of Battle, at a time unspecified, 'copied the escutcheons and nems that were left clere into a book for cause that they shuld be there founden in remembrance for ever, that al men myght find there their armes if thei hem not knew'. This book was kept in Battle Abbey 'until the tyme that Kyng Henry the Vte shuld passe in-to Normandie to conquere his right and toke wiyth hym al the gentill-men which had forgeton their armes; wherfore the Kyng sent unto the Abbot of Bataile for to sende hym that boke of Armes'. The book thus left the abbey never to return. It was subsequently lost, and the rest of the painted chamber collapsed, but fortunately the names were recorded in a table 'which is of recorde in the Abbay of Batail'. The *Brut* then includes a version of what has become known as the Battle roll, a list of those supposed to have crossed with the Conqueror. There are many mid to late fifteenth-century copies and versions of this roll. Some are preceded by four lines of verse which conclude by calculating the time which has passed since 1066.[51] The earliest of these datable lists, although not yet traceable in its manuscript original, appears to have been compiled in 1419.[52] If this is indeed the earliest text then the date is surely significant and may demonstrate a revival of interest in the Norman Conquest of England occasioned by Henry

[48] *Brut*, ii, p. 384, from Cambridge University Library, MS KKI-12.

[49] Ibid., ii, p. 404 from BL, MS Galba EVIII, with other mentions listed in Allmand, *Henry V*, p. 125 n. 91.

[50] *Brut*, ii, pp. 534-37.

[51] For instance, BL, MS Royal 14 B1, where the mention of 370 years since the battle suggests a compilation date of 1436.

[52] Thomas Hearne, *Liber Niger Scaccarii* (2nd edn. Oxford 1728). pp. 522-24. It apparently had on its dorse 'To my most welbeloved and trusty friend William Worcestre'. See also E. Searle, *The Chronicle of Battle Abbey* (Oxford, 1980), p. 19. The history of the Battle roll deserves further study.

V's successes, although we must remember that only the MS Harley 53 *Brut* explicitly links the two together.[53]

It would be going too far, however, to see Henry's actions in Normandy on the second campaign as a deliberate conquest in reverse. Admittedly, he did grant Norman lands to his supporters, but it cannot be shown that he consciously allocated them so that they matched the landholdings of their supposed Norman ancestors. It is unlikely that he had any sources which would have enabled him to do this. Moreover, Henry seems to have chosen to allocate only those titles in current use, as can be seen in his peerage creations in Normandy which focused on those Norman nobles who were dead or loyal to the Valois.[54] Whilst he did revive feudalism by demanding military service and renders of military equipment, it has proved impossible to find any links in terms of quotas or conditions of service with the Anglo-Norman ducal past.[55] In some land grants Henry demanded that feudal renders were to be paid on 1 August.[56] This was a commemoration of the date of Henry's landing in Normandy at Touques in 1417. In his subsequent rule of the duchy much was made of this date, and of the *descente* (or *journée*) which he had made on it. The choice of the first of August may be accidental – merely the product of the prevailing wind –[57] although there could be some significance in the fact that it was the feast of St Peter ad Vincula, a commemoration of the day the Apostle escaped from prison through angelic intervention. Was Henry wishing to imply that he had come with God's aid to liberate the Normans or, more cynically, to liberate the duchy into his own hands and those of his English supporters? Whatever the symbolic virtues of the precise date, Henry undoubtedly intended his conquest to mark a new beginning for both the Normans and himself, and it certainly did so particularly in terms of land law, tenurial rights, and legal memory.[58] In some ways we might take it as a parallel gesture to that of Edward III at Ghent in January 1340 when he formally assumed the title and arms of France and started the dating of his French regnal years. Two reservations should be applied, however. The first is that Henry was not consistent in the use of 1 August for feudal renders: many land grants named

---

[53] It may be significant that vernacular chronicles also give much space to the surrender of Falaise in January 1418, e.g. *The Great Chronicle of London*, ed. A.H. Thomas and I.D. Thornley (London, 1938), pp. 97-103, where the treaties of surrender of the town and of the castle are given verbatim. None mention it as the birthplace of William.

[54] *CP*, v, p. 177 note f.

[55] R.A. Newhall, *The English Conquest of Normandy, 1416-1424* (New Haven, CT, 1924), p. 211. See in general A.E. Curry, 'Le service féodal en Normandie pendant l'occupation anglaise, 1417-1450', *La France anglaise au moyen age: actes du IIIe congrès national des sociétés savantes (Poitiers 1986)* (Paris, 1988), pp. 234-57.

[56] See for instance the grant of the county of Aumale to the earl of Warwick, May 1419 (*CP*, i, appendix J). I am grateful to Dr Massey for discussion on this point.

[57] It is possible that he had intended the first campaign to land on 1 August.

[58] Allmand, *Henry V*, p. 194; see also BN, MS fr.5964, fo. 205v onwards;

other days, such as Michaelmas or the Nativity of St John the Baptist. Secondly, Henry did not introduce a specific ducal or regnal dating system.

In his second campaign, however, he did call himself duke of Normandy. Although the earliest usage discovered is on a document dated 24 November 1417,[59] it is highly likely that he was using the title from the date of his landing for there are references in the interim to the term 'ducatus noster'.[60] Certain aspects of the use of the title need to be pointed out. First, Henry used it alongside rather than instead of his French royal title. It is thus difficult, if not impossible, to distinguish between his exercise of authority as duke and as a claimant of the French crown. Did the people of Normandy surrender to him and accept his authority as their duke or as their king? Henry may not have wished them to distinguish, for as we have seen his only real claim to Normandy stemmed from his claim to the French throne. Thus he spoke of his invasion as both a conquest and a recovery of his lost rights. Hence too his abolition of the *gabelle* in May 1418 spoke of the recovery of 'notre pais et duchie de Normandie et autres lieux et pais appartenans a nostre corone et seignorie royale de France', implying that his claim to the duchy was part of his right to France as a whole.[61] On this occasion, he expressed his desire that his officials should behave well 'aux usages et coustumes qui estoient en notre pais au temps de nos predecesseurs'. But who were these predecessors supposed to be? The confirmation of the liberties of Rouen following its surrender in January 1419 shows again how Henry wished to have the best of all worlds, for it referred not only to those liberties granted in the time of his progenitors of famous memory kings of England and dukes of Normandy but also those granted by his predecessors as kings of France up to the time of Philip of Valois. In practice of course, here as elsewhere, Henry did accept privileges granted by the Valois kings of France.[62] A further, related, problem concerns the consistency with which Henry used the title 'duke of Normandy'. Here we are not helped by the following of standard chancery practice in the Norman rolls where the king's title is abbreviated to 'Rex etc.'. Where copies of these enrolments survive, Henry's style sometimes includes the ducal title, but sometimes it does not. Most treaties of surrender, for instance, name him only as king of France and England, possibly confirming that the Normans were submitting to his authority as king rather than as duke. The treaty concerning Coutances, for example, gives the earl of Huntingdon's power to take the surrender as deputed from Henry, king of France and England and duke of Normandy, yet states that the submission is to be made to Henry as king of

---

[59] BN, MS fr.26042/5334.

[60] E.g. Rymer, *Foedera* (third edn), IV, iv, p. 16 (12 September 1417). The title was not used, however, in his summons to Charles VI at Touques on 13 August where he asked for the crown of France 'non minori jure quam haereditario nobis spectantia' (ibid., p. 12)

[61] Ibid., p. 51.

[62] Ibid., pp. 82-83.

France and England.[63] It may be, of course, that the inconsistency in usage is insignificant and merely the result of different scribal practices. One particular problem is that the use of the title seems to disappear completely from the early summer of 1419. Is this symptomatic of a real change in policy or simply the result of the uneven survival of unenrolled documents? Official documents suggest that Normandy continued to be called 'our duchy' to the end of Henry's reign and beyond even though neither he nor his son used the title of duke after the treaty of Troyes.[64] The Valois kings had also used the term 'our duchy' even when there was no titular duke. Moreover, before 1419 Henry frequently used the term 'ducatus regis', reminiscent of recent French usage when the duchy was in royal rather than ducal hands.

Indeed it is not clear what duchy Henry was attempting to recreate, that of the Anglo-Norman past, that of the French past and present, or something else of his own creation which aimed at having Normandy, like Gascony and Calais, as an appendage of the English crown. It is difficult to pinpoint anything in his administration which was redolent of the ancient duchy. Only in 1423 did the appointment of the seneschal deliberately echo the powers of the pre-1204 position, being drawn from the *Coutumier*.[65] Likewise, it was only after Henry V's death that the *Charte aux normands*, the symbol of liberties won from the kings of France over the last century or so, was confirmed.[66] Most of the privileges, for instance those of the towns, which Henry and his successors confirmed and which had their roots in the ducal past had previously been accepted by Capetian and Valois rulers of the duchy after 1204. Yet Saint-Etienne and La Sainte-Trinité at Caen along with a few other Norman monasteries were anxious to have noted in confirmations of their privileges the fact that they had been founded by Henry's ancient predecessors.[67] Henry's willingness to allow this may be a manifestation of his piety and of his sense of his own Norman inheritance, but the clauses could equally well have been included at the behest of the recipients, thus fuelling the king's own pretensions. It is intriguing to think that Saint-Etienne sought to ingratiate itself by presenting Henry with a copy of part of the chronicle of Orderic Vitalis, although Camden may be correct in saying that it formed part of Henry's booty from the capture of Caen.[68] Most significantly, confirmations of monastic lands and rights specifically excluded their claims to their erstwhile

---

[63] Ibid., p. 40.

[64] By the early eighteenth century at least, it was thought that Henry V's tomb in Westminster Abbey bore an inscription which included 'dux Normannorum', but this is unlikely to have been of fifteenth-century origin; see print of tomb in Rapin de Thoyras, *The History of England* (2nd edn, London, 1732), after p. 530.

[65] R. Sauvage, 'Une procédure devant la sénéschaussée de Normandie en 1423', *Mémoires de l'Académie Nationale des Sciences, Arts et Belles-Lettres de Caen* (1910), pp. 141-42.

[66] See above pp. 225.

[67] Rymer, *Foedera* (third edn), IV, iv, p. 16.

[68] Orderic, i, p. 121; iv, p. xiv.

possessions in England, lands which had been seized in the wars of Edward III and which had been established once and for all as English possessions earlier in Henry's own reign. Petitions for restitution, presented once the monasteries had accepted Henry's rule in Normandy, fell on deaf ears in his capacity as king of England.[69]

Much of the administration of Normandy under Henry V and his son remained as it had been under the Valois, even though only the lower offices remained in the hands of Normans. Admittedly, Henry established a *chambre des comptes* at Caen, but this was essentially modelled upon that at Paris to which Norman revenues had previously been directed. In the appointments of lieutenants and of the admiral of Normandy French practice was again followed. In certain other respects, however, Henry V's administration in Normandy was essentially English in style. His chancellor of Normandy paralleled the English chancellor and used a duplicate of the English royal seal. The Norman rolls were in the style of chancery enrolments, similar to the patent and close rolls and to the Gascon rolls. The treasurer general of Normandy acted according to exchequer practices; up to Henry's death his accounts were audited in England. Henry's seneschals of Normandy may well have been modelled on their counterpart in Gascony.

The impression one ends up with is that Henry was not a slave to the past, and that both he and his administrators had a rather feeble knowledge of the Anglo-Norman ducal past. Henry did not become carried away by the notion of ducal revival but used it to serve his overwhelming desire to have Normandy. Until the treaty of Troyes his propaganda remained very English in tone, aimed both at encouraging his English supporters and showing the Normans that they now had a new master. Feudal renders were thus sometimes ordered to be paid on St George's Day. Although a deliberate policy is difficult to prove, surrenders of towns were strikingly often effected on English saints days, for instance Caen on the feast of St Cuthbert, Rouen on that of St Wulfstan. When Rouen was taken, to shouts of St George, banners were placed at key points. On the Porte Saint-Hillaire were put those of the Trinity, on the Porte Cauchoise of the Virgin (conveniently the Virgin was as much Norman as she was English), on the Porte de Martainville that of St George and on the castle the arms of England and France.[70] There is no proof that Henry himself adopted any specific arms as duke of Normandy, although the *Croniques de Normandie* claim that he wore ducal robes at Rouen at Candlemas 1419.[71] What those robes looked like is anybody's guess, and even more intriguing is whether they had any real or perceived link with those of the ducal

---

[69] For such a petition see D.J.A. Matthew, *The Norman Monasteries and their English Possessions* (Oxford, 1962), pp. 172-73.

[70] *Brut*, ii, p. 421.

[71] *Les croniques de Normandie* (Rouen, 1505), p. 174. Hellot suggests this was written fairly close to the event although not made up into a final redaction till 1422-24, *Les croniques de Normandie, 1223-1453* (Rouen, 1881), p. xii.

past. Indeed we are here faced with another problem. What were the arms of Normandy in the late twelfth century? The Valois dukes of the fourteenth century had sported two lions passant regardant, but there is no absolute proof that such ducal arms date back to the twelfth century, although tradition has it that they were worn by Henry II.[72] The Lancastrians certainly introduced the two lions into the seals of some Norman offices and institutions, often replacing or sidelining the fleur de lys found on the pre-1417 seals.[73] William the Conqueror was portrayed in two early to mid fifteenth-century manuscripts wearing two lions.[74] The English may well have seen them as the ancient ducal coat, and of course it is the perception rather than the reality of the situation which is all important. On some duchy seals, however, they introduced the quartered arms of England and France. Again, what was crucial above all was the statement of English control. In the English parliament of November 1417 the conquest of Normandy was said to be to the glory of Henry 'et de tout son royaume dAngleterre'.[75] In October 1419, whilst he was negotiating for the French crown itself, his conquests in Normandy were described as 'parcelle de son droiturelle demande', and part of the recovery and restitution of the rights of the English crown overseas.[76] In this respect, too, it is interesting that there was no move to create a Normandy herald: the chapter of English heralds which met at Rouen in January 1420 stated their offices to be 'du royaume d'Angleterre et de l'obeissance dicelle'.[77]

In his campaigns Henry wished to portray Normandy as a 'pays subgiet dAngleterre'. To this end he used whatever arguments he could, including those dependent upon a somewhat shaky perception of the ancient ducal past. His stance presented a considerable problem when the terms of the treaty of Troyes were being drawn up. This helps to explain the awkwardness of the treatment of Normandy in the treaty. Henry was loathe to give up the duchy yet he probably also realised the dangers that its removal from his potential French crown could produce. On his death bed he may have come to regret his agreement at Troyes that Normandy should be reunited with the French crown

[72] N.V.L. Rybot, 'The Arms of England and the Leopards of Normandy', *Coat of Arms*, 6 (1960), p. 162. I am grateful to Adrian Ailes for this reference.

[73] See particularly the section on the seals of the *vicomtés* in G. Demay, *Inventaire des sceaux de la Normandie* (Paris, 1881). Only the sixteenth-century chronicler, Hall, claims that Henry V's funeral cortège bore a coat of two lions, W.J. St John Hope, 'The Funeral, Monument and Chantry Chapel of King Henry the Fifth', *Archaeologia*, 2nd series, 5 (1913-14), p. 135.

[74] Bod Lib, MS Lyell 22, fo. 6v, reproduced in *Domesday: 900 Years of England's Norman Heritage*, National Domesday Committee (London, 1986), and BL, MS Cotton, Faustina B VII, reproduced as the frontispiece to *Early Yorkshire Charters*, iv, ed. C.T. Clay, Yorkshire Archaeological Society, record series, extra series (1935). See Plate 26.

[75] *Rot Parl*, iv, p. 106.

[76] Ibid., iv, p. 116

[77] L.S. London, *The Life of William Bruges, the First Garter King of Arms*, Harleian Society, 91, 92 (London, 1959-60), pp. 78, 98-107.

when Charles VI died.[78] What we do not know, of course, is whether the duke of Burgundy and the other advisers of Charles had put paid to any plans Henry might have had during the Troyes negotiations for the permanent separation of Normandy from France.[79] Nor, as Waugh pointed out, can we know exactly what Henry's plans were for Normandy in the event of his own accession to the French crown.[80]

The status of Normandy remained complex after 1422. One can argue that it was never fully part of Lancastrian royal France, nor was it kept totally separate, nor was it ever integrated with the kingdom of England. It was anomalous. Guy Thompson has pointed to the fact that the conscious development by Henry V and VI of Rouen as the basis of their rule undermined relations with Paris and the claim of the Lancastrians to be kings of France.[81] Maurice Keen has reminded us of problems in the late 1440s when Normandy was the principal English holding:[82] whilst it was by then much ruled from England, like a colony, there was also a strong sense of quasi-independence on the part of those in Normandy who had devoted their careers to settlement in and defence of the duchy. We could perhaps reflect upon what might have happened had Normandy remained in English royal hands in this fashion. Would there have been demands for self-government? Would we have had Irish-style struggles between Normans, Anglo-Normans and English? All hypothetical but not so incredible: the English had the examples both of the Channel Islands, the rump of the first Norman Conquest, which had gradually slipped further and further into idiosyncratic yet theoretically dependent rule, and of Gascony where the preservation of local liberties was crucial to and yet problematic for English control. Henry V's policies both before and after Troyes had ensured that there was continuing English confusion over the status of Normandy. Was it a separate duchy annexed to the English crown, or was it part of the French crown? These confusions, accompanied by the overbearing nature of the Troyes settlement as a whole, contributed to the failure of negotiations in the 1430s and 40s which might have created a territorial settlement based upon an English Normandy, Gascony and Calais. In 1450 Normandy was still a 'jewel in the crown', but now the crown was emphatically that of a *Valois* king of France, Charles VII.

---

[78] *Proceedings and Ordinances*, ed. Nicolas, iii, p. 248.

[79] It is interesting to note that in a letter to Llanthony Priory in December 1419 the countess of Stafford, acting no doubt on information from her husband who was in France with the king, wrote that Henry was to have all Normandy, Gascony and Guienne with the county of Ponthieu for himself and his heirs both during the life of the king of France *and after his decease*, and that after the death of the king of France the crown was to go to King Henry, PRO, C 115 K2/6682, fo. 142r. See also Hardyng's comment referred to in note 8 above.

[80] Waugh, 'Administration', p. 350.

[81] G.L. Thompson, *Paris and its People under English Rule: The Anglo-Burgundian Regime, 1420-1436* (Oxford, 1991), pp. 19, 22-25, 38.

[82] 'The End of the Hundred Years War: Lancastrian France and Lancastrian England', *England and her Neighbours, 1066-1453: Essays in Honour of Pierre Chaplais*, ed. M.C.E. Jones and M.G.A. Vale (London, 1989), p. 310.

18

The English Army and the Normandy Campaign of 1346

Andrew Ayton

If Edward III's newsletter of 3 September 1346 is to be believed, the camp of the victors of Crécy was a solemn, humourless place. The English army, according to this document, spent the night after the battle 'fasting and without eating or drinking'.[1] An altogether more likely story is told by Jean Le Bel. He has the English king invite the great men of his army to dine with him. It seems to have been an occasion for mutual congratulation: 'Or poeut bien sçavoir chascun en quelle joye le noble roy et tous ses barons et seigneurs souperent et passerrent la nuit, regraciant Dieu de leur belle fortune, que à sy petite compaignie avoient tenu contre toute la poissance de France champ et deffendu.'[2]

The Liègeois chronicler's depiction of Crécy as the triumph of a 'little company' over 'all the power of France' makes for a good story but is a little misleading. Although numerically inferior to Philip of Valois' host, the English army was, nevertheless, a substantial and potent force. For all their 'good fortune' on the day of Crécy, there could have been few on the morrow of that battle who doubted the fighting ability of King Edward's army, its adaptability, brutal professionalism and sheer élan in a tight corner. The distinctive tactical combination of archers and men-at-arms, well-rehearsed in a variety of battlefield conditions, from Dupplin Moor and Halidon Hill to Sluys and Morlaix, proved decisive in the defensive battle at Crécy; but most of the fights during the Normandy campaign saw the English assuming the offensive and the forced passage of the Somme at the Blanchetaque ford was quite as remarkable a display of fighting ability as the great battle fought two days later. There was a wealth of combat experience at all levels of the army hierarchy: from the king's principal lieutenants, like the earl of Northampton, the victor of Morlaix, down to inconspicuous men-at-arms, like the Norfolk squire William de Thweyt, a regular and versatile soldier since Halidon Hill.[3] These

---

[1] R. Barber, *The Life and Campaigns of the Black Prince* (Woodbridge, 1986), pp. 22-23.

[2] J. Viard and E. Déprez, ed., *Chronique de Jean Le Bel*, 2 vols (Paris, 1905), ii, p. 107.

[3] For Thweyt's career, see A. Ayton, 'William de Thweyt, Esquire: Deputy Constable of Corfe Castle in the 1340s'. *Notes and Queries for Somerset and Dorset*, 32/329 (1989), pp. 731-38.

veterans gave the army its steely core, but its cohesion rested squarely on its homogeneity, for as Joshua Barnes observed, 'There were but a few Strangers at this time with King Edward'.[4] But a greatly reduced dependence on foreign troops did not leave Edward III with a small army, since in the spring and early summer of 1346 his kingdom bore the weight of a massive mobilisation of men, ships and supplies. That it was not in any sense a 'happy few' that landed with Edward III at Saint-Vaast La Hougue can be judged from the size of the transport fleet.[5] Whilst assembling in the Solent, the armada of vessels drawn from ports around the coast of England stretched, according to the *Acta bellicosa*, from Yarmouth to the Needles.[6] Small wonder that it took five days to complete disembarkation at La Hougue.

It was not difficult to convey an impression of the scale of the expedition of July 1346 in general terms; but reconstructing the precise dimensions of the army, ascertaining its size, structure and composition in detail, is an altogether more demanding task. The problem is that the sources, though impressive in volume and variety, are also both indigestible and frustratingly incomplete. This is certainly the case with those that can contribute significantly to the compilation of a nominal roll for the army. The enrolled lists of men who received letters of protection or charters of pardon provide the largest numbers of names: about 800 men obtained protections during the early summer of 1346 prior to leaving England,[7] whilst well over a thousand received charters of pardon during the march across Normandy or in the early autumn after the army had arrived at Calais.[8] So, even without the survival of muster rolls or horse inventories, it is still possible to compile a nominal roll of respectable length. Although this is usually the case with fourteenth-century armies, for the Normandy campaign the evidence from protections and pardons is complemented by the richly detailed records generated by a short-lived military assessment of landowners on the basis of their income.[9] These are the records that make the study of the personnel of Edward III's army in 1346 a particularly rewarding exercise. There are several types of document. The original returns, drawn up by commissioners appointed in October 1344 and January 1345, are organised by county and consist of lists of landowners,

---

[4] J. Barnes, *The History of that Most Victorious Monarch Edward III* (Cambridge, 1688), p. 340.

[5] The chroniclers' estimates, which range from 750 to 1,500 vessels, are conveniently summarised in J. Viard, 'La campagne de juillet-août 1346 et la bataille de Crécy', *Le moyen âge*, 2nd series, 27 (1926), p. 8 n. 1.

[6] Barber, *Life and Campaigns of the Black Prince*, p. 27.

[7] PRO, C 76/22; C 76/23. Cf. captains' bills requesting the issue of protections: e.g. M.C.B. Dawes, ed., *Register of Edward the Black Prince*, 4 vols (London, 1930-33), i, pp. 13, 115; and suspensions of assizes of novel disseisin: *CCR, 1346-49*, pp. 83, 85, 139, 143, 155, 156, 170.

[8] *CPR, 1345-48*, pp. 483ff.

[9] On this new assessment, see M, Powicke, *Military Obligation in Medieval England* (London, 1962), pp. 194ff; G. Harriss, *King, Parliament and Public Finance in Medieval England to 1369* (Oxford, 1975), pp. 392-95.

together with the estimated annual value of their property, expressed as round sums: 100s., £10, £25 and so on up to £1,000.[10] The land values were the basis of the military assessment: a 100s. landowner was to be (or to provide) an archer; a £10 one a hobelar; a £25 man was to be a man-at-arms. Landholdings worth more than this, up to a ceiling of £1,000, were to provide proportionate numbers of additional personnel. Although in all likelihood presenting consistently low valuations, the original returns are nevertheless a remarkable source,[11] opening a door in particular onto the lower levels of the landowning community. Correlation of the county returns in order to produce a national picture of landownership, aggregating the wealth of the many individuals who held in more than one shire, is sadly frustrated by the uneven survival of the returns and the poor state of many that have been preserved; but to some extent the lost information can be recovered by recourse to records generated after the assessed manpower was summoned to Portsmouth to serve for wages in the king's army. On the one hand, there are letters from interested parties, including certificates of service from captains;[12] and, on the other, there are the writs of exoneration, enrolled on the treaty, patent, fine and memoranda rolls, which record the performance of military service,[13] pardons from assessment,[14] reductions in assessment and fines paid in lieu of service[15] – or, as occurs quite frequently, a combination of these for a single man. The need to document the fulfilment of military obligation, whether the personal performance of service or the reasons why it need not be done, gave rise to a body of records revealing a wealth of detail about military service undertaken during the mid 1340s: about the circumstances and fortunes of a host of individuals, and about their attitudes to war. Here is a rare opportunity to examine the relationship between landed wealth and military service, for all levels of the landowning community, from the elderly earl of Warenne assessed at forty men-at-arms and forty archers, to a man of rather more modest means, Richard de Thorp, who was assessed at an archer for his land in Leicestershire.[16]

The varied collection of military assessment records can contribute much to the Normandy campaign roll. Many of the assessed landowners served in person on the march from La Hougue to Crécy – or later at the siege of Calais.

---

[10] *CPR, 1343-45*, pp. 414-16, 427-28. For the original returns and related records, see PRO, C 47/2/31, 34, 36-41, 52, 58.

[11] For perceptive comment, see N. Saul, *Knights and Esquires: The Gloucestershire Gentry in the Fourteenth Century* (Oxford, 1981), pp. 33-34.

[12] E.g. the earl of Warwick's confirmation that William Charnels had found an archer called William Warde, who had served since the landing at La Hougue, PRO, SC 1/39, no. 180.

[13] Many of the relevant treaty roll and memoranda roll entries are calendared in G. Wrottesley, *Crecy and Calais* (London, 1898), perhaps the most useful material in a flawed volume.

[14] *CPR, 1345-48*, pp. 94, 202.

[15] See *CFR, 1337-47*, pp. 497-524; *CFR, 1347-57*, pp. 16-17. Scale of fines; usually 10 marks for a man-at-arms, 5 marks for a hobelar and 40s for an archer.

[16] Wrottesley, *Crecy and Calais*, pp. 149, 184.

Certificates of service and writs of exoneration, issued before, during or after the expedition, reveal where and with whom the service was performed.[17] Perhaps more interesting are the frequent cases of men serving in fulfilment of the military obligation of other landowners, for here some of the more shadowy members of the military community emerge for a moment into the light: ordinary men-at-arms, hobelars and archers – men like Henry Sturhup, an archer serving for the Northamptonshire landowner Henry de Fortho.[18] Some landowners found relatives to wield the sword for them. Thomas Meverell sent his brother Guy as a man-at-arms. He was not to see him again, for Guy died in the siege-camp outside Calais.[19] Sir John de Cherleton sent his three sons,[20] one among many instances of young men fulfilling the obligations of middle-aged landowners. Glimpses of this kind of younger aristocratic warrior, in many cases taking up arms for the first time, complement the rather better-known evidence furnished by the court of chivalry records of the later fourteenth century. Give the time that had elapsed since 1346, it is not surprising that only thirty-two of the court of chivalry deponents of the 1380s claimed to have participated in the march from La Hougue to Crécy;[21] but few of these men can be seen to have been Normandy campaign veterans from other sources. Some of them were already seasoned soldiers by 1346, but five stated that they had begun their careers in arms with the expedition to Normandy and up to dozen more may also have been initiates. Unfortunately few were as explicit as Sir Bernard Brocas who stated that he was first armed 'on the seashore at La Hougue'.[22]

The military assessment records, and particularly the writs of exoneration, also offer glimpses of changes in the composition and structure of King Edward's army during the Normandy campaign and the siege of Calais. A desire to document the precise circumstances of a man's service has allowed us to see men switching from one retinue to another, or establishing their own. Reasons are rarely given, but the changes appear to be less a reflection of innate restlessness or volatile interpersonal relations within retinues, having more to do with the death or temporary absence of captains. When Sir Maurice de Berkeley died during the siege of Calais, in February 1347, one of his men, Sir John de Palton, joined the retinue led by Berkeley's friend, Sir Thomas de

---

[17] Apart from the other continental theatres of war, obligations were also discharged by service in Ireland, the 'maritime land' of England and in garrisons, both in the north (e.g. Berwick, PRO, C 81/1710, no. 7) and in the south (e.g. Dover, PRO, C 76/22, m. 18d; C 76/23. m. 18d; and Windsor, PRO, C 76/23, mm. 24d, 25d.

[18] Wrottesley, *Crecy and Calais*, p. 172.

[19] Ibid., p. 151.

[20] Ibid., pp. 143, 167.

[21] Seventeen from the Lovel-Morley case (PRO, C 47/6/1); and sixteen from the Scrope-Grosvenor case: N.H. Nicolas, *The Scrope-Grosvenor Controversy*, 2 vols (London, 1832). One of these men, Sir Richard de Sutton, testified in both heraldic disputes.

[22] Nicolas, *Scrope-Grosvenor Controversy*, i, p. 180.

Bradeston, whilst another, Sir Gerard Burdet, transferred to Sir Richard Talbot's company.[23] Changes in the composition of the army could be brought about in other ways. It is useful to be reminded occasionally of the Englishmen who were taken prisoner during the Hundred Years War: men like the unfortunate pair, Sir Robert de Tyford and Sir James de Haumville, who fell into French hands at Crécy.[24] Then, of course, there were the casualties. The losses suffered by fourteenth-century English armies are usually poorly documented: the pay-rolls are often silent, the chronicles and inquisitions *post mortem* extremely selective. Had we been reliant upon such sources, our knowledge would have been woefully incomplete for the campaign of 1346-47. Death on active service is noted in the inquisitions *post mortem* of only four men during these years,[25] and only one of these cases concerns a casualty of the Normandy campaign: Sir Edward Atte Wode, who was killed during the assault on the castle of Roche Guyon. His death is also mentioned by several chroniclers,[26] but as usual the narrative sources for this campaign provide no more than a sprinkling of similar references. Altogether more revealing are the writs of exoneration. Here we find dozens of unfortunates, killed, wounded or falling sick during the Crécy-Calais campaign – and not just aristocratic casualties. For example, Thomas de Stonlye, a hobelar, was killed in the abortive attack on the fortified bridge at Meulan; and Richard Whet, an archer, was slain during the assault on Caen.[27] At Crécy, English casualties appear to have been light.[28] One of the few men-at-arms to be killed was Sir James Audley's *valet*, Robert de Brente, a man performing in person the service due from his property in Somerset.[29] But the losses through sickness during the siege of Calais were of an altogether different order of magnitude. The fortunate ones were invalided home, but many died in the siege-camp and like the newly created knight, Sir Ralph Abenhale, were buried on the spot.[30] The writs of exoneration reveal more than just the names and fortunes of some of those who served in the king's armies. Those who sought to avoid their military assessment, or at least to have it reduced, are quite as interesting as

[23] Wrottesley, *Crecy and Calais*, pp. 141, 146; cf. Saul, *Knights and Esquires*, pp. 76-77.

[24] Wrottesley, *Crecy and Calais*, pp. 134, 165.

[25] William de Wauton, Robert de Lacy, Edward Atte Wode, Edmund de St. John: *CIPM*, viii, no. 682; *CIPM*, ix, nos 2, 35, 52. The inquisitions of several other known casualties of this campaign are unspecific about the circumstances of death.

[26] *Acta bellicosa* (Barber, *Life and Campaigns of the Black Prince*, p. 35); F.S. Haydon, ed., *Eulogium historiarum sive temoris*, Rolls Series (London, 1858-63), iii, p. 208, notes that he was 'unus nobilis miles de novo factus' and was killed by 'una petra jactata de castello'. Cf. Viard, 'La campagne de juillet-août 1346', pp. 40-42.

[27] Wrottesley, *Crecy and Calais*, pp. 105, 165; 155.

[28] For a survey of chroniclers' estimates, see Viard, 'La campagne de juillet-août', p. 81 n. 3.

[29] PRO, SC 1/39, no. 178; Wrottesley, *Crecy and Calais*, pp. 125, 146; *Eulogium historiarum*, iii, p. 211, offers the name of a further casualty: Eymer de Rokesley, 'novus miles'.

[30] PRO, SC 1/39, no. 187; *CIPM*, ix, no. 13. Abenhale was assessed at a hobelar for his lands in Gloucestershire: cf. Saul, *Knights and Esquires*, pp. 34, 51, 79 (and n. 84).

those who quietly conformed. There were all kinds of excuses. Some men, with land partially or wholly located within six leagues of the sea, were legitimately employed in the defence of the 'maritime land'.[31] Many others claimed that their landed income was less than the value returned.[32] Sir John Folville claimed to have nothing, since he had delivered all his property to his son, John – who, appropriately enough, was on active service with the earl of Warwick.[33] Some men secured the intercession of influential patrons. The earl of Suffolk wrote to the chancellor on behalf of Robert Curzon, 'un des noz povres tenantz', assessed at a hobelar in Norfolk, who was 'graundment charge des enfauntz'.[34]

The records created as a consequence of the short-lived military assessment of the mid 1340s contribute hundreds of additional names to the roll of men known to landed at La Hougue in July 1346: names drawn, as we have seen, from several levels of the military community. Yet taken as a whole, the roll of identifiable combatants is not a representative sample of the army's personnel, for most of the sources contributing to it offer a very 'aristocratic' view of King Edward's host. This is particularly the case with the narrative sources. For all their lively portrayals of individual exploits, like that of Sir Thomas de Colville,[35] the chronicles, focusing in the main on the most prominent combatants, contribute very little unique nominal evidence.[36] The enrolled letters of protection also provide a distinctly skewed sample, even of the aristocratic section of the army, for the majority of protection recipients were possessors of landed property. There are few landless younger sons among them: none of the virgin soldiers in 1346 who were to give evidence before the court of chivalry in the 1380s bothered with a letter of protection before they embarked. Recipients of charters of pardon were spread more evenly throughout the army (if anything, there is a bias in favour of the non-chivalrous fighters), but it is often unclear whether a pardon recipient is a man-at-arms, an archer or a non-combatant. Not only is our nominal roll not a random sample, it also includes many individuals who can, at best, be described as 'probable' combatants. Securing a protection represented an intention to serve; confirmation of the service of lesser men-at-arms is possible in only a minority of cases[37] and some certainly defaulted.[38] Charters of pardon may

---

[31] Writs to this effect: PRO, C 76/22, m. 18d (April 1346); PRO, C 76/23, m. 18 (September 1346). Cf. *CFR, 1337-47*, p. 505 (Thomas de Cheddeworth).

[32] E.g. John de Greyvill: *CFR, 1337-47*, p. 469.

[33] Wrottesley, *Crecy and Calais*, p. 104.

[34] PRO, C 81/1710, no. 14.

[35] V.H. Galbraith, ed., *The Anonimalle Chronicle, 1333-1381* (Manchester, 1927), p. 22; and *Eulogium historiarum*, iii, p. 210.

[36] The *Acta bellicosa* provides the fullest and most accurate nominal evidence (e.g. Barber, *Life and Campaigns of the Black Prince*, p. 29), but few of the men named are minor players. For corrupt name-forms, mistakes or perhaps pure invention, see *Froissart*, iv, pp. 377, 380-81.

[37] E.g. John de Colby, protection recipient (Wrottesley, *Crecy and Calais*, p. 114), took the order of knighthood at Crécy, PRO, E 159/121, m. 228.

[38] E.g. *CPR, 1345-48*, p. 190.

offer firmer evidence, but the precise period of service is not always made clear with enrolled pardons;[39] and this is a particular problem with the Crécy-Calais campaign, where we would ideally like to disentangle the pardons issued for service in Normandy from the very large numbers earned for sitting in the siege-camp outside Calais.

That neither muster rolls nor horse inventories have survived for any part of this army prevents us from uncovering the identities of many combatants, but perhaps a more serious problem is the absence of precise information on the size and structure of either the whole army or its constituent retinues and companies. Most estimates of the size of the army that landed at La Hougue have fallen within the range of 10,000-15,000 men, although the most recent, that suggested by Jonathan Sumption, is rather lower: 7,000-10,000.[40] the fact that Sumption's figure is based essentially upon the *estimated* carrying capacity of an English fleet of *estimated* size arises from the fact that there exists for this army neither a collection of indentures of war, which would give us the proposed dimensions of individual retinues,[41] nor a full pay account, which would present a systematic captain by captain schedule of the army's constituent units, with details of personnel numbers, the period of service and pay due. Pay rolls of this kind cast light on many of the armies of Edward III's reign, but the pay accounts which we know were drawn under the supervision of Walter de Wetwang, keeper of the king's wardrobe, no longer survive for King Edward's most celebrated expedition. The other documents generated by the pay process cannot adequately fill the gap. The records of 'prests' made to army commanders, usually advances on their retinues' wages,[42] confirm the participation of a number of retinue commanders; but they do not provide a complete register of captains,[43] and they are a poor guide to manpower numbers and periods of service.[44]

---

[39] Bills from captains authorising pardons are often more explicit: e.g. PRO, SC 1/39, no. 185; Dawes, *Register of Edward the Black Prince*, i, p. 125.

[40] J. Sumption, *The Hundred Years War: Trial by Battle* (London, 1990), p. 497. At the other extreme, Wrottesley suggested 19,500 men (*Crecy and Calais*, pp. 9-10).

[41] The one known indenture of war for the Normandy campaign records the proposed service of a company of German men-at-arms: PRO, E 101/68/3, no. 64 (dated 20 May 1346).

[42] It is necessary to combine the evidence from two sources: Wetwang's book of receipts (PRO, E 101/390/12: extract printed in Wrottesley, *Crecy and Calais*, pp. 205-14) and an issue roll (PRO, E 403/336). The latter is generally more detailed and includes some pay advances not to be found in the book of receipts; but since no issue roll survives for the Easter term 1346, the book of receipts is our only systematic record of prests from 25 April. Wardrobe debentures (PRO, E 404/496) offer very little additional information and there are no surviving warrants for issues dating from the spring or summer 1346 which relate to the Normandy campaign (PRO, E 404/5/31); but cf. E 404/5/33 for warrants concerning the Crécy-Calais campaign as a whole, issued several years after the expedition.

[43] Notably absent are the earls of Arundel, Huntingdon and Suffolk. There are numerous noncombatants among the prest recipients.

[44] With very few exceptions (e.g. PRO, E 403/336, m. 49: Sir Giles de Beauchamp; PRO, E 404/496, no. 100), personnel numbers are not stated. The earl of Oxford's prest (PRO, E 403/336, m.

continued

The dearth of precise data on the size and structure of Edward III's army in 1346 is particularly striking, since in many other respects, this phase of the war is well-documented. The itinerary of the English march through Normandy, over the Seine and the Somme to Crécy, can be pieced together very fully, from a combination of record and narrative sources.[45] A great deal is known about English forces in other theatres of war during the summer of 1346. Henry of Grosmont's army in Aquitaine and Sir Thomas Dagworth's much smaller force operating in Brittany are illuminated by pay accounts and a selection of muster rolls.[46] For Sir Hugh Hastings' few hundred troops in Flanders, the core of an army drawn mainly from Flemish towns, there is an enrolled pay account.[47] We are equally well-informed about the paid element of the army which mobilised at short notice to confront the Scots at Neville's Cross;[48] as also we are about troops in Ireland and the Channel Islands.[49] and indeed those under Sir Thomas Spigurnell's command at Dover Castle at the time that the king's army was gathering at Portsmouth.[50] The lack of systematic pay records for the Normandy campaign stands in stark contrast with the corpus of materials which document so fully the other dimensions of the English war effort at this time; but at least we can be sure of some of those who *cannot* have been with the king in Normandy in 1346, because they were quite definitely somewhere else. As regards direct evidence for the army that landed at La Hougue, there remains one further source requiring careful consideration. Although Walter de Wetwang's pay accounts have been lost, we do have a number of documents, dating from the fifteenth and sixteenth centuries (and later), which appear to be partial transcripts from Wetwang's originals. There is much variety in the content of these manuscripts, but what they all purport to show is the army assembled for the siege of Calais. Few of these transcripts retain the appearance of a pay roll: the material is too abbreviated and there are no indications of the duration of service or the amounts of money owed in wages. But for all the reservations that historians must have felt about

continued

42) is the only one to state explicitly that it is a 'first quarter' payment; it would be unsafe to assume this of the others.

[45] The fullest narrative is Viard, 'La campagne de juillet-août 1346'; the most recent, Sumption, *The Hundred Years War: Trial by Battle*, pp. 497-534; (p. 500, no. 24 for sources).

[46] On Grosmont's expedition, K. Fowler, *The King's Lieutenant* (London, 1969), pp. 222-24 (muster rolls: PRO, E 101/25/9, m. 3; E 101/24/20). On Dagworth, A.E. Prince, 'The Strength of English Armies in the Reign of Edward III', *EHR*, 46 (1931), pp. 364-65 (PRO, E 101/25/17, 18 and 19).

[47] PRO, E 371/191, m. 49.

[48] PRO, E 101/25/10; J.E. Morris, 'Mounted Infantry in Medieval Warfare', *Transactions of the Royal Historical Society*, 3rd series, 7 (1914), pp. 98-102.

[49] R. Frame, 'The Justiciarship of Ralph Ufford: Warfare and Politics in Fourteenth-Century Ireland', *Studia hibernica*, 13 (1973), pp. 7-47. Channel Islands: PRO, E 101/25/6; E 403/336, m. 43 (Castle Cornet, Guernsey, garrison).

[50] PRO, E 101/531/21.

these transcripts, few seem to have doubted their essential authenticity;[51] and so the 'Calais roll', this very curious shadow of Wetwang's original accounts, best known from the version published in Wrottesley's *Crecy and Calais* (though parts had been printed before),[52] has become one of the documentary pillars of fourteenth-century military studies. It is, for example, the source of the often-quoted figure of 32,000 men assembled at the climax of the siege of Calais in 1347. But how useful are these transcripts as a guide to the army which fought the campaign in Normandy a year earlier?

In answering this question, it is important to distinguish two elements in King Edward's army: firstly, the retinues of men-at-arms and archers, led by aristocratic captains; and secondly, the companies of archers, hobelars and spearmen raised in the shires and towns of England and Wales. The Calais roll is of no practical use as far as the shire and urban levies are concerned. The manpower figures are not disaggregated to the county-company level and the total muster of foot archers indicated, about 15,000 men, is far higher than the projected number to be raised from the English counties for the Normandy campaign. Clearly there had been a massive expansion in this section of the army during the course of the siege. Our only guide to the numbers in the arrayed contingents of the army in July 1346 is an unsatisfactory one, offering us not the totals actually mustered and paid for service, but the numbers which the government originally hoped could be arrayed. Twenty-nine English shires lying south of the Trent were to supply, in all, 3,900 foot archers, with individual county targets ranging from 280 for Kent to forty for Rutland.[53] In like fashion, 142 towns, also from the south and midlands of England, were allocated individual quotas, ranging from London's, which stood at 600 men, to that of more modestly sized communities like Chippenham, which was required to find two. Overall the government planned initially to raise just under 2,000 men, mainly hobelars, from the towns.[54] But the most productive

---

[51] See Galbraith, *Anonimalle Chronicle*, p. 161.

[52] Wrottesley, *Crecy and Calais*, pp. 191-204. Robert Brady, *History of England* (London, 1700), ii, appendix, pp. 86-88. E.R. Mores, *Nomina et insignia gentilitia nobilium equitumque sub Edoardo I militantium: accedunt classes exercitus Edoardi III Caletem obsidentis* (Oxford, 1749), pp. 89-101. *Collection of Ordinances and Regulations for the Government of the Royal Household* (London, 1790), pp. 1-12. J.J. Champollion-Figeac, ed., *Lettres de rois, reines et autres personnages des cours de France et d'Angleterre*, 2 vols (Paris, 1847), ii, pp. 82-85. J. Gairdner, ed., *Three Fifteenth-Century Chronicles*, Camden Society, new series, 28 (1880), pp. 81-85 [London, Lambeth Library, MS 306]. F.W.D. Brie, ed., *The Brut*, 2 parts, EETS, 131 and 136 (1906-8), ii, pp. 538-41 [part of Wetwang embedded in a fifteenth-century version of the English Brut: BL, MS Harley 53]. Of the numerous manuscript copies of Wetwang, those showing the arms of captains are conveniently listed in Sir A. Wagner, ed., *Catalogue of English Medieval Rolls of Arms*, Harleian Society, 100 (1950), pp. 159-60.

[53] PRO, C 76/21, m. 9; C 76/22, m. 29 (Wrottesley, *Crecy and Calais*, pp. 58-60, 72-73). Special arrangements were specified in the case of Cambridge and Lincoln, ibid., pp. 62, 65.

[54] 1, 963 men: PRO, C 76/22. m. 35 (10 February 1346; Wrottesley, *Crecy and Calais*. pp. 66-68). All were to be hobelars (*armati*), except one hundred of London's quota, who were to be men-at-arms. Subsequent urban assessment lists were shorter (5 March: PRO, C 76/22, m. 30; 20 April: C 76/22, m. 15).

recruiting ground was to be Wales, which it was hoped would provide no fewer than 7,000 men, half of them archers and half spearmen. The Marcher lords were to supervise the array of half the total, with the prince of Wales being responsible for the other half from 'his lands and lordships' in the principality.[55] The price was also to raise one hundred archers from Cheshire.[56]

These were very ambitious targets and it is unlikely that many of the individual quotas were actually met. There were the usual cases of arrayers receiving a hostile reception in the counties: John de Lodebrok, an arrayer in Warwickshire, was roughly handled at Birmingham, for example.[57] Some, no doubt were 'tardy' and 'negligent' in fulfilling their commissions;[58] and we encounter the familiar problem of arrayed troops being unwilling to set off for the port of embarkation until they had been given an advance on their wages.[59] Since the French war had not yet shown itself to be a particularly attractive proposition, the caution of the recruits is hardly surprising. A few fragments of solid evidence cast doubt on the success of the arrayers in the English shires to meet their quotas. Edmund Blount received the wages for 129 archers from Norfolk, for the journey from London to Portsmouth, whilst the array target for this county had been 200 men. About two-thirds of the projected numbers then, had been found, a proportion which accords quite well with the evidence for the Cheshire contingent.[60] Similarly, Thomas Scarle received payment for forty archers from Kesteven, which is probably fewer than were hoped for from this part of Lincolnshire, when the array target for the whole county had been 200 men.[61] Whilst there seem to have been no significant changes to the shire array quotas, many town assessments were substantially reduced or completely remitted during the months following the initial writ of 10 February. Norwich, for example, was permitted to array sixty rather than 120 *armati* and overall perhaps as much as half of the urban assessment was discharged either by order of the council or by lump sum payments by individual towns.[62] All this tends to suggest that the numbers of arrayed troops actually mustering at Portsmouth were well below the original projections. It has been argued that the delayed departure from England 'enabled considerable numbers of men . . . to join the expedition up to 11 July',[63] but in truth the delay is more

[55] Wrottesley, *Crecy and Calais*, pp. 69, 80-81: 3,450 from the earl of Northampton and twenty-eight other lords; 3,550 from the Prince of Wales. The two contingents marched to Portsmouth separately: PRO, E 403/336, m. 44.

[56] Wrottesley, *Crecy and Calais*, pp. 58, 80.

[57] *CPR, 1345-48*, p. 113.

[58] Dawes, *Register of Edward the Black Prince*, i, p. 14.

[59] PRO, SC 1/54, nos 52-54.

[60] This 'may have been made up of as few as seventy-one men', whereas the target was 100: P. Morgan, *War and Society in Medieval Cheshire, 1277-1403* (Manchester, 1987), p. 104.

[61] PRO, E 403/336, m. 42. Forty of the 200 were to be supplied by the city of Lincoln: Wrottesley, *Crecy and Calais*, p. 65.

[62] Ibid., pp. 65, 68, 70-72; *CFR, 1337-47*, pp. 497, 500-504.

[63] J.E. Morris: review of Wrottesley, *Crecy and Calais* in *EHR*, 14 (1899), p. 768.

likely to have had the opposite effect on the great crowd of soldiery kicking their heels in the Portsmouth area. Some men at least did indeed 'return home without leave'.[64] Moreover, efforts were made to raise reinforcements for the king's army only a couple of weeks after it had arrived in Normandy. On 26 July 1,240 further archers were ordered from the English shires.[65] Even if the fifty mounted archers ordered from Shropshire, Worcester and Hereford, to act as a royal bodyguard,[66] are taken into consideration, it would seem unlikely that the arrayed troops in Edward III's army in July 1346 numbered as many as 9,000 men (and there may have been significantly fewer), whereas the original target had been about 13,000.

Turning to the other section of the army, to the retinues raised in the main by aristocratic captains, here it is perhaps possible to use the transcripts from Wetwang's original accounts, the so-called 'Calais roll'. In most of the transcripts the bulk of the text is devoted to listing the retinues of magnates and lesser captains, and at first sight it seems that these data might well serve as a guide to part of the army that landed at La Hougue. A method of proceeding was outlined long ago by J.E. Morris, the father of Edwardian military studies.[67] He identified those of the captains on the Calais roll who had previously fought at Crécy and, assuming little net change in retinue numbers ('that . . . reinforcements did not more than suffice to fill up the losses made by death and desertion'), he totalled the numerical strength of their retinues. Morris' result, in round figures, was 2,500 men-at-arms and 2,500 mounted archers, a result which, very comfortingly, was confirmed by reference to the nominal roll of known combatants for the army. He found that the names of 500 knights were to be extracted from the records printed in Wrottesley's *Crecy and Calais* and 'adding 100 for possible omissions and multiplying to allow for three men-at-arms to each knight' – and assuming a 1:1 ration of men-at-arms to archers – he 'got nearly the same result' as he had through his calculations from the Calais roll.

There are a number of problems with Morris' methodology. The second confirmatory method, using nominal roll evidence, is reliant upon several assumptions, the most significant of which concerns the proportion of the army's knights that are likely to be known by name. The calculation based upon figures on the Calais roll, although seemingly very straighforward,

[64] Dawes, *Register of Edward the Black Prince*, i, p. 9.

[65] Wrottesley, *Crecy and Calais*, pp. 101-102. Cf. Dawes, *Register of Edward the Black Prince*, i, pp, 9, 13-14. On 29 July, the king (at Caen) ordered that men and supplies should be sent to Le Crotoy, at the mouth of the Somme: K. Fowler, 'News from the Front: Letters and Despatches of the Fourteenth Century', in P. Contamine et al., ed., *Guerre et société en France, en Angleterre et en Bourgogne, XIVe-XVe siècle* (Lille, 1991), pp. 78-79, 83-84.

[66] Wrottesley, *Crecy and Calais*, pp. 61, 65.

[67] Morris, *EHR*, 14 (1899), p. 767; and idem, 'Mounted Infantry in Medieval Warfare', pp. 97-98.

involves more pitfalls than confronted the French cavalry at Crécy. Determining which of the captains on the Calais roll had previously landed at La Hougue at the head of retinues is not as easy as might be thought. Firstly, a proportion of the Calais roll captains had arrived during the siege, and these men are not all as easy to identify as the earl of Lancaster. Secondly, some of the Calais captains had risen in status and military responsibility since disembarking at La Hougue. Moreover, some of the captains who had served in Normandy are not to be found in the Calais roll. There is always the possibility of clerical omission with these Wetwang transcripts, but some captains had certainly left the scene, having died, like Sir Alan de la Zouche,[68] or returned permanently to England. There were also retinues which had been absorbed by others and thus lost to view. Lastly, not all of the continental knights in King Edward's army remained steadfastly in his service. The Norman, William de Groucy did,[69] but his compatriot, Godfrey de Harcourt, who played such a prominent part in the Normandy campaign, returned to the Valois camp soon after Crécy and does not appear on the Calais roll.[70]

Regarding those captains who did serve throughout the campaign and who can be found on the Calais roll, are we really to assume, as Morris did, that their retinues remained essentially the same size, with reinforcements filling the gaps left by casualties? Bearing in mind the prevalence of camp-sickness during the siege of Calais, surely it would have been extremely difficult for captains to maintain manpower numbers in the way Morris has suggested. Many of the retinues on the Calais roll may, therefore, have been bigger, perhaps substantially bigger, on the day of their arrival in Normandy. Unfortunately very little concrete evidence can be brought to bear on this matter. What appears to be a verbatim transcript of a small fragment of Wetwang's original pay roll, concerning the companies of the brothers Otes and Thomas Holand, has been preserved on a memoranda roll. The manpower figures, which cover the period from June 1346 to the end of the following January, and which for both retinues remain unchanged during this time, are identical with those supplied on the Calais roll;[71] but the numbers of men involved, about a dozen for both companies combined, are very small. A similar opportunity for comparison, this time concerning Sir Thomas de Haukeston's retinue, also offers an exact match of personnel numbers, but on this occasion the period of service covered by the memoranda roll entry is January to April 1347.[72] Haukeston was still in England on the day that Crécy was fought. Not only is there very little hard evidence to support Morris' assumption, there are strong

---

[68] *CIPM*, viii, nos 662, 715.

[69] Wrottesley, *Crecy and Calais*, pp. 148, 198; *CPR, 1345-48*, p. 228.

[70] In January 1347 orders were issued for the seizure of Harcourt's goods and men in England: *CFR, 1337-47*, pp. 490, 495; cf. *CCR, 1346-49*, p. 189.

[71] Wrottesley, *Crecy and Calais*, pp. 176-77; BL, MS Harley 3968, fo. 120r.

[72] Wrottesley, *Crecy and Calais*, pp. 176, 201; BL, MS Harley 3968, fo. 128v. But cf. Brie, *The Brut*, ii, p. 540.

indications that in the case of some retinues it would be quite wrong to assume continuity of manpower numbers. The formidable Thomas de Hatfield, bishop of Durham, witnessed both the battle of Crécy and the siege of Calais, but his return to England after the battle was accompanied by the break-up of his retinue. Some of the men who had served with him in Normandy transferred to other retinues; and four of his knights, Thomas de Colville, Philip Despenser, William de Felton and William Marmion, established their own separately paid companies and appear as captains on the Calais roll. There is no compelling reason to believe that the bishop served with the same number of men at Calais as he had from La Hougue to Crécy; and the same applies to the earl of Huntingdon, who retired sick to England shortly after the capture of Caen, but returned to the army during the course of the siege.

J.E. Morris' reliance on the Calais roll as a guide to the army that landed at La Hougue and fought the battle of Crécy also involves another assumption: that the personnel figures in Wetwang's original accounts have been faithfully preserved in the surviving copies. However, comparison of the fuller transcripts reveals many instances of disparity.[73] The differences are of various kinds. Perhaps the most significant involve the omission of material. The best known of the long versions of the Calais roll, the College of Arms manuscript printed in Wrottesley's *Crecy and Calais*, which was the basis of Morris' calculations,[74] omits no fewer than twenty-two retinues which are to be found in another version, BL, MS Harley 3968.[75] These retinues, mainly those of royal household knights, range in size from four men to fifty. Overall, 166 men-at-arms and 155 archers can be added from the Harley manuscript. But Harley 3968 is very far from perfect. It has several duplicate entries and is particularly prone to corrupt name-forms; and it is not complete, since further fragments from Wetwang's original accounts can be added from other texts.[76] The other really significant form of disparity between the various copies of the Calais roll concerns the personnel numbers attributed to individual retinues. For example, the College of Arms manuscript gives Sir John Darcy *père* forty-eight esquires whilst Harley 3968 assigns sixty-eight to his retinue. In both manuscripts, he has sixty archers, but in the 'Brut copy', Darcy has eighty.[77]

---

[73] By 'fuller transcripts' I mean those which have at least the semblance of completeness; the shorter texts either summarise Wetwang's accounts (e.g. BL, MS Harley 53) or quote only selected extracts from them (e.g. Brady, *History of England*, ii, appendix; London, Lambeth Palace, MS 306).

[74] London, College of Arms, MS 2 M 16.

[75] BL, MS Harley 3968, fos 114r-131v (printed in abbreviated form, with numerous misreadings, in Champollion-Figeac, *Lettres de rois, reines et autres personnages*, pp. 82-85); cf. other BL copies: MS Stowe 574, fos 28r-42v; MS Add. 38823, fos 59r-69r; MS Harley 246, fos 9v-17v.

[76] E.g. the copy of Wetwang embedded in a fifteenth-century version of the Brut includes a retinue led by the clerk Philip de Weston, consisting of no fewer than sixty men, Brie, *The Brut*, ii, pp. 540-41.

[77] Wrottesley, *Crecy and Calais*, p. 195; BL, MS Harley 3968, fo. 121v; Brie, *The Brut*, ii, p. 539.

There are disparities like this for most of the bigger retinues and for a proportion of the smaller ones. There appear to be no obvious patterns in these or indeed the other types of inconsistency exhibited by these texts, and so it is difficult, if not impossible, to arrange the various copies of Wetwang's accounts into a 'family' of documents and thereby determine the most reliable set of figures.

Morris' method of calculating the size of Edward III's army at Crécy from the figures on the Calais roll involves a further assumption: that pay rolls like those drawn up for the Crécy-Calais expedition provide an accurate record of manpower numbers, including changes in numbers brought about by reinforcements and casualties. This is not always a safe assumption, as far as fourteenth-century pay rolls are concerned. All too often, these records present a suspiciously neat and tidy view of an army, disguising the intricate mosaic of companies, some independent, some forming part of larger retinues, and concealing the constantly changing shape of these companies, as men arrived, departed or died. In many cases this documentary tidiness was the result of heavy summarisation by clerks drawing up the final accounts.[78] Manpower numbers have been adjusted to ensure 'fit' with the sums of money due to captains; fighting men have become accounting units. If Wetwang presided over this kind of summarising process – and the presumed scale of the full draft accounts, combined with demonstrable wardrobe accounting practice, makes this likely – then it follows that the compilers of the Calais roll, in its various versions, had access to less than perfect data, and that the roll's personnel figures for the period of the siege should be treated with appropriate caution. The copyists, in their turn, abbreviated their material still further. Perhaps most significantly, they excluded all reference to the time-span of each retinue's service. By doing this they gave the roll a very misleading appearance, so that it has been taken by modern historians to be a snap-shot of the strength of King Edward's army at a single moment during the siege, whereas it is in fact a list of the captains who had been in the king's service at some stage during the long investment of Calais. That the Calais roll is not a snap-shot can be easily enough demonstrated. The earl of Kildare, who is listed with a retinue of fifty-three men-at-arms and hobelars, was a very late arrival in the siege-camp, crossing to the Continent in mid July 1347.[79] Some historians have assumed that the earl's inclusion indicates that the roll records the state of King Edward's army at the end of July, just prior to the surrender of the town.[80] But the Calais roll also lists several captains who are known to have died during the siege, before the earl of Kildare's arrival. These include Sir Maurice de

---

[78] This summarising process can be seen when both draft and final versions of accounts have survived; for examples, see A. Ayton, 'The Warhorse and Military Service under Edward III' (unpublished Ph.D. thesis, University of Hull, 1990), pp. 190-94.

[79] Wrottesley, *Crecy and Calais*, p. 183.

[80] E.g. Morris, *EHR*, 14 (1899), p. 768.

Berkeley, Sir Thomas de Bourne and Sir William de Kildesby.[81] Their retinues broke up following their deaths. Some at least of the dispersed personnel joined other retinues; others, including several of Kildesby's men, established their own companies and duly appear as captains on the Calais roll.[82] Either way it looks as though they and their companies are being counted twice on the roll. So whatever the copyists of Wetwang's pay accounts were seeking to achieve, what they actually compiled cannot be taken to be a record of the size and structure of the English army at the climax of the siege, or indeed at any other single point. The end result, including the familiar figure of 32,000 men supplied by the College of Arms manuscript, should therefore be treated with extreme caution – not least because two other versions of Wetwang's accounts offer a more modest overall total of around 26,000 men.[83]

Despite the absence of a pay roll, the identities of most of the captains at the time of the landing at La Hougue can be established from the records of prests and the notes of warranty associated with enrolled lists of protections, service pardons and writs of exoneration. But numbers of retinue personnel cannot be ascertained from these records. All they can do is to offer confirmation of the general order of magnitude – and the order of precedence – of those retinues that appear on the Calais roll. So we are left with that enigmatic document, the Calais roll, and the frustrating conclusion that, despite its methodological flaws and questionable assumptions, Morris' method of calculating the contribution of the retinue personnel to King Edward's army in Normandy and at Crécy would seem to be the only means of achieving a quantified answer to the problem. It is possible at least to correct some of Morris' errors, especially his omissions, which include the retinues not listed in the College of Arms version of the Calais roll and some captains who do not appear on any version of the roll – men like Sir Robert de Colville and Sir Alan de la Zouche, along with a number of foreign captains, of whom the most significant is Godfrey de Harcourt.[84] We can also avoid some of the double counting of personnel on the Calais roll, and one of two misinterpretations, which seem to have inflated Morris' estimate. A rerun of Morris' method suggests that the retinues of magnates, knights and royal servants may have contributed about 2,700 – 2,900 men-at-arms, along with a similar number of mounted archers, to King Edward's army at the time of the landing at La Hougue. It is impossible to be more precise. Uncertainty surrounds the presence of some minor captains at the landing in July and it is difficult to make proper allowance in the calculation for captains who are not on the Calais roll. But bearing in mind all that has

---

[81] *CIPM*, ix, no. 46; Wrottesley, *Crecy and Calais*, pp. 153, 157.

[82] E.g. Sir Adam de Asshehurst from Kildesby's retinue, ibid., pp. 85, 92, 200.

[83] Brie, *The Brut*, ii, p. 541; Gairdner, *Three Fifteenth-Century Chronicles*, pp. 81-85.

[84] Harcourt's prests totalled nearly £670 (PRO, E 403/336, mm. 41, 42, 43); only four captains received more than this before the start of the expedition.

been said about the reliability of the Calais roll, anything other than imprecision would be inappropriate.

In conclusion, Edward III's army at La Hougue may have comprised as many as 14,000 or 15,000 men, including rather fewer than 3,000 men-at-arms, a larger number of mounted archers and hobelars[85] and perhaps as many as 8,000 foot soldiers, along with several hundred paid non-combatants.[86] This was one of the largest armies raised during Edward III's reign, founded upon an impressive turnout of aristocratic warriors – the consequence, in part, of government pressure – and upon the recruitment of large numbers of infantry. It is possible that the size and composition of this army were shaped by a strategy aiming at the establishment a permanent military presence in Normandy.[87] However, Edward may simply have felt that to challenge Philip of Valois effectively he needed a large army at his back. In 1346 this still meant an army resting heavily on the mass recruitment of infantry by commission of array. 'Mixed' retinues of men-at-arms and mounted archers, led by aristocratic captains, were becoming the cutting edge of the English military machine. It was with such 'horse soldiers' that the future lay and they were, as we have seen, far from insignificant in the king's army of 1346. But it was the foot soldiers who left the greater mark on the course of the Normandy campaign: through their indiscipline – displayed in apparently uncontrollable bouts of looting and burning, and in their recklessness in battle, as in the assault on Caen; and through their lack of mobility which, having retarded the march to the Somme, almost brought disaster to King Edward's army. Such an army was beginning to appear outmoded; it was certainly not suitable for a true *chevauchée*. For the moment, it seems, the king had to make do with the resources at his disposal, with a military machine still in the process of transformation.

---

[85] Some of the 'mounted archers' in the retinues were probably actually hobelars: both were paid 6p. per day and hobelars were supplied by many landowners in fulfilment of their military obligation. The Calais roll allows for only 528 hobelars (Wrottesley, *Crecy and Calais*, p. 204).

[86] Including the company of forty carpenters led by William of Winchelsea (PRO, E 101/390/12, fo. 8r; Wrottesley, *Crecy and Calais*, pp. 62, 65, 80), the heroes of the bridge repair work at the Vire, Douve and especially at Poissy. Bridging the Seine at Poissy was 'a feat which the French had thought impossible', R.A. Newhall, ed., *The Chronicle of Jean de Venette* (New York, 1953), p. 42; cf. *Chronique de Jean Le Bel*, ii, p. 86.

[87] J. Sumption has suggested that 'what began as a campaign of conquest became a *chevauchée*': *The Hundred Years War: Trial by Battle*, pp. 532-33. The garrisons established at Carentan and Caen were soon overwhelmed by the French.

19

Lancastrian Rouen: Military Service and Property Holding, 1419-49

Robert Massey

The aim of this essay is to examine the relationship between military service and property tenure during the thirty-year period when Rouen was in the possession of men and women loyal to Henry V and to Henry VI. For Lancastrian Rouen was a major French city garrisoned by an occupying force comprising mostly, but by no means exclusively, Englishmen, a force which was itself only one element of a sustained military presence in a Lancastrian France of ever-shifting frontiers.[1] The sources for the history of both Valois and Lancastrian Rouen are rich and worthy of exploration over periods much longer than that attempted here. A near-complete series of registers of the *Tabellionnage de Rouen* down to 1445 is especially worthy of note. The *tabellion* was a notary public who entered in an official register details of property sales, leases and exchanges, loans of money, the appointment of *procureurs* and much else beside; these notarial records for Rouen and Caen (for which no equivalent exists in England) allow a picture to be drawn in fine detail of an urban occupation.[2] Muster rolls for the four major Rouen garrisons and nearby Monte-Sainte-Catherine have been examined and the names of all mounted and foot lances have been entered on a computer database.[3] These rolls do not form a complete series, garrison musters for the years 1419-22 and after 1443 being particularly scarce, but patterns of military service can now be reconstructed and set beside what is known of property tenure and ownership locally.

---

[1] BL, MS Add. Ch. 8023, a Rouen muster roll recording a large Welsh presence among archers and lances. On the problem posed by nationality see A.E. Curry, 'The Nationality of Men-at-Arms Serving in English Armies in Normandy and the *Pays de Conquête*, 1415-1450: A Preliminary Survey', *Reading Medieval Studies*, 18 (1992), pp. 135-63.

[2] A. Dubuc, 'Le Tabellionnage rouennais durant l'occupation anglaise (1418-1445)', *Bulletin philologique et historique (jusqu'à 1610), année 1967* (Paris, 1969), pp. 797-808; A. Barabé, *Recherches historiques sur le tabellionage royal, principalement en Normandie* (Rouen, 1863), pp. 132-35.

[3] Database compilation was made possible by the generosity of a British Academy Personal Research Award to Dr Anne Curry. I am happy to acknowledge the information she has made available to me and the support she has offered.

Rouen held a strategic importance to the Lancastrians which would be difficult to exaggerate. It was a seaward-looking settlement resistant to centralising forces, to the extent that Braudel has termed it a frontier city 'both in France and out of France', a town on the periphery.[4] Its orientation after capture would arguably be as much towards London as Paris. The House of Lancaster was heir to a multiplicity of urban roles, ecclesiastical, legal, commercial and military which are perhaps best summed up by Charles VII's tribute in 1451 to 'la mere et metropolitaine de nostre pais et duchié de Normandie'.[5] To its occupiers Rouen was the historic capital of a duchy of Normandy which assumed a leading place among their demands in 1415 by virtue of a claim which, according to the *Gesta Henrici Quinti*, dated from the time of William the Conqueror.[6] The treaty of surrender in January 1419 spoke of the king's predecessors, kings of France and dukes of Normandy.[7] Like William, Henry V derived legal justification for his actions both from history and by right of conquest. Normandy was his and he was entitled to be called its duke;[8] its people were his rightful subjects and its territories were his possessions to do with as he wished. Rouen took its place alongside Harfleur, an exclusive English colony, Caen, the capital of lower Normandy and, within a matter of months, Paris, as centres of a Lancastrian urban occupation in which each played at times competing and at times complementary roles; it is probable that in terms of numbers of resident civilians and soldiers Rouen took precedence for most of the period under discussion. The *bailliage* of Rouen attracted the largest number of settlers for most of this period too.[9] It should also be stressed that Rouen was occupied without interruption for thirty years, unlike Harfleur or Dieppe, a favourable circumstance which made possible the emergence of a second generation of locally-born settlers in conditions identical to those noted by Christopher Allmand at Caen.[10] The Rouen population has been estimated at 40,000 in the late fifteenth century,[11] but this was at a

---

[4] F. Braudel, *The Identity of France*, 2 vols (London, 1988-90), i, p. 249.

[5] *Ordonnances des roys de France de la troisième race*, 23 vols (Paris, 1723-1849), xiv, p. 131.

[6] *Gesta Henrici Quinti: The Deeds of Henry the Fifth*, ed. and trans. F. Taylor and J.S. Roskell (Oxford, 1975), p. 16.

[7] Rymer, *Foedera*, IV, iii, p. 83; A. Cheruel, *Histoire de Rouen sous la domination anglaise au quinzième siècle* (Rouen, 1840), part ii, p. 47.

[8] C.T. Allmand, *Henry V* (London, 1992), p. 187.

[9] R.A. Massey, 'The Lancastrian Land Settlement in Normandy and Northern France, 1417-1450' (unpublished Ph.D. thesis, University of Liverpool, 1987), appendix IV.

[10] C.T. Allmand, *Lancastrian Normandy, 1415-1450: The History of a Medieval Occupation* (Oxford, 1983), pp. 103-4. Robert Loy of Canterbury, described as a tailor, required letters of denization in 1448 because of his birth in the parish of Saint-Maclou, Rouen (*CPR, 1446-52*, p. 123).

[11] M. Mollat, *Le commerce maritime normand à la fin du moyen âge: étude d'histoire économique et sociale* (Paris, 1952), p. 529; P. Benedict, *Cities and Social Change in Early Modern France* (London, 1989) p. 9; G. Bois, *Crise du féodalisme: économie rurale et démographie en Normandie occidental du début du XIVe siècle au milieu du XVIe siècle* (second edn, Paris, 1981), translated as *The Crisis of Feudalism* (Cambridge and Paris, 1984).

time when Rouen was on the verge of becoming the second city of the kingdom and after the *vicomté* had enjoyed what Guy Bois terms 'un jaillissement', a demographic spurt. Prior to this, Bois suggests for the city and its surrounding countryside a catastrophic fall in population during the years 1415-22, a rapid recovery until 1434-35, and then a further wave of military, biological and economic disasters until 1442.[12] The fragmentary nature of the *feux de monnéage* and other population sources means that caution must be exercised in their interpretation, but this argument does correspond with other evidence for an influx of refugees from the *plat pays* which Rouen experienced prior to the 1418-19 siege, forced and voluntary departures during and immediately after it, and with the sorry sight of families from the *pays de Caux* driven into the city's squares and hospitals following the revolt of 1435.[13] A Lancastrian Rouen with a core population of 10-15,000 inhabitants (the figure can be little more than a guess) but subject to considerable fluctuations would not be unreasonable; this would put Rouen comfortably ahead of all contemporary English cities except London.[14]

Garrison organisation in Rouen underwent change during the period under discussion but typically there was a garrison for the town and one for the gates and walls, organised into four *quartiers*, mustered accordingly. In addition there were garrisons at the castle, the Seine bridge, from 1439 at the royal palace, at Mont-Sainte-Catherine outside the walls and a force forming the retinue of the *bailli*, all responsible to the captain and his lieutenant. Surviving muster rolls for all these garrisons provide us with the names of 1031 men-at-arms, mounted and on foot, who at one time or another served in Rouen.[15] The typical garrison size, including archers, was 200-300 at any one time. A very approximate ratio of soldiers to civilians of 1:40 (allowing for a population of 10,000 people) may therefore be suggested, a ratio which rose sharply after 1424, when the garrison was reduced in number, and fell in 1429 in response to French military threats to Louviers and the lower Seine.[16] It is important to state at the outset that only approximately 1 per cent of that population comprised Lancastrian owners or tenants of houses. The urge to quantify must not, however, be taken in hand lightly, wantonly or unadvisedly. First, taking a broader definition of military service than garrison membership, as I think we should, to include Lancastrian civilians resident within the city, would slightly

---

[12] Bois, *Crise*, pp. 58-67.

[13] Thomas Basin, *Histoire de Charles VII*, ed. and trans. C. Samaran, 2 vols (Paris, 1933, 1944), i, p. 222; Rouen, BM, tiroir 15, no. 1.

[14] L.R. Delsalle, *Rouen et les Rouennais au temps de Jeanne d'Arc, 1400-1470* (Rouen, 1982), p. 22; R. Holt and G. Rosser, *The English Medieval Town: A Reader in English Urban History, 1200-1540* (London and New York, 1990), p. 6.

[15] A.E. Curry, 'Military Organization in Lancastrian Normandy, 1422-1450' (unpublished Ph.D. thesis, CNAA/Teesside Polytechnic, 2 vols, 1985), ii, appendix XI.

[16] Ibid., i, pp. 218-20. For ratios in other towns see Curry, 'The Impact of War and Occupation on Urban Life in Normandy, 1417-1450', *French History*, 1 (1987), p. 169.

increase the soldier-civilian ratio. An exclusively military or civilian career in Lancastrian service was the exception rather than the rule. Fletchers might be deemed military personnel, but what about men in household service, carpenters or purveyors? Secondly, Anne Curry has shown that concepts of nationality within Lancastrian France were fluid and that a garrison composition which might include Normans, Frenchmen, Dutchmen and Lombards presents a further obstacle to distinguishing in hard and fast terms occupier from occupied.[17] Thirdly, turnover rates were generally high in a city well located to receive and supply reinforcements and where troop movements of a regional or local nature were frequent and long periods of service rare.[18] So Lancastrian Rouen was not the home of a static force of English soldiers employed to enforce a strict military occupation: at one and the same time it could resemble a transit camp, with large troop movements into and out of the city, a colonial settlement in which a small number of soldier-civilians owning property locally assumed a significance out of all proportion to their numbers, and an urban melting-pot attracting men of diverse origin in common service. Rouen was no 'Englishry', populated exclusively by settlers. Rather, houses were acquired by dint of royal grant, marriage or inheritance and later sold, exchanged, sub-let and leased in a myriad of private transactions in the local land market sometimes recorded by the local *tabellion* at the time or shortly afterwards. Assimilation and integration are evident from the time immediately following the city's capture in January 1419.

This urban occupation took different forms. Harfleur was first and foremost a military settlement peopled by soldiers, tradesmen and their suppliers; Caen grantees had a much broader occupational range of which men valued for their skills as administrators formed the largest group. Rouen required all this and more. Some seventy-six settlers can be identified as tenants of Rouen houses, men customarily described as 'demourant à Rouen'. There are certainly more awaiting discovery. These tenants appear in the *tabellionnage* registers and elsewhere as individuals or family members renting property on a private basis from a fellow-countryman or from the cathedral chapter, for example, or as one among multiple occupants of a single property often in the crowded and poorer parts of the city. They were in some cases temporary residents, passing through Rouen on their way to and from the ports and the major garrison towns and England; some may have had official reason to travel; others still were part of that floating population of refugees, casualties and the disaffected which characterises all warfare. Occupations listed included a number of merchants, a pursuivant, a master carpenter and a priest. From an early date the merchants, purveyors and those with commercial interests made an impression on the local land market. The Londoner Thomas le Clerc, living in Saint-Maclou parish, rented nine shops from the crown in 1421 for three years,

[17] Idem, 'Nationality', pp. 151-57.
[18] Idem, 'Military Organisation', p. clxxviii.

no mean commitment.[19] For the most part these tenants and lessees had at least an indirect involvement with military matters, as illustrated by the fletcher John Dirvic of the parish of Saint-Maclou.[20] A more overt relationship between military service and property holding can be observed at archer level. In 1426 John Magnitourne sold to his fellow archer John Coutin and his French wife a house and garden in the parish of Saint-Jean-sur-Renelle for 30 *livres tournois* and 20 *sous* for wine; it may be that Magnitourne and others had benefited from the distribution of small land grants by Bedford after the Anglo-Burgundian victory at Verneuil two years previously.[21] John Leicester was reputedly 'demourant à Rouen comme l'un des souldoyers du chastel', but whether as an archer or lance is not known, while one would expect Roger Rowen, houseowner and esquire of the garrison, to have served among the latter.[22] Men holding a minor interest in property would have included those lacking the means to make an outright purchase or the influence to secure for themselves a share of Lancastrian patronage, and the populous eastern parishes of the city, especially that of Saint-Maclou, were home to a number of such men.[23] Put another way, a metropolis offered unrivalled space and opportunity for tradesmen, often engaged in war-related activities, to pursue their livelihoods within the relative safety of city walls under the protection of soldiers, some of whom were themselves aware that a Rouen posting was a means to pursue residential or commercial ambitions. It may be tempting to characterise all such tenants and lessees as men of low status or class but, quite apart from the inherent impossibility of defining such terms, the sources imply such a variety of reasons for the holding of any interest in property, great or small, that such a classification would be meaningless. Variety in accommodation, variety in occupants, variety of motives; Rouen was no more and no less to Lancastrians than to Valois.

Some fifty-nine settlers are known to have owned property within the city, as opposed to holding a tenancy. They again testify to a wide range of backgrounds and occupations. On the military side they included Sir John Handford, who in 1433 was living in 'l'ostel où pend l'ensaigne de la cuillier à pot' in the parish of Saint-Pierre-le-Portier at a time when he was captain of the city bridge.[24] Thomas Beaufort, duke of Exeter, Thomas Lord Scales and Sir John Fastolf were other senior soldiers acquiring Rouen houses for residence, status or investment, but it should not be thought that those at the top, either soldiers or civilians, necessarily took only the grandest hotels or developed the largest interests in property. That many of the best hotels on named streets fell, as in

---

[19] ADSM, Tabellionage de Rouen, 1421-22, fos 79r-79v.

[20] ADSM, G 158, fo. 13r.

[21] ADSM, Tabellionage de Rouen, 1425-26, fo. 223v.

[22] Ibid., 1421-22, fos 213v, 290r.

[23] M. Mollat, 'Une expansion différée par la guerre (1382-environ 1475)', *Histoire de Rouen*, ed. Mollat (Toulouse, 1979), p. 137.

[24] ADSM, Tabellionage de Rouen, 1430-31, fo. 108v.

Paris,[25] to the great and the good should come as no surprise, but in terms of long-term residence and the patient acquisition of houses, tenements, gardens and vacant plots it was men of middling rank who thrived and contributed most to this foreign urban environment. The process could be helped by marriage to a Frenchwoman holding property in her own right. Richard Bic married the daughter of a Rouen *bourgeois* and the marriage settlement included the grant of a house which was to return to the donors if the newly-weds died without heirs, a positive encouragement to a further generation of settlement.[26] Thomas Halliday went one better. His name does not feature in the lists of known Rouen mounted foot lances, but the presence of a Thomas Halyday on the Agincourt campaign was twice recorded, once in the service of Sir William Cromwell and once as a minstrel attached to the royal household.[27] However he earned his living later, it was evidently to the satisfaction of the authorities. In 1434 as a *bourgeois de Rouen* he bought from the Rouen *bailli* Sir John Salvain a tenement in the parish of Saint-Vincent for 50 *saluts d'or* which he subsequently sold; Halliday was also a landholder and served in the early 1440s as *vicomte* of Pont-Authou and Pont-Audemer.[28] Bourgeois status by definition required the tenure of property and residence for at least part of the year.[29] Settlers who held *lettres de la bourgeoisie* were no longer *arrivistes* but respected figures in a community whose interests were now their own. Aspirants to the rank gained privileges and exemptions in return for specified obligations which went well beyond those of a narrow interest in local property tenure. Everyone thought they knew what citizenship meant, Susan Reynolds has told us, and 'everyone' meant settler and native alike.[30]

Caen was more than a match for its rival in terms of numbers of Lancastrian *bourgeois* (twenty are known as opposed to ten) and, by virtue of its position away from major campaigning areas and its important role early in the occupation, was better able to retain residents for periods of twenty years or more.[31] Rouen was much more the frontier city offering greater risk and greater potential reward to greater numbers of soldier-settlers, and indeed settler-soldiers, those recruited to garrison or campaign army as a result of

[25] G.L. Thompson, *Paris and its People under English Rule: The Anglo-Burgundian Regime, 1420-1436* (Oxford, 1991), pp. 131-45.

[26] ADSM, Tabellionage de Rouen, 1440-41, *sub* 14 October 1440.

[27] *History of the Battle of Agincourt*, ed. N.H. Nicolas (third edn, London, 1971), pp. 356, 389.

[28] ADSM, Tabellionage de Rouen, 1434-35, fo. 82r; ibid., 1435-36 fo. 205v; AN, Collection Lenoir MS 4, fo. 263r.

[29] *Le coustumier de la vicomté de Dieppe par Guillaume Tieullier*, ed. E. Coppinger (Dieppe, 1884), pp. 19-20; *Ordonnances*, i, p. 315; M.-T. Caron, *La société en France à la fin du moyen âge* (Paris, 1977), pp. 85-87.

[30] S. Reynolds, *Kingdoms and Communities in Western Europe, 900-1300* (Oxford, 1984), p. 187.

[31] Allmand, *Lancastrian Normandy*, p. 89.

invitations to staff the garrisons primarily with Englishmen.[32] The Seine Valley was strategically difficult to defend, as was shown most dramatically by the loss of Paris in April 1436, which confirmed the Norman capital as the heartland of Lancastrian France. Houses and *hôtels* appropriate to the status and position of those displaced were purchased from the Rouennais, sometimes in transactions which dragged on for years before all the necessary rights of ownership were established; the possibility of contested claims and the difficulty of successfully asserting definitive title to the many tiny gardens, plots and alleys which made up the city remind us that urban property acquisition could be no more straightforward than that of large estates in the Norman *bailliages*. A good business sense, exercised in person or by proxy, was a distinct advantage. Such was one of the qualities which took the celebrated Nicholas Molyneux into financial service in a private capacity with Fastolf, Bedford and York and publicly as a *maître* in the *chambre des comptes* and as a royal councillor.[33] What is less well known is that Molyneux bought and sold Rouen property and was as capable in looking to his own interest as those of his respective masters. In July 1440 he bought the *Hôtel du Moulinet* in the Saint-Sauveur parish and seems to have paid only 100 *sous tournois* for the *décret*, the order passed by a court for the sale of seized property. Molyneux sold the hotel three years later to a Rouen merchant for 410 *livres tournois*.[34] Outright profit this was not, since he was accountable for any outstanding debts and charges on the property. Nevertheless Molyneux had exploited a legitimate means to supplement his life annuity from Fastolf's English estates and from his wages of office in Normandy. He also acquired 'ung tènement de maisons contenant plusieurs éstages, édiffices, jardins et le fons de la terre' in the parish of Saint-Pierre l'Onoré.[35] Rouen property dealing may therefore have helped, in a small way, to finance the process described by McFarlane of the acquisition of heritage in Camberwell and other places south of the Thames, an example on a small scale of the celebrated practice of financing English land purchase from the profits of French war which is so readily associated with the name of Molyneux's master, Sir John Fastolf. Nicholas Molyneux was no longer, in McFarlane's phrase, an active fighting man if, indeed, he had ever been one. He was an accountant and homeowner in the Rouen of the 1440s, a brother-in-arms turned non-combatant, a property dealer able to earn gains of war from immovable goods, a long-term resident professional among others of that ilk.

Turning specifically to the relationship between military service and property ownership, it should be remembered that sanctions existed from as early

---

[32] R.A. Newhall, *Muster and Review: A Problem of English Military Administration 1420-1440* (Cambridge, MA, 1940), pp. 119-20.

[33] K.B. McFarlane, 'A Business-Partnership in War and Administration, 1421-1445', *EHR*, 78 (1963), pp. 290-310.

[34] ADSM, Tabellionage de Rouen, 1439-40, *sub* 1 July 1440; ibid., 1442-43, *sub* 8 August 1443.

[35] ADSM, Tabellionage de Rouen, 1440-41, *sub* 13 January, 23 June 1441.

as 1419 against garrison soldiers taking up quarters in towns.[36] Again in 1423 on the advice of the *grand conseil* and Bedford ordinances were issued in the name of Henry VI declaring that residence by soldiers outside their garrisons in town or countryside was to be punished by imprisonment at the king's pleasure. In general terms such residence was declared an inconvenience which set back and impeded royal business; in particular, captains wishing to take men out to campaign against enemies and brigands would not be able to find them.[37] Good military practice suggested that soldiers frequently absent from their bases pursuing personal commercial interests could not be thought of primarily as upholding the defence of Normandy. It was also preferable to avoid enforced billeting of soldiers in civilian properties wherever possible, in the interests of establishing and then maintaining good working relations with townspeople. No town welcomed a foreign garrison, still less one that spilled over into its own houses.[38] The cathedral chapter protested when the duke of York's men occupied canons' houses and chaplains' colleges.[39] The more important reason for the exclusion, however, was surely a financial one. Garrison wages put an enormous strain on the revenue-raising powers of the Norman estates in particular: there simply was not money enough for large static garrisons and for the field armies necessary for specific campaigns. It was therefore the intention that those mustered each quarter in Rouen as else- where in Normandy should be bona fide soldiers dependent solely on crown wages for their living. Those fortunate enough to have an alternative liveli- hood were not to be subsidised at public expense. A muster ordered at Caudebec in 1430 specifically excluded those holding property for trade purposes.[40] This referred to the common practice among Lancastrian settlers of so using a small house as a shop, tavern or suchlike in addition to its residential function. This muster roll demonstrated the effects of a series of restrictions imposed or reaffirmed during the years 1428-30 on recruitment to garrisons and the employment of householders and land grantees in them.[41] The particular instruction to refuse muster to town-dwellers engaged in the retail trade dated from September 1430 at which time Henry VI's council had supplanted Bedford's authority, and was part of a general tightening up of

---

[36] 'ad evitandum pericula et inconveniencia que forte, quod absit, possent evinere', PRO, C 64/ 11, m. 25d; 'Rôles normands et français et autres pièces tirées des archives de Londres par Bréquigny en 1764, 1765 et 1766' [thereafter Bréquigny], ed. L. Puiseux, *Mémoires de la société des antiquaires de Normandie*, 3rd series, 23 (1858), no. 648.

[37] BL, MS Birch 4101, fo. 65v, published by B.J.H. Rowe, 'Discipline in the Norman Garrisons', *EHR*, 46 (1931), pp. 201-6; see also Cheruel, *Histoire de Rouen*, part ii, p. 87.

[38] B.G.H. Ditcham, ' "Mutton Guzzlers and Wine Bags": Foreign Soldiers and Native Reactions in Fifteenth-Century France', *Power, Culture, and Religion in France c. 1350-1550*, ed. C.T. Allmand (Woodbridge, 1989), p. 10.

[39] L. Fallue, *Histoire politique et religieuse de l'église métropolitaine et du diocèse de Rouen*, 4 vols (Rouen, 1850-51), ii, p. 435.

[40] BN, MS fr. 26053/1395.

[41] Curry, 'Military Organization', i, pp. 246-48.

military organization. Elsewhere garrison wages were paid but then returned because one Norman and one Englishman 'ont terres et menent merchandises dont ilz peuvent bien avoir vescu pour le dit quartier sans prendre gaiges'.[42]

To hold land and simultaneously to engage in trade was to erect a double exclusion to crown emolument. There was something of a conflict of interest here. On the one hand, the authorities officially frowned upon residence in towns outside the garrisons, with security thoughts and good community relations uppermost in their minds. On the other, the desirability of reducing demand on the public purse caused such regulations to be overlooked in practice. It was thus unusual that a Rouen Castle muster of 1437 specifically identified mounted foot lances holding a *don de roy*.[43] They numbered only four out of twenty-five lances. It was perhaps the misfortune of this particular garrison in its showpiece location to fall under the eagle eye of a royal secretary, Ralph Parker. At other times and in other places such instructions were quietly ignored. What has been said above about restriction on extra-garrison residence helps to explain why military property-holders in the city were often office-holders rather than men-at-arms. Richard Clerc was a long-serving garrison controller who between 1427 and 1444 was recorded variously in the retinues of the town, bridge, castle and gates. Another long-resident controller, this time of the town and, following its completion in the late 1430s, of the palace, was Richard Coole (or Cooles), who stayed until 1449.[44] Both were small-scale property-holders, Coole probably by virtue of his marriage to a Frenchwoman.[45] The tenure of office over what might amount to twenty years or more made house acquisition desirable and necessary, often through purchase or marriage, since a controller was expected to be resident and not absent.[46] Anne Curry has suggested that men-at-arms might typically serve for shorter periods than their officers.[47] If to this one adds the high turnover rate thought probable for the Rouen garrison as a whole, compared with known turnover elsewhere, then the virtual exclusion of men from the ranks from the known list of the propertied in the city comes as no surprise. Controllers were in the unusual position of being answerable to the Lancastrian civilian authorities and not to individual captains.

It might be thought that the search for a distinct relationship between military service and property tenure must be fruitless, since by royal policy the two were mutually exclusive. But the relationship was not one based solely on narrow financial considerations, nor, in practice, was it as strictly enforced as the ordinances demanded. It is clear that by giving military service a broader definition than that of purely garrison membership, to embrace that normal

---

[42] BN, MS Clairambault 169, no. 18.
[43] ADSM, MS Danquin, carton 11, MS 83.
[44] Curry, 'Military Organization', ii, clxxix.
[45] ADSM, Tabellionage de Rouen, 1431-32, fos 200v-201r; ibid., 1440-41, *sub* 16 January 1442.
[46] BN, MS. fr. 26074/5315 for Thomas Dixon.
[47] Curry, 'Military Organization', ii, pp. clxviii-clxxix.

degree of commitment to the defence of the occupied territories expected of virtually all Lancastrian and their Norman allies, there were many in Rouen from the earliest date with property interests due to purchase, marriage, gift, rent or inheritance who at the same time can be regarded as part of the occupying presence in the city. How else to describe Sir Robert Babthorpe, a Yorkshireman who was controller of Henry V's household in 1416 and again in 1418 and who was granted an hotel in Rouen 'ubi Ursus habetur insignum'? Babthorpe could point to his presence on the battlefield at Agincourt as part of his military *curriculum vitae* and, no less than fellow-owners Thomas Lord Scales or Sir John Gray of Heton, was a professional soldier to his boot-straps.[48] But he was not this alone, and attachment to a household or employment in royal service would scarcely make him less of a soldier. With Rouen and other Norman towns there developed what may be termed a semi-civilian lifestyle, whereby an individual could defy the letter of official ordinances and leave garrison quarters on a temporary or long-term basis in order to live locally, marry, set up shop or tavern, lend money and so on, while at the same time being expected, should the need arise, to take up arms in the defence of the city against external attack or internal revolt. This was very much the tenor of the 1423 ordinances which clearly stated that all men were to keep themselves armed and ready to assemble and fight as required of them.[49] It is important to note that those holding royal grants of houses in Rouen were expected as a condition of their grant to keep watch there as required, either in person or by deputy.[50] Town houses were to be lived in by their new owners or a proxy, and were to be maintained and repaired, just as residence on French soil by settlers holding fiefs was increasingly insisted upon. At Harfleur I have tried to show elsewhere that a rough correlation existed between property value and guard duty: property owing 20d in rent owed half a night's watch, that owing 3s. 4d owed one night and so on.[51] At Caen and Rouen the obligations were not as precisely stated but obtained nonetheless, and the maintenance of the *guet et garde*, first in military and then civilian hands, was a cause of great concern to the Lancastrian government over many years.[52]

There were indeed several major threats to Rouen's safety from within, chiefly the seizure of the castle by Ricarville in 1432.[53] From without, the

[48] PRO, C 64/11, m. 43; Bréquigny, no. 590.

[49] BL, MS Birch 4101, fo. 68v.

[50] Bréquigny's transcripts of the Norman Roll entries often exclude such requirements.

[51] Massey, 'Lancastrian Land Settlement', p. 259.

[52] Rouen, BM, tiroir 245; Bréquigny, no. 653; Cheruel, *Histoire de Rouen*, part ii, pp. 131-35; R.A. Newhall, 'Bedford's Ordinance of the Watch of September 1428', *EHR*, 50 (1935), pp. 50-54.

[53] *La Chronique d'Enguerran de Monstrelet*, ed. L. Douët d'Arcq, 6 vols (Paris, 1863-4), v, pp. 12-16; C. de Robillard de Beaurepaire, 'Notes sur la prise du château de Rouen par Ricarville en 1432', *Précis analytique des travaux de l'académie impériale des sciences, belles-lettres et arts de Rouen*, 58 (1856), pp. 306-29.

revolt of the *pays de Caux* threatened the city described by Thomas Basin as the seat of almost all English power in the French kingdom.[54] Although one cannot accurately gauge the degree of responsibility felt by settlers towards the security of their new home, especially after some years of enjoyment of a quasi-indigenous life which fostered family and communal ties, yet we can be sure that in practice such long-term urban settlement by soldiers was officially countenanced. There was never any question of soldiers being confined to barracks for years at a time on the pain of loss of wages or goods for any who moved into the town. Those who did make the move, however, were expected to support themselves and their dependents by whatever legal means they chose. Some did so successfully. We can also be sure that a few slipped the net and persisted in drawing wages whilst also deriving private incomes. For the most part these were primarily office-holders acting with official sanction, not members of the rank and file.

Of all the privileges held by the Rouen *bourgeois*, that of appointing their own captain had been among the most jealously guarded. It was a right lost in 1382 to the detriment of the independence of the duchy and to a local say in the city's defence, and its restoration in 1449 was the subject of remark.[55] The office was the senior garrison appointment in Lancastrian France. To take the muster of its occupants is to survey the aristocracy of Lancastrian France: Exeter, Warwick on three occasions, Willoughby, Bedford, York and Edmund Beaufort twice, Talbot.[56] It was held exclusively by Englishmen and was in the keeping of lieutenants-general and governors of Normandy acting for Henry VI, who often held the two positions concurrently.[57] Its rewards included an annual salary of 1,000 *livres tournois* paid by the inhabitants and not by the *chambre des comptes* and, evidently, a house, but residence in the castle built by Philip Augustus was more likely.[58] In most cases the Rouen captains were indeed city property owners, but not necessarily by virtue of this position alone. They were essentially itinerant figures, not the least among their responsibilities being their extensive holdings of Norman estates, and had ready access to official accommodation suited to their rank in the castle. The day-to-day military government of the city fell to lieutenants of garrison, town, castle, bridge, palace or Monte-Sainte-Catherine. Putting the names and service records of forty-one known lieutenants alongside those of city property owners produces little correlation. The lieutenants' turnover rate was often brisk and it may well be that the responsibilities of this office required a

[54] Basin, *Histoire de Charles VII*, i, pp. 213-27; Monstrelet, *Chronique*, v, pp. 104-5.

[55] Rouen, BM, MS A7, Délibérations de la Ville, 1447-53, cited by C.T. Allmand, 'Local Reaction to the French Reconquest of Normandy: The Case of Rouen', *The Crown and Local Communities in England and France in the Fifteenth Century*, ed. J.R.L. Highfield and R. Jeffs (Gloucester, 1981), p. 149.

[56] Curry, 'Military Organization', ii, pp. cxxiii-cxxxi.

[57] Richard, duke of York, claimed this privilege in 1445: BN, MS fr. 26074/5336.

[58] Delsalle, *Rouen et les Rouennais*, p. 56.

military, not a civilian billet. An interesting exception to the rule was John Clay, esquire, a name familiar to students of Talbot or York and a man in whose career one can witness an accumulation of properties which ran concurrently with his promotion from man-at-arms to garrison lieutenant. By virtue of fortuitous presence at Verneuil he received a small land grant, and in 1430 he bought a modest Rouen house; by the late 1440s when he held senior positions he had rented from the city a much more substantial property, the Hôtel de Jouy.[59]

This brings us to the office of *bailli*. Following the revolt of La Harelle this was again a crown and not a local appointment, and whereas in some Norman towns there was no effective division of civilian and military authority since one man could serve simultaneously as captain and *bailli*, at Rouen the offices were separate.[60] *Baillis* were protected by a personal retinue varying in number, in the case of Walter Beauchamp, esquire, recorded as four men-at-arms, twelve mounted archers and six foot archers.[61] Would they all have been accommodated in the hotel in the rue Grand-Pont given to him as a life-grant?[62] It is unlikely. For much of the Lancastrian occupation the post was held by the ubiquitous John Salvain (Salvayn). This was a remarkable continuity. With only a short interval between 1430 and 1431 Salvain was *bailli* from 1422 almost until the French reconquest; he was a pluralist, being captain of Dieppe between 1423 and 1435 and of Château-Gaillard from 1444 until 1445 but there was no doubt where his main duties lay.[63] His name pervades local records to the extent that one might be forgiven for thinking that he was really two men, and at the very least his surname can have presented few difficulties of pronunciation or spelling than some of his English or Welsh contemporaries. Of Yorkshire provenance, in 1436 he married Eleanor, sister of Robert Lord Willoughby, himself an erstwhile captain of Rouen.[64] Salvain held multiple grants of Norman fiefs, chiefly located in the *vicomté* of Pont-Audemer within the Rouen *bailliage* but also in the Contentin and near Caen.[65] He must also be classed a major Rouen property-holder. In piecemeal manner he acquired an *hôtel* here, in the parish of Saint-Andrieu to the west of the city, a modest house there, in Saint-Vincent in the city centre and, with a

---

[59] A.J. Pollard, *John Talbot and the War in France, 1427-1453* (London and New Jersey, 1983), p. 81; Rouen, BM, MS xxi, fo. 18v; ADSM, Tabellionage de Rouen, 1430-31, fo. 91v; AN, Collection Lenoir MS 21, fo. 319r.

[60] Curry, 'Impact of War', p. 172.

[61] M. Veyrat, *Essai chronologique et biographique sur les baillis de Rouen (de 1171 à 1790)* (Rouen, 1953), p. 122.

[62] PRO, C 64/10, m. 39; Bréquigny, no. 278.

[63] *Gallia Regia, ou état des officiers royaux des bailliages et des sénéchausées de 1328 à 1515*, ed. G. Dupont-Ferrier, 7 vols (Paris, 1942-66), v, pp. 108-10; ibid., ii, p. 67 and iii, p. 399.

[64] *DKR*, 44, p. 617; *CPR, 1429-36*, p. 378; ADSM, Tabellionage de Rouen, 1436-37, *sub* 13 October 1436.

[65] AN, Collection Lenoir MS 8, fo. 393r; ibid., MS 27, fos 361r-62r.

stake in houses in several other parishes, he seemed indeed to be everywhere.[66] Where then did he live? Perhaps in the centrally-located Hôtel de la Fontaine on the rue du Bec, or close to the seat of the *bailliage* to the northwest of the city.[67] Salvain was a man with a good eye for property speculation inside and outside the city, selling his Saint-Andrieu *hôtel* for 550 *saluts d'or* to a fellow-countryman in 1435, picking up fiefs outside the city very cheaply, collecting rents and revenues all the while.[68] A *bailli* would expect tangible benefits in the form of landed interests as a regard for past and anticipated services, and Salvain's responsibility, together with that of the garrison, for city security earned him a direct benefit following the failure of a plot by Richard Mites to betray Rouen to the Valois by the grant in 1427 of Mites' not inconsiderable properties locally.[69]

The distribution of English settlers was partly a matter of chance and partly one of choice. It was the larger parishes of Saint-Maclou, Saint-Vivien and Saint-Godard which housed the largest concentration of tenants and others 'demourant à Rouen'. Purchasers were most numerous in the western parishes, though it should be stressed that almost all the thirty-one parishes within the city walls housed settlers at some time. One group of people readily identifiable in western Rouen after 1436 are officials of the *chambre des comptes*. The auditor William Wymyngton had a house on the rue des Béguines close to the royal palace, a street name owed to the monastery of that order demolished to make way for Henry V's palace.[70] As we have seen, Nicholas Molyneux's holdings included property nearby in the parish of Saint-Sauveur. Sir William Milles, also an auditor later promoted to *maître*, bought a house in the parish of Saint-Laurens.[71] Given that the *chambre des comptes* was located on the rue aux Ours it can be suggested that residence in the central western parishes was favoured by these senior officers at least in part as a matter of convenience for their place of work.[72] To attach too much emphasis to a particular location would be to assume actual residence there, which we cannot do with certainty. What can be said with confidence is that close ties existed between service in the *chambre*, direct crown employment and attachment to a noble household which Rouen residence could and surely did foster.

[66] ADSM, Tabellionage de Rouen, 1434-35, fo. 82r; C. de Robillard de Beaurepaire, *Notes et documents concernant l'état des campagnes de la haute Normandie dans les derniers temps du moyen âge* (Evreux, 1865), p. 153.

[67] N. Periaux, *Dictionnaire indicateur et historique des rues et places de Rouen* (Rouen, 1870), p. 37; *Rouen au temps de Jeanne d'Arc et pendant l'occupation anglaise (1419-1449)*, ed. P. Le Cacheux (Rouen and Paris, 1931), p. 343. For the residences of a possible mistress within Rouen, and his wife at the castle of Tancarville, see A.E. Curry, 'Sex and the Soldier in Lancastrian Normandy, 1415-1450', *Reading Medieval Studies*, 14 (1988), p. 35 and n. 82.

[68] ADSM, Tabellionage de Rouen, 1434-35, fos 238r-238v; ibid., G 9195, fos 19r-24r.

[69] AN, Collection Lenoir MS 22, fo. 47r.

[70] Periaux, *Dictionnaire*, p. 18.

[71] ADSM, Tabellionage de Rouen, 1433-34, fo. 161r.

[72] *Rouen au temps de Jeanne d'Arc*, ed. Le Cacheux, pp. 66, 333-34.

Milles was attached to the Bedford household in a financial capacity;[73] two royal secretaries, Ralph Parker and John Profoot, bought houses in the parish of Saint-Godard to the north of the city for identical sums, with Profoot succeeding Molyneux in the office of receiver-general of the estates of York and his son.[74] Property-holding was reward for and acknowledgement of good service by administrative staff over a number of years, and it is not too fanciful to suggest that whether one reads into evidence of common location coincidence or choice the net effect was to help engender those shared communal values which contributed in Rouen, arguably as much as the monetary values attaching to properties, to long-term service there.

It is often difficult to say where English royalty and aristocracy lived. Kings required security and comfort, but the symbolic importance also attached to a royal residence was not lost on the Lancastrians. Henry V instructed the mason Jean Salvart to build what was quite precisely termed a *palatio* in the south-west corner of the city facing the Seine; this had been a condition of surrender.[75] Sometimes described by contemporaries as 'le palais emprès Saint-Jacques' and later as the Vieux Palais, it was clearly intended to serve as a royal residence and not simply as a fortress.[76] The English were in Rouen, after all, to stay. Its connection with the land settlement was twofold. First, building work was financed in part from a one-off payment by grantees of one-tenth of their annual landed revenues in respect of grants in tail male and one-twentieth of life grants.[77] Secondly, the crown reserved to itself in an exemption clause in certain land grants the quarries near Caen and Falaise whose stone was to be used for its construction. Unfortunately, building work in fine Caen stone took a long time and only neared completion in the late 1430s when a garrison took up home there.[78] In the meantime the preferred residence was the Château Bouvreuil, begun by Philip Augustus in the early thirteenth century and home to Henry V following the city's capture, but others, as Monstrelet reported, presumably meaning those not part of the king's immediate household, had to find bed and board as best they could.[79] Such practices were likely to lead to abuses of hospitality, and the ordinance of 1423 referred to above announced that noblemen attending meetings in towns should not lodge their households in nearby villages without permission and without

---

[73] BL, MS Add. Ch. 120, fo. 161r.

[74] ADSM, Tabellionage de Rouen, 1439-40, *sub* 28 July 1440; ibid., 1442-43, *sub* 21 June 1443; BN, MS fr. 26076/5703.

[75] See above, n. 7.

[76] *Chronique normande de Pierre Cochon*, ed. C. de Robillard de Beaurepaire (Rouen, 1870), p. 281.

[77] Massey, 'Lancastrian Land Settlement', p. 257.

[78] C. de Robillard de Beaurepaire, 'Notice sur le Vieux-Palais de Rouen', *Nouveau recueil de notes historiques et archéologiques* (Rouen, 1888), p. 334; *Rouen au temps de Jeanne d'Arc*, ed. Le Cacheux, pp. 318-20.

[79] Monstrelet, *Chronique*, iii, p. 307.

payment. The king, it seems, had set a bad example.[80] Following his entry to the city in 1430 Henry VI retired to the archiepiscopal palace and thence to Bouvreuil where the duke of Bedford had already refurbished apartments.[81] As is well known, Bedford spent time and money in his last years acquiring land and building on it his Joyeux Repos. Evidently the manor of Chantereine, as the property was previously known, had once been a *maison de plaisance* of the dukes of Normandy.[82] The duke of York and earl of Warwick probably acquired *hôtels* in a private capacity and certainly had the use of the official residences to which their position entitled them;[83] Edmund Beaufort certainly did have local interests, chief among them the Hôtel de Harcourt.[84] This *hôtel* provides one of the best examples in the city of continuity of tenure: as part of the *comté* of Harcourt it was given to Thomas Beaufort, duke of Exeter before Rouen had even been besieged;[85] it passed to Anne, duchess of Burgundy for life; to Bedford, and thence, after a long dispute with Bedford's second wife, to Edmund Beaufort.[86] Beaufort also commissioned the building of an elaborate ducal residence at Elbeuf upstream from Rouen but prior to this apparently lived at Joyeux Repos until he granted his rights there to the Célestins.[87] The extended or travelling households of these men were evidently accustomed to a nomadic existence[88] and, although in a few cases their points of contact with Rouen property tenure can be identified, they were not in large number house owners there.

How did settlers regard the properties granted to them? First of all, some buildings were in a poor state of repair at the time of their issue, and there were instances of a marked reluctance to mend and maintain. One does not have to look far to be reminded that in Rouen, as in Paris, housing stock had been damaged or ruined by war or neglect, a matter of loss to the crown and against '*la chose publique*'.[89] Houses often owed small sums of rent which could be difficult to collect because of tenant absence, in spite of the best efforts of the city authorities to seize anything moveable which could stand for the missing

---

[80] BL, MS Birch 4101, fo. 66v.

[81] Fallue, *Histoire politique*, ii, p. 372; *Rouen au temps de Jeanne d'Arc*, ed. Le Cacheux, pp. 152-54.

[82] Fallue, *Histoire politique*, ii, p. 434.

[83] *Rouen au temps de Jeanne d'Arc*, ed. Le Cacheux, pp. 372-73.

[84] Located on the *rue de la vicomté* (Periaux, *Dictionnaire*, p. 651).

[85] 'in quantum se extendit in longitudine et latitudine' (PRO, C 64/10, m. 35; Bréquigny, no. 205, 1 July 1418).

[86] AN, Collection Lenoir MS 22, fo. 49r; AN, P 1905/2, nos 6069, 6090; M. K. Jones, 'The Beaufort Family and the War in France, 1421-1450' (unpublished Ph.D. thesis, University of Bristol, 1982), pp. 317-320.

[87] Ibid., pp. 325-27.

[88] See the testimony of William Zeman in C.T. Allmand and C.A.J. Armstrong, ed., *English Suits before the Parlement of Paris, 1420-1436*, Camden Society, 4th series, 26 (London, 1982), p. 273.

[89] *Ordonnances*, xiii, pp. 49-51; Bréquigny, no. 793.

sums.[90] It is doubtless the case that some new owners at least hoped that houses would serve as rewards to be enjoyed and exploited rather than as necessary financial commitments. Profit-seeking should not be underestimated as an incentive to house acquisition – the examples we have noted of bargain purchases and lucrative sales can probably be multiplied as illustration of the tangible rewards still available to the fortunate and the cunning. But there were surely few fortunes to be made from Rouen firesides. The *tabellionnage* registers speak of rents to be paid and charges and mortgages resting on grantees' properties, of walls running with water and buildings being put up without permission, or knocked down without permission, indeed, all matters which make up the familiar litany of expense and dispute to the homeowner. To those unfamiliar with local customs and practice, the tenure of property whether by royal grant from dispossessed Normans deemed to be 'rebels' or by purchase or other means could prove a very mixed blessing and was in all instances a matter of some seriousness.

For these houses were given to Lancastrians primarily 'pour remunéracion de [leurs] services',[91] and their upkeep was a condition of tenure. For three decades Rouen hotels engendered and helped preserve a commitment to the Lancastrian cause in city, duchy and beyond, and there was a resultant blurring of interests between the conditions characteristic of peace and a civilian lifestyle and those typically redolent of war and a military lifestyle. The preservation of an intact estate could thereby become a priority of war and the pursuit of material gain a priority of peace; conventional priorities were neatly reversed.[92] Property bought status, title and peer respect and satisfied symbolic and utilitarian needs. Indeed it was this compatibility of private and public interests which helped ensure the longevity of the settlement in Rouen. The ready availability of housing of widely varying type and value in the local land market was a direct consequence of military success, a spoil of war in a new sense, that of immovable goods held on foreign soil with binding obligations to a Norman local community. Such responsibilities were well understood by those – a very small minority of the total numbers of soldiers and civilians who went to France – who decided to stay; they might be bewildering to those who did not. That separation of interests between Lancastrian England and Lancastrian France to which Maurice Keen had drawn attention was in part a result of the success of a policy of conquest which attached to the mundane matter of property-ownership in Rouen and elsewhere an importance which it could scarcely warrant back in England.[93] To use the term 'success' would be

---

[90] Rouen, BM, MS xxi, fo. 44v.

[91] *Ordonnances*, xiii, p. 139.

[92] M. Hicks, 'Introduction', *Profit, Piety and the Professions in Later Medieval England*, ed. M. Hicks (Gloucester, 1990), p. xvii.

[93] M.H. Keen, 'The End of the Hundred Years War: Lancastrian France and Lancastrian England', *England and her Neighbours, 1066-1453. Essays in Honour of Pierre Chaplais*, ed. M.C.E. Jones and M.G.A. Vale (London, 1989), pp. 297-311.

meaningless if restricted to consideration of the small number of beneficiaries under discussion. But in terms of the extent and duration of personal and familial responsibility – wardships, inheritance rights, presentations to bene-fices, watch and guard duty – built up in Caen or Rouen, often as intangible and as immobile as they were indescribable to those not familiar with them in this foreign context, these obligations had an importance which was not lost to those, on both sides of the sea, aware of the paradox which had long lain at the heart of the Lancastrian settlement policy. This was that settlers' interests must inevitably diverge from those of their homeland unless they could be protected by a long-term commitment of money and personnel which ultimately lay beyond the will of Henry V's successors.

More Rouennais than the Rouennais? It would be easy in arguing here for a pattern of integration and assimilation of incomers with residents to give a false impression of social harmony and good relations. However much one allows for a basic institutional stability and the relative safety of life behind city defences it cannot be forgotten that Rouen was in a state of occupation following a bitterly-fought siege and the renewal of a protracted conflict. Lancastrian merchants, craftsmen and clerics had followed in the footsteps of soldiers; their presence did not form part of a commercial colony in a manner common throughout western Europe in the later middle ages or indeed in Rouen itself only a century later.[94] Hatred, anger, frustration and non-cooperation have left proportionately fewer traces in the record than coexist-ence and collaboration, but were nonetheless surely evident. Rouen soldiers were no less prone than others to leave their garrison to live off the surround-ing countryside, or to commit outrages.[95] Henry Gregory, a member of Salvain's retinue between 1423 and 1429 who also served the same man in a civilian capacity as a *procureur*, was pardoned for the murder of a Frenchman whom he surprised one night drinking with Gregory's wife in the city.[96] At individual and family level it must be emphasised, however, that the number and variety of types of contact between the two races were such that for some Rouennais at least business continued as usual, while for some Englishmen at least the city meant more than *une place de séjour*. A baptism may be interpreted to indicate nothing more than convenience: the duke of York had a son, Edmund, and a daughter, Elizabeth, baptised in the cathedral;[97] a marriage may be ascribed to bigamous opportunism;[98] a burial too, might be more a matter of necessity than choice of resting-place;[99] bequests of money,

[94] P. Benedict, *Rouen during the Wars of Religion* (Cambridge, 1981), pp. 21-22.

[95] BN, MS fr. 26066/3936.

[96] *Actes de la chancellerie d'Henry VI concernant la Normandie sous la domination anglaise (1422-1435)*, ed. P. Le Cacheux, 2 vols (Rouen and Paris, 1907-8), ii, p. 358.

[97] F. Farin, *Histoire de la ville de Rouen*, 6 vols (3rd edn, 1738), iii, p. 158; P.A. Johnson, *Duke Richard of York, 1411-1460* (Oxford, 1988), p. 47.

[98] ADSM, G 249, G 250.

[99] Talbot buried his son, John, in the chapel of the Virgin in Saint-Ouen: ADSM, G 9195, fos 11v-12v; Farin, *Histoire*, v, p. 215; C. de Robillard de Beaurepaire, 'Notes sur des ornements

continued

plate and robes may be read as merely fulfilling contemporary expectations of the aristocracy.[100] Taken together, such testimony suggests something more than martial rule by garrison soldiers. In different ways and at different levels of society contact between occupiers and occupied took traditional and new forms which defy neat generalisations about profit and loss, conquest and defeat. Anecdotal evidence for local assimilation may not convince us that in Lancastrian Rouen the '*paix finale*' of the Treaty of Troyes was close to realisation but nor should it be characterised as, for example, mere pious gesture or the cynical pursuit of local favour. In secular matters and spiritual, in private and public capacities, Valois and Lancastrian came to an accommodation in many cases to their mutual benefit.

We would be justified in regarding this model of settlement as the norm rather than the exception. Whether instigated by accident or design, and whether witnessed in a small town such as Caudebec or larger centres such as Caen and Rouen, a pattern based on the inclusion rather than the exclusion of military personnel within pre-existing social and economic structures of urban Normandy was preferred and pursued, and Rouen is the most conspicuous instance of it. Individual and collective fortunes were bound up in the continuance of good relations between townsmen, their governors (still largely Norman) and the English. Property tenure or ownership affected only a small minority of those in Lancastrian military service, but such service, broadly defined, assumed a political importance which belied the numbers involved. We might end by considering the cautionary tale of Stephen Drop, archer of the Rouen garrison. He petitioned the crown that he had served on various expeditions and *chevauchées* since Henry V's landing at Touques in 1417 but had received no grant of land to help him live. His '*pouvres gaiges d'archier*' were expected to support himself, his wife and seven children, but his quarterly wages had been docked because he was reported to be earning a living as a barber during this period, which he denied. Could he please have his deduction restored? He could.[101] Expectation of reward, pursuit of livelihood, a close and complex relationship between military service, civilian life and personal circumstances; an unglamorous business, war.

---

continued

d'église donnés par Talbot à la chapelle Saint-Georges de Rouen', *Derniers mélanges historiques et archéologiques* (Rouen, 1909), p. 46.

[100] ADSM, G 2124, fo. 137r for bequests by Salisbury; ibid., G 2126, fos 60r-61r for those of Bedford; Farin, *Histoire*, i, pp. 351-52 for those of Edmund Beaufort.

[101] ADSM, MS Danquin, carton 9, liasse D.

20

The English and the Church in Lancastrian Normandy

Christopher Allmand

The title given to this essay is a general one; the text needs to be more specific. We have to ask how, in the circumstances of the time, in particular in a period of occupation, the English dealt with the church and its personnel in Normandy. What factors influenced their attitude towards it? What could they hope from it? In short, if they had a policy, did it succeed or fail?

Let us recall some of the problems which the English faced as they first conquered, and then ruled for a period of some thirty years, the duchy which had been lost over two centuries earlier. Their main problem was to get themselves accepted as *de facto*, if not *de jure* rulers of Normandy; they had to keep order in time of war; and they had to draw upon the clergy in their search for at least some of the personnel who would serve in the highest levels of administration. The church was an ally of great potential to the English, if it could be won over to their side.

What was expected of the clergy of the duchy which, step by step, was brought under English rule between the summer of 1417 and the early spring of 1419?[1] Henry V was anxious that they should be well treated; so much is clear. The reasons lay not merely in the king's well-known respect for the church and his regard for the clergy, nor, necessarily, in his determination that the clergy, as well as women, children, and old men should receive proper treatment at the hands of his soldiers. The king was motivated by an important political consideration (the political factor must be borne in mind all the while): Henry wanted the compliance and cooperation of the clergy; he wanted to secure their influence, and he wanted it to work for him. In this situation, unpromising as it might be, he held two excellent cards: one, the fear experienced by the clergy that, should they oppose him, they would lose their benefices and their revenues; the other, the power of ecclesiastical patronage which Henry acquired as his conquest developed, patronage which could be used to further the careers of men who might be persuaded to join him.

The evidence of the Norman rolls, in the Public Record Office, underlines some of these points. The lists of parish clergy leading their parishioners into

---

[1] See C. Allmand, *Henry V* (London, 1992), ch. 9, and in particular pp. 191, 195-98.

the presence of the king or of one of those delegated to receive the oath of fealty to the new regimes constitute evidence of two things to be noted:[2] the early acceptance (at least at its most superficial level) of the reality of the English occupation by many of the parochial clergy; and, secondly, the emphasis on the leadership role played by the clergy in these difficult and abnormal times, a role which recognised the place of the parish and its church as a stabilising factor in the situation, one which may have had more influence than any secular or feudal authority in bringing the people to formal acceptance of English rule. In a small, local society such as the parish, the influence of the priest could be considerable: his pulpit might be used as a means of persuasion; his confessional, although private, might be used to do the same. The priest was a man whose influence had to be won, whose importance it was perilous to neglect.[3]

The same Norman rolls also contain evidence of the power which the new conquerors held over the clergy. It is clear that not a few of the clerical estate refused to accept the invader and fled. Whether they did so out of fear or determination not to submit to English rule we do not know. What is certain is that their publicised absences from their spiritual and public role will have done no good to their parishioners; no good either, to their new political masters. Over a long period attempts were to be made to persuade the clergy (and others) who had fled to return.[4] While at first appearing to be patient, the English found that their patience could not last for ever. A priest who abandoned his benefice, especially if it involved residence, was a rebel, and a well-known one in the locality of his church. Absentee priests had to be enticed back for another reason, a provision of spiritual services. The cure of souls had to be assured as far as possible in these difficult times when with scarcely a bishop in residence, the administration of the duchy's seven bishoprics must have been in turmoil.

So the English played one of their strong cards. Clergy who refused all blandishments to return were gradually deprived and replaced. By acting in this way, largely through the exercise of the regalian right in vacant sees as well as that of much secular patronage which they had acquired, the English achieved two things: they demonstrated their authority over the Norman church and its personnel; and, perhaps more important for the future, they ensured that the clergy appointed to replace those who had abandoned their cures were ready to accept the reality of the conquest by taking the oath of

---

[2] *Forty-first Report of the Deputy Keeper of the Public Records* (London, 1880), pp. 692, 721-22, 725, 743.

[3] 'C'est par l'entremise des prêtres qu'il [Henry V] s'efforce de se concilier les habitants des campagnes et de les rattacher à son gouvernement.' L. Puiseux, *L'émigration normande et la colonisation anglaise en Normandie au XVe Siècle* (Paris, 1865), p. 26.

[4] C. Allmand, 'The Relations between the English Government, the Higher Clergy, and the Papacy in Normandy, 1417-1450' (unpublished D. Phil. thesis, University of Oxford 1963), pp. 11-12, 32.

fealty to the English king. In this way, at least in theory, both the clergy who continued undisturbed and those replacing men who had forsaken their churches were formally committed to the acceptance of English rule.[5]

Such, briefly, was the situation which developed in the early years of the occupation. Was it all as straightforward as it appeared? Unhappily, we know all too little about what happened in the rural areas, and are left to judge what the reaction may have been from patchy evidence, much of it legal in character and not necessarily typical of the duchy as a whole. We are forced back on impressions. The overriding one is of the clergy unwilling to take too many risks for fear of losing their benefices and, in some cases, seeking favour with the new political masters who might secure them promotion and advancement within the ecclesiastical hierarchy. Of resistance by these men of high local profile, something, but relatively little, is known. Of course, as Roger Jouet pointed out in his study of resistance to English rule, a few clergy became *brigands* or *résistants*. Yet as a class they had too much to lose to do this other than on a small scale, so that it is scarcely surprising that the chapter devoted to clerical opposition is the shortest in Jouet's book.[6] To be sure, Mont-Saint-Michel stood out as a bastion of defiance to the English (while, ironically, its abbot, Robert Jolivet, served the enemy in Rouen), and it even managed to raise levies of money, or *appatis*, from certain areas within the duchy, which suggests support for what it stood for. Nor will the Franciscans of Falaise have been the only religious body to have given shelter to members of the clergy on the run from authority. We learn, too, that there were clergy who refused to accept orders to pray in public for the new government, and that there were those accused of having been *adversaires du roy* or purveyors of *mauvaises paroles*. Jouet makes a valid point when he stresses the tension which sometimes arose when a clerical court claimed authority over a member of the clergy accused of a secular offence, such as treason, arguing that when this form of tug-of-war between spiritual and secular jurisdictions arose it reflected a pro-French attitude on the part of the ecclesiastical authorities anxious to protect one of their own.[7] Whether one accepts this argument depends on how one interprets the complex evidence available. But one thing is clear. Although the clergy doubtless included men – perhaps many – who were antipathetic to the English presence and who, given the chance, helped in secret ways either to undermine English authority or, more positively, to further the Valois cause, there is precious little evidence of a considered and hostile attitude on the part of the Norman clergy of this period to the reality of English rule.

---

[5] Allmand, *Henry V*, pp. 195-96.

[6] R. Jouet, *La résistance á l'occupation anglaise en Basse-Normandie, 1418-1450* (Caen, 1969), pp. 73-77, where most of the examples cited here are to be found.

[7] See, for instance, ADSM, G 860, 1167, 1188, 1191, 1196, 1278.

Let us leave generalisation for a particular example, the relationship between the English and the chapter of the metropolitan cathedral at Rouen. There are good reasons for choosing Rouen. The archives there contain a fine, unbroken series of capitular records which covers the entire period under consideration.[8] In addition, there are many other documents which throw light on the chapter's relationship with the occupying power. Such records assume even greater importance when it is appreciated that the series is unique for Normandy at this period. To be able to follow what was decided at the regular capitular meetings is significant for other reasons. We have here the record of how the most important and distinguished gathering of secular clergy in Normandy in the first half of the fifteenth century carried out its business and, to a certain extent, how it reacted to the English presence over a long period of years. It should also be emphasised that, for the first years of the occupation, the chapter's influence was greatly enhanced by the absence of the archbishop, Louis d'Harcourt, and that, thereafter, the diminishing influence of his successors (at least until the election as archbishop in 1444 of Raoul Roussel, a long-standing member of the chapter) led to the moral leadership of the clergy within the see of Rouen passing to 'messieurs du chapitre de Notre Dame de Rouen'. In the particular political conditions prevailing at the time, the chapter had no ordinary role to play.

It was, therefore, vitally important for the English to establish a good working relationship with that body, and to avoid doing this through overt control which might be fiercely resisted. The accumulated evidence of records housed today in London, Rouen and at the Vatican demonstrate how many of those, including some Englishmen,[9] who became members of the metropolitan chapter (and, indeed, members of other cathedral chapters in Normandy) during these years owed their nomination to royal patronage exercised by the English, who built up a fount of indebtedness from the clergy thus promoted. Other records, in some instances supported by the evidence of the chronicle compiled by Pierre Cochon, a member of the city's clergy, suggest that there were moments of tension between the secular and spiritual authorities. Two cases of what was regarded as profane behaviour by Englishmen, one in 1419, another in 1436, were probably the result of ignorance of local customs rather than direct attacks upon the church's privileges.[10] In 1423 we witness the first example of disputed jurisdiction between chapter and archbishop attracting the unwelcome attention of John Salvain, the Yorkshireman who was *bailli* of Rouen, who was not always tactful in his handling of the clergy.[11] Two years

---

[8] ADSM, G 2121-34.

[9] See C. Allmand, 'Alan Kirketon: A Clerical Royal Councillor in Normandy during the English Occupation in the Fifteenth Century', *Journal of Ecclesiastical History*, 15 (1964), pp. 33-39; idem, 'Some Effects of the Last Phase of the Hundred Years' War upon the Maintenance of Clergy', *Studies in Church History*, ed. G.J. Cuming (Leiden, 1966), 3, pp. 179-90.

[10] ADSM, G 2122, fo. 100v; G. 2127, fo. 181v.

[11] ADSM, G 1191.

later chapter and archbishop took joint action against an overzealous royal official in a dispute important enough for the record, *procès-verbal*, to be included in the cathedral's main cartulary, and for the event to be recorded by Pierre Cochon among the main ones of that year.[12]

Surviving evidence tells us of a variety of other disputes, Who exercised jurisdiction over clergy accused of violence or, as it was sometimes regarded by what was at times a nervous English administration, *lèse-majesté* or treason, cases, for instance, in which clergy were accused of involvement in attempts to undermine or destroy English authority?[13] Who was to have the final word in testamentary cases?[14] What would happen if the English, deliberately or out of ignorance of local customs, refused to grant the chapter its ancient privilege of visiting the prisons on Ascension Thursday to claim the release of a prisoner, the exercise of the historic privilege of Saint-Romain, as it was called?[15] Then, too, there were occasions for conflict arising from disputed nominations to one of the main offices within the church. In 1432 there was trouble over who should be named archdeacon of the Grand Caux, the chapter refusing the royal nominee and stating its determination to defend 'les drois, libertés, ou franchises de notre dicte eglise ou de nous' against even the royal authority.[16] By 1446, however, in a similar sort of dispute, the canons felt it more prudent to cede to the wish of the civil power, expressed by the forceful presence of the lieutenant of the *bailli* who appeared before the chapter to support the election of the royal nominee.[17]

How should such evidence be interpreted? Was opposition to royal nominations to specific offices simply a predictable reaction on the part of the chapter anxious, at a time when ecclesiastical reform was in the air, to assert its corporate identity and defend its historic rights and those of its church against royal intervention, as the texts suggest? Or should they be read as opportunities to oppose the 'enemy' occupier, as opposition, therefore, to the English. Perhaps not. In the duchy as a whole, relations between the government and the cathedral chapters remained generally cordial.[18] In Rouen, in 1430, they reached new heights with the personal election of John, duke of Bedford, as a canon of the cathedral, his formal reception being marked by ceremonies of considerable pomp.[19] Once more we may ask how this event should be

---

[12] ADSM, G 7, fo. 480; *Chronique normande de Pierre Cochon*, ed. C. de Beaurepaire (Rouen, 1870), pp. 294-95 (under 1426).

[13] Allmand, 'Relations', pp. 90-93.

[14] See, for example, ADSM, G 1195.

[15] ADSM, G 2122, fo. 88; A. Floquet, *Histoire du privilège de Saint Romain* (Rouen, 1833), ii, pp. 628-47.

[16] ADSM, G 2126, fos 167v-170.

[17] ADSM, G 2131, fos 28, 67, 69.

[18] Except, perhaps at Sées, situated near the duchy's more remote southern frontier, C. Allmand, 'L'évêché de Séez sous la domination anglaise au XVe siècle', *Annales de Normandie*, 11 (1961), pp. 301-07.

[19] ADSM, G 2126, fo. 59.

interpreted. Certainly it was an honour for Bedford himself, a man known for his piety. We would like to know whether it arose from a demand or suggestion put to the chapter by the English or, conversely, whether it should be regarded as a rather subtle way of engaging the moral support of the duke (who was regent of France) against those of his administrators who were inclined to be less than understanding in their dealings with the church in Rouen. Wherever the answer may lie, the honour accorded to Bedford suggests that relations between the chapter and the English were already on a sound footing and that, if anything, the members of the chapter were ready to see them improve further. The fact that a decade or so later the duke of York would also enjoy a good relationship with the capitular body suggests that, far from depending on individuals, the understanding between *château* and *cathédrale* was founded upon a coincidence of interest, that of peace and order.[20]

The maintenance of stability through just and effective rule was probably the political ideal which forged and supported the understanding between the chapter and the English, the chapter being well aware that the duke of Bedford had the attainment of social and political order high on his list of priorities. Bernard Guenée has recently shown how, in the works of Thomas Basin, who came from Caudebec (near Rouen) and was to become bishop of Lisieux in 1447, the notion was put forward that rule which lacked full legitimacy should none the less be obeyed if it achieved justice and order, that is if it fulfilled the purpose for which it was exercised.[21] If, at the end of their rule, the English lost much support, this was chiefly because they were failing in their self-assumed obligation of ruling the duchy in peace. Earlier, however, Bedford had done his best to curb abuses, not least those perpetrated by his own soldiers, in his attempt to achieve a peaceful society. Was the relative compliance of the Rouen chapter and, as far as we can tell, that of other ecclesiastical corporations in the duchy influenced by ideas not dissimilar to those of Basin, who was prepared to accept English rule because it was reasonably effective? It was the view expressed by the Religieux de Saint-Denis about French acceptance of Henry V: 'S'il est le plus fort, eh bien! qu'il soit notre maître, pourvu que nous puissions vivre au sein de la paix, du repos, et de l'aisance.'[22] Doubts about legitimacy were being overcome by a realisation that, under English rule, France was experiencing a greater level of political and economic stability than she had experienced for many years.

In addition to that which it wielded within the duchy, the chapter exercised great influence within Rouen itself. In the circumstances, its attitude to the English cannot have been far divorced from the wider interests and attitudes of

---

[20] ADSM, G 2129, fo. 163; 2130, fos 106, 142, 147v, 193.

[21] B. Guenée, *Between Church and State: The Lives of Four French Prelates in the Late Middle Ages* (Chicago and London, 1991), p. 303.

[22] Cited by G. Ascoli, *La Grande-Bretagne devant l'opinion française depuis la Guerre de Cent Ans jusqu'à la fin du XVIe siècle* (Paris, 1927), p. 12.

the city itself. As such one would expect it to support policy initiated by the English to revive the economic prosperity and political fortunes of the Norman capital. In this respect relations with Paris, the national capital likewise under English rule, assumed great importance. It is well known how the economy of Rouen, like that of Paris closely linked to the prosperous fluvial traffic of the Seine, had, over the past years, come to be dominated by Paris to the detriment of Normandy. From the early days of the conquest it became English policy to help redress the balance. It was also English policy to stand up for a measure of Norman judicial independence against the pretensions of the parlement of Paris, largely by encouraging Normans to bring their appeals from inferior courts either before the duchy's *échiquier* (on the few occasions on which that body met during these years) or, on an increasingly regular basis, before the cour du conseil, a conciliar court established by the English to hear appeals in suits concerning Normans or Norman interests (lands, benefices) which, it was claimed, should be decided not in Paris but in Rouen. In such matters the duchy and the English enjoyed a significant congruity of interest, helped by a fairly consistent English policy of encouraging the duchy to stand up for itself against the domination of the capital.[23] When the supporters of Charles VII retook Paris in 1436, thus forcing the English to retreat to Rouen, the policy was to be continued with the creation of a *chambre des comptes* and a *cour des aides* for Normandy, as well as by the foundation of the university of Caen, which took place during these years.[24] That the Rouen chapter approved of this attitude of independence is underlined by the fact that it was that body which was to be at the forefront of resistance to complete political control by the French after the reconquest of 1449-50. It is in the capitular register of the day that the statement of demands aimed at safeguarding the independence of separate Norman institutions, approved by the chapter in November 1452 and presented to Charles VII by the estates of the duchy, is to be found.[25] The English, not without thoughts of self-advantage, had appreciated and given their support to a number of practical expressions, some economic, others institutional and political, of Norman particularism. In this they made common cause with the people of the duchy and those of Rouen in particular, whose ambitions to some extent survived the French reconquest of 1450.

In order to influence the government and administration of the church in Normandy it was important for the English to have a say (the greater the say, the better) in the promotion of the higher clergy and, in particular, of those who were to become bishops. In this matter English policy was to come under a

---

[23] C. Allmand, *Lancastrian Normandy, 1415-1450: The History of a Medieval Occupation* (Oxford, 1983), ch. 5.

[24] For the origins of the university, see idem, *Lancastrian Normandy*, pp. 105-21.

[25] Idem, 'Local Reaction to the French Reconquest of Normandy: The Case of Rouen', *The Crown and Local Communities in England and France in the Fifteenth Century*, ed. J.R.L. Highfield and Robin Jeffs (Gloucester, 1981), ch. 8 and especially pp. 155-57.

number of different influences, reflecting both the situation in France and that in the church as a whole. The Great Schism (1378-1417) had greatly weakened the power of the papacy, not least the aim which it had been pursuing for the past century of increasing its control over the appointments made to high offices within the church, an attempt which had provoked considerable reaction in France, in particular in the closing years of the fourteenth century. The election of Martin V in November 1417 (just at the moment when Henry V was launching his conquest of Normandy) may have ended the search for a single pope. Whether, with the immediate reassertion by the new pope of claims to the exercise of rights enjoyed by his fourteenth-century predecessors, the election would mark the end of the dispute between the papacy and the local churches was another matter.

The schism had encouraged men to think. High on both the intellectual and the practical agenda was 'reform'. In France, as elsewhere, this was often taken to mean the encouragement of local autonomy in ecclesiastical matters, with a particular emphasis on the rights of local patrons and electors. In France, this was called 'Gallicanism', a kind of French church for the French, whose ideals were enshrined in a series of *ordonnances*, registered by the parlement of Paris, which reflected the hostile attitude of the Armagnac party (which had dominated French political life in the first years of the fifteenth century) to papal pretensions. Not all were in sympathy with this 'hands off' reaction to papal claims. By late 1418, with an administration of Burgundian sympathies in Paris now regulating relations with the papacy according to a recent concordat, or agreement,[26] whose terms reflected a much more moderate approach to papal pretensions on such matters as ecclesiastical appointments and the payment of papal taxes, Armagnac attitudes, although far from dead, were no longer influential in policy making. More important in this respect would be the link between the Burgundians and the university of Paris whose graduates had experienced lean years in the benefice 'market' in the days of schism and Armagnac legislation. In the circumstances, all the parties needed the help of the others: but at a price. As the newcomers to the French political scene, the English needed Burgundian support, which implied seeking the backing of the pro-Burgundian university of Paris, anxious to further the interests of its members. One consequence, then, of the entente with Burgundy established by Henry V and later developed by Bedford was their acceptance of the broad points of Burgundian policy towards the papacy which was more tolerant (for reasons of self-interest) of papal pretensions than had been that of the rival Armagnac party. In their search for able clergy who might enter their service, the English were to adopt a policy towards Rome inspired by the pro-papal attitude of the Burgundian group in the royal council,[27] as well as by the need to maintain the support of the university of

[26] J. Mansi, *Sacrorum conciliorum nova et amplissima collectio*, xxvii (1784), cols 1184-89.

[27] B.J.H. Rowe, 'The *Grand Conseil* under the Duke of Bedford, 1422-35', *Essays in Medieval History Presented to H.E. Salter* (Oxford, 1934), pp. 207-34.

Paris and its graduates whose careers it was to favour. The duke of Bedford, in particular, found it to his interest to adopt an attitude to Rome acceptable both in Parisian circles, where Burgundian influence was considerable, and in Rouen, where sympathy for the Burgundian cause had once been strong and where the cathedral chapter already numbered many Parisian graduates among its members. We should not be surprised that the policy followed in the years to come should have given the renewed papacy considerable powers over the church and the careers of churchmen in Normandy.

This was to be shown very quickly. In 1418 the duchy was badly in need of new bishops. Three had been victims of the great anti-Armagnac massacre which occurred in Paris in the early summer of that year; others, for a number of reasons, were absent 'in partibus'. In these early days, however, Henry V had, as yet, no wish to trust the rule of the church in Normandy to Frenchmen – or so it was reported from Rome.[28] In the meantime, the sees of Coutances, Evreux, and Lisieux were given to Italians, papal appointments all,[29] a way of proceeding which enabled the king to make a gesture to the new pope while ensuring, since the nominees were not likely to reside, that the new English administration would be able to exert practical influence in those dioceses for at least a few years.

It needs to be emphasised that English ecclesiastical policy in Normandy was free of certain factors which dominated anglo-papal relations with regard to England. There was never any threat, for instance, of applying the regulations of the statute of Praemunire to Normandy.[30] The duchy was seen as part of France, so that French, not English factors controlled consideration of policy towards papacy. Thus Henry V tried to secure Martin V's seal of approval for the treaty of Troyes largely by making concessions to the pope regarding ecclesiastical appointments in the duchy. But in this respect neither he nor his successor got what he wanted. The concessions went for nothing.

The English were prisoners, on the one hand, of their own requirements, of the political and ecclesiastical circumstances within France to which they were heirs, and, on the other hand, of growing sympathy for reform which emerged from the period of schism and the meetings of the two great councils at Constance and Basel which followed. They wanted clergy, above all bishops and high ecclesiastical office holders, whom they could trust and in whose appointment they could have at least some say. They wanted, too, to advance

---

[28] 'Quia . . . nullum in dicta ecclesia gallicum patietur quousque terra ipsa magis confirmata fuerit', Bod Lib, MS. Arch. Seld. B. 23, fo. 68v; cited by E.F. Jacob, 'To and from the Court of Rome in the Early Fifteenth Century', *Studies in French Language and Medieval Literature Presented to Professor M.K. Pope* (Manchester, 1939), pp. 167-68.

[29] Pandolfo di Malatesta (Coutances); Paolo da Capranica (Evreux); and Cardinal Branda da Castiglione (Lisieux). Two more members of the Castiglione family, Zano and Giovanni, were to become bishops of Lisieux (and then Bayeux) and Coutances respectively in 1424 (and 1432) and 1445.

[30] Margaret Harvey, 'Martin V and Henry V', *Archivum historiae pontificiae*, 24 (1986), p. 49.

university graduates (a problem familiar from experience in England) by securing promotion for them within the hierarchical structure of the church in Normandy as well as within their own, secular administration. Both these aims, whose fulfilment would strengthen links with the Burgundian court whose pro-papal sympathies were well known, could be furthered by allowing the papacy an important, if not decisive role in the matter of high clerical appointments in Normandy. Against this stood the parlement, the traditional defender of the Gallican liberties (hence rather hostile to papal pretensions), now increasingly aware of the growing demand for reform, one aspect of which was to be its defence of the rights of local electors, such as cathedral chapters or monastic communities, in ecclesiastical appointments. Neither Henry V nor Bedford was against reform as such. Political considerations, however, had to come first. So it was that both men pursued a policy which allowed them maximum control over the Norman church, a policy best achieved by permitting papal intervention to the detriment of local claims. Bedford might use the threat of 'Gallican' legislation (as he did in 1424, after the great confidence-boosting victory won against the Franco-Scottish army at Verneuil that year) to try to force the papacy to introduce certain reforms.[31] But the threat was only half-hearted. Encouraged by domestic factors and by the clergy of Burgundian background at that time influential in the royal council, Bedford decided that he had little to gain by antagonising the papacy. Although a blow to Norman autonomy and to the hopes of local patrons, a new papal constitution for the provision of benefices through the application of the 'alternative' system (first used in France a quarter of a century earlier) which enabled the papacy to nominate to benefices which fell vacant during the eight months of the year was nonetheless accepted in 1425.[32] By then it had become clear to Bedford that, both in the matter of the appointment of bishops and other dignitaries, such as cathedral deans, and in the promotion of graduates to positions of influence within the church in Normandy, the system which favoured the papacy also favoured the English. By and large, it was already promoting the kind of people they wanted. It should be allowed to continue.

Bedford had probably judged it right. By following a policy of cooperation with, but not total submission to Rome (for the policy was never so firm as to ignore totally the rights of canonical electors and patrons), the regent was demonstrating his appreciation that the support which he might get from individuals was more important to him than the defence of the political

---

[31] On 4 October 1424 the chancellor, addressing the estates in Paris, claimed that the present religious policy was allowing large sums of money to be taken from France to the Roman curia; that, acting as he did, the pope was contravening both decrees of past councils and royal ordinances on the subject; he finished by stating that it was 'l'intencion du dit de Bedford . . . de maintenir et faire maintenir l'église de France et les personnes ecclesiastiques de ce royaume en leurs libertés et franchises anciennes, selon la teneur des dictes ordonnances . . . ', AN, X1a 1480, fos 308v-309; cited by S. Luce, *Jeanne d'Arc á Domremy* (Paris, 1886), pp. 127-28.

[32] AN, X1a 8605, fos 24-24v.

principles enshrined in Gallicanism. Protests from the parlement could be ignored or quickly forgotten. The justification of the policy was to be found in the tragic episode of the trial of Joan of Arc. Many of those who took part in it, men such as Pierre Cauchon and certain members of the Rouen chapter,[33] were alumni of the university of Paris and, in politics, pro-Burgundian in sympathy. All had accepted the reality of the English occupation; all had personally benefited from it. Their participation in the trial, political in motive while ecclesiastical in form, shows that the English had chosen their men well. They had used their influence to draw in those who would support them in time of difficulty. The policy appeared to have worked.

The church in Normandy during the English occupation is here presented in a particular way but one which is justified by much of the surviving evidence. The aim has been to provide, in a short compass, some kind of an answer to some of the questions raised at the start of this essay. We need to know how the occupation was managed, and how the English regarded and confronted the problems of government and order which they faced. Equally, we need to appreciate how the Normans, in particular the clergy, reacted to the presence and rule of the English. It is not difficult to find information regarding opposition to English rule over a period of a generation or more. Not unnaturally, French historians have given much attention to the trial of Joan of Arc, and to those who took part in it. Their verdicts, above all when declared by those of the old nationalist school, have not been favourable. Today, a greater tolerance prevails. It can now be seen more readily that the past has shown too little historical understanding of the real coincidence of interest between what the English demanded of the clergy, especially its university educated members, and what such men could hope for in return for their support of English rule. Furthermore, our discernment of English policy towards Rome, and the reasons which lay behind it, add to our appreciation of how the papacy reasserted itself after the Schism and how the movement for reform failed to make much headway. Above all, it should be apparent that a subject such as this was influenced by many considerations. The English had to decide what they wanted for the church in Normandy, what part it should play in the society they had come to rule, and what could be expected in terms of political advantage from a careful handling of the church's personnel. This brief consideration should suggest both the complexity of the situation and the relative success which the English achieved in their management of these intricate problems.

[33] P. Wolff, 'Le théologien Pierre Cauchon de sinistre memoire', *Economies et sociétés au moyen âge: mélanges offerts à Edouard Perroy* (Paris, 1973), pp. 553-70.

21

English Patrons and French Artists in Fifteenth-Century Normandy

Catherine Reynolds

In 1981 a contemporary English patron, Dr Nellie B. Eales, presented the University of Reading Library with a fifteenth-century Book of Hours illuminated by French artists.[1] The Eales Hours, MS 2087 in the University Library, originally had a full programme of illustration, with fifteen large miniatures marking the major divisions of the text, of which six remain (Plate 18), twenty-four marginal roundels illustrating the calendar and twenty-one small miniatures for the memorials to the saints. All the surviving miniatures are in a style known as that of the Master of the Munich Golden Legend, from a copy of the French translation of the *Legenda aurea* in Munich (Bayerische Staatsbibliothek, MS gall, 3).[2] Pen and ink reinforce contours and define details and parallel hatching supplements more painterly tonal modelling. The linearity of the style lends itself to easy duplication and economy of effort so that motifs and whole compositions are sometimes repeated. Figures conform to a limited range of types, sharing emphatically drawn facial features and a rather stunted physique. Although at the centre of a style's development there is likely to be one individual, or conceivably two or even three on the model of the de Limbourgs, systems of apprenticeship, paid assistance by journeymen and collaboration between masters make it difficult to distinguish *the* Master as a definable individual among the painters working in the Munich Golden Legend style.

The Eales Hours, like many of the books sharing the style, is of the Use of Paris and both it and the Munich *Golden Legend* were probably produced in Paris. The *Golden Legend* contains a long illustrated addition on the Saint Voult of Lucca, indicating an original patron either from the Lucchese community in Paris or someone associated with their confraternity in Saint-

---

[1] J.A. Edwards, *A Gift and its Donor* (Reading, 1984). I am very grateful to the University Archivist, Michael Bott, for his assistance with photographs.

[2] J. Plummer, *The Last Flowering, French Painting in Manuscripts 1420-1530 from American Collections* (New York and London, 1982), pp. 6-7, with bibliography; Eleanor P. Spencer, who reconstructed the Master, generously shared unpublished research.

Sepulchre dedicated to the Saint Voult.[3] On stylistic grounds, the *Golden Legend* can be dated to *c.* 1420 and the Eales Hours to the 1440s. Between these dates, the main practitioner of the Golden Legend style temporarily abandoned the capital for the greater security and prosperity of Normandy.[4] Miniatures in the Golden Legend style are found in two Books of Hours for the Use of Rouen (Naples, Biblioteca Nazionale, MS I B 27, and Minneapolis, Private Collection), one for the Use of Evreux (Cambridge, Fitzwilliam Museum, MS McClean 82) and one for the Use of Bayeux (Caen, Musée des Beaux-Arts, Mancel MS Collection 139).[5] There are no original marks of ownership in the two Rouen Hours and it is likely that they were made for the open market, aimed at a French, rather than English, clientele. The English apparently preferred their native Use of Sarum, since Sarum hours, incorporating prayers to specifically English saints, were manufactured for the English market in sufficient quantity to have a lasting effect on Norman devotional practice. In the Naples Hours, the Memorials to the Saints follow Lauds within the hours of the Virgin, a Sarum convention which became a regular feature of Rouen books of hours.[6] Although practitioners of the Munich Golden Legend style seem not to have been so heavily involved in the English market as some of their colleagues, at least one Sarum Hours was decorated in this style (London, Quaritch, June 1907, no. 1112).[7]

A French Use, however, would not necessarily deter an English customer from acquiring an existing book of hours to personalise in order to reflect his or her identity and concerns. Painters in the Munich Golden Legend style were employed for a member of the family of Ralph Neville, 1st earl of Westmorland, and a member of the family of Burgh to alter a book of hours of Paris Use, with a calendar and litany indicative of Brittany (BN, MS lat. 1158).[8] A new gathering of six bifolios with two added unruled single leaves, fos 27 and 34, making up fos 27-40, was inserted before the hours of the Virgin to carry

---

[3] L. Mirot, *Etudes lucquoises* (Paris, 1930), pp. 18-19.

[4] C. Reynolds, ' "Les Angloys, de leur droicte nature, veullent touzjours guerreer": Evidence for Painting in Paris and Normandy, *c.* 1420-1450', *Power, Culture and Religion in France c. 1350 - c. 1550*, ed. C.T. Allmand (Woodbridge, 1989), pp. 37-55.

[5] M. Rotili, *Miniatura francese a Napoli: Miniatura e arte minori in Campania*, Collana di saggi e studi, 2 (Benevento, n.d.), p. 42, no. 7, pls xvii-xix; Minneapolis, University of Minnesota Gallery, *Medieval Illumination, Glass, and Sculpture in Minnesota Collections*, by A. Stones and J. Steyaert (Minneapolis, MIN, 1978), no. 14, pp. 58-66, figs 45-46; M.R. James, *A Descriptive Catalogue of the McClean Collection of Manuscripts in the Fitzwilliam Museum, Cambridge* (Cambridge, 1912), no. 82, pp. 169-72, pl. 53; Bibliothèques de la ville de Caen, *Livres d'heures de Basse Normandie* (Caen, 1985), pp. 53-54, no. 10, illustrations on cover and pp. 21, 33, 36, 40, 52.

[6] L.M.J. Delaissé, 'The Importance of Books of Hours for the History of the Medieval Book', *Gatherings in Honor of Dorothy E. Miner*, ed. U. McCracken, L. Randall, R. Randall, (Baltimore, MD, 1973), p. 217.

[7] Bernard Quaritch, *Catalogue of Works of Standard English Literature* (London, 1907), appendix, no. 1112, p. 112 and pl.

[8] V. Leroquais, *Les livres d'heures manuscrits de la Bibliothèque Nationale* (Paris, 1927), i, pp. 72-75; iv, pl. xxxv.

additional prayers,[9] That on fo. 28 opens with a miniature of the Trinity and that on fo. 35 with a miniature of Christ of the Last Judgement, both above four lines of text on the model of the original miniature page layouts. Painted over the border decoration on fo. 28 is a kneeling man whose surcoat bears azure three fleur de lys ermine, the arms of at least two branches of the Burgh family, differenced with an annulet or, and a badge of a wing emerging from a crown with the motto 'sans ne puis', also superimposed on the marginal decoration of fo. 35. These arms without difference were used by Thomas Burgh (dead by 1434), heir to his elder brother, John Burgh of Colthorpe, Yorks;[10] he married the heiress of Gainsborough, inherited by his only son, Sir Thomas, created Lord Burgh in 1487.[11] Thomas and John had two younger brothers, Peter and Roger, and an uncle Robert. A branch, apparently of the same family since bearing the same arms, possibly with a chevron for difference,[12] said to have come from Westmorland where the Burghs of Colthorpe owned land, prospered through the marriage of Hugh Burgh (died 1430) to the heiress of Wattlesborough, Salop.[13] Their son, Sir John Burgh (1417-71), is an appealing candidate for the Hours as he campaigned in France, probably under Talbot, the family's patron, and was rewarded with the seigneurie of Ollande near Cherbourg.[14] The two single leaves, both unruled, were inserted so that on fo. 27v is a miniature of Ralph Neville, earl of Westmorland, who died in 1425, with nine male and three female members of his family, his banderole addressed to the Trinity on fo. 28, and on fo. 34v is a miniature of his second wife, Joan Beaufort in widow's weeds, with six female members of the family, her banderole addressed to Christ of the Last Judgement on fo. 35 (Plates 20, 21).

While the Nevilles can be identified individually, in a way not yet possible with the common name of Burgh, it is still uncertain for which member of the

[9] The Calendar, fos 1-12, forms 1[12] and the Gospel extracts, *Obsecro te* and *O intemerata*, fos 13-26, form 2[8]-3[6], with the *O intemerata* ending on fo. 26r following by the rubric *Cy apres sensuivent les heures de nre dame selon lusage de Paris*; fo. 26v was left unwritten; the hours of the Virgin, beginning a new gathering, now follow on f. 41.

[10] For Burgh of Colthorpe, *Testamenta eboracensia*, i, Surtees Society (1836), pp. 447-48; J.C. Wedgwood, *History of Parliament: Biographies of the Members of the Commons House* (London, 1936), p. 316; R. Eden Cole, 'Pedigree of the Lords Burgh of Gainsborough', *Genealogist*, 12, pp. 233-35.

[11] Glass given to Gainsborough parish church, presumably during Sir Thomas's lifetime, by his daughter, Elizabeth, Lady Fitzhugh, and Sir George Tailbois, his daughter Mary's husband, showed his and his father's Burgh arms without difference, while those of his son, Edward, had a label of three files argent, ed. R.E.G. Cole, *Lincolnshire Church Notes made by Gervase Holles, 1634-1642*, Lincolnshire Record Society, 1 (Lincoln, 1911), p. 151.

[12] *The Visitation of Shropshire 1623*, ed. G. Grazebrook and J. Rylands, Harleian Society, 28 (1899), i, pp. 59-61 and 104.

[13] J.S. Roskell, L. Clark, C. Rawcliffe, *The House of Commons, 1386-1421*, The History of Parliament Trust (Stroud, 1992), pp. 417-19.

[14] Wedgwood, *Biographies*, p. 134; J. Brickdale Blakeway, *The Sheriffs of Shropshire* (Shrewsbury, 1831), p. 70.

family the book was adapted.[15] On fo. 34v are the shields of Joan Beaufort, Ralph Neville's second wife; of their daughters, Cecily, duchess of York, Catherine, duchess of Norfolk, Eleanor, countess of Northumberland, and Anne, countess of Stafford; and of two of Ralph's daughters by his first wife, Margaret Stafford, Alice, Lady Grey of Heton, and Margaret, Lady Scrope of Bolton. Of the impaled coats on fo. 27v, only the middle one is certainly identified as that of Philippa, Lady Dacre of Gilsland, another daughter of Margaret of Stafford. The other two must represent, incorrectly, her remaining married full sisters: Matilda, Lady Mauley, and Anne, Lady Umfraville. The eldest daughters of both wives were nuns and are excluded. On fo. 27v, the first undifferenced saltire is for Joan's husband, Ralph Neville. The plain label of three points argent should belong to either Ralph's eldest son, John, who died in 1423, or John's son, another Ralph, who succeeded his grandfather as earl of Westmorland. The label of three points gobony argent and azure was used by Joan's eldest son, Richard, earl of Salisbury. The plain saltire between the differenced shields is presumably for Ralph of Oversley, the first earl's other son by Margaret. One of the saltires must be for Robert Neville, shown in episcopal robes, who became bishop of Salisbury in 1427 and bishop of Durham in 1438. Four must be meant for Joan Beaufort's other sons who survived infancy: William, Lord Fauconberg; George, Lord Latimer; Edward, Lord Bergavenny; and, apparently, Thomas. For the remaining saltire there are two candidates, Henry and Cuthbert. The countess and five daughters wear the Lancastrian collar of SS, while all the men, except the bishop, wear collars of a stag jumping through a fence. A desire to emphasise family solidarity may have encouraged the omission of the younger sons' marks of difference.

The miniatures must postdate 1427, the costume indicating the 1430s,[16] and can probably be dated to before 1440, when Joan Beaufort, the most likely Neville owner, died; her will, however, mentions her mother's psalter to be preserved by her male heirs but not an Hours.[17] Her step-children can be excluded as possible patrons since there was a bitter feud between them, their stepmother and their half-siblings;[18] it was for two of Margaret's daughters that the illuminator lacked accurate heraldic information. One of Joan's children is likely to have wanted more attention paid to his or her own family, although one could have had the book altered for her, as a gift or acting on commission. All the miniatures and the figure with the Burgh arms are in the

---

[15] For the amendments to C. Couderc, *Les enluminures du moyen âge* (Paris, 1927), pp. 86-88, see R. Surtees, *The History and Antiquities of the County of Durham* (London, 1840), iv, pp. 158-62; B. Burke, *The General Armory* (London, 1884); E. Ashmole, *History of the Order of the Garter* (London, 1672).

[16] M. Scott, *The History of Dress Series: Late Gothic Europe, 1400-1500* (London, 1980), pp. 110-12.

[17] *Historiae Dunelmensis scriptores tres*, ed. J. Raine, Surtees Society (1839), p. cclviii.

[18] E.F. Jacob, *The Fifteenth Century* (Oxford, 1961), pp. 319-23.

style of the Munich Golden Legend and it is difficult to define whether Burgh or Neville owned the book first. The Neville miniatures are unusual in commemorating an entire family in a book of hours through portraits and in their technique. The elaborate modelling of the faces of the Neville men over a green underpaint is more usual in Netherlandish miniatures or in panel painting. Such exceptional miniatures could have been planned on detached leaves at the same time as the rest of the gathering; single leaves simplified procedures for the painter and were standard in Netherlandish book production.

Similarities between the Neville miniatures and the monumental votive panel, painted between 1444-1449 for the funerary chapel of the Jouvenel des Ursins family in Notre-Dame in Paris,[19] and the origins of the Munich Golden Legend style in Paris led to the assumption that the miniatures were also products of the capital.[20] Given their likely date, in the 1430s, and the fact that practitioners of the Munich Golden Legend style worked in Normandy, it seems more likely that they were commissioned there, probably in Rouen. Several members of the Neville family could have had direct access to the Rouen book trade. Richard led reinforcements in the summer of 1431 for Henry VI's French coronation and in 1436 accompanied his brother-in-law, Richard, duke of York, to Normandy; William served in France from 1428 until his release as one of the hostages taken as security for the treaty surrendering Rouen in 1449.[21]

Although the chief Master of the Munich Golden Legend moved on, probably through Brittany, before returning to Paris, his style influenced that of the Hoo Master named from the Book of Hours made for Sir Thomas Hoo, created Lord Hoo in 1445, and his second wife, Eleanor, daughter of Lionel Lord Welles (Dublin, Royal Irish Academy, MS 12 R 31).[22] They were married by about 1444 when Hoo's direct access to French painters would have been restricted to Normandy, where he held lands and high offices, including that of chancellor; he only returned to England in 1450. A weak practitioner of the Munich Golden Legend style was responsible for the miniatures in the Hours for the Use of Evreux (Fitzwilliam Museum, MS McClean 82), illuminated for the Norman George de Clere and his wife Marguerite de Bigny.[23] The date of their marriage has not been discovered but George de Clere's third cousin, Renaud de Chartres, archbishop of Reims, and his uncle Guillaume de Hellande, bishop of Beauvais, were his guardians during his minority and he is

[19] C. Sterling, *La peinture médiévale à Paris*, ii (Paris, 1990), pp. 28-35, figs 7 and 8 in colour; Denis Jouvenel omitted from transcription of inscription.

[20] Reynolds, 'Les Angloys', p. 52.

[21] *CP*, xi, pp. 393-98, v, 281-87.

[22] L.L. Williams, 'A Rouen Book of Hours of the Sarum Use *c.* 1444 Belonging to Thomas, Lord Hoo, Chancellor of Normandy and France', *Proceedings of the Royal Irish Academy*, 75, section C (1975), pp. 189-212.

[23] James, *McLean Collection*, pp. 370-72.

unlikely to have commissioned his Hours in Lancastrian Normandy. English patronage may have encouraged the Master of the Munich Golden Legend to leave Paris for Normandy, but it was not essential to the style's survival in the duchy, where the leading Rouen painter of the next generation, the Master of the Echevinage de Rouen (or of the Geneva Latini) formed his style under the influence of that of the Munich Golden Legend.[24]

The anonymous illuminator called the Master of the Harvard Hannibal is also found first in Paris and then in other areas, including Normandy. He was named by Millard Meiss from one miniature in a Livy now in Harvard (Houghton Library, MS Richardson 32).[25] Many of the manuscripts Meiss attributed to this artist would not appear to be by the same hand and it seems preferable to follow Pächt and Alexander in taking a copy of the Alexander Romance in the British Library, MS Royal 20 B XX, as the starting-point and to name the artist the Master of the Royal Alexander.[26] In marked contrast to the linear Munich Golden Legend style, that of the Royal Alexander is characterised by a thoroughly painterly technique, with figure drawing of greater variety and architectural and landscape settings of greater complexity.

The Master was involved in adapting a pre-existing book for an English owner, a psalter (BL, MS Cotton, Domitian A XVII), decorated originally for a dauphin of France depicted as a child, identifiable from the style of the manuscript as Louis born in 1397. The dauphin's arms were overpainted to convert the figure into that of Henry VI,[27] who must still have been a child for this to be appropriate. He was aged between seven and nine when he made his only visit to France from April 1430 to January 1432, a likely period for such an acquisition on his behalf, or gift to him. A series of miniatures, some, as fo. 122v (Plate 19), by the Master of the Royal Alexander, illustrating the recitation of the psalms were probably added at the same time to make the book more attractive to a child.[28] The Master could have worked on the psalter in Paris but he had probably already moved to Normandy. There are miniatures in his style in an hours of Rouen Use (Baltimore, Walters Art Gallery, MS W.259)[29] and in an Hours of Sarum Use (BL, MS Sloane 2468) perhaps made in Rouen for the English market. It came to be owned by John and

[24] C. Rabal, 'Artiste et clientèle à la fin du moyen âge: les manuscrits profanes du maître de l'échevinage de Rouen', *Revue de l'art*, 84 (1989), p. 58.

[25] M. Meiss, *French Painting in the Time of Jean de Berry: The Boucicaut Master* (London, 1968), pp. 57, 142, ill. 433; idem, *French Painting in the Time of Jean de Berry: The Limbourgs and their Contemporaries* (New York, 1974), pp. 390-392; Plummer, *Last Flowering*, pp. 5-6.

[26] O. Pächt and J.J.G. Alexander, *Illuminated Manuscripts in the Bodleian Library, Oxford. German, Dutch, Flemish, French and Spanish Schools* (Oxford, 1966), p. 52, no. 663; G.F. Warner and J.P. Gilson, *Catalogue of the Western Manuscripts in the Old Royal and King's College Collections* (London, 1921), ii, pp. 369-70; iv, pl. 116.

[27] J. Porcher, *Les Belles Heures de Jean de France, duc de Berry* (Paris, 1953), pp. 26-27; Meiss, *Limbourgs*, pp. 375 and 405, attributing all the added miniatures to his Master of St Jerome.

[28] Reynolds, 'Les Angloys', p. 51.

[29] R.S. Wieck, *The Book of Hours in Medieval Art and Life* (London, 1988), pp. 184-85, fig. 87.

Eleanor Umfray, who added to the calendar notes, subsequently erased, of their marriage in 1453 by 16 April and the birth of their first child, Joanna, in 1454 by 15 February.[30] The owner may be identified with the John Umfray or Humfrey of Barton Seagrave, Northants, whose widow, Eleanor, and her second husband, Robert Fenn, were pardoned in 1468.[31] Barton Seagrave was inherited by John and Eleanor's son, William, who had two younger brothers, Edward and Richard.[32] The Umfrays of Barton Seagrave could have married in 1453 but with firm evidence for neither the date of their marriage nor for the existence of an eldest child, Joanna, their ownership of the hours cannot be proved. The manuscript was not specially made for the Umfrays, whether of Barton Seagrave or elsewhere, and could have reached England with another owner or professional trader.

In a compilation made for the échevinage of Rouen (BN, MS fr. 126) is a miniature which, if not by the Master of the Royal Alexander, was produced under his influence (fo. 121, Plate 22), the remaining miniatures being in the style of the Talbot Master, as fo. 7 (Plate 23).[33] As the texts include Alain Chartier's *Quadrilogue invectif* and *Le curial*, they are unlikely to have been commissioned under English rule, showing that the styles of the Royal Alexander and Talbot Masters continued under French patronage despite the expulsion of the English.[34] The Talbot style is also found in earlier books of Norman Use, such as the hours of Rouen Use in Paris (BN, MS lat. 13283) and the hours of Coutances Use in Cambridge (Fitzwilliam Museum, MS 61).[35] The Master takes his name from John Talbot, earl of Shrewsbury, based in Rouen after the fall of Paris, who commissioned three books with miniatures in the style: the Shrewsbury Book, presented to Margaret of Anjou in 1445 (BL, MS Royal 15 E VI), and two hours of Sarum Use (Fitzwilliam Museum, MS 40-1950 and Aberdeen, Blairs College, deposited at Edinburgh, National Library of Scotland, MS Dep.221/1).[36] With the Talbot style it is particularly difficult to

[30] J. Backhouse, *Books of Hours* (London, 1985), p. 52, pl. 51.

[31] Wedgwood, *Biographies*, pp. 895-96, 317.

[32] *The Visitations of Northamptonshire made in 1564 and 1614-19*, ed. W.C. Metcalfe (London, 1887), p. 28; J. Bridges, *The History and Antiquities of Northamptonshire* (Oxford, 1791), p. 218; Victoria County History, *Northamptonshire*, iii (London, 1930), p. 177.

[33] Rabal, 'Artiste et clientèle', p. 49 and n. 14.

[34] Chartier's appeal to the English developed after the loss of English possessions in France, M.S. Blayney, *Fifteenth-Century English Translations of Alain Chartier's 'Le Traité de l'Espérance' and 'Le Quadrilogue Invectif'*, ii, EETS, 281 (1980), pp. 1-3; his appeal to the échevinage, newly united to the French crown, seems self-evident.

[35] Leroquais, *Livres d'heures*, ii, p. 85, pls xxxvi, xxvii; M.R. James, *A Descriptive Catalogue of the Manuscripts in the Fitzwilliam Museum, Cambridge* (Cambridge, 1895), pp. 154-56; for this style, C. Gaspar and F. Lyna, *Les principaux manuscrits á peintures de la Bibliothèque Royale de Belgique*, Société française pour la reproduction des manuscrits à peintures (Paris, 1948), ii, pp. 38-40.

[36] C. Reynolds, 'The Shrewsbury Book, London, British Library, Royal MS 15 E VI', *Medieval Art, Architecture and Archaeology at Rouen*, ed. J. Stratford, *BAACT*, 12 for 1986 (Leeds, 1993), pp. 109-16, with bibliography.

discern one dominant hand in the mass of productions, which vary from the meticulous and stiff, yet pleasing, to the ludicrously incompetent. The style shares certain characteristics with that of the Master of the Munich Golden Legend. Like the Munich Golden Legend style, the Talbot style relies on line and outline, using flat areas of comparatively unmodelled colour but often varying plain colours with simple patterns: day or night, skies are usually spattered with golden stars.

Other books illuminated in the Talbot style were ordered by or aimed at English patrons, such as an hours of Sarum Use (sold Christie's, London, 2 December 1987, lot 160),[37] which bears the arms of Sir Robert Conyers of Finningham, Suffolk, fos 42v-43 (Plate 24)[38] and his second wife, Maud, daughter of John Fitzralph of Pebmarsh, Essex. His first wife was apparently alive in 1438;[39] he and Maud were married by January 1446.[40] Sir Robert died c. 1465,[41] leaving his eldest son by his first marriage, Thomas Conyers, as heir to the Conyers lands,[42] while Maud made her will during her husband's lifetime in 1460 to secure her inheritance in Norfolk to her son, John Conyers, for whom it was proved on 30 June 1467.[43] In 1449 Sir Robert Conyers of Norfolk successfully petitioned that he should not be put in office nor have any goods taken in purveyance against his assent because of his service in the wars of Henry V and Henry VI; although his service cannot be attested before 1423, he appears in France throughout the 1420s and 1430s, being last recorded in 1441 in Rouen where his hours was probably made.[44] It may have been

[37] Christie's, London, *The Doheny Collection*, 2 December 1987, lot 160 with pls.

[38] Descendants used the arms of the Yorkshire Conyers, azure a maunch or, to represent their Conyers ancestry, e.g. D. Gurney, *The Record of the House of Gournay* (London , 1848), pp. 414-14, 440-41; a chevron with three pierced cinquefoils is given as Sir Robert's arms by Robert Glover, Somerset Herald 1570-88, BL, MS Lansdowne 205, fos 43v-44; Nicholas Conyers, holder of Finningham in 1416, *CCR, Henry V*, i, p. 264, almost certainly Sir Robert's father, used the same charge on his seal, BL, Harley Ch. 48 G 46 of 1421. Sir Robert sealed PRO, A 7396, with the crest used in the hours and possibly the same motto, *Descriptive Catalogue of Ancient Deeds*, iv, (London, 1902). the rabbit supporters – conies – are a canting reference to Conyers. For an incomplete Fitzralph and Conyers genealogy, A. Campling, *East Anglian Pedigrees*, ii, Harleian Society, 97 (London, 1946), p. 32.

[39] *Ancient Deeds*, iv, PRO, A 7544.

[40] Will of Maud's mother transcribed by Davy, BL, MS Add. 19129, fo. 294.

[41] Wedgwood, *Biographies*, pp. 214-15.

[42] *CIPM*, 20 Edward IV, 74.

[43] London, PRO, PROB 11/5. 19, summarised by N.H. Nicolas, *Testamenta vetusta* (London, 1826), i, p. 298, bequeathing a mass book and chapel furnishings.

[44] I am indebted to Dr Anne Curry for generously supplying references to Conyers' French service from her data base of men-at-arms and captains, funded by the British Academy: petition, PRO, E 28/79/20; Robert Conyers serving under John Harpeley 1423, BN, MS fr. 25767/49; Sir Robert Conyers under Harpeley 1430, BN, MS fr. 25769/465; Sir Robert Conyers in Rouen, captain in York's expeditionary army 1441, PRO, E 101/54/9. See also BL, Add. Ch. 1419; AN, K 62/11/19, K 59/10; BN, MSS fr. 25772/945, 998, 1036, fr. 26050/796, fr. 4488, pp. 227-28, fr. 26056/1967 for further references to Conyers' service in France. Harpeley was married to Robert's sister Alice, BL, MS Harley 10, fos. 274v-275.

through advancement in France that he was able to secure the heiress, Maud Fitzralph, whose grandmother was half-sister to Sir John Fastolf.[45] Fitzralph connections included the de la Poles,[46] which may explain the passage of the Conyers Hours to Dorothy de la Pole by the late fifteenth century, when Catherine de la Pole's name was also inscribed. They are presumably the daughters of John de la Pole, 2nd duke of Suffolk, and Elizabeth of York; little is known of them despite, or because of, their possible importance to the Yorkist succession.[47]

The Talbot style in the Conyers Hours is very close to that of the Fastolf Master, named from a copy of Christine de Pisan's *Epitre d'Othea* with the *Livre des quatre vertus* written for Sir John Fastolf in 1450 (Oxford, Bodleian Library, MS Laud Misc. 570).[48] Fastolf had left France almost a decade before the fall of English Normandy and his book was illuminated by an artist who had moved from France to England. The Fastolf Master seems to have begun his career in Paris, as did the Munich Golden Legend and Royal Alexander Masters. His activity in Normandy is substantiated by books of hours with miniatures in his style, two for the Use of Coutances, (Cambridge, St John's College, MS N. 24, and Paris, Bibliothèque de l'Arsenal, MS 560) and two for the Use of Rouen (Chicago, Tripp Collection and New York, Pierpont Morgan Library, MS M.27).[49] The Morgan Hours bears the arms of the Guérin or Garin of Rouen and it has been suggested that the manuscript was made for Jean Guérin, who died in 1433, canon of Rouen Cathedral from 1422 and one of the panel who tried Joan of Arc.[50] A cleric with an obligation to recite the breviary seems unlikely to have wanted an hours intended for the laity, and another member of the family could have commissioned the manuscript. The

[45] Fastolf's kinsman, Robert Fitzralph, was probably the son of Sir Thomas, younger son of Sir John and Fastolf's half-sister, Margery Mortimer, *Paston Letters and Papers of the Fifteenth Century*, ed. N. Davis, 3 vols (Oxford, 1971), ii, pp. 260, 534-35, etc.

[46] Maud's brother, John Fitzralph, married Alice Walesborough, first cousin of the half-blood to Alice Chaucer, countess of Suffolk, see Sir H.C. Maxwell Lyte, *Historical Notes on Some Somerset Manors Formerly Connected with the Honour of Dunster*, Somerset Record Society, extra series (1931), pp. 369-71, 79-81; the marriage was at the request and desire of the earl and countess, BL, MS Harley 970, fo. 27v; the earl was godfather to their son, R. A. Griffiths, *The Reign of Henry VI* (Berkeley, 1981), p. 362.

[47] Dorothy, the third daughter, is only a name; Catherine, the eldest, was thought to have married William 5th Lord Stourton, W. Dugdale, *The Baronage of England* (London, 1676), p. 190; F. Sandford, *A Genealogical History of the Kings of England and Monarchs of Great Britain* (London, 1677), p. 380; by 1502, Stourton was definitely married to Thomasine, daughter of Sir Walter Wriothesley, Lord Mowbray, Segrave and Stourton, *The History of the Noble House of Stourton*, 2 vols (London, 1899), i, pp. 275-79.

[48] J.J.G. Alexander, 'A Lost Leaf from a Bodleian Book of Hours', *Bodleian Library Record*, 8 (1971), pp. 248-51; Plummer, *Last Flowering*, pp. 1-2, 15-16.

[49] For these manuscripts, see Alexander 'Lost Leaf', pp. 249-50, with bibliography.

[50] Plummer, *Last Flowering*, p. 15, no. 21; for Jean Guérin, *Procès de condemnation de Jeanne d'Arc*, ed. P. Tisset, ii, Société de l'histoire de France (Paris, 1970), p. 403.

Coutances Hours in Cambridge came to be owned by Lady Margaret Beaufort, perhaps having been acquired by her father, John Beaufort, duke of Somerset, during his French service.[51]

The English in France directly commissioned manuscripts illuminated in the Fastolf style, such as the hours of Sarum Use, thoroughly French in appearance, which incorporates the arms and owner portrait of Sir William Porter (Pierpont Morgan Library, MS M.105).[52] Porter was knighted at Harfleur in 1415 and returned to France in August 1417. Present at the capture of Vernon in 1420, he seems to have been in England from at least 1422 as one of the executors of Henry V's will. From 1428, he was attendant on Henry VI as a household knight, returning to France with Henry in 1430. He died in 1434.[53] It is less clear whether another Sarum Hours with miniatures in the Fastolf style (Plate 25) in the Getty Museum (MS 5, 84 ML. 723), was made in France or England.[54] Michael K. Jones identified its first known owner, John de Vere, earl of Oxford, from his autograph *Oxenford* under the miniature of the national patron, St George, fo. 35v.[55] The book would seem to have been intended for the open market and subsequently acquired by Oxford, possibly in France. The earl helped to relieve the siege of Calais in 1436, was one of the ambassadors to treat for peace in 1439 and accompanied the duke of York to Normandy in 1441.[56] The *Cecyl Dorsett*, inscribed fo. 83, is presumably Cecily, daughter of William Bonville, Lord Harrington, married in 1474 to Thomas Grey, Marquess of Dorset, who made her will as 'Cecill, Marquess of Dorset', despite a second marriage.[57] Her mother and the wife of Oxford's son and successor were sisters, daughters of Richard Neville, earl of Salisbury.[58]

Although the Fastolf Master left Normandy to concentrate on his English patrons in their native land, his art had been equally acceptable to the French under English rule. The Masters of the Munich Golden Legend, of the Royal Alexander and of Lord Talbot, whether they remained in Normandy or moved elsewhere, continued to find French clients, newly French French in Normandy or of longstanding loyalty further south. The most easily traced

---

[51] M.K. Jones and M.G. Underwood, *The King's Mother: Lady Margaret Beaufort, Countess of Richmond and Derby* (Cambridge, 1992), pp. 160, 284, pl. 7.

[52] Plummer, *Last Flowering*, pp. 15-16, no. 22.

[53] J.H. Wylie, *The Reign of Henry V*, i (Cambridge, 1914), pp. 343-44; Griffiths, *Henry VI*, pp. 51, 55, 57, 65.

[54] *The J. Paul Getty Museum Journal*, 15 (1987), pp. 202-3, no. 124; H.P. Kraus, *Illuminated manuscripts: Catalogue 159* (New York, 1981), p. 38, no. 16, pl. XVI; Sotheby's, London, *Sale Catalogue*, 5 July 1976, lot 80, ills, identifies the scribe as Ricardus Franciscus, in England when he wrote Bod Lib MS Laud Misc. 570 and the Sarum hours, BL, MS Harley 2915, also with Fastolf style miniatures, see Backhouse, *Books of Hours*, pp. 30-31, pl. 26. It is not clear whether this partnership was earlier operative in France.

[55] I am greatly indebted to Michael K. Jones for generously allowing this communication.

[56] *CP*, x, pp. 236-39.

[57] *CP*, iv, p. 418; Nicolas, *Testamenta vetusta*, p. 631.

[58] *CP*, ii, p. 219; x, p. 236.

transition from English to French France is by the illuminating workshop named for the duke of Bedford, although only lesser practitioners of the style seem to have worked in Rouen itself.[59] The manuscript known to have been made in Rouen for the Duke, a medical treatise dated 1430 (BN, MS fr. 24246), is illuminated in the flat outline style characteristic of Rouen,[60] not unlike that in the book of the Rouen confraternity of the Holy Sacrament of 1435 (BS, MS Add 19734).[61]

Even an English artist is known to have continued in Rouen after 1449: Thomas Brydon, embroiderer of the duke of Bedford.[62] In 1427, with the mercer Jouen de Rodemare, his partner, both natives of England, Brydon was producing elaborately worked costumes for the earl of Salisbury.[63] In 1458 when the Rouen embroiderers' guild drew up its statutes. Thomas Bridon (*sic*) was represented by his grandson, Robinet des Chasteaulx.[64] Other English artists were active in Normandy. It has been surmised that the painter, Richart Decestre, employed in December 1420 by Robert Alorge to decorate the family chapel in Saint-Martin-du-Pont and a room in his *hôtel* may have been of Exeter and an Englishman.[65] If so, Alorge was probably not deliberately anglicising his chapel and *hôtel* since he was executed for plotting against the English in the following year. Conquest was not a prerequisite for the presence of foreign artists in a town,[66] although war generated work for artists in providing the trappings which identified and consolidated armies.[67] In 1427 the Rouen painter, Etienne Guyot, successfully argued that he required a window opening onto the cemetery of Saint-Nicholas-le-Peinteur, despite the church's opposition, because he needed to be able to dry works of painting, particularly banners, by hanging them out of the window.[68] The banners are unlikely all to have been ecclesiastical and the English armies must have been important customers for Guyot's wares.

---

[59] See Reynolds, 'Shrewsbury Book'.

[60] Illustrated in J. Stratford, 'The Manuscripts of John, Duke of Bedford: Library and Chapel', *England in the Fifteenth Century: Proceedings of the 1986 Harlaxton Symposium*, ed. D. Williams (Woodbridge, 1987), pp. 329-50, pl. 16.

[61] A.G. Watson, *Dated and Datable Manuscripts, c. 700-1600, in the Department of Manuscripts in the British Library* (London, 1979), i, p. 55, no. 218; ii, pl. 423.

[62] J. Stevenson, *Letters and Papers Illustrative of the Wars of the English in France during the Reign of Henry VI, King of England*, Rolls Series, 22 (London, 1861-1864), II, ii, p. 415.

[63] C. de Beaurepaire, *Derniers mélanges historiques et archéologiques concernant le département de la Seine-Inférieure et plus spécialement la ville de Rouen* (Rouen, 1909), p. 246.

[64] De Beaurepaire, *Derniers mélanges*, pp. 248-49.

[65] De Beaurepaire, *Derniers mélanges*, pp. 45-46; a distinction is made between Richart 'paintre demourant à présent en la paroisse Saint-Pierre-l'Honoré de Rouen' and his colleague Pierre Huache dit Daniel 'paintre de la paroisse Saint-Pierre-du-Chastel d'icelle ville'.

[66] For a Scottish sculptor in Rouen in 1405 and an embroiderer from Brussels in 1411, De Beaurepaire, *Derniers mélanges*, pp. 78 and 243.

[67] Reynolds, 'Les Angloys', pp. 47-48.

[68] P. Le Cacheux, *Rouen au temps de Jeanne d'Arc (1419-1449)*, Société de l'histoire de Normandie (Rouen and Paris, 1931), pp. 110-16.

Both the war effort and the civil administration required the English leaders to live with appropriate state. Henry VI's lieutenants in Normandy, and the household of the king himself from 1430-32, needed to appear plausible as the representatives of the legitimate king of France and duke of Normandy.[69] Even before the loss of Paris in 1436, Normandy, with Rouen as its capital and trading centre and with Caen as a centre of English settlement and of the new university, was increasingly regarded and used as the base of English France.[70] In 1430-31 Jeanne du Pont was unable to find a buyer in Paris for a set of vestments and altarcloths so that she took them to Rouen where they were purchased by either Cardinal Beaufort or Cardinal Louis of Luxembourg.[71] It was a centre for those, English and French, who were expected to maintain their accustomed standards of living, which necessarily involved the employment of artists. The duke of Bedford's retinue in 1429 included the London painters, Thomas Rich and Gilbert Melton, who may have been the two painters who dined at the earl of Warwick's house in Rouen in April 1431.[72]

The magnates' households and retinues would add to their lords' honour by themselves living honourably, in the eyes both of their fellow men and of God. Sir William Oldhall and his wife Margaret, daughter of William, Lord Willoughby de Eresby, who were married by 1423, needed their Hours (BL, MS Harley 2900), to secure their salvation as well as to maintain their status.[73] They employed their own priest and, while prepared to put business before mass, were careful to secure a plenary remission of sins in the Jubilee Year of 1450. Oldhall began his career in France in 1416 in the retinue of Thomas Beaufort, duke of Exeter. In 1436-37 he joined the duke of York and under York's patronage became one of the chief English landholders in Normandy. In 1441 he was appointed to York's council in Rouen. He was summoned to England to advise the king's council 'in such things as shall be occurent and touche our Reaume of France and Duchie of Normandie as he that of reason shuld have moost perfecte knowledge in the same, considering his long abode

[69] For Bedford see J. Stratford, 'John, Duke of Bedford, as Patron in Lancastrian Rouen', *Medieval Art, Architecture and Archaeology at Rouen*, ed. Stratford, pp. 98-108; for York, T.B. Pugh, 'Richard Plantagenet (1411-60), Duke of York, as the King's Lieutenant in France and Ireland', *Aspects of Late Medieval Government and Society: Essays Presented to J.R. Lander*, ed. J.G. Rowe (Toronto, 1986), pp. 107-41; for Warwick, J. Harvey, *Gothic England* (London, 1947), pp. 93 and 173-78 and H.A. Cronne and R.H. Hilton, 'The Beauchamp Household Book', *University of Birmingham Historical Journal*, 2 (1949), pp. 208-18; for Edmund Beaufort, M.K. Jones, 'War on the Frontier: The Lancastrian Land Settlement in Eastern Normandy, 1435-50', *Nottingham Medieval Studies*, 33 (1989), pp. 113-14.

[70] See C. T. Allmand, *Lancastrian Normandy, 1415-1450: The History of a Medieval Occupation* (Oxford, 1983).

[71] G. Thompson, *Paris and its People under English Rule: The Anglo-Burgundian Regime, 1420-1436* (Oxford, 1991), pp. 22-23.

[72] *DKR*, 48 (London, 1887), p. 266; Harvey, *Gothic England*, p. 84.

[73] Backhouse, *Books of Hours*, p. 73, fig. 66; J.S. Roskell, 'Sir William Oldhall, Speaker in the Parliament of 1450-1', *Nottingham Medieval Studies*, 5 (1961), pp. 87-112.

with you there'.[74] Oldhall's 'long abode' meant that he commissioned his book of hours in France, probably *c*. 1430, but it did not alter his adherence to the Sarum Use.

Although the English affected the content of liturgical books and thus the range of subject matter requiring illustration, it is difficult to discern an English influence on the style of illumination or a specifically English taste: English, English French, and French French patrons turned to the same artists and the artists accepted the available jobs. In the first half of the fifteenth century many of these were commissions from the English or works produced for the English market, whether for local purchasers in Normandy or for export to England. The commercial relationship between English or Welsh patron and French artist might be very clear. In March 1420 in Rouen, Jacquet le Caron, born in the parish of Châtel-la-Lune near Bernay, was hired by William Bradwardine, seigneur of Saint-Vaast and La Poterie, to serve him 'de son . . . mestier d'escripre et enluminer au mieulx que il pourra et saura', all his materials provided, for three years for the sum of 20 *livres tournois* a year, his food, drink, heating, appropriate lodging and one robe and one chaperon a year.[75] Bradwardine, consistently called esquire, was a surgeon, first documented in 1394.[76] In 1415, with Thomas Morstede, he was responsible for the casualties of the French campaign, a charge renewed the following year. He was prosperous, engaging in various property deals and, it would seem, in trade. On 14 September 1420 at Rouen, letters of attorney to Bradwardine from Roger Sapurton and Ralph Holland, citizen and clothier of London, were registered.[77] From June 1421, he seems to have been in London. His relationship with Jacquet le Caron was almost certainly a trading arrangement. Bradwardine would have financed the scribe and marketed his works, perhaps providing models of Sarum Use texts to exploit the English market. An illuminated manuscript was a natural souvenir to acquire in France just as it was natural for the French, and the Normans in particular, to import Nottingham alabasters from England.[78]

With the decline of Paris, English patronage helped to make Rouen a great book-producing centre, geared to markets both at home and abroad, which

[74] J.S. Roskell, *The Commons and their Speakers in English Parliaments, 1376-1523* (Manchester, 1961), p. 243.

[75] C. de Beaurepaire, *Nouveaux mélanges historiques et archéologiques* (Rouen, 1904), p. 361; cited in R. Watson, *The Playfair Hours* (London, 1984), pp. 23-24.

[76] For Bradwardine, C.H. Talbot and E.A. Hammond, *The Medical Practitioners in Medieval England: A Biographical Register*, Publications of the Wellcome Historical Medical Library, new series, 8 (London, 1965), pp. 387-88; R.A. Griffiths, *The Principality of Wales in the Later Middle Ages: The Structure and Personnel of Government, I, South Wales 1277-1536*, Board of Celtic Studies, University of Wales, History and Law Series, 26 (Cardiff, 1972), pp. 263-64, 396-97.

[77] *DKR*, 41 (1880), p. 796.

[78] F. Cheetham, *English Medieval Alabasters* (Oxford, 1984), pp. 45-49.

continued and flourished in the age of printing.[79] A distinctive Rouen style of manuscript illumination had evolved by the later fifteenth century to which artists patronised by the English had contributed: the Masters of the Munich Golden Legend, of Sir John Fastolf, of Lord Talbot and of Lord Hoo. These styles, comparatively economical in time and materials, were suited to the conditions created by the Anglo-French wars and, in this limited sense, English intervention in France could be seen as having a far-reaching influence on the work of French artists, an influence, however, not inherently English. The Burgundian-Armagnac fighting had produced similar economic circumstances. There was no apparent cross-fertilisation of French painting by English painting and stylistic similarities between French and English illuminators may be the result not of direct interaction but of shared dependence on the Netherlands, the dominant force in the pictorial arts throughout Europe.

It is very probable that some, at least, of the painters employed by the English came from the Netherlands and were not French by birth. They can, however, be considered French in terms of artistic style, a complicating contribution to the debate over the significance of terms of nationality. English patrons are easier to define. Generally, those with sufficient wealth to buy works of art had lands and property on both sides of the Channel and, while benefiting from Norman grants, regarded England as home. Permanent settlement is most obviously expressed in the arts by architecture and here, following the lead of Henry V, the duke of Bedford was the most active patron, both in Paris and Rouen. While Edmund Beaufort planned to build a luxurious *maison forte* at Elbeuf on the Seine and Fulkes Eyton contributed to the rebuilding of the church of Caudebec,[80] many English seem to have taken a shorter-term view, one in which their essential Englishness and separateness from France was not lost. This is very apparent in where those rich enough to choose decided to be buried.

The duke of Bedford was, as usual, exceptional in electing to be buried on that side of the Channel where he happened to die, the more realistic Rouen replacing his first choice of Amiens.[81] Of the other patrons of French artists, Talbot, killed at Castillon, had asked to be buried at Blackmere and was finally interred at Whitchurch;[82] his elder brother, killed at the siege of Rouen, had only his entrails buried there, although even his tomb involved an effigy and employment for artists; only Talbot's son, John, who died in childhood in January 1439, was left to lie *in toto* in Rouen.[83] Talbot's father-in-law, the earl of Warwick, was returned to his chapel in Warwick and the earl of Salisbury to

---

[79] Watson, *Playfair Hours*, pp. 23-34.

[80] Jones, 'War on the Frontier', pp. 113-14.

[81] C. de Beaurepaire, 'Fondations pieuses de duc de Bedford à Rouen', *Bibliothèque de l'Ecole des Chartes*, 34 (1873), pp. 343-86.

[82] H. Talbot, *The English Achilles* (London, 1981), pp. 172-78.

[83] De Beaurepaire, *Derniers mélanges*, p. 47; since John's tomb bore the arms of Talbot quartering Tyes, he was presumably a son of Margaret Beauchamp.

his at Bisham. There was no question of burial in France for Fastolf, Hoo, Oldhall, Porter and Conyers who had returned to England before death. Lower down the social scale, where finances restricted freedom, there must have been more families, like that of the embroiderer Thomas Brydon, who settled permanently in France. Whether Brydon contributed something specifically English to Rouen manufacture cannot now be known. Certainly in the illuminated manuscripts, where the visual evidence does survive, it is hard to see English patronage as a determining factor of style. The English did provide new markets and a level of stability which attracted refugee artists from Paris into Normandy and helped to make Rouen a centre of illumination and book production, with patterns of trade sufficiently established to survive the resurgence of Paris. Within those trade patterns, the English market continued to be of importance, even if, after 1450, French artists in Normandy had to export to reach their English patrons.

Index of Names and Places

(References to plates are in bold)